COMPARING WELFARE STATES

D311 COURSE TEAM

John Baldock, Consultant author

Pam Berry, Compositor

Kum Kum Bhavnani, External assessor

David Boswell, Open University author

Juliette Cowan, Course Manager

John Clarke, Open University author

Allan Cochrane, Open University author

Donna Collins, Secretary

Rosemary Collins, Tutor panel

Helen Cowie, Tutor panel

Rudi Dallos, Open University author

Jonathan Davies, Designer

Alison Edwards, Editor

Janet Fink, Reading member

Sally Foreman, Consultant author

Sharon Gewirtz, Open University author/ Course Team Chair

Norman Ginsburg, Consultant author

Hilary Graham, Course assessor

Peggotty Graham, Staff Tutor

Pauline Harris, Staff Tutor

Jill Humphrey, Reading member

John Hunt, Designer

Chris Jones, Course assessor

Nicole Jones, Secretary

Hilary Land, Consultant author

Mary Langan, Open University author

Jack Leathem, Producer, BBC/OU

Vic Lockwood, Senior Producer, BBC/OU

Caroline McKinlay, External assessor

Eugene McLaughlin, Open University author

Dorothy Miell, Audio-cassette presenter

John Muncie, Open University author

Sharon Pinkney, Open University author

Lynne Poole, Consultant author

Roger Sapsford, Open University author

Esther Saraga, Open University author

Lynne Segal, Consultant author

Jane Sheppard, Designer

Richard Skellington, Open University author

George Taylor, Consultant author

Raymond Taylor, External assessor

Margaret Wetherell, Open University author

Fiona Williams, Consultant author

Roberta Woods, Open University author

COMPARING WELFARE STATES

EDITED BY
ALLAN COCHRANE, JOHN CLARKE
AND SHARON GEWIRTZ

SAGE Publications
LONDON • NEWBURY • NEW DEHLI

IN ASSOCIATION WITH

TheOpen
University

This publication forms part of the Open University course D311, *Family Life and Social Policy*. Details of this and other Open University courses can be obtained from the Call Centre, PO Box 724, The Open University, Milton Keynes MK7 6ZS, United Kingdom: tel. +44 (0)1908 653231, e-mail cesgen@open.ac.uk

Alternatively, you may visit the Open University website at http://www.open.ac.uk where you can learn more about the wide range of courses and packs offered at all levels by The Open University.

To purchase this publication or other components of Open University courses, contact Open University Worldwide Ltd, The Berrill Building, Walton Hall, Milton Keynes MK7 6AA, United Kingdom: tel. +44 (0)1908 858785; fax +44 (0)1908 858787; e-mail ouwenq@open.ac.uk; website http://www.ouw.co.uk

 Sage Publications Ltd
6 Bonhill Street
London EC2A 4PU

Sage Publications Inc
2455 Teller Road
Newbury Park, California 91320

Sage Publications India Pvt Ltd
32, M-Block Market
Greater Kailash-1
New Dehli 110 048

Edited, designed and typeset by The Open University.

Printed and bound in the United Kingdom by The Bath Press, Bath.

British Library Cataloging in Publication Data
A catalogue record for this book is available from The British Library.

Library of Congress catalogue record available.

ISBN 0 7619 7089 4 (hbk)
ISBN 0 7619 7090 8 (pbk)

2.1

CONTENTS

PREFACE   vi

CHAPTER 1   COMPARING WELFARE STATES   1
ALLAN COCHRANE, JOHN CLARKE AND SHARON GEWIRTZ

CHAPTER 2   THE CONSTRUCTION OF THE BRITISH
WELFARE STATE, 1945–1975   29
JOHN CLARKE, MARY LANGAN AND FIONA WILLIAMS

CHAPTER 3   REMAKING WELFARE: THE BRITISH
WELFARE REGIME IN THE 1980S AND 1990S   71
JOHN CLARKE, MARY LANGAN AND FIONA WILLIAMS

CHAPTER 4   US WELFARE: VARIATIONS ON THE
LIBERAL REGIME   113
JOHN CLARKE

CHAPTER 5   GERMANY: A CONSERVATIVE REGIME IN
CRISIS?   153
LYNNE POOLE

CHAPTER 6   SWEDEN: THE SOCIAL DEMOCRATIC
CASE   195
NORMAN GINSBURG

CHAPTER 7   IRELAND: FROM CATHOLIC
CORPORATISM TO SOCIAL PARTNERSHIP   223
EUGENE McLAUGHLIN

CHAPTER 8   LOOKING FOR A EUROPEAN WELFARE
STATE   261
ALLAN COCHRANE, JOHN CLARKE AND SHARON GEWIRTZ

ACKNOWLEDGEMENTS   291

INDEX   292

PREFACE

Our aim in *Comparing Welfare States* is to show the value of adopting a comparative approach to the analysis of social and family policy by setting the British experience in a broader (largely European) context. Such an approach is not only important because it introduces us to a wider range of welfare regimes, but also because it helps to clarify the nature of the British system itself. After discussing some of the principles of comparative study, we use them in practice by looking at the contrasting experiences of welfare states in Britain, the USA, Germany, Sweden and Ireland. As well as highlighting the diversity of national experiences we explore the shared features of these countries, and conclude by considering whether a transnational European welfare system is emerging. Each chapter moves between national and comparative issues, emphasizing the need to bring the two together if we are to grasp the full complexity of existing and developing welfare regimes.

This second edition of the book has been extensively rewritten in order to reflect and analyse the changes in welfare states and systems taking place at the end of the twentieth century. Changing national and international contexts, new or intensified social, economic and political pressures, and shifting views about the proper relationship between states and welfare have created flux and uncertainty. We have made one other change for the second edition, substituting a chapter on welfare in the USA for one on Hong Kong that appeared in the first edition. The change in Hong Kong's status after its return to China meant that it could not play the same role as a comparative case in this edition. We believe the USA is a valuable alternative focus of attention.

The period between 1993 (when the first edition appeared) and 2001 has seen significant developments in all of the welfare systems considered in this book, necessitating substantial rewriting of all the chapters. It is, of course, the challenge of analysing such dynamic processes – and their social consequences – that provides one of the core fascinations of studying social policy. We hope this book conveys something of the interest and significance of comparative work in social policy.

This book is one of a series published by Sage that is concerned with the relationships between families and the development and practice of social policy. The other three books in the series are *Understanding the Family* (edited by John Muncie, Margaret Wetherell, Mary Langan, Rudi Dallos and Allan Cochrane), *Social Problems and the Family* (edited by Rudi Dallos and Eugene McLaughlin), and *A Crisis in Care? Challenges to Social Work* (edited by John Clarke). Each of the books in the series looks at the ways in which professional and state-sponsored interventions help to shape the experience of family life in different contexts. And each also considers the ways in which particular notions of the family influence the development of social policy. We believe that only by bringing these debates together is it possible to understand ways in which welfare systems were being reconstructed at the end of the twentieth century.

This series of books was initially written as part of an Open University course, D311 *Family Life and Social Policy,* which is, as its title implies, principally concerned with the complex inter-relationships between the family and the state. The family is frequently understood as a private arena within which individuals are essentially free to determine how they live their own lives. The state, on the other hand, is often presented as the complete antithesis, at worst seeking to interfere in matters that should be left to private decision-making, at best helping to provide a wider – public – context within which individuals and families may interact.

The course questions these dichotomies and explores complexities of family life in the United Kingdom, using insights from psychology, social policy and sociology to develop its arguments, starting with a focus on the internal life of families, moving through a consideration of forms of social and professional intervention towards a comparative analysis of social policy in Europe and a consideration of possible futures. At the core of the course are concerns about the relationship between the public and private spheres, about the need to acknowledge and explore diversity in the lived experience of families and about the ways in which power and inequality work themselves out within and between families. These concerns are also central to all of the books in this series.

The chapters of this book have been substantially informed by debates within the Course Team, drawing on ideas, evidence and methods from a range of disciplines. In other words they are the products of a genuinely interdisciplinary process in which we have all learned from each other. Without these debates and regular discussion it would have been impossible to produce this book. In such a collaborative process it should be clear that important contributions have been made to all of the chapters by people who are not explicitly named as authors.

An Open University Course Team stretches far beyond the core of academics who write for it, it include consultants, tutor-testers and assessors who give invaluable advice, a course manager who somehow brings the pieces together, editors and designers who make it all look good, and secretaries who manage – against all odds – to produce high-quality manuscripts to deadlines that everybody else does their best to forget. The work of all of these people is reflected in this book as well as in other parts of the course. We thank them for it.

Allan Cochrane
John Clarke
Sharon Gewirtz

CHAPTER 1
COMPARING WELFARE STATES

ALLAN COCHRANE, JOHN CLARKE AND SHARON GEWIRTZ

CONTENTS

INTRODUCTION   2

1   DEFINING WELFARE STATES   5

2   MOVING TOWARDS COMPARISON: STATISTICS
    AND WELFARE REGIMES   7

3   STATES, REGIMES AND MIXED ECONOMIES   12

4   INCLUDING THE EXCLUDED   14

5   MODELS AND STRUCTURE   18

6   CONVERGENCE OR DIFFERENCE?   22

    REFERENCES   24

INTRODUCTION

This book has two main aims. The first is to show the value of cross-national comparison in the analysis of social policy. Whilst recognizing the difficulties of this, we aim to show not only that comparative analysis is possible, but also that it can deliver useful insights by highlighting alternatives to existing arrangements which are frequently taken for granted. This leads directly into the second aim, which is to develop a fuller understanding of welfare systems in a range of countries, both to see whether broad international trends can be identified and to use the experiences of others to inform domestic (British) debates.

If the growing number of books (and journals) promising comparative analysis is anything to go by, it is perhaps no longer necessary to make the case for a comparative approach to the study of social policy. On the contrary, it may now be single-country studies that need to be justified. It is increasingly assumed that reaching a full understanding of developments in any particular country is only possible if its experience is set in the context of the experiences of other countries. It is also increasingly acknowledged that developments in any single country cannot be explained without setting them in the context of wider – global – changes. Thus, for example, Clasen (1999, p.4) has argued that 'Growing interdependence between and similar challenges across countries have put into question social policy research which remains locked into analysing developments within one country'. Yet there is a danger that the new orthodoxy may make it rather too easy to espouse a comparative approach without ever being quite clear why, or what questions can be most helpfully illuminated through comparison. We need to be clear about the reasons for adopting this approach.

The value of comparison can be illustrated negatively by considering the way in which the development of the British welfare state has generally been interpreted. Traditionally, its growth until the late 1970s has been explained as a more or less inexorable progression from the Poor Law to the Department of Health and Social Security, with the welfare state receiving its endorsement in the implementation of the ideas of Beveridge and Keynes by successive governments after 1945. This has been described as an evolutionary process (Fraser, 1973) and, however modified by the consideration of historical detail, it has always read like a story of the triumph of rational social administration over the forces of darkness – or, in its least determinist form, of reluctant collectivism over anti-collectivism (George and Wilding, 1986). It was easy to believe in the uniqueness and perfection of the British welfare state, at least until the governments of Margaret Thatcher began to 'reform' it in the 1980s. But this approach missed the extent to which similar moves were taking place at the same time in many of the countries of the developed capitalist world, especially in Western Europe and North America. It also ignored the extent to which other models of welfare might have been more effective than that of Britain, whether judged in terms of income maintenance, social support or the reduction of social and economic inequalities. In practice, a narrow focus on Britain made it easier to perpetuate the myths that helped to sustain Britain's peculiar form of political consensus after 1945, despite the tensions within it (see, for example, Johnson, 1977, Chapters 1 and 2; Leys, 1989, Chapters 4 and 6). Equally importantly, analysis of this kind tended to ignore the global context within which the development of the British welfare state took place. Once this is taken into account, it is difficult to ignore the extent to which events in Britain were part of a wider international settlement, dominated by the economic and political power of the USA, but also influenced by the perceived military and ideological threat from the Soviet Union. The advantage of such a global focus is that it encourages an interest in the framework, structural constraints and dynamics within which welfare states were constructed in the developed capitalist countries after 1945, and then challenged in the 1980s and 1990s (Mishra, 1990; Kuhnle, 2000).

Paradoxically, perhaps, it also makes it easier to explore some of the special and equally important features of individual welfare states. Staying with Britain for the moment, the experience of the Second World War confirmed its secondary status, setting up a continuing debate about whether it should continue to seek an international (global) role as deputy to the USA or accept an apparently more modest role as part of Europe (see, for example, Brett, 1985). '1945' also heralded a gradual retreat from the formal trappings of Empire, often under pressure from national movements in the old colonies. The new welfare state implied a recognition that the UK's citizens (particularly the working class) could no longer rely on an empire to provide economic and social benefits. The move towards a welfare state was not accompanied by similar reforms in its remaining colonies, but rather by increasingly restrictive controls on entry to the UK, thus effectively excluding their residents from welfare citizenship.

Most single-nation studies have conventionally focused on the specific points and institutional features associated with the development of a particular form of welfare state. Attention has concentrated on questions of political mobilization and political parties, or on issues of institution-building and the creation of paths of policy development (see, for example, the discussion in Amenta, 1998). Such approaches have also dominated much comparative analysis, contrasting political forces in the development of different welfare states, or examining divergent historical paths in the construction of welfare institutions (Castles, 1989). However, these political-institutional views of welfare state development have prioritized internal, national dynamics and tended to give limited attention to external (international or global) contexts and conditions.

Alternative approaches have given greater weight to international or global contexts, particularly in relation to challenges to welfare states that emerged in the 1980s and 1990s. The changing relationships of the global economy were identified as placing new pressures on welfare states: driving through a crisis 'of welfare states' (Mishra, 1990); pushing governments into a retreat from, or retrenchment of, welfare spending (Pierson, 1991), or creating a shift towards 'post-fordist welfare systems' that were subordinated to the demands of a more global capitalism in search of new 'flexibilities' (Burrows and Loader, 1994; Jessop, 2000).

These approaches tend to highlight the international political and economic forces that have come to bear on developed welfare states. In particular, they stress the role of a more global economy in reducing the autonomy of nation states to determine social and economic policy. They also point to the intense political and ideological attacks on public spending – on welfare in particular – that have been so influential through the 1980s and 1990s. Finally, they suggest that we have seen an increasing subordination of social policy objectives to economic interests and objectives (especially in creating or encouraging more 'flexible' labour markets). There are different variants offering divergent views of the global context and its relationship to national welfare states, and we will return to these later in the book. At this point, we want to emphasize how the greater attention to the international/global dimensions within comparative social policy has been closely associated with the challenges to – or retreat from – developed welfare states.

Although most of these approaches foreground economic and political processes, Kersbergen (2000) has suggested that there may be a range of common processes that affected most of the western capitalist societies with welfare states. He argues that political and economic dynamics combined with demographic and social changes to put pressure on and challenge welfare states:

> First, the relatively stable balance between generations is being challenged by an ageing population ...

> Second, the traditional family, towards which so many social policies were targeted, is no longer dominant ...

> Third, slacking economic growth and the post-industrialization of labour markets ... have decreased job security and continuity of employment generally ... Consequently, the financial logic of social security arrangements are jeopardized.

> Fourth, changing relations between men and women with respect to the division of labour within and outside the family ... have challenged the gender assumptions of many welfare state arrangements.

> Fifth, politically recognized systems of interest intermediation and centralized collective bargaining, which historically have accorded a firm social and economic base to the welfare state, have been eroded to a considerable extent ...

Finally, relatively fixed relations between nation states are in a state of flux as a result of the end of the Cold War, continuing and accelerating globalization and the intensification of European economic and monetary union.

(Kersbergen, 2000, pp.21–2)

While these processes represent common challenges to welfare states, Kersbergen suggests that national political and institutional factors may have been significant in resisting these processes, and in shaping different national responses (pp.23–4; see also Esping-Andersen, 1996). Working through the intersection of national and international forces and processes is a central task for comparative social policy.

In this book, we address both sides of the comparative process. The first is the strictly comparative one, which identifies and explores the similarities and differences between countries and their experiences. The second has the rather different (though related) aim of setting those experiences within a wider global context, both to highlight what is specific to individual countries and to help us understand transnational trends and processes.

I   DEFINING WELFARE STATES

The chapters that follow examine countries that have been described as having welfare states, but the implications of such a description may not always be clear, since the differences between them sometimes appear to be as important as any similarities. It is important not to impose any excessively tight definitions at the start, because, if we do, the conclusions are likely to follow inescapably from the definition. Some countries will meet the standard and others will not. However, a loose working definition is required to make comparison possible in the first place. So, what do we mean by 'welfare state'?

Mishra (1990) argues strongly that a commitment to full employment needs to be seen as a central component of welfare states. Clearly, one of the most effective ways of reducing poverty (if that is one of the aims of welfare) is to ensure that access to paid employment is easily available. Furthermore, where social insurance is a major feature of a welfare system, it is difficult to see how benefits can be maintained at reasonable levels without close to full employment (thereby ensuring that contributors outnumber beneficiaries). However, we have excluded a commitment to full employment as a defining characteristic of a welfare state, not least because the general move away from full employment policies is so well recorded in all but a very small (and reducing) number of countries. In that sense it is already clear what the direction of change has been, and we would immediately have to find a new term for the states in which we are interested. There is also a more fundamental problem with a focus on full employment, and that is its inherent gender bias. Most definitions of 'full employment' generally exclude women in low-paid and part-time work on the continued assumption that most of them will be married and that the welfare needs of married women will be met through 'their breadwinner husbands' (Chamberlayne, 1991/2, p.7).

This difficulty with 'full employment' is a particular expression of a more general problem in the analysis of welfare, when attempts are made to differentiate clearly between the public and the private domains – so that, for example, care that is undertaken by those employed by the state (in the public domain) is likely to be understood as part of the welfare state, whilst care undertaken in the domestic sphere (and probably not, or only marginally, funded by the state) is likely to be considered as outside the welfare state. As a result, Dominelli (1991, p.9) chooses to work with a much broader definition, suggesting that 'the welfare state comprises those public and domestic relationships which take as their primary objectives the well-being of people'. We have a great deal of sympathy with this definition, but in this case find it difficult to know quite how to use it in practice. In one interpretation this could include almost every sphere of human activity: even the most profit-maximizing of entrepreneurs might justify their activity in terms of providing services to people. In another it could exclude most of human activity: even the most apparently selfless of individuals might explain her (or his) actions in terms of dedication to God, or to the benefits she got from her relationship to the person being helped. At least some of those working in the welfare state do so for the money, or because of an 'urge to meddle or control others' (Sevenhuijsen, 1998, p.20) rather than out of any concern for the well-being of others. Moreover, institutions ostensibly concerned with the provision of care may also be sites of control, abuse and oppression (Shakespeare, 2000).

As a result, we have chosen to take a rather more limited definition as our starting-point. We shall principally (though not solely) be concerned with those policy areas generally associated with a relatively narrow use of the term 'welfare state', namely the involvement of the state in the provision of welfare services and benefits. So, while acknowledging the potential importance of labour-market policies, we plan to start by looking, more modestly, at areas which are more widely understood as being to do with social welfare, rather than those connected with the development of macroeconomic policy and the maintenance of full employment. Because we acknowledge the dangers of sharply distinguishing between public and private, we shall focus particularly on the ways in which different welfare states have developed (implicit or explicit) family policies. This should make it easier to explore the complex relations between social policy and people's lives, while acknowledging that states themselves help to define the distinction between public and private realms.

This definition and its associated focus should not be taken to imply that direct state provision is a necessary or defining characteristic of welfare states. On the contrary, we start from the assumption that there is likely to be a 'mixed economy' of welfare, whose precise mix will itself be different in different countries, involving the state, commercial (or for-profit) providers, non-statutory (or voluntary) organizations and 'informal' carers. In other words it will be possible to identify different mixes in different countries. However, we also accept Mishra's argument that the move from a state-dominated system to a more 'mixed' economy of welfare may not simply be a neutral one, in which one set of providers is seamlessly replaced by another. On the contrary, Mishra suggests, it may mean a shift in emphasis: in some cases, for example, a 'disentitlement' to services may be buried within a process labelled 'privatization' (Mishra, 1990, p.111). One of the reasons for developing a comparative approach is to explore the implications of these different mixes for the production and distribution of welfare in different countries.

Our concern with 'family' policies has both a pragmatic and a more basic justification. Pragmatically, it makes it possible to be a little more consistent about the examples developed and explored in the different countries considered in the book. But our emphasis on family policies in particular reflects our understanding that a central feature of social policy in developed capitalist countries is to be found in the way such policies define and construct families as sources of informal welfare supply and – when families 'fail' – as causes of social problems. This focus makes it easier for us to consider the extent to which changes in 'mixed economies' of welfare may be encouraging disentitlement for some families and shifts towards placing new (or additional) responsibilities on some members (usually women) of some families. Looking more closely at these policies helps to confirm the significance of gender-based differences in the operation of the welfare system, and to call into question the gender-neutral language of benefits, entitlement and citizenship in which social policies are often framed and discussed.

2 MOVING TOWARDS COMPARISON: STATISTICS AND WELFARE REGIMES

If there is widespread agreement about the need to develop comparative analysis, there is much less on quite how this should be done or on the implications of doing it. One widely acknowledged pitfall of comparative work is that it is difficult to avoid interpreting the experience of other countries in terms of the country with which we are most familiar. There is a risk that the home country of the researcher becomes some sort of a norm against which everything else is judged. This is compounded by the difficulty of understanding the social and political 'rules' that are simply taken for granted in apparently similar, as well as widely different, systems. Similar terms may have quite different social meanings in different places. Although most countries have local governments, for example, their role within different national political structures may be subtly different. For example, Ashford (1980) draws

a contrast between the historically subordinate status of local government in the United Kingdom and its higher status (if not greater
power) in France. In official discussions within the UK it is frequently
suggested that its mechanisms of democratic decision-making at local
level may interfere with the local government's efficiency in delivering
nationally agreed services. Ashford (1980, p.96) argues that such a
distinction could not be made in France, where mayors think of
themselves as 'part of the democratic fabric of Republican France' with
their own specific legitimacy. In Germany the Constitutional Basic Law
guarantees local government autonomy within the framework of law; in
the UK it is assumed that the responsibilities of local government are
delegated from the centre.

It will be clear to anyone who has travelled outside their own country
that we understand the unspoken 'rules' of our own countries, but feel
less secure about apparently similar situations in other countries. We
are often unsure how to behave, even where – as in the case of the USA
for English-speaking visitors – language is not a problem. Language
differences highlight and intensify these difficulties. At its most basic,
all translators of foreign languages know that words which 'mean' the
same may conjure up quite different images in different societies. Even
apparently straightforward words such as 'flat' or 'apartment' may
imply significantly different living arrangements (or social relations) in
different countries, although we generally use them as if they mean the
same; and some words, such as *Schadenfreude* and *Weltanschauung*,
are often described as untranslatable. If these problems arise with
ordinary language, how much more complicated are things likely to be
in the highly contested fields of welfare and social policy. The danger of
pursuing this acknowledgement of differences too far is that it makes
comparison impossible: everything becomes unique and little can be
shared across cultures. So, in general, social scientific teeth are gritted,
problems acknowledged and comparisons undertaken. But the legacy of
these fears often survives and is reflected in collections of case studies
of individual countries in which little attempt is made to explain how
they link together, or even why they have been put together, except in
the most general terms. Simply cataloguing different experiences is
assumed to be worthwhile, encouraging readers to move from narrow
parochialism, to open their eyes to the importance of difference. This is
a justifiable but inherently limited position, since collections of case
studies rarely allow enough space to explore differences effectively.
Often attempts are made to draw out superficial similarities, while key
differences are missed. Unless it is clear that chapters really are
focusing on equivalent activities, comparison becomes impossible. A
great deal of supposedly comparative work looks rather too much like
an unconnected series of chapters (usually written by national experts),
each summarizing the experience of one country and expecting the
reader to draw his or her own conclusions.

One way out of this impasse has been to move away from the detailed
study of individual countries, which are later brought together in a

linked series of case studies, towards the study of more aggregated data, which are increasingly available from international agencies such as the United Nations and the Organization for Economic Cooperation and Development (OECD). Using such data makes it possible to develop comparisons across a range of indicators, such as public expenditure on particular activities (for example, levels of social and defence spending) and patterns of income distribution. With the help of statistical analysis it is possible to draw conclusions about some of the factors that might have influenced differences, exploring a range of hypotheses including 'the impact of economic growth, the openness of the economy, demographic structure, the role of political parties, forms of interest mediation and so on' (Castles, 1989, p.5). One conclusion of this research has been that party political control has had an impact on levels of social expenditure, with parties of the right resisting its growth and social democratic parties encouraging its increase (see Castles, 1982; Esping-Andersen, 1985; Heidenheimer *et al.*, 1990).

The advantage of approaches that utilize existing, internationally available aggregate data is that it is possible to identify broad trends and draw equally broad conclusions, but the gaps they leave remain frustratingly large. Whilst accepting the existence of a correlation between party political control of governments and levels of welfare spending, for example, one still wants to know what factors caused different parties to succeed in different places, and whether overall levels of spending conceal significant differences in the form of spending. This may be compounded by problems with the data used for comparisons. It is not always clear whether the data are strictly comparable, since different countries may use slightly different definitions: the exclusion, for example, of publicly regulated insurance schemes in one country and their inclusion in another may make it difficult to assess the allocation of resources to welfare. Allowances can be made for some of these (for example, by translating spending levels into standardized international units) but there remains a continuing concern because the data are supplied by the governments whose spending is being compared. It may be the case (as Castles suggests) that there is a high degree of standardization, but it does not take a very cynical observer – particularly one who has seen the ways in which definitions of unemployment were changed in the UK during the 1980s and 1990s – to imagine how figures could be manipulated to suit the interests of governments. Even without manipulation, serious problems may arise if aggregate figures are simply taken for granted. As we have already indicated, support for full employment can be seen as a central element of some welfare states, yet one consequence of high levels of unemployment might be increased expenditure on unemployment benefit. In the aggregate figures, therefore, a move away from a commitment to full employment (one measurement of the existence of a welfare state) may be reflected in terms that suggest an increased commitment to welfare spending (another measure of the existence of a welfare state). Again taking the UK as an example, although the governments of the 1980s and 1990s were committed to and implemented a range of policies intended fundamentally to reshape the welfare state, the rise of welfare spending to meet the income support and benefit costs of rising unemployment may have obscured the actual extent of this shift.

Concerns such as these can perhaps be dealt with through careful – and sceptical – analysis of the readily available data. More importantly, however, as Castles acknowledges, the data do not cover all those areas of interest in the comparison of welfare states. As Castles explains:

> The initial thrust of comparative policy analysis had a very strong tendency to be concerned with topics for which comparable, and most specifically, quantitative data were readily available – public expenditures and macroeconomic outcomes in particular. Far less was it concerned with qualitative issues or intrusion into areas in which governments had not seen fit to provide standardized data. In other words, the appropriate domain of comparative analysis was conceptualized in terms of officially defined functions of the modern state, not so much because of the values that social scientists brought to their analysis, but rather because governments were themselves deeply implicated in those aspects of the domestic political economy and considered it useful to gather information on such matters. Until quite recently, it is fair to say that comparative policy analysis followed the primrose path of doing what it was easiest to do on the basis of information gathered by others.
>
> (Castles, 1989, p.5)

Despite these concerns, at its best this method has been highly productive, making it possible to develop typologies as a framework for exploring particular cases. Esping-Andersen (1990, pp.26–30) used it to identify what he calls three regimes of welfare capitalism – conservative, liberal and social democratic – around which he suggests most welfare states could be clustered.

Conservative welfare regimes are those in which 'corporatist' arrangements are most pronounced. Esping-Andersen defines these in terms which stress the ways in which state welfare is used to maintain (and even reinforce) existing class and status differentials, thus encouraging social and political stability and continued loyalty to the state. The state (rather than the market) is likely to be important in the delivery of welfare, but not in ways that encourage redistribution or equalization. These welfare regimes tend to dominate in those countries in which Catholic parties are strong, parties of the left weak, and there has been a history of absolutism and authoritarianism. Because such regimes tend to be highly influenced by the Church, they are also usually committed to the maintenance of traditional family forms, and the state intervenes only when it is felt that the family cannot resolve the problems of its members. The entry of married women into the labour market is discouraged, and benefits tend to encourage motherhood, while collective forms of childcare provision are underdeveloped.

Esping-Andersen suggests that Austria, France, Germany and Italy could all be seen as regimes of this type.

Liberal welfare regimes are principally characterized by an emphasis on market-based social insurance and the use of means-testing in the distribution of benefits. Levels of universal transfer payments and forms of social insurance are 'modest', and welfare is largely oriented towards a class of the poor dependent on the state. Benefits are limited and stigmatized, because the model assumes that higher levels of benefit will reduce incentives to work. Private schemes are encouraged for those who wish to go beyond the minimum, and in some cases may be actively subsidized. Such regimes are, therefore, highly differentiated and stratified, with 'a blend of a relative equality of poverty among state-welfare recipients, market differentiated welfare among the majorities, and a class-political dualism between the two' (Esping-Andersen, 1990, p.27). Examples of this type are said to include the USA, Canada and Australia.

In contrast to the other two, the social democratic regime is characterized by principles of universalism and equality. This regime tends to encourage equality across classes, based on high standards, rather than the minima endorsed elsewhere. In order to achieve this, services and benefits have to be provided at levels acceptable (and attractive) to middle-class groups, and members of the working class need to have access to the same rights as those of the middle class. According to Esping-Andersen (1990, p.28), 'This model crowds out the market, and consequently constructs an essentially universal solidarity in favour of the welfare state. All benefit; all are dependent; and all will presumably feel obliged to pay'. The attitude to the family within this model contrasts with those of the other two, because the state takes on and socializes many aspects of traditional family responsibilities (such as in providing support for children and old people), effectively encouraging individual independence, particularly for women who choose to work. Full employment is a central element in this regime, both because it provides income support and because it makes it possible to pay the costs of welfare. The Scandinavian countries provide the best examples of such regimes.

The power of such comparison is clear. It enables analysts of social policy to develop a picture both of patterns of difference and of broad directions of change. It allows them to raise their heads above the details of legislative programmes and their implementation in individual countries and to consider the importance of more general tendencies which cut across national developments. It provides a starting-point from which the significance of differences can be explored more fully. As Esping-Andersen makes clear, none of the regimes he identifies could be found in a perfect or pure form. Instead, each particular welfare state may have elements of all three in its make-up, and some may have quite distinctive features which are not reflected in the types he has identified. Britain provides a good example of a system that fits uneasily into any of the three regime types, although Esping-Andersen (1990, p.26) suggests that it is closest to the liberal one.

Thus, taking a typology as a starting-point for analysing welfare states does not necessarily mean that one has to present an overtidy account. Nor should it imply that one has to conceptualize welfare regimes as static entities. In fact typologies may constitute a useful starting-point from which to explore the dynamics of welfare change. Indeed, a more recent collection edited by Esping-Andersen (1996) is entitled *Welfare States in Transition*. This explores the changing pressures on, and developments in, different 'welfare regimes' in a changing global context. The transitional nature of welfare states is a distinctive focus of this volume, too. While some countries may still broadly conform to one of Esping-Andersen's regime types, all of the welfare states discussed in the chapters that follow are in a state of flux, experiencing changes that are contested and unfinished. Some of these changes may be away from particular regime types, towards hybrids of types or altogether new types of regime. Whilst Esping-Andersen's regime types do provide a useful starting-point for comparing welfare states, his typology does have its limitations, which we discuss below. First, however, we want to draw attention to and clarify some of the key concepts that have been referred to so far in this chapter.

3   STATES, REGIMES AND MIXED ECONOMIES

So far we have used three different labels for the systems of welfare that are the focus of this book – welfare states, welfare regimes and mixed economies of welfare. This raises the question of what precisely the object of analysis is in the national studies that follow. Are we examining states, regimes or mixed economies? The short answer is all three. As our discussion above of the problem of defining welfare states indicates, terms such as these are contested. Such terms are sometimes also used interchangeably, or one term can be used by the same author to mean different things in different contexts. In this book the term welfare state is used in a very general sense to refer to collections of policies and institutional arrangements within particular national territories for which the state has some kind of responsibility. As we have already argued, the use of the term welfare state does not necessarily imply that the state is involved as a direct provider of welfare services. Nevertheless, it does suggest that the state plays a role in shaping the context within which welfare is provided.

In some instances, the term welfare regime is used interchangeably with welfare state as we have defined it here. However, it is also used in a more specific way to refer to the particular constellation of features that an author believes to be salient and helpful in enabling us to distinguish between one type or model of welfare state and another.

Thus, for Esping-Andersen, the significant dimensions of welfare regimes that we need to look out for when comparing them are:

- the extent of decommodification of labour – that is, 'the degree to which individuals, or families, can uphold a socially acceptable standard of living independent of market participation' (i.e. without paid employment) (Esping-Andersen, 1990, p.37); and

- the extent of stratification – that is, the degree to which the welfare state differentiates between social groups (for example on the basis of occupational status).

In Esping-Andersen's usage, the concept of welfare regime has provided the basis for his typology of 'three worlds of welfare capitalism', which we discuss further in the next section. However, there is a third concept that has become increasingly influential in comparative social policy: the idea of mixed economies of welfare. As we noted earlier, the concept of mixed economies draws attention to the existence of multiple sources or providers of welfare (rather than an exclusive focus on the state). Two different strands in the study of social policy have contributed to the growing significance of this concept. First, feminist approaches to social policy have long sought to make the place of the family and a gendered division of labour in welfare more visible. In comparative social policy these approaches have argued that the focus on the institutions, politics and policies of welfare states has led to the role of the family and gender relations being either ignored or normalized as part of the undiscussed social context of welfare (see, for example, Langan and Ostner, 1991; Lewis, 1992, 1997; Sainsbury, 1994). As Jane Lewis has argued,

> the recent literature on modern welfare regimes has tended to pay insufficient attention to the significance of the mixed economy of welfare provision. Such provision means that the state, the voluntary sector, the market and the family all play a part, and although the balance among them has shifted over time, the amount of informal provision through the family has remained remarkably constant.
>
> (Lewis, 2000, p.38)

Second, some of the changes to systems of welfare provision in the 1980s and 1990s have made other providers more visible to social policy analysts, especially where the state has withdrawn from the direct provision of public services – see, for example, Rao's (1996) view of 'welfare pluralism'. Such changes, promoting the greater involvement of private, voluntary and family provision of both benefits and services in welfare, has made the mixed economy a more central concept for both welfare provision in general and in relation to specific services such as social care (Kuhnle and Alestalo, 2000; Wistow *et al.*, 1994). Both of these strands have played important parts in directing attention beyond the state in the study of welfare.

There are a few problems of categorization and terminology associated with studying mixed economies of welfare. For some studies, the critical distinctions are between the state and the market (for example Deakin, 1994; Johnson, 1995; Loney et al., 1991), reflecting the stark choice posed by neo-liberal challenges to the state in the 1980s and 1990s. Others have drawn a binary distinction between public and private provision (for example Burckhardt and Hills, 1999). Such binary distinctions tend to conceal significant differences and make the infor-mal/familial provision of welfare less visible. More conventionally, the mixed economy of welfare is seen as composed of multiple sectors. For example, Wistow et al. (1994) differentiate between the *public* sector, the *voluntary* sector, the *private* sector and the *informal or household* sector, while Kuhnle and Alestalo (2000) distinguish between the state, the market, civil society and the family and identify different patterns of welfare mix in European welfare systems. Their four elements clearly parallel the four sectors of Wistow et al., but the differences in terminology imply some significant issues for the analysis of mixed economies. For example, is 'the family' the same as the 'informal or household sector'? Does 'the family' imply a normative view of kin relations that might obscure other intimate relationships that are not part of a 'family system'? Is either the family or the household part of a 'sector' comparable to public, private or voluntary organizations? Finally, is the public sector the same as the state? It might be worth drawing a distinction between the public sector (as service provider) and the state (as the agency of policy-making, financing, regulation and control). Such a distinction helps to separate out the mixed economy of welfare (and its changing balance) from the political and policy calcu-lations made in the state which play a central part in determining the mix of the mixed economy (Clarke, 1996; see also Turner and Corbacho, 2000). These considerations suggest that although the 'mixed economy of welfare' has been a valuable addition to the conceptual repertoire of social policy, it needs to be approached and used with care. Despite this, it is clear that it is a concept that opens up dimensions of social welfare that take us beyond the concepts of welfare state and welfare regime. Because each of them highlights different aspects of social policy (and because terminological purity is not attainable, even if it was desirable), the authors in this book use all three concepts in exploring the changing politics, conditions and consequences of welfare.

4   INCLUDING THE EXCLUDED

Comparative social policy has continued to be dominated by approaches that centre on large-scale aggregate data that are mostly concerned with cash transfers and with issues of inequalities (and transfers) between socio-economic groups. Despite its overall strengths, some of the weaknesses associated with research based on international stat-istics are also apparent in Esping-Andersen's work. The main policy areas he explores are social security and pension expenditure and labour-market policies (Esping-Andersen, 1990). These are the areas in which his conclusions about the importance of class alliances and politics might be expected to find their greatest support. They are also the areas for which internationally comparative data are most likely to be available in a reasonably standardized form. If one were looking for policy areas in which non-class interests might be mobilized, or indeed those in which other forms of class politics were important (for example in the workplace), then other sources of evidence would be required. This is perhaps most obvious in areas such as family policies, childcare provision or reproductive rights, in which one might expect the role of women's organizations to have been significant but which are not well represented in international statistics.

The most striking absences from these statistical approaches – and (except in asides) from Esping-Andersen's regimes – are those relating to gender. Yet it is clear that the welfare arrangements in different countries are all based on key assumptions about the different positions of men and women in the labour market and the domestic economy. One of the problems with Esping-Andersen's approach is that it tends to underplay this. Although, as we noted above, he points to some important differences between the ways in which the regimes he identifies deal with families, and women within them, he does not follow up these issues in his more detailed analysis of statistics. Langan and Ostner (1991, p.130) have argued that 'Women appear almost by accident and then vanish again', because they are not central to the theoretical framework utilized by Esping-Andersen, and they only appear when the statistics make that necessary, for example in the discussion of labour markets. More often the discussion deals with apparently non-gendered categories, focusing on, for example, the extent to which different regimes allow a greater or lesser 'decommodification' of labour – that is, the degree to which social policies enable individuals to enjoy an acceptable standard of living without paid employment (Esping-Andersen, 1990, p.37). Of course, this fails to acknowledge the extent to which women's social position is shaped by being in a 'non-commodified' setting: the domestic or family economy (Orloff, 1993). Their role there is neither commodified (as waged labour) nor decommodified (as the condition of social benefits). Any binary distinction between the market and the state misses this realm. Langan and Ostner (1991, p.131) argue that 'men and women are "gendered commodities", with different experiences of the labour market resulting from their different relationship to family life', and stress the importance of appreciating the domestic division of labour 'in understanding the gendered nature of the welfare state and its associated social stratification'. Taylor-Gooby (1991, p.101) points to the way that 'the gender division of care coincides with patterns of access to and status in paid employment that, despite national variations, deny women equal opportunities in this sphere'. Drawing on Taylor-Gooby, Jane Lewis (2000, p.38) insists that social policy analysis needs to explore 'the relationships between paid work, unpaid work and welfare'.

These points are reinforced when consideration is given to 'welfare services provided free by women in the domestic economy' (Dominelli, 1991, p.8). These, of course, find no expression in aggregate statistics, yet may be of crucial importance in making judgements about who gains and who loses within particular welfare regimes – or particular 'mixed economies of welfare'. One attempt, by the Family Policy Studies Centre, to estimate what it would cost to pay wages to those involved in providing unpaid care in the UK put it at between 15 and 24 billion pounds per year (Evandrou *et al.*, 1990, p.258). If anything, this was probably an underestimate. As Dominelli goes on to argue, this makes it necessary to move away from approaches that distinguish sharply between the public and private spheres, since 'treating these worlds as unconnected to each other enables non-feminist theories to ignore the contribution the domestic economy makes to sustaining and repro-ducing public welfare relationships' (Dominelli, 1991, p.9).

In response to these criticisms of mainstream comparative research, feminist scholars have reworked orthodox typologies (for example Orloff, 1993) or devised new ones as a basis for comparing welfare states in such a way as to enable issues of gender to be foregrounded (for example Lewis, 1992, 1997; Sainsbury, 1994). These have sought to facilitate exploration of:

- the significance of the unpaid work that women do and the problem of securing social entitlements for these providers (Jane Lewis, 2000, p.37);

- the interrelationships between the various providers within the mixed economy of welfare;

- the dynamics and shifting boundary between the private and public spheres;

- the influence of familial ideology on social policies;

- how social policies reproduce the division of labour between the sexes; and

- the impact that the state as an employer and provider of welfare has on women's experiences as workers, consumers, mothers and clients (Sainsbury, 1994, p.152).

If gender is one element that is absent in much comparative work, 'race' is another. In fact, as Williams (1995) has pointed out, even gendered typologies have tended to neglect the dimensions of 'race' and ethnicity. Yet a crucial element in most modern welfare states is that they have developed to a large extent in response to changing under-standings and interpretations of 'race' and 'nation'. In turn, they have helped to shape and reshape the ways in which racialized divisions are understood in the societies of which they are part (Baldwin-Edwards, 1991a, 1991b; Williams, 1995; Gail Lewis, 2000). The Western European welfare states were created in part as a means of defining the continued status of their residents and citizens, in sharp contrast to the outsiders for whom access was to be limited. Since 1945 one of the recurrent themes of popular newspapers in most Western European countries has been the extent to which outsiders of one sort or another (usually black and frequently defined as 'immigrants') have been seeking to 'take advantage' of their welfare benefits and other provisions. Welfare citizenship has been a means of including some people, while excluding others (Morris, 1998).

As with the case of gender, the racialized division of labour within the welfare system has also served to reinforce and reproduce fundamental divisions. Since a high proportion of the support and service jobs within Western European welfare states are performed by black people, and these jobs are usually low paid, this helps to confirm their position at the bottom of the social system, within what Fiona Williams (1989) has called 'a racially and patriarchally structured capitalism'. Dominelli (1991) has listed a number of factors that need to be considered in the analysis of welfare in this context. They include: 'the exclusion of black people from access to positive welfare resources; the over-representation of black people in its punitive elements; [the] use of black people's labour to finance welfare provisions on the cheap; and the detrimental impact of policies on black families' (Dominelli, 1991, p.2). Few of these issues can be identified in the readily available international statistics. However, qualitative studies of the experiences of particular racialized groups have demonstrated the ways in which processes of social exclusion and subordination operate within a range of welfare regimes. For example, White (1999) has identified four main ways in which racially or culturally differentiated migrants are excluded: legal restraint; ideologies of 'othering' which de-legitimate the claims of migrant groups; failure to provide services that cater to the needs of these groups; and poverty and economic exclusion. From a different starting-point, Castles and Miller (1998) have devised a typology of western welfare states that distinguishes between three kinds of 'race regime': the assimilationist multicultural model associated with Australia, Canada, Sweden and the USA; the quasi-assimilationist post-colonial model exemplified by Britain, the Netherlands and France; and the guest worker, exclusionary regimes of Austria, Germany and Switzerland.

These concerns mark the beginning of a shift in comparative social policy. The move to broaden the concerns (and forms of evidence) away from the large-scale data sets dealing with financial transfers and labour markets has been a slow and uneasy one. The demands for comparison that is attentive to differentiated populations (not just socio-economic hierarchies); to the interplay of unpaid work, paid work and welfare (not just work and welfare); and to the forms of domination and subordination, inclusion and exclusion that are constructed through welfare policy and practice (not just income inequality), are significant challenges to the comparative study of social policy. This book reflects these challenges – and the problems of addressing them effectively.

5 MODELS AND STRUCTURE

Comparative work based on aggregate statistics produces a useful starting-point, as much for the questions it raises as for the conclusions it offers. But the gaps – what is not explained – are as important as what is explained. In order to move on, it becomes necessary to return to more detailed studies of individual countries or groups of countries, both in order to go below the level of official statistics and explore the content of welfare policies, and to fill in some of the gaps, to understand why particular welfare states do not quite fit the various types. In moving in this direction we are following the route advocated by Castles in his discussion of comparative public policy. He argues that although comparative analysis cannot deliver a model of welfare able to identify convincing and continuing statistical regularities, it is able to identify 'puzzles' that need to be explained and looked at in the context of a more limited number of cases (Castles, 1989, p.10). In other words, if one starts from a belief that there are substantial differences between two countries and the available statistics suggest their welfare out-comes are similar in some particular respects, then it might be worth asking why. Conversely, where similarities are expected and differences become apparent, questions may need to be asked. This is a more modest form of comparison, but not a retreat back to a belief in the need for an endless catalogue of unique cases. On the contrary, it is only recognition of the interdependence of welfare states within a wider set of international arrangements that provides the basis for a return to particular cases.

Despite the weaknesses that have been considered above, the three welfare regimes identified by Esping-Andersen are helpful in providing a starting-point for comparative analysis, particularly if they are not restricted to the areas of policy on which he concentrates. It is possible, for example, to point to ways in which the different regimes might also imply different positions for women within them (Taylor-Gooby, 1991, pp.102–3). They may also provide the starting-point for a more system-atic analysis of particular welfare states. This is the method we have adopted here, setting out to follow the approach described by Ginsburg (1992) as 'structured diversity'. This acknowledges the wide range of differences between welfare states but also understands that they exist within wider economic, social and political frameworks that help to structure that diversity.

It is in order to emphasize the importance of this that we start with an extended investigation of the development of the British welfare state since 1945. This may seem rather paradoxical: a return – despite all our high ambitions – to the usual quick run-through from Beveridge to Thatcherism and beyond. But our argument does not take Britain for granted as a focus of study, as a paradigm of the 'welfare state' against which those of other (less fortunate) countries have to be judged. On the contrary, we set out to use Britain as a case study of a welfare state both in order to help us to understand what is distinctive about it and

what it shares with other welfare states. We seek to explore and
identify what was historically specific about Britain within a wider set
of international arrangements. Our starting-point is the wider international settlements that were reached in the wake of the Second World
War. The bases of these are, of course, to be found in earlier periods,
but '1945' effectively settled the ground rules for the next three
decades, endorsing already apparent directions. These will be explored
more fully in Chapter 2, but it should be clear that European welfare
states developed in the context of the economic and political dominance
of the USA and the perceived threat of conflict with the Soviet Union.
An important justification for our approach is to explore the consequences of the break-up of these arrangements and the coterminous (if
not necessarily causally related) crises faced by many of the modern
welfare states.

Chapters 2 and 3 highlight the ways in which the British welfare
system has been shaped and reshaped since 1945, questioning the
notion that there was a welfare consensus that was unchallenged until
1979. Writing in 1990, Esping-Andersen noted that Britain's welfare
regime was a rather uneasy mix of universalism and the market.
Chapter 3 questions whether it has shifted to a new hybrid, combining
neo-liberal and social democratic approaches with traces of corporatism.
This chapter highlights the dynamic nature of welfare state development in the late twentieth and early twenty-first centuries.

Chapters 2 and 3 also explore many of the implicit assumptions made
about gender, 'race' and class which helped to define the meanings of
welfare 'citizenship' in Britain. In approaching these issues the chapters
draw on Williams's (1989, 1995) analytical framework, which is
organized around the interconnected themes of family, nation and work.
As Williams (1993, pp.82–3) has argued, 'particular and changing ideas
about what constitutes family life, what constitutes nationhood, culture
and national unity and the ways in which people are brought into (or
excluded from) particular forms of production, have a major bearing on
the formation and outcomes of welfare policy, provision and practice'.

Using this framework, it is possible to trace shifts in the assumptions
underpinning social policy in Britain which may have significant
consequences for how different groups experience the welfare system.
Thus we are able to see that the Beveridgean welfare state was
constructed around a particular vision of the white, English, 'respectable' working-class family, headed by an able-bodied, heterosexual, male
breadwinner. By the end of the twentieth century we can see a shift
towards a more ambiguous set of assumptions, in which an acceptance
(albeit limited) of diverse family forms and cultural traditions is
combined with a belief in the value of restrictive and punitive immigration and asylum laws and the active promotion of paid work as the
passport to social inclusion.

We then move on to consider other cases, which have been chosen
partly to exemplify the regime types developed by Esping-Andersen, but
with the clear understanding that these types only provide a starting-

point and that the actual experience of welfare in each may bear little relationship to what might be expected from the model. The chapters do not focus on Esping-Andersen's own relatively narrow concerns with pension rights and labour markets, but instead seek to consider a wider range of social relations and welfare provisions, in order to provide more rounded discussions of the particular cases, without losing sight of our broader comparative ambitions. Two examples of conservative-corporatist states are considered, in order to help clarify the range of differences that may exist within one model (see Table 1.1). In addition, the cases chosen are intended to help clarify the extent to which there is a degree of convergence between welfare states within Europe and, ultimately, as Chapter 8 asks, whether it is possible to identify the first signs of the development of a European welfare state. We have not attempted to produce a comprehensive survey of all possible forms of welfare regime, but have retained a more limited focus, with Britain at its centre. This means that we explicitly chose not to include any substantive discussion of the post-communist regimes of central and Eastern Europe or of the developing welfare systems in Southern European states, or of welfare arrangements in the South (Latin American, Asian or African states).

TABLE 1.1   States and welfare regimes

State	Regime type
USA	Liberal/neo-liberal
Germany	Conservative
Sweden	Social democratic
Republic of Ireland	Conservative

Chapter 4 turns our attention to the USA. The USA has often been presented as the clearest example of a liberal welfare regime and as the model to which many European welfare states are increasingly aspiring or being driven. However, by exploring the diverse social forces and political conflicts that have shaped the development of welfare in the USA, Chapter 4 suggests that the term liberal may not be adequate to capture the complexities of the US welfare regime, particularly in its current form. For example, an over-emphasis on the USA's liberal features – its emphasis on means-testing, its modest social benefits and its reliance on the market as the primary source of welfare – may lead us to underplay the significance of the moralistic and authoritarian influences associated with neo-conservative political forces that have played such a dominant role in US politics since the 1980s (Lo and Schwartz, 1998). Thus when the USA is presented as a model that

European welfare regimes are moving towards, we need to understand that this is a model which is itself in a state of transition.

Chapter 5 focuses on Germany as an example of more corporatist arrangements. Like the USA, Germany is a country fundamentally committed to market capitalism yet with quite a different set of arrangements in the welfare field. If the USA offers a mixed economy dominated by the private sector, the mixed economy of welfare in Germany is a rather different one, deeply rooted in a wider range of voluntary and church-based organizations, and organized around a clear notion of 'partnership' between the different sectors. The German system is explicitly based on the notion of 'subsidiarity', according to which welfare provision should always be the responsibility of the most basic unit possible, on a range from individual through family and voluntary sector to the different levels of the state. The state will only intervene when the family is unable to support its own members. But there is also an equally clear understanding that the state retains an important role in maintaining social norms and encouraging particular social relationships – for example, in constructing gender relations and also in defining those who may be accepted as 'German'. The absorption of East Germany by West Germany (the German Democratic Republic by the Federal Republic of Germany) in the early years of the 1990s has highlighted some of the tensions within the system, since although the Eastern model (of enforced universalism) was largely rejected, it continues to raise questions about attitudes to childcare, abortion rights and support for women in paid employment. It also draws attention to some of the difficulties of giving rights to insurance-based benefits to those who have never been part of insurance schemes and to the differentiated ways in which different social groups and differently racialized sections of the population are positioned by and experience the welfare system. The unification of East and West Germany also raises questions about the durability of Germany's conservative system, thus emphasizing once again that contemporary welfare regimes cannot be understood as static, stable or impervious to change.

Chapter 6 turns to Sweden, which has generally been cited as the classic example of the social democratic (universalist or socialist) model. Many of the aspects of the model are indeed to be found in the Swedish welfare state, particularly in the extent to which the middle class as well as the working class benefits from the welfare state, and the extent to which women have greater access to the labour market and there is more support for childcare than in other countries. There is also an emphasis in Swedish policy discourses on the active promotion of mutli-cultural awareness in order to facilitate the incorporation of minority ethnic communities into Swedish society and the welfare state. But the difficulties of sustaining the social democratic model in a time of economic difficulties are increasingly apparent, as are tensions in the underlying assumptions of universalism, the promise of economic independence for women and the emphasis on the incorporation and assimilation of minority populations.

The fourth case, the Republic of Ireland, is an example of a Catholic corporatist regime which, like Germany, has historically placed an emphasis on maintaining status differentials with extensive involvement from the Church. Up until the 1990s, conservative attitudes to the position of women dominated, and these severely restricted women's economic, social and reproductive rights. However, Chapter 7 shows how Ireland's Catholic corporatism has been radically redefined in recent years. Unlike in Germany, where economic and social pressures associated with unification have cast doubt on the durability of the welfare regime, the pressure for change in Ireland has come, at least in part, from an opposite direction – the dramatic improvement in economic fortunes associated with the development of the 'Celtic Tiger' economy. This has given rise to the consolidation of corporatist approaches to economic and social issues, combined with new commitments to combating poverty, inequality and social exclusion of the kind that have been more commonly associated with social democratic regimes. Most explicitly of all the cases under consideration, Ireland's welfare system has begun to be influenced by its relationship to a wider European context through membership of the European Union. For example, women's groups have increasingly been able to utilize EU legislation to challenge welfare policies and practices which discriminate against or oppress women. This begins to raise questions about convergence at a European level that are discussed more fully in the book's final chapter.

6   CONVERGENCE OR DIFFERENCE?

Running through all the cases and through the book as a whole is a concern to understand the nature of the crises through which all the welfare states under discussion have been passing, with a view to assessing how far these crises have been resolved, in what ways, to whose benefit, and at whose expense. An underlying issue in a great deal of comparative study is the extent to which welfare policies are becoming more or less similar. As we saw earlier, this issue also implies questions about what sets of conditions or forces are the predominant ones in shaping the direction of welfare states.

One argument that has been put strongly (for example by Esping-Andersen, 1990) is that the US-influenced liberal model is becoming, or is likely to become, dominant across welfare states. In the face of this perceived shift, others have argued for a form of social corporatism as a viable alternative that should be adopted more widely (see, for example, Mishra, 1990). The conclusions of Esping-Andersen's 1996 survey of welfare state developments are rather more circumspect about claims of convergence. Esping-Andersen argues that 'global economic competition does narrow policy choice', but that 'standard accounts are exaggerated and risk being misleading. In part, the diversity of welfare states speaks against too much generalization' (Esping-Andersen, 1996, p.2). Other studies have drawn similar conclusions (for example Kuhnle,

2000; Sykes, Palier and Prior, 2001). Kersbergen (2000) is surely right to conclude that welfare states remain the focus of continuing and new pressures. As a result, we cannot assume that welfare states (or mixed economies of welfare) will remain stable types. Indeed, many of the chapters in this book address the unsettled and uncertain prospects for the welfare systems that they examine.

It might, however, be possible to draw rather more definite conclusions about some continuing features of welfare states which are widely shared. In their different ways all of them make assumptions about the roles to be played by women and informal carers (also often women), and in the early twenty-first century it looks as if that role is going to be of increasing importance, with increased pressures on those performing it. It is also increasingly clear that welfare – however universally it is defined – is only available to those recognized as citizens. Different groups have different rights and different access. Paradoxically, it is frequently those employed at the lowest levels of the welfare system who are most explicitly excluded from its benefits.

Western Europe is becoming more integrated economically, and this is having fundamental impacts on systems of welfare, some of which are discussed more fully in the final chapter of this book. One aspect of this has been described as the development of 'Fortress Europe' – that is, a Europe whose main justification is to sustain high levels of welfare and employment within it, while excluding those from outside who also wish to benefit (see Gordon, 1989). As Hudson and Williams (1998, p.20) have pointed out, 'Whereas labour migration was encouraged in the expansionary 1950s and 1960s, there has subsequently been a progressive closure to both temporary and permanent immigration in the face of growing unemployment'. Most EU countries have effectively moved towards a model (pioneered by the Benelux countries, France and Germany) characterized by strict immigration control, permitting only economically necessary guestworkers and humanitarian considerations of family reunification and refugees (Baldwin-Edwards, 1991a, p.19). At the same time, refugee status is becoming increasingly tightly defined throughout Europe as a means of restricting the numbers able to seek asylum in these countries.

The promises (or threats) of harmonization of social as well as economic policy within the EU reinforce the urgency of clarifying the different models in contention. The current dominant expectation seems to be that the welfare regimes of the northern parts of the EU will appear too costly in comparison with the cheaper welfare regimes of the poorer south, even as the southern states seek to create more expansive welfare systems. This would then be a critical pressure leading towards the victory of liberal approaches within Europe (Sykes, Palier and Prior, 2001). Even if these are the dominant pressures, however, it is not clear that liberal market approaches will necessarily be the most effective (or cheapest) in delivering welfare. It is possible to envisage residualized versions of all the welfare regimes, even if it is not always easy to see how each would be able to sustain social and political legitimacy in such a context. It may be more appropriate to acknowledge that the complexity of the mix between regime types is likely to increase. There may also be pressures working in other directions, resisting moves to residualization. It may be too early to dismiss the positive benefits to employers as well as welfare citizens from welfare states closer in form to social democratic and conservative regimes, and Esping-Andersen (1996, p.267) holds out the hope that coalitions may be forged for the construction of welfare systems based on 'an alternative, post-industrial model of social citizenship and egalitarianism'. Such alternatives might be available if alliances are built which recognize the particular position and needs of women and of racialized minority populations within existing welfare states. We hope that this book will make its own contribution to informing debates about future welfare strategies in Britain and more widely within Europe.

REFERENCES

Amenta, E. (1998) *Bold Relief: Institutional Politics and the Origins of Modern American Social Policy*, Princeton, NJ, Princeton University Press.

Ashford, D. (1980) 'A victorian drama: the fiscal subordination of British local government', in Ashford, D. (ed.) *Financing Urban Government in the Welfare State*, London, Croom Helm.

Baldwin-Edwards, M. (1991a) 'The socio-political rights of migrants in the European Community', in Room (1991).

Baldwin-Edwards, M. (1991b) 'Immigration after 1992', *Policy and Politics*, vol.19, no.3, pp.199–211.

Brett, E.A. (1985) *The World Economy since the War: The Politics of Uneven Development*, London, Macmillan.

Burckhardt, T. and Hills, J. (1999) 'Public and private welfare', in Dean, H. and Woods, R. (eds) *Social Policy Review 11*, London, Social Policy Association.

Burrows, R. and Loader, E. (eds) (1994) *Towards a Postfordist Welfare State?*, London, Routledge.

Castles, F. (ed.) (1982) *The Impact of Parties: Politics and Policies in Democratic Capitalist States*, London, Sage.

Castles, F. (1989) 'Introduction: puzzles of political economy', in Castles, F. (ed.) *The Comparative History of Public Policy*, Cambridge, Polity Press.

Castles, S. and Miller, M. (1998) *The Age of Migration*, Basingstoke, Macmillan.

Chamberlayne, P. (1991/2) 'New directions in welfare? France, West Germany, Italy and Britain in the 1980s', *Critical Social Policy*, no.33, pp.5–21.

Clarke, J. (1996) 'The problem of the state after the welfare state', in May, M., Brunsdon, E. and Craig, G. (eds) *Social Policy Review 8*, London, Social Policy Association.

Clasen, J. (ed.) (1999) *Comparative Social Policy: Concepts, Theories and Methods*, Oxford, Blackwell.

Deakin, N. (1994) *The Politics of Welfare: Continuities and Change*, Hemel Hempstead, Harvester Wheatsheaf.

Dominelli, L. (1991) *Women Across Continents: Feminist Comparative Social Policy*, Hemel Hempstead, Harvester Wheatsheaf.

Esping-Andersen, G. (1985) *Politics Against Markets: The Social Democratic Road To Power*, Princeton, NJ, Princeton University Press.

Esping-Andersen, G. (1990) *The Three Worlds of Welfare Capitalism*, Cambridge, Polity Press.

Esping-Andersen, G. (ed.) (1996) *Welfare States in Transition: National Adaptations in Global Economies*, London, Sage.

Evandrou, M., Falkingham, J. and Glennerster, H. (1990) 'The personal social services', in Hills, J. (ed.) *The State of Welfare*, Oxford, Clarendon Press.

Fraser, D. (1973) *The Evolution of the British Welfare State*, London, Macmillan.

George, V. and Wilding, P. (1986) *Ideology and Social Welfare*, first published 1976, London, Routledge and Kegan Paul.

Ginsburg, N. (1992) *Divisions of Welfare: A Critical Introduction to Comparative Social Policy*, London, Sage.

Gordon, P. (1989) *Fortress Europe? The Meaning of 1992*, London, Runnymede Trust.

Heidenheimer, A.J., Heclo, H. and Adams, C.T. (1990) *Comparative Public Policy: The Politics of Social Choice in America, Europe and Japan*, third edition, New York, St Martin's Press.

Hudson, R. and Williams, A. (eds) (1998) *Divided Europe*, London, Sage.

Jessop, B. (2000) 'From the KWNS to the SWPR', in Lewis, G., Gewirtz, S. and Clarke, J. (eds) *Rethinking Social Policy*, London, Sage/The Open University.

Johnson, N. (1977) *In Search of the Constitution: Reflections on State and Society*, Oxford, Pergamon.

Johnson, N. (ed.) (1995) *Private Markets in Health and Welfare: An International Perspective*, Oxford, Berg.

Kersbergen, K.V. (2000) 'The declining resistance of welfare states to change?', in Kuhnle (2000).

Kuhnle, S. (ed.) (2000) *Survival of the European Welfare State*, London, Routledge.

Kuhnle, S. and Alestalo, M. (2000) 'Introduction: growth, adjustments and survival of European welfare states', in Kuhnle (2000).

Langan, M. and Ostner, I. (1991) 'Gender and welfare', in Room (1991).

Lewis, G. (2000) *Race, Gender, Welfare: Encounters in a Post-Colonial Society,* Cambridge, Polity Press.

Lewis, J. (1992) 'Gender and the development of welfare regimes', *Journal of European Social Policy,* vol.2, no.3, pp.159–73.

Lewis, J. (1997) 'Gender and welfare regimes: further thoughts', *Social Politics,* vol.4, no.2, pp.160–77.

Lewis, J. (2000) 'Gender and welfare regimes', in Lewis, G., Gewirtz, S. and Clarke, J. (eds) *Rethinking Social Policy,* London, Sage/The Open University.

Leys, D. (1989) *Politics in Britain: From Labourism to Thatcherism,* second edition, London, Verso.

Lo, C. and Schwartz, M. (eds) (1998) *Social Policy and the Conservative Agenda*, Oxford, Blackwell.

Loney, M., Bocock, R., Clarke, J., Cochrane, A., Graham, P. and Wilson, M. (eds) (1991) *The State or the Market: Politics and Welfare in Contemporary Britain*, second edition, London, Sage/The Open University.

Mishra, R. (1990) *The Welfare State in Capitalist Society: Policies of Retrenchment and Maintenance in Europe, North America and Australia*, Hemel Hempstead, Harvester Wheatsheaf.

Morris, L. (1998) 'Legitimate membership of the welfare community', in Langan, M. (ed.) *Welfare: Needs, Rights and Risks,* London, Routledge/ The Open University.

Orloff, A. (1993) 'Gender and the social rights of citizenship: state policies and gender relations in comparative research', *American Sociological Review,* vol.58, no.3, pp.303–28.

Pierson, C. (1991) *Beyond the Welfare State?*, Cambridge, Polity Press.

Rao, N. (1996) *Towards Welfare Pluralism: Public Services in a Time of Change*, Aldershot, Dartmouth Publishing Company.

Room, G. (ed.) (1991) *Towards a European Welfare State?*, Bristol, School for Advanced Urban Studies.

Sainsbury, D. (ed.) (1994) *Gendering Welfare States*, London, Sage.

Sevenhuijsen, S. (1998) *Citizenship and the Ethics of Care: Feminist Considerations on Justice, Morality and Politics*, London, Routledge.

Shakespeare, T. (2000) 'The social relations of care', in Lewis, G., Gewirtz, S. and Clarke, J. (eds) *Rethinking Social Policy*, London, Sage/ The Open University.

Sykes, R., Palier, B. and Prior, P. (eds) (2001) *Globalization and European Welfare States: Challenges and Change*, Basingstoke, Palgrave.

Taylor-Gooby, P. (1991) 'Welfare state regimes and welfare citizenship', *Journal of European Social Policy*, vol.1, no.2, pp.93–105.

Turner, F. and Corbacho, A. (2000) 'New rules for the state', *International Social Science Journal*, no.163, pp.109–20.

White, P. (1999) 'Ethnicity, racialization and citizenship as decisive elements in Europe', in Hudson, R. and Williams, A. (eds) *Divided Europe*, London, Sage.

Williams, F. (1989) *Introduction to Social Policy*, Cambridge, Polity Press.

Williams, F. (1993) 'Gender, "race" and class in British welfare policy', in Cochrane, A. and Clarke, J. (eds) *Comparing Welfare States: Britain in International Context*, first edition, London, Sage/The Open University.

Williams, F. (1995) 'Race/ethnicity, gender and class in welfare states: a framework for comparative analysis', *Social Politics*, Summer, pp.127–59.

Wistow, G., Knapp, M., Hardy, B. and Allen, C. (1994) *Social Care in a Mixed Economy,* Buckingham, Open University Press.

CHAPTER 2
THE CONSTRUCTION OF THE BRITISH WELFARE STATE, 1945–1975

JOHN CLARKE, MARY LANGAN AND FIONA WILLIAMS

CONTENTS

	INTRODUCTION	30
1	THE EARLY YEARS	32
2	REBUILDING THE NATION	34
2.1	THE BRITISH WELFARE REGIME: STATE, MARKET, VOLUNTARY SECTOR AND FAMILY	36
2.2	NATIONALIZING INFRASTRUCTURE: HEALTH AND EDUCATION	38
2.3	WELFARE IN THE POST-WAR ECONOMY	39
2.4	MEANS-TESTING: RESIDUAL NEEDS AND RESIDUAL BENEFITS	40
2.5	CITIZENSHIP: THE COSTS AND BENEFITS OF WELFARE	41
2.6	1945 AND ALL THAT	43
3	EXPANSION AND MODERNIZATION	44
3.1	THE EXPANSION OF STATE WELFARE	44
3.2	NEEDS AND PRIORITIES: THE CHANGING SHAPE OF WELFARE	50
3.3	MODERNIZATION AND REORGANIZATION: THE CORPORATE MANAGEMENT STATE?	57
3.4	THE FAMILY AND THE STATE	59
4	THE IDEAL, THE REALITY AND THE PATHOLOGY	61
4.1	CONTRADICTIONS IN WELFARE	64
4.2	THE BEGINNING OF THE END?	66
	REFERENCES	68

INTRODUCTION

This chapter and Chapter 3 deal with the organization of social welfare in Britain in the period since the Second World War. They examine how different institutions – the family, the market, the voluntary sector and the state – have been co-ordinated in a 'mixed economy of welfare' and how the balance of that mixed economy has changed during the period. Although we are concerned with the relationship between the four institutions in this mixed economy, in both chapters we give distinctive attention to the state. This is not because the state necessarily plays the primary role in *providing* welfare, but because the state is the *organizing* force that establishes the 'mix' between the sectors: the balance of familial, market, voluntary and public provision.

Our concern, then, is to highlight the political choices, the settlements between different interests, that have shaped and re-shaped the composition of the mixed economy of welfare. In these two chapters we have referred to the different patterns or mixed economies of welfare as 'welfare regimes'. This is not only a less cumbersome phrase, but it also highlights our concern to focus on political choices and the state's role in co-ordinating the different components of welfare provision. Partly as a result of this focus, these two chapters are specifically about Britain rather than the UK. Although Northern Ireland is subject to the same welfare legislation, the changing nature of the state and the forms of political organization there have meant that welfare has a relatively distinct organizational character (see, for example, Ditch and Morrissey, 1992). Even though the chapters focus on the British welfare system, this masks some differences that have existed within Britain. Some fields of welfare – and the law – differ significantly between Scotland and England and Wales, while education at all levels and the personal social services are organized through different structures and policy frameworks in England and Wales. This issue is a significant reminder that the process of studying and comparing national welfare systems or regimes implies paying some attention to the conditions, boundaries and constructions of nations. In the period covered by this chapter, the UK and Britain denote different geographical and political entities and ones that increasingly became the focus of forms of controversy and conflict.

In our survey of the developing construction of the welfare state we are also concerned to draw out the often unstated gendered and racialized assumptions within welfare policy about the role of the family, the position of women, and the nature of social citizenship. As we show, these assumptions have their roots in late nineteenth- and early twentieth-century welfare provision that was implemented to support the norm of the white, respectable working-class family, headed by a securely employed father with a subordinate, financially dependent wife and children. We pay close attention, therefore, to the ways in which particular ideas and norms about family, work and nation shaped the conceptualization of the rights and needs of citizens in early policy-

making, and highlight the extent to which these ideas became embedded in the post-war welfare regime. Drawing on Williams's (1989)
analysis of the centrality to social policy of assumptions about family,
work and nation, in this chapter and the next we will be examining the
changing – and contested – sets of assumptions in British social policy.
The triangle shown in Figure 2.1 sets out this framework and will be
used here and in Chapter 3 to summarise these assumptions and their
changes.

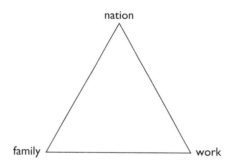

Figure 2.1   Structuring assumptions of welfare

A distinctive feature of the early post-war years was the expanded role
of the state in economic management and in providing benefits and
services by comparison with the pre-war period. The comprehensive
package of reforms affecting education, health, housing and social
security that was introduced between 1944 and 1949 established a
welfare regime in which the state promoted the principles of
universalist provision. However, the market, the voluntary sector and
the family continued to fulfil important welfare functions, while the
state sector retained important elements of an earlier individualist and
selectivist model of welfare alongside a wider commitment to collectivist
and universalist principles. Although this post-war welfare regime came
under growing pressure as a consequence of rising unemployment and
other social and economic changes from the mid 1970s onwards, it
remained substantially intact until the arrival of the Conservative
governments of the 1980s. We discuss these changes in Chapter 3.

This chapter begins with a discussion of the constellation of international and domestic political conditions that formed the context
within which the welfare regime emerged. We then divide the period
into two phases, the first from the mid 1940s up to the mid 1960s,
during which the broad framework of the welfare state was established,
and the second from the mid 1960s to the mid 1970s, when considerable
expansion and modernization took place on the foundations established
in the immediate post-war decades. Any attempts at periodizing social
history in this way always creates problems, implying too neat a
distinction between phases or periods. Social change is rarely organized
in forms of years or decades. Some processes have a long duration (the
struggle to create welfare rights runs from the late nineteenth century),
while others are intermittent or are of a briefer time-span. However,

periodizations are helpful as a way of concentrating attention on particular trends or tendencies. By focusing attention on the particular trends, tensions or conflicts of a period, they also show us how to escape a view of welfare history as a long and unbroken process of steady improvement. In this context, this periodization allows us to concentrate explicitly on the changing relationships between the state, the market, the voluntary sector and the family in the provision of welfare.

I THE EARLY YEARS

The most significant expansion of the British welfare state is generally traced from 1945. However, the period from 1880 to the 1930s saw both the consolidation of some collectivist forms of state organization and social regulation, and a crucial shift in the balance of the country's welfare regime. During the late nineteenth century, the delivery of basic welfare provision had been organized through a 'partnership' between the state and the voluntary sector, which included both working-class voluntary organizations such as friendly societies, and middle-class philanthropy. The two sectors operated in different spheres of action, but 'the voluntary sector was seen as part and parcel of the body politic, working with the same principles as government in respect of social problems' (Lewis, 1999). But increasing state involvement in welfare provision during the first decades of the twentieth century changed both the character of voluntary action and the relationship between the two sectors. By the 1930s voluntary organizations were no longer considered to be in 'partnership' with the state; rather their role was to influence and supplement public services (Lewis, 1999). From this point the state became the primary organizing force in welfare provision.

However, welfare policies introduced from the first decade of the century – old-age pensions, health and national insurance, school meals, the supervision and control of 'mental deficiencies', maternity and child welfare, public housing and the various employment benefits after 1919 – were not only concerned with meeting social need. They were also part of the attempts by the state to appease, supervise and control an increasingly militant working class and, thereby, maintain the social and economic conditions of Britain's stability, power and reputation.

They represented an attempt to ensure the fitness of British soldiers to defend the Empire and the skills and health of a labour force to maintain British industrial supremacy in the world markets, which were increasingly under threat from competition from the USA and other European nations. At the same time these policies began to consolidate particular images and conditions of family life and work practices and their relation to national and imperialist interests in ways which subordinated, marginalized and excluded certain social groups.

In the case of women, social policies focused on their needs as mothers over and above their needs as wage-earners. This can be seen in the development of maternity and child welfare services after 1918, which met some of women's very real needs but which also served to position women more firmly within the home. Such policies elevated motherhood to a new dignity. 'It was', as Anna Davin (1978, p.13) explains, 'the duty and destiny of women to be "mothers of the race", but also their great reward'. Women's role in the family became tied to the development of 'race' and nation through the assumption that nation meant the same as 'race': the 'British people' were also the 'British race' (Hall, 1998). Moreover, this elevation reinforced the restriction of women to the home and the separation of home from paid work, a process also reflected in the exclusion of women from some of the new insurance and unemployment benefits. In the health insurance scheme of the National Insurance Act 1911, women were only eligible for three-quarters of the rate; they were also penalized by not being able to claim for time off for childbirth (see Land, 1978).

Policies around income maintenance also marked the beginnings of a popularly accepted idea that entitlement to forms of welfare provision would be restricted by nationality, which in practice meant 'white', Christian and English-speaking. In addition, they illustrate how the close connection was forged between welfare provision and immigration control. This worked in two ways: denial of access to welfare acted as a form of control by threatening a so-called 'alien' who turned to public funds with deportation, or by using the welfare agencies themselves to police the access of 'aliens' to benefits. The Aliens Act of 1905 imposed restrictions on Jewish immigrants who had begun arriving, many as refugees from Eastern Europe and Russia, from the 1880s onwards. The campaigns for immigration control often included abusive anti-semitism, and found support from all the major political parties as well as from trade unionists like Ben Tillet, the dockers' leader. The Aliens Act demanded that no person who could not support her- or himself, or who might need welfare provision, should be allowed in, and that anyone who within 12 months was homeless, or living in overcrowded conditions, or living off poor relief, be deported. Following this, the Pensions Act 1908 denied a pension to anyone who had not been both resident *and* a British subject for twenty years. In the health insurance scheme of the National Insurance Act 1911, non-British citizens who had not been resident for five years received lower rates of benefit (seven-ninths), even though they had paid contributions (Cohen, 1985).

In the subsequent development of welfare policies, appeals to notions of the family, to national identity and British culture, and to the centrality of the work ethic for men continued. However, there were changes in how these ideals were constituted. Until the Second World War, national identity and British cultural supremacy tied the development of welfare policy to imperialism abroad. In particular, the economic imperatives of imperialism were consistently interleaved with the social and cultural mission to spread (British) civilization. To some on the left, like John Strachey, there was hope that the welfare state could replace the old imperial ideal in sustaining national cohesion. The welfare state became central to the reconstruction of post-war Britain. Britain's 'civilizing mission' as an imperial power was to be brought home. The welfare state embodied this spirit of reform and improvement. It was to be built with the bricks of the family and the mortar of national unity, by the labour of low-paid women and newly arrived black workers. Ironically it was often these groups of workers to whom the benefits of the new welfare state were restricted. Black male workers may have built council houses, but discriminating allocation criteria meant that they weren't eligible to live in them (Jacobs, 1985). Working-class white and black women may have cleaned hospitals but they were not necessarily entitled to sickness benefit in their own right.

2   REBUILDING THE NATION

Like the other western nations, Britain faced major tasks of social and economic reconstruction at the end of the Second World War. The form of welfare regime that emerged was the outcome of the particular balance of international and domestic social forces in the immediate post-war period. A complex combination of conditions framed the new world order that took shape in the late 1940s. Although the Allies emerged victorious from the war, popular confidence in the capacity of unrestrained market forces to guarantee either economic or political stability had been severely undermined by the events of the pre-war decades. Free market economies had been seriously discredited by the worldwide slump of the 1930s and by the slide of much of Europe first into fascist dictatorship and then into war. By contrast, the Soviet Union had emerged with unprecedented prestige from the war, its system of state planning apparently vindicated. A wave of popular radicalization throughout the west insisted on 'no return to the thirties' as the price to be paid for the sacrifices of the war years. Such demands meant that social, as well as economic, reconstruction were central issues for post-war governments.

The issue for capitalist societies in the west was how to combine the 'economic engine' of the free market with arrangements for ensuring domestic social peace. Reconciling these needs focused attention on economic management (rather than state ownership as in the Soviet model) to minimize the fluctuations of the free market and on social policies directed at the promotion of social harmony. As Esping-Andersen (1990) has shown, different countries developed different solutions to these problems, creating a variety of 'welfare capitalisms'. The creation of the British welfare regime was framed by these same conditions, shaped by the structure of its pre-war welfare system and overlaid by its position in the world order that emerged at the end of the Second World War. A central feature of this position was Britain's subordinate place in the 'Western Alliance' under US leadership, an alliance whose defining characteristics were increasingly sharply etched in opposition to the 'eastern' or 'Soviet' bloc in the cold war. US leadership of this alliance combined military, economic and political power, most clearly expressed in its domination of the post-war reconstruction of Europe: rebuilt using US funds, shaped by US concerns about the Soviet threat, and enthusiastically courted as a market for US economic expansion. Britain was locked tightly in that alliance – the 'special relationship' celebrating close military, economic and cultural ties that linked Britain and the USA and creating an 'Atlanticist' rather than 'European' orientation in British politics (Calvocoressi, 1987).

This new world order provided the framework within which the British welfare state was constructed. The traditional British establishment was deeply tarnished by bitter memories of the long depression years, by the shame of appeasement and by its early incompetence in the conduct of war, symbolized by Dunkirk and savagely caricatured in the figure of 'Colonel Blimp'. Even Churchill's wartime role could not save the Conservative Party from the landslide defeat of 1945. The leadership of the Labour Party, experienced in earlier minority governments and in the war cabinets, now stepped forward to implement a national revival programme largely drafted by two Liberals – John Maynard Keynes and William Beveridge. The legislative reforms that inaugurated the welfare state met some of the social needs of economic reconstruction. They also addressed the demands of a labour movement which articulated an egalitarian and democratic ethos engendered by the experience of wartime mass mobilization.

The creation of the welfare state was to play an important role in enhancing national prestige abroad, compensating to some extent for the loss of status to the USA and for imperial decline. In the post-war period Britain placed great emphasis on its capacity to give the world a moral lead, through the vitality of its democratic institutions (which had stood firm against fascism) and the values of citizenship and social solidarity (upheld by its comprehensive and progressive welfare system). The eugenic themes of the Beveridge Report, with its imperialist emphasis on the role of mothers in 'ensuring the adequate continuation of the British race and British ideals in the world', reflected this outlook (Cohen, 1985). Richard Titmuss, the pre-eminent figure in post-war social administration, endorsed the prevailing concern about the 'future of the white peoples' and drew attention to the way in which western civilization had 'slowly evolved a higher way of life', insisting that it was 'our duty to help and guide the teeming millions of India and Africa to a more abundant life' (quoted in Jacobs, 1985, p.10).

At the same time, the terms of Britain's subordination to the USA constrained the development of the welfare state. In the late 1940s US economic pressure reinforced domestic political opposition to social reform and spending on social services (Brett, Gilliatt and Pople, 1982). As early as 1947 the burden of financing US loans precipitated a balance-of-payments crisis, leading to the curtailment of the government's council housing and school-building programmes (Morgan, 1984). By 1950–1 the high defence budget required to sustain British support for US involvement in Korea resulted in further welfare cuts and the imposition of charges for false teeth and prescriptions. From the outset, the British post-war welfare regime was circumscribed by Britain's subordinate position in the Atlantic Alliance.

These economic and political conditions framed the internal reconstruction of the British economy and state. They form the boundaries of the post-war political consensus which oversaw the creation and development of the British welfare state. While the consensus allowed scope for considerable domestic political disagreement, keeping the major dimensions of party alignment alive and active, the external conditions were accepted by all three major parties (Conservative, Labour and Liberal) as establishing the limits within which governments were able to act. More than this, the consensus extended to agreement over the major directions that governments would pursue within those limits. At the core was an acceptance that some form of government intervention in economic management was necessary to overcome the inherent instabilities of a free market economy and to promote full employment.

Macroeconomic policies aimed to achieve a number of objectives: to promote Britain's competitiveness in a more complex world market; to minimize the economic and social disruptions brought about by the cycles of slump and boom to which unregulated free markets seemed prone (and to which the crises of the 1930s presented stark testimony); and to encourage the politically significant goal of full (male) employment. While parties differed on the level and form that such macroeconomic management might take (for instance, over whether nationalization of key sectors was desirable), the principle of intervention was widely shared. This commitment to intervention owed much to the experience of the wartime 'command economy' and its perceived effectiveness in promoting national efficiency.

The state was accepted as having a national 'co-ordinating role' in both economic and social management. Nonetheless, the stress both in wartime and the subsequent decades was firmly on the principle of co-ordination: improving the functioning of what was to remain a fundamentally capitalist or free enterprise economy in which nationalized or public-sector production was to play, at most, a supporting or infrastructural, rather than leading, role. Equally, the Keynesian policies of economic management adopted in the post-war period were geared to smoothing the workings of a free market through affecting the conditions of demand which formed the economic environment of individual enterprises, rather than the direct management of production implied in a fully fledged 'command' economy.

2.1 THE BRITISH WELFARE REGIME: STATE, MARKET, VOLUNTARY SECTOR AND FAMILY

In assessing the post-war reconstruction of welfare in Britain, it is useful to think of welfare provision not as a unitary structure ('the welfare state') but as a complex and changing pattern of relationships between the state, the market, the voluntary sector and the family. It is probably best captured by an analogy with the term used to describe the British economy in the same period – the 'mixed economy'. What was constructed between 1944 and 1948 was a new mixed economy of welfare. Nevertheless, the term 'welfare state' that was used widely to describe these developments was profoundly significant, both politically and ideologically. There was no 'welfare state': welfare was organized and provided through a range of departments, institutions and different tiers of government. Nevertheless, the popularity of the term suggests that it captured something of a shift in the relationships between state and citizen, centred on the commitment to collective welfare provision.

Although most attention has been given to the expansion of state provision in this period, this expansion was framed by the presumption that most welfare needs would be satisfied by the family and the market. Only in some instances, notably education and health, was it the state's role to be the primary agency of provision, and even here private provision continued alongside the work of the state. As we have seen, Britain's relationship with the USA established an external constraint on welfare spending that influenced both the structure and standards of the welfare state from the outset. Limited organizational and financial resources were directed into local welfare services, and consequently the voluntary sector continued to play a major role alongside local authorities in the provision of 'personal social services'. Equally importantly, the social relations of the market-place permeated the new system, creating a 'social division of welfare' that reflected deep-rooted class inequalities in British society (Titmuss, 1958). To the extent that welfare remained a matter of 'private' concern, the structural inequalities of individual income and family wealth were able to exercise a significant influence on access to 'welfare goods'.

In addition to its direct role in the provision of healthcare and education, the state was required to support the institutions of the market and the family, filling gaps where the market and the family failed, but with no intent to replace them as the main source of support to individuals. In their different ways the programmes of public housing, income maintenance, services to neglected children and so on, assumed that needs would be met primarily through (male) waged work and the services that a wage can buy, and through the services provided within the family by wives/mothers. Even in the income maintenance programmes, the predominant mode of providing for benefits was to be social insurance, which presumed a pattern of sustained employment in order to accrue a contribution record.

In these ways the construction of the post-war welfare state assumed a particular type of 'mixed economy' of support for the individual's well-being based on an economic and social architecture in which the 'family wage' was the lynchpin, linking the labour market to the distribution of social roles and dependency by age and gender within the family. Embedded in this structure is a clear view of a gendered division of labour. The idea of the 'family wage' justified differentials between male and female wage rates, men's higher rates reflecting their role as 'breadwinner' for dependants. Within the family, women traded house-work, childbirth and child-rearing and physical and emotional caring as 'labours of love' in return for economic support (Finch and Groves, 1983). In practice, much 'welfare work' was expected to be undertaken within the family either by spending some of the 'family wage' (on insurance policies or at the chemists) or by women 'looking after' young children, ill family members or dependent relatives. The provision of state welfare was intended to supplement and support this hidden welfare work and the family economy.

2.2 NATIONALIZING INFRASTRUCTURE: HEALTH AND EDUCATION

In the areas where the state intervened most extensively through the post-war welfare reforms – health and education – 'market' or private provision was marginalized but not abolished. Both the Education Act 1944 and the National Health Service Act 1946 extended and integrated previously existing state provision in their respective fields, creating national systems which were, significantly, free at the point of use. Universal access to secondary education and health provision marked major advances over pre-war patterns of provision and access, in particular the structures of class advantage associated with being able to pay privately for education and health services.

Nonetheless, these developments rearranged rather than removed the private sector in education and health services. The development of both proposals ran into strongly entrenched interests intent on defending private-sector provision. In health, this resistance was mar-shalled by the British Medical Association, which preserved the right of both hospital consultants and general practitioners to continue with private practice outside of or alongside National Health Service work. In education the Fleming Committee reported on the future of the private sector, recommending the continuation of 'independent schools' together with their closer integration with the state sector. Although permissive powers were established, allowing for the use of up to a quarter of private places for pupils from the state sector in return for subsidies to private schools, these powers were little used. As later research was to reveal (for example Westergaard and Resler, 1975), the architecture of both class and gender inequalities was reconstructed rather than dismantled within the new secondary education. The independent sector retained its privileged position and was supplemented by the creation of the grammar school stream. For most working-class children the expansion of access to secondary education led straight to the gates of the secondary modern (see the discussion in Halsey, 1978).

The changes in both health and education bore the marks of wartime experiences. The 'home front' had revealed the limitations of the pre-existing systems of healthcare and education, while the co-ordination of wartime services (such as the Emergency Medical Service and the evacuation of schoolchildren) indicated the possibility of the state playing a more enhanced role in the organization and provision of welfare. Although such possibilities were doubtless moved forward by particular political interests and lobbies, the experience of state co-ordination during the wartime economy provided a springboard for post-war reforms. The reconstruction of education and health around principles of universal state provision resembled the processes of 'economic' nationalization. Both were prefigured by state direction of the economy during wartime, but post-war this was concentrated on the nationalization of infrastructural industries or what were identified as core public utilities. Health and education can be seen as major infrastructural provisions in the social rather than economic field – being taken into 'public ownership' and thereby 'socializing' the costs of providing the minimum national health and educational standards seen as essential to the post-war reconstruction of British society.

2.3 WELFARE IN THE POST-WAR ECONOMY

The key economic foundation of the post-war welfare regime was the presumption that a managed economy would deliver full (male) employment as a political objective. Such conditions were the starting-point for William Beveridge in *Social Insurance and Allied Services* ('The Beveridge Report', 1942), which established the principles of an integrated system of welfare benefits. This report placed the insurance principle at the heart of welfare, drawing on the earlier systems of old-age, sickness and unemployment insurance introduced during the Liberal governments of 1906–14. The Beveridge reforms integrated these into a more systematic approach to social insurance, on the principle that contributions paid by employers and employees would fund basic insurance for the three main categories of need: old age, ill health and unemployment.

Embedded in this system were three core assumptions. First, it rested on the view that waged work was the primary source of income and that the state's role was to provide a limited substitution for loss of income suffered by individuals through no fault of their own (right from the start those making themselves 'voluntarily unemployed' were penalized). The principle of limited substitution was important in the way it assumed that the level of state provision should not act as a disincentive to either looking for employment or making individual provision for misfortune or the future (for example, by individual investment in private pensions).

Second, it embodied the assumption that the political task of maintaining full employment would be achieved, thereby minimizing the costs of one element of the insurance scheme: Unemployment Benefit. Without the maintenance of full employment, the insurance principle would be very severely tested, both by demands made upon it by those out of work and by the lack of incoming contributions from those who would have been in employment. Furthermore, the failure to achieve full employment would mean an inability on the part of individuals to build up the record of contributions necessary to fund the benefits which they might claim in the future (affecting pension rights in particular).

Third, it assumed that full employment meant full *male* employment. Despite the expansion of women's waged work during the war, both the Beveridge Report and the benefit system flowing from it viewed women's waged work as a secondary or peripheral activity. The assumption was that although women might work for a period before marriage, this would be merely a transitional phase on the way to their 'normal' condition of housewives and mothers. On this basis, women were structurally positioned in the benefit system as dependants, in that their access to income was assumed to be via men. In 'normal' conditions men would be the wage-earners, bringing in the 'family wage' from which the wife and other dependants would be maintained. In 'abnormal' conditions (such as sickness or unemployment) the interruption of earnings would be substituted by state benefits payable to the wage-earner and *his* dependants. One index of this gendered hierarchy was that married women were not expected to be separately insured for sickness benefit, since their sickness was assumed to involve no loss of income. As a result, it was anticipated that most women who were in paid work would pay reduced National Insurance contributions, since they were not expected to be claiming benefits in their own right.

2.4   MEANS-TESTING: RESIDUAL NEEDS AND RESIDUAL BENEFITS

From the outset, the benefits system rested on the assumption that income was normally to be derived from labour-market activity or its linked substitute, insured benefits. For Beveridge, an increasingly residual role was to be played by a further layer of non-insured benefits, namely National Assistance. This was intended to fill the gaps left by employment income and insured benefits and was to be strictly means-tested. Like the insured benefits, National Assistance embodied a set of assumptions about gender relations and the family. It continued what had been known as the 'liable relative' rule in Public Assistance, whereby men were assumed to be financially responsible for the women with whom they lived. This barred 'cohabiting' women from independent access to the National Assistance system, deeming that they would be economically supported by their male cohabitees.

A variety of changes between Beveridge's conception and the implementation of the National Insurance and Assistance programmes ensured that Beveridge's original view that means-tested benefits would play a declining role was never fulfilled. From the start, the benefit rates for National Insurance were set below the carefully calculated subsistence levels worked out by the Beveridge Committee, affecting unemployment and sickness benefits and state pensions. This led to recipients having to apply to the means-tested National Assistance for 'topping up' to bring their benefits up to the subsistence level determined by National Assistance criteria. Unemployment benefits were then time-limited to 52 weeks, requiring the long-term unemployed to resort to means-tested benefits after that point. A range of benefits directed to what Beveridge termed 'the marriage needs of women' (relating to widowhood, divorce, separation and sickness) were withheld, tightening the economic dependency of married women on their husbands.

Finally, the introduction of family allowances, for which feminist groups had campaigned since the late nineteenth century, established them below the realistic cost of child maintenance, requiring both National Insurance and Assistance to build in allowances for dependent children to their benefit rates. This was to have particular significance for National Assistance (and its later incarnation as Supplementary Benefit) as the numbers of lone-parent households grew (a category of need to which Beveridge had attached low priority). The combined effect of these changes was to ensure that means-tested benefits were to play a central rather than peripheral role in the British state's provision of income support during the post-war decades.

2.5   CITIZENSHIP: THE COSTS AND BENEFITS OF WELFARE

The post-war construction of welfare enormously extended the range of the state's support for individual welfare. It created wider access to the basic health and education services, increased access to public-sector rented housing, extended the numbers covered by insurance benefits, and extended access to uninsured benefits (National Assistance). In 1938, 1.3 million people were in receipt of some form of state income support, while by 1950 this had risen to 2.3 million (Parker and Mirlees, 1988, pp.494–5).

The expansion of services meant a continued enlargement of the share of gross national product devoted to public spending. Central government spending was the area of substantial post-war expansion, followed by growth in the local government share. The funding of state activities followed wartime trends, based on increasing rates of both personal and corporate taxation and lowering the thresholds at which personal taxation became payable. This expanded tax base combined with the revenue from National Insurance contributions to establish the financial settlement for the development of state welfare.

The combination of NI contributions and taxation in funding welfare expenditures is reflected in tensions about the nature of welfare 'rights' in the British welfare state which are particularly visible in relation to income support. On the one hand, the insurance or contributory system is associated with the idea of benefits being 'earned', since claims on such systems are legitimated through a contribution record. On the other hand, non-contributory benefits are funded from general taxation and represent cash transfers from taxpayers to the non-working population. This distinction underpins the more grudging nature of the 'rights' of individuals to non-contributory benefits. From the outset, non-contributory benefits involved an apparatus of means-testing and investigation designed to prevent fraudulent claiming, which continued pre-war attitudes to the 'undeserving' poor (those who had not 'earned' their benefits). Many surveys undertaken during the intervening years have confirmed that the social stigma associated with means-testing, combined with a relative lack of knowledge about entitlements, resulted in substantial underclaiming of non-contributory benefits.

Such processes raise significant questions about the nature of the status of 'citizenship' which is commonly identified as being expressed in the creation of the post-war welfare state. The idea of 'citizenship' reaches back to the 'New Liberalism' movement of the early twentieth century, in whose hands it became a key term for defining the expanded responsibilities of the state in establishing the conditions for all members of society to take a full and productive role in the nation's life (Langan and Schwarz, 1985). Beveridge himself was much influenced by New Liberalism and by the development of the idea of citizenship within Fabian thinking in the inter-war years. His use of it in the Beveridge Report echoed a wider view of post-war social reconstruction as making Britain a more egalitarian society (Calder, 1969).

The classic view of citizenship, formulated by Marshall (1950), describes the development of three fields of rights established between the state and its subjects which promote a formalized system of equality. The first is the field of *legal* rights (equality before the law), the second the field of *political* rights (universal suffrage) and the third the field of *social* rights (universal access to welfare benefits and services). The post-war welfare state, although often conceived of as establishing the last of these conditions, fell some way short of establishing universal access. We have seen that, in some respects, benefits were conditional rather than unconditional. We have also seen that, in the case of married women, access was as dependants rather than as individual citizens in their own right. (This parallels the uneven gender development of both legal and political rights in British history.)

Citizenship also imposed limitations based on birth and residence through the nationality tests that have been used to distinguish citizens from aliens in defining eligibility for benefits and services (see Gordon and Newnham, 1985). The 'universalism' of citizenship was, in these ways, deeply circumscribed – it was a highly conditional universalism which presumed a family-based social and economic structure. It addressed an indigenous population at whose heart were wage-earning males supporting families surrounded by a set of dependent populations positioned by age (both young and old), by gender (the 'anomaly of the married woman'), by infirmity and by 'race' (the 'alien' non-citizen). Assumptions about family, work and nation were integral to this view of welfare citizenship. These assumptions are linked by expectations about key processes in welfare: the family wage, the insurance principle, and the reproduction of the British people (see Figure 2.2).

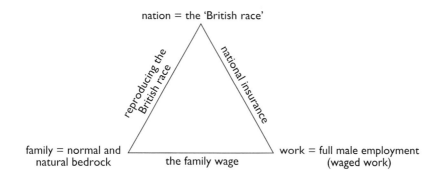

Figure 2.2   Structuring assumptions of the post-war welfare regime

2.6   1945 AND ALL THAT

In the preceding sections we have been attempting to establish some of the structural conditions and limitations of the immediate post-war welfare reforms. One reason for this focus is that the 'moment of 1945' is profoundly wrapped up in what might be called myths of recent British history which make it difficult to discern the precise character of the welfare regime that was created. On one side, '1945' is a triumphal moment – the point at which British society was transformed and a peculiarly British variety of 'socialism' was installed. Here, the welfare state, nationalization and the managed economy are seen as a decisive break with the bad old days of pre-war Britain. Opposed to this mythology is a demonology of '1945' which treats it as the point of origin of a British version of the 'totalitarian' state: an excessive and excessively interfering structure which undermined British freedoms, and the free market in particular (Hayek, 1944). Although the triumphal tone of '1945' as the start of a new Golden Age dominated public and political discourse in the 1950s and 1960s, the demonology of '1945' came to occupy an increasingly significant role in the 1970s and 1980s as the welfare consensus constructed around the post-war settlement came apart.

Our attention to the structural conditions and limitations of the creation of the British welfare regime is intended to offer a more circumspect view of the achievements of '1945'. What was created was considerably more cautious, partial and conditional than either of the mythologies about the creation of the welfare state allows. It is also important to trace the structural conditions under which the state involved itself in welfare, because many of the subsequent changes in welfare in Britain represent attempts to come to terms with different aspects of the legacy of '1945'. Subsequent events only make sense in the context of this settlement. The limited nature of British 'universalism'; a recognition that the 'welfare state' was only part of a larger mixed economy of welfare; the problems implied by lower than projected National Insurance benefit rates; and the dependence of this mixed economy of welfare on conditions of economic growth and the subordinate economic and political place of Britain in the post-war international system – these mark out the founding conditions of the post-war welfare regime. The following sections explore what happened when the unravelling of these founding conditions met changing social and economic circumstances.

3   EXPANSION AND MODERNIZATION

The international economic boom of the post-war decades allowed a dramatic expansion in the scope of welfare services within the framework established in the 1940s – a pattern that was common throughout the west. Demographic trends in advanced capitalist society – a combination of a baby boom and a growing number of older people – increased demands for welfare benefits and services. At the same time growing prosperity and, in the sphere of health in particular, scientific and technological advances encouraged higher expectations, but also spiralling costs. However, the welfare state in Britain came to occupy a distinctive political position in the 1960s because of the fact that, although the British economy had grown consistently in the post-war decades at a faster rate than at any time in the twentieth century (at an average of 3 per cent a year), it was still falling behind its major industrial competitors (whose average rates of growth were around 5 per cent a year). In response to the widespread perception of relative decline, the Labour Party put welfare services at the heart of a programme of modernization and national revival. These themes were to recur at the end of the 1990s, when a later Labour government identified 'modernization' as its core political task. This view of 'modernization' identified different conditions, problems and solutions from the programme of modernization developed in the 1960s.

In Harold Wilson's vision of the 'white heat' of technological revolution, an expanded and improved education system (including the harnessing of 'wasted talent' by The Open University) had a vital role to play. Grand housing and development schemes would remove the slum housing and inner-city blight that had resulted from 'thirteen years of Tory misrule'. Even social security policy – with the introduction of earnings-related sickness and unemployment benefits – was linked to the modernization project: 'in a period of rapid industrial change it is only elementary justice to compensate employees who, through no fault of their own, find that their job has disappeared', declared Labour's 1964 manifesto (quoted in MacGregor, 1981, p.112).

3.1   THE EXPANSION OF STATE WELFARE

If '1945' marked the foundation of the welfare state in Britain, the following thirty years saw its development into a systemic structure. That pattern of development changed little by way of the basic principles around which the mixed economy of welfare was originally structured. In those domains where the state had taken on the role of primary provider (especially education and health), the state continued to expand – particularly in secondary, further and higher education. In part, the expansion of the state's role in education and health reflected Labourist commitments to greater egalitarianism and increasing access to educational and health services.

But even where the state was the primary provider, voluntary and private sector alternatives continued and, in some areas, flourished. From 1948 local authorities were given responsibility for the development and provision of personal social services to some of the most vulnerable groups in society, including children and elderly, disabled and mentally ill people. However, these 'residual categories' of social need were accorded a low priority in the development of the welfare state, with 'the goals of universal access, uniform standards and comprehensive provision' (Brenton, 1985) being applied to the state's national priorities – the improvement of health and education services. As a result, local welfare services' share of 'public expenditure in the decade before 1965 grew from 0.6 to only 0.8 per cent, while health expenditure grew from 9.4 to 10.1 per cent and education grew from 8.8 to 12.4 per cent in that time' (Brenton, 1985).

Such inadequate financial resources meant that local authorities were not able to recruit personnel or develop the necessary expertise to meet their new responsibilities. The voluntary sector continued, therefore, to provide a range of personal social services which were drawn upon and part-financed by local authorities across the country. Figures for 1956, for example, showed that '87 per cent of local authorities utilised the services of voluntary organisations for the blind, 83 per cent for the elderly, and 70 per cent for the unmarried mother' (Finlayson, 1994). The slow growth in statutory welfare services thus ensured a continuing role for voluntary organizations within the country's mixed economy of welfare, with the voluntary sector being recognized as 'an integral part of the health and welfare services ... needed now and in future to supplement statutory provision and to undertake work beyond the scope of legislation' (Younghusband, 1959).

The private sector was also active in this same period. Table 2.1 records the growth of occupational pension schemes and private health insurance in the post-war period, together with the survival of private education. We have not discussed housing within this chapter, but it is worth noting that although the number of properties in the public rented sector increased from 2.5 million in 1951 to 7 million in 1980, the number of owner-occupied properties rose from 4.5 million to 12 million over the same period (*Social Trends*, 1982, p.149). That growth was heavily subsidized by a little regarded 'welfare benefit' – mortgage tax relief – which represented a major transfer from the public to the private sector in terms of tax revenue forgone.

Mortgage tax relief is one reminder of the continued presumption that it was through the market that most needs would be satisfied. Changes in the systems of income support were made within the continuing

TABLE 2.1 Private welfare in the United Kingdom, 1951–80

	Pensions (percentage of labour force in occupational pension schemes)		Healthcare (millions of members of private health insurance schemes)		Housing (millions of houses in tenure categories)			Education (percentage of pupils in independent schools)
	Men	Women	Subscribers	Pensions insured	Owned	Council rented	Private rented	
1951	30	12	0.06	0.1	4.5	2.5	7.5	5.0
1956	39	19	0.32	0.7	–	–	–	6.2
1961	50	25	0.50	1.1	6.5	4.5	5.5	7.7
1966	62	26	0.75	1.6	–	–	–	7.2
1971	55	34	1.0	2.1	9.0	6.0	4.0	6.1
1976	65	50	1.1	2.2	–	–	–	5.6
1980	68	55	1.6	3.4	12.0	7.0	2.5	5.8

Source: Taylor-Gooby, 1984, Table 5; data from *Social Trends*, 1981 (pensions); Seldon, 1981, p.56 (healthcare); *Social Trends*, 1982, p.149 (housing); *Social Trends*, 1982, p.47 (education)

underlying assumption that waged work was the primary source of economic support. What did change, though, were the numbers of people who were excluded from the labour market – by virtue of age, responsibilities for dependants, disability or (in the shape of things to come) unemployment. This growth of the dependent population (rather than substantial increases in the level of benefits) underpinned the substantial rise in spending on social security between 1945 and 1975.

In other respects changes in the nature of insurance benefits underscored the importance of the market. The shift to earnings-related contributions and benefits tied a person's prospects for income support more closely to their fortunes in the labour market and less to their 'universal' position as a citizen. Given the structuring of the labour market by patterns of class, gender and racialized inequality, the effect of introducing earnings-related benefits was to ensure the reproduction of labour-market inequalities inside the system of state income support.

TABLE 2.2   The relative growth of different categories of public expenditure, United Kingdom, 1910–1975

| | As percentage of gross national product | | | | | | |
	Social services	Economic services	Environ-mental services	Defence	Debt service	Other services	Total
1910	4.2	1.8	0.7	3.5	0.9	1.7	12.7
1938	11.3	2.9	1.0	8.9	4.0	1.9	30.0
1955	16.3	3.2	1.1	9.6	4.2	2.1	36.6
1970	23.2	6.1	4.0	5.6	4.6	3.7	47.1
1975	28.0	8.2	4.2	5.6	4.5	4.3	54.7

| | As percentage of total public expenditure | | | | | |
	Social services	Economic services	Environ-mental services	Defence	Debt service	Other services
1910	33.1	14.2	5.5	27.6	7.1	13.4
1938	37.7	9.7	3.3	29.7	13.3	6.3
1955	44.5	8.7	3.0	26.2	11.5	5.7
1970	49.1	12.9	8.4	11.9	9.8	7.8
1975	51.2	15.0	7.7	10.2	8.2	7.8

Note: totals may not be exact due to rounding.

Source: Sleeman, 1979, Table 3.1

Between 1950 and 1975 the share of GNP taken by public expenditure (that is, by central and local government spending) rose fairly steadily. Given that GNP itself was growing on average by 3 per cent per annum through much of this period, this meant a simultaneously larger slice of a larger cake. Within this framework, it was spending on welfare services that accounted for the largest part of the growth of public spending. Figure 2.3 shows the changing shares of GNP taken by different elements of public spending up to the mid 1970s. Spending on welfare services rose from a share of 11.3 per cent in 1938 to 16.3 per cent by 1955 and to 28 per cent by 1975 (see Tables 2.2 and 2.3).

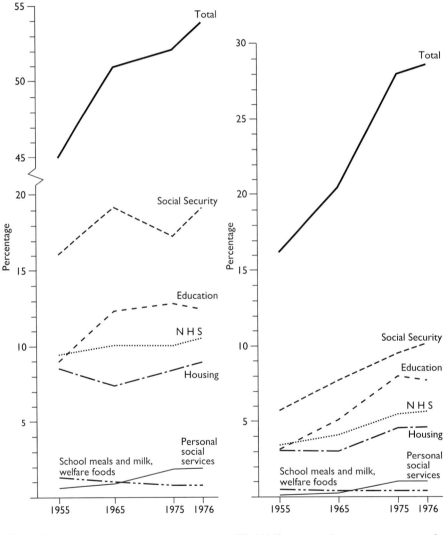

(a) Welfare expenditure as percentage of total public expenditure

(b) Welfare expenditure as percentage of Gross National Product

Figure 2.3   The growth of expenditure on the main branches of the social services, United Kingdom, 1955–76

Source: based on data from Sleeman, 1979, Table 3.2

TABLE 2.3   Total social welfare expenditure as a percentage of total public expenditure and GNP, United Kingdom, 1955–76

	Expenditure as percentage of:							
	Total public expenditure				Gross national product			
	1955	1965	1975	1976	1955	1965	1975	1976
Total social welfare	44.9	50.9	51.2	53.9	16.3	20.6	28.0	28.6
Total public expenditure	–	–	–	–	36.4	40.8	54.7	53.1

Source: Sleeman, 1979, Table 3.2

Figure 2.3 shows how different elements of the welfare system experienced divergent patterns of growth within the overall expansion of welfare up to 1975. In subsequent sections we shall consider some of the changing patterns of needs and priorities that account for these divergences. However, it is important not to take the bare economic facts of the growth of state spending and its share of GNP at face value, since there are specific political and economic decisions which shape that growth, in particular the means by which the state appropriates a proportion of the GNP for its own use. Public expenditure in general, and welfare spending in particular, is funded by a combination of four sources of finance:

1   National Insurance contributions;

2   general taxation (both direct and indirect);

3   local taxation (rates/community charge/council tax);

4   borrowing by the government.

Although employers' and employees' contributions nominally covered the expenditure on insured benefits, the bulk of welfare spending was funded from general taxation. In the mid 1960s, local taxes and NI contributions accounted for only 16 and 15 per cent respectively of the state's income (Sleeman, 1979, p.67). In part, the general economic growth experienced during the period provided a steadily increasing flow of money to the state without any change in taxation policies. But, in order to divert an increasing share of GNP to state spending, taxation patterns had to change.

Figure 2.4 indicates one significant area of change in taxation policies: the steady lowering of tax thresholds relative to average male earnings. The effect of such changes was to widen the tax base (the number of people paying income tax) by drawing in greater numbers of those on below-average earnings. Lower thresholds were accompanied by a tendential increase in the *rates* of taxation through the period, although

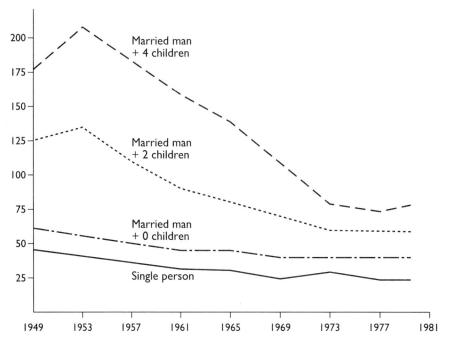

Figure 2.4   Tax thresholds as percentage of average male earnings

Note: the diagram takes family support through family allowance, Child Benefit and child tax allowance into account so that it is comparable over the whole period.

Source: Taylor-Gooby, 1984, Figure 2

these were subject to regular variations from government to government, particularly between Labour and Conservative terms of office. The expanding range of personal taxation made it clear that, if the newly discovered citizenship brought social rights, it also brought economic obligations.

3.2   NEEDS AND PRIORITIES: THE CHANGING SHAPE OF WELFARE

The expansion of welfare through to the mid 1970s can be seen as the product of the conjunction of three elements: changing patterns of need, changing state priorities and changing costs of welfare. Demographic patterns affect the level of demand for welfare. As Figure 2.5 reveals, one of the key demographic shifts that has borne increasingly upon the welfare state has been the growth in the proportion of the population beyond retirement age. This shift has two key features. One is the overall growth in the numbers of people over 65, and the other is the effect of increasing longevity such that some analysts find it appropriate to distinguish two age groups beyond retirement age: pensionable age to 74, and 75 and beyond.

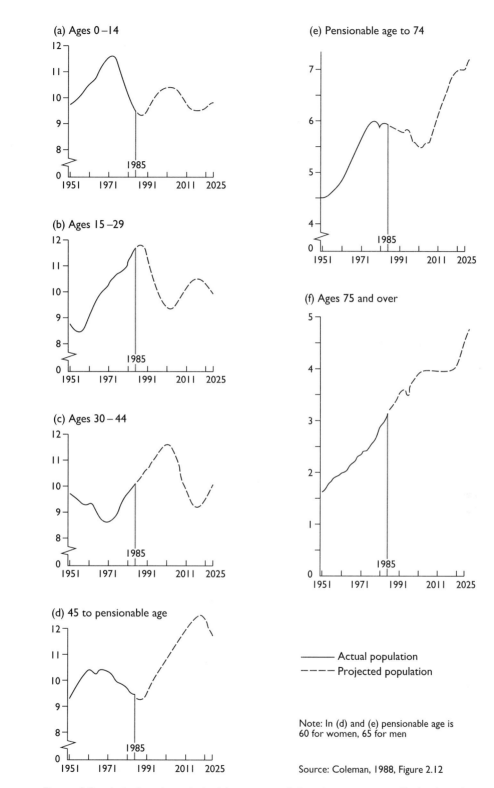

Figure 2.5   Actual and projected home population by age-group, England and Wales, 1951–2025 (millions)

Such changes have multiple implications for the provision of welfare. First, there are increasing numbers of people eligible for pensions. Second, there is an increasing demand from an older population on health services. Third, an ageing population implies more demand for social as well as healthcare, ranging from accommodation to personal support, which may be forthcoming from a variety of sources – kin, voluntary groups, personal social services or purchased from the private sector. Finally, as the proportion of the population beyond retirement age (and not merely the absolute numbers) increases, so the social costs of a growing non-working sector have to be met from the revenue generated by a relatively smaller economically active sector.

Poverty and inequality first re-emerged as political issues in the USA, partly in response to the black civil rights movement and partly as a result of a growing recognition of the persistence of poverty in an age of affluence. The complacency of the post-war world order, with its theories of 'convergence', 'post-industrial harmony' and the 'end of ideology', was undermined by the emergence of new forms of social conflict and widespread evidence of a decline of social cohesion. In the USA a series of social investigations, notably Galbraith's indictment of 'private affluence, public squalor' in *The Affluent Society* in 1958 and Michael Harrington's *The Other America: Poverty in the United States*, published in 1962, contributed to the 1964 'war on poverty' launched by the Johnson administration. Parallel studies of poverty and anti-poverty initiatives were undertaken in Australia, Canada, Sweden and France (see Atkinson, 1975).

In Britain 'the rediscovery of poverty' resulted from the pioneering work of Dorothy Wedderburn, Brian Abel-Smith and Peter Townsend. The publication of *The Poor and the Poorest* by Abel-Smith and Townsend in 1965 had a major public impact and put social security policy back on the political agenda for the first time since the Beveridge Report. It also led directly to the launch of the Child Poverty Action Group, which, as well as spearheading a forceful 'poverty lobby', influenced the growth of a wider 'welfare rights' movement over the next two decades (see Alcock, 1987). This movement included professional associations (representing groups working within the welfare state), charitable bodies (representing particular kinds of need, such as neglected children or forms of disability), activist groups emerging around new needs (such as those of the homeless and lone-parent families) and groups contesting patterns of discrimination (around 'race', gender and sexuality), newly defined welfare constituencies (people in mental hospitals, older people, claimants) and groups emphasizing links between First World industrialized affluence and Third World poverty and dependency. The expansion of the 'voluntary sector' added the political tasks of raising public consciousness and political lobbying to the work of direct provision of assistance which had historically been the focus of voluntary agencies. These 'dissenting voices' articulated a complex set of demands on, and challenges to, the welfare system. Some were demands for improvement in *levels* of benefits and services; some were demands for better *access* to benefits and services; others challenged the conditions, statuses and relationships that were assumed by – or reproduced in – welfare provision. The meanings of social citizenship took on increasing politicized significance. Characteristically, groups challenged what they saw as their marginalization or exclusion as 'second-class citizens'. Many of those challenges exposed the assumptions about family, work and nation that underpinned social welfare.

The impact of these pressure groups and the 'social administration' lobby on Labour policy may be discerned in the introduction of earnings-related benefits, the replacement of the limited family allowance scheme with the more comprehensive Child Benefit, and the strengthening of entitlements to means-tested benefits (see Hills, 1990). However, it must also be noted that real benefit levels were little improved, and Child Benefit in particular fell far below the costs of childcare, while the rising numbers of the long-term unemployed and lone-parent families produced growing reliance on means-tested benefits with their concomitant problems of stigma and lack of take-up.

Other demands on the welfare system also increased substantially between 1950 and 1970. Tables 2.4 and 2.5 show the changing pattern of income maintenance benefits paid out by the state in the post-war years. With few exceptions, most categories of benefit reveal steady increases between 1950 and 1970, with the largest rises being for pensions in both the insurance and means-tested benefit payments. The growth of needs for income support of all kinds enlarged the share of public expenditure taken by income maintenance (sometimes referred to as 'transfers'). But other services encountered rising demand as well in a complex mixture of new or growing needs (health), changing population patterns (numbers of children entering the education system) and changing political priorities. Substantial rises in education spending, for example, followed two major initiatives – the major expansion of higher education begun in the 1960s, and the raising of the school-leaving age (ROSLA) for secondary schooling, combined with moves towards comprehensivization.

At the same time, it is clear that not all the rise in welfare expenditure could be attributed to the processes of meeting new or expanding needs. The welfare state suffered from differential price inflation – the costs of providing its services rose faster than the national rate of inflation through the 1960s and 1970s. This phenomenon was visible for welfare services in all the western industrialized countries during this period and is based on the way in which costs are incurred in the provision of such services. Figure 2.6 provides a breakdown of the factors involved in the rising public expenditure on three areas of welfare between 1965 and 1975 in Great Britain. It separates out four elements:

1   the 'real increase' per person;

2   the 'population effect' (changing demographic patterns);

3   the relative price effect; and

4   general inflation.

TABLE 2.4   Number of persons receiving insurance grants, 1950-80, Great Britain (thousands)

	Insurance benefits					Maternity benefits		Children attracting family allowances[4]	War pensions
	Retirement pensions[1]	Widows, orphans, guardians, etc.	Average number[2] incapacitated by sickness and injury	Industrial/ disablement pension	Unemployment Benefit[3]	Maternity grants awarded during year	Maternity allowances awarded during year		
1950	4,152	474	917	59	226	757	124	4,756	1,047
1960	5,563	549	957	173	192	867	198	5,764	724
1970	7,363	551	978	207	305	829	233	6,955	519
1980	8,918	457[5]	1,096	196	709	664	351	13,304	354

Notes: [1] Men over 65, women over 60. [2] Not including death benefit. [3] Average number of claims during the year. [4] Before April 1977 family allowance was payable to a family with two or more children; Child Benefit, introduced in April 1977, applies to all children. [5] 1979 figures.

Source: Parker and Mirlees, 1988, Table 12.25; data from CSO, Statistical Abstract for the United Kingdom, relevant years; Ministry of Labour, Abstracts of Labour Statistics; Ministry of Labour Gazette; Treasury, Return of Expenditure on Public Social Services; DHSS, Social Security Statistics, 1976 and 1985

TABLE 2.5   Number of persons receiving National Assistance/Supplementary Benefits, 1950–80, Great Britain (thousands)

	Total persons benefiting from assistance	Total no. of weekly allowances	Dependants		Old[1]		Sick		Unemployed		Others		Non-contributory pensions in payment without supplement
			Adults	Children	With*	Without*	With*	Without*	With*	Without*	With*	Without*	
1950	2,289	1,350	272	351	677	106	114	102	38	39	96	178	316
1960	2,724	1,857	385	436	1,075	111	139	128	43	85	65	211	46
1970	4,238	2,739	674	825	1,745	156	164	159	71	157	274		–[2]
1980	4,972	3,115	692[3]	1,165[3]	1,590	101	57	148	176	678	365		–

Notes: *With/without contributory benefit. [1] Men over 65, women over 60. [2] No longer separately counted. [3] Includes Northern Ireland figures.

Source: Parker and Mirlees, 1988, Table 12.24; data from Ministry of Health, *Annual Reports*; National Assistance Board, *Annual Reports*; CSO, *Statistical Abstract for the United Kingdom*, for relevant years; DHSS, *Social Security Statistics*, 1976 and 1985.

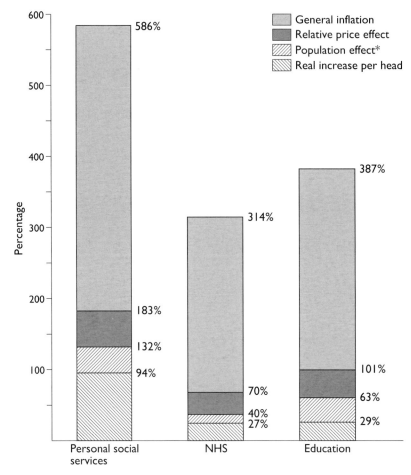

Figure 2.6   Percentage increases in government expenditure on services, 1965–75

*This assumes the following increases in 'need' stemming from population changes alone: education +27%, derived from a calculation of the increase in the 5–14 year-old age group; NHS +10%; and personal social services +20%, using the figures in *The Government's Expenditure Plans* (1977), vol. II (HMSO), p.80, for the second half of the 1970s.

Source: Gough, 1979, Figure 5.2

It can be seen that a significant proportion of the increased costs of each service are generated by the 'relative price effect' of the provision of public services. Gough (1979) argued that this effect primarily results from the comparatively labour-intensive nature of such services. Where other forms of economic activity were increasingly substituting machinery for labour, many of the services provided by the state offered few opportunities for such substitution, in that they involved what might loosely be termed 'people work' and did not fit the general industrial and commercial trend towards 'labour-saving devices' (for example, teachers were not displaced by teaching machines, nor nurses by robots). Such conditions meant that welfare services were disproportionately affected by rising labour costs throughout the post-war decades, although this only became visible as a political issue in the period of more militant public-sector trade unionism in the middle and late 1970s (Gough, 1979, pp.85–6). Nevertheless, the potential impact of labour costs on the provision of welfare services was mitigated by its characteristic employment patterns. The expansion of the public-sector services in the three decades following the war involved the staffing of such services drawing disproportionately on women and black people, whose position in the labour market meant that average wage rates remained significantly lower in the public compared to the private sectors of the economy. Without such wage differentials, deriving from the effects of gendered and racialized discrimination in the labour market, the costs of welfare would have been considerably higher.

3.3   MODERNIZATION AND REORGANIZATION: THE CORPORATE MANAGEMENT STATE?

The response of the state to this complex network of needs, priorities and costs was to focus on the need to modernize the organizational structures through which welfare was provided. Between the early 1960s and the mid 1970s, the British state underwent a fevered range of restructuring and reorganization affecting central government, local government and the NHS. All of these reforms aimed at creating administrative and managerial systems in place of what were identified as archaic and ramshackle systems that had evolved over the previous 150 years and whose lack of integration presented a major stumbling-block to the efficient co-ordination and management of public services.

The modernizing impulse of the Labour governments under Harold Wilson in the 1960s produced a major reorganization of government ministries into a new departmental structure of 'super ministries', starting with the creation of the Department of Education and Science in 1964 and, most significantly, the creation of the Department of Health and Social Security in 1968, which brought together the main structures of welfare services and benefits. This followed on from the reform of the National Insurance and National Assistance systems of income maintenance. Both government reports and other research had demonstrated structural flaws in the system of income support: the inadequate level of insurance benefits which meant recourse to National Assistance; the inadequacy of family allowances; and the problems of low take-up and stigma associated with means-tested National Assistance.

The Labour reforms brought some significant changes, most notably the extension of graduated benefits and contributions in the National Insurance scheme affecting sickness and unemployment benefits, and, in 1970, pensions through the introduction of the State Earnings Related Pension Scheme (SERPS). The National Assistance Board mutated into the Supplementary Benefits Commission, though much of its personnel, methods and rules remained the same. The resulting schemes of income support were not as redistributive in their effects as the original plans, nor did they accomplish sufficient increases in benefit levels (or family allowances) to remove the reliance on 'top-ups' from means-tested benefits. In fact, the decade of the 1960s saw an increasing reliance on means-tested benefits: among pensioners from 1.3 million in 1961 to 1.9 million in 1971; among unemployed people from 140,000 to 400,000; among sick and disabled people from 280,000 to 320,000; and among women with dependent children and no insurance entitlement from 80,000 to 220,000.

Local government was also a major object for reform, not least because a wide range of welfare services – education, housing and personal social services – were delivered through the local state. The Kilbrandon Committee (Scotland) and the Seebohm Committee (England and Wales) produced plans for the integration of what had been widely scattered aspects of personal social services, creating integrated social work or social services departments delivering a range of provision to a variety of client groups. The expansion of state welfare involved local authorities spending a greater share of GNP, rising from 9.8 per cent in 1951 to 18.6 per cent by 1975 (Gough, 1979, p.97). At the same time as local authorities' share of public expenditure was rising, the proportion of government revenue raised by local taxation (rates) declined, the gap being filled by increasing transfers from central to local government. A variety of reports addressed the changing role and position of local government, eventually resulting in a major restructuring in 1974 which created new and larger authorities responsible for the bulk of service provision. The aim was to create better management structures, which, combined with larger client populations, would produce more efficient service delivery.

The National Health Service was also to undergo major reforms through the same period, culminating in a major restructuring in 1974. In 1962 a substantial hospital building programme was inaugurated, and the hospital sector laid claim to a rising share of NHS expenditure through the 1960s. As in local government, concerns with the efficient allocation and use of resources dominated policy discussions through the period – originally around the concentration of services through district hospitals and eventually emerging in the form of regional and district tiers of management in the 1974 reorganization. The concern with the organizational structure of the NHS was paralleled by concern over the way resources were distributed in relation to health needs. The pattern of resources and needs at the inception of the NHS and for much of the ensuing period gave rise to what was known as the 'inverse care law', which described the concentration of services in the areas of lowest need and the relative lack of services in areas of highest need. The reorganization of 1974 followed previous initiatives aimed at redistributing resources to a closer fit with need, and was accompanied by the establishment of the Resource Allocation Working Party (RAWP), whose purpose was to establish new principles for matching needs and resources.

All of these reforms shared significant common features. They involved greater *centralization* and a commitment to a view of *managerial efficiency,* and were part of a movement towards greater *public expenditure and resource planning* by central government. The response to the growth of state spending, and the coterminous growth of the state as the largest employer in the country, was to look for mechanisms that would improve co-ordination. Increases in scale (whether in the form of the 'super' departments, larger local authorities or the regionalization of the NHS) represented public-sector adaptations of the economic wisdoms of the private sector – that large corporations represented the best integrated and most cost-effective form of organizing production.

Similar lessons were learned from the private sector in the view that such large, integrated organizational structures were best steered through systems of 'corporate management' – a cadre of senior managers capable of developing and carrying out long-term planning and of managing the efficient allocation of resources to accomplish the plans. This view of integrated planning also applied at the highest level of national government, with an increased commitment to both long-term economic planning and greater economic management in which the Treasury played a leading role. The result was a system in which centralized planning and budgetary systems took on a central role in the organization of public services.

3.4   THE FAMILY AND THE STATE

By 1975 the family occupied a rather more complex position in relation to state welfare than might have been predicted from the comfortable assumptions of 1945. The core presumption of the conventional nuclear family as the cornerstone of social care still prevailed, and the demeaning conceptions of heterosexual cohabitation still dominated social security provisions. But there were increasing signs that reality was failing to live up to this ideal, which led some commentators to criticize reality. Among the causes for concern were: the increase in married women's employment (concern that children were not being looked after properly); the rising divorce rate (concern about the possible collapse of the family); the growing number of lone-parent families (concern about the possible disappearance of the family); the growing numbers of illegitimate births (concern about growing immorality); and the increasing numbers of older people dependent upon public rather than familial care (concern about the loss of 'family feeling' and obligation on the part of younger generations). The bracketed comments here identify the most pessimistic and 'traditionalist' interpretations of these changes.

This growing gulf between the ideal and the reality of family life placed contradictory demands on social policy. On the one hand, state provision of care had developed around the assumption that the family would normally provide support for its members and therefore state support would be the exception. As the exceptions (and the concomitant demands on the state) increased, there was concern that the very existence of state support itself was producing the deviations from the ideal. This argument, sometimes referred to as the 'perverse incentives' of insurance (Parker, 1983), was expressed with especial vigour in relation to lone-parent families. Critics claimed this was a deviation encouraged by the knowledge that Supplementary Benefit was available to compensate for the loss of male income (the vast majority of lone-parent families being headed by women).

At the other extreme efforts were made to ensure that some sections of the population did not have families or, more accurately, did not have dependants who might seek to benefit from state provision. Although, as we have noted, public services benefited disproportionately from the employment of migrant workers, the 1960s and 1970s saw a constant tightening of restrictions on immigration to Britain, from the Common-wealth Immigration Act of 1962 through to the Immigration Act of 1971. The growing restrictiveness of the legislation was disproportion-ately directed at black and Asian migration. This oppressive trend culminated in the 1971 Act's distinction between 'patrials' and 'non-patrials': only those who had a parent or grandparent with UK citizenship were eligible for the right to live in the UK. Others wishing to enter became simply migrant workers with no rights of settlement or citizenship. 'Dependants' became a major focus of attention, with increasingly rigorous and discriminatory tests being applied to prevent entry of those who might become 'a charge on the public purse'. In these conditions, proving 'citizenship' became an increasingly significant test of eligibility for services or benefits – a test to be taken by those from ethnic minorities whose skin colour was taken to suggest that they were 'alien' rather than British (Gordon and Newnham, 1985).

The family also played an ambiguous role in one of the other significant policy developments of the 1960s and 1970s – the expansion of personal social services. The creation of local authority social services depart-ments (social work departments in Scotland) focused explicitly on the provision of a 'family service', which positioned the family in a number of different ways. Like other policy domains, it assumed both the normality and desirability of the nuclear family, and aimed to address concerns about 'family failure' by providing social work services to improve family functioning (**Clarke, 1993**). In an uneasy alliance with the NHS, social services were also responsible for those who, for one reason or another, were not being cared for by or within families and thus required (or were seen to need) residential care in public institutions.

The dual function of personal social services, linking family inter-vention and institutional care for dependent populations of older, young and disabled people, put social workers at the forefront of the move-ment towards 'community care'. This policy combined critiques of the ineffectiveness (and costs) of institutional regimes with a view of the desirability of individuals living 'independently' in the community. At its heart was an assumption that networks of care would or could be available within the community to provide support. This rested on the belief that networks of 'primary carers' rather than professional carers would play the dominant role in providing such support. In that context, primary care was identified with the family and – through the usual gendered logic of familialism – with women as wives, mothers, daughters and sisters of those who needed care.

4   THE IDEAL, THE REALITY AND THE PATHOLOGY

Throughout this chapter we have emphasized the importance of ideological assumptions about family, work and nation. These assumptions formed a context for the construction and development of the post-war welfare system, and they also shaped specific welfare policies. But such assumptions played a significant part in shaping experiences of welfare and the tensions or contradictions that the welfare system encountered.

In the immediate post-war period there was a substantial labour shortage, especially in the manufacturing industries and the developing welfare services. The state was faced with two possible solutions: to draw on married women as workers, or to draw on migrant labour from the colonies or the poorer parts of Europe. The first solution contradicted the ideals of motherhood and implied meeting the costs of socialized childcare, a provision which had been ill-organized and patchy during the war (Riley, 1983). The second solution posed problems to the state in terms of the costs that migrant workers would incur (housing, etc.). But it also evoked problems of racism and nationalism. The 1949 Royal Commission on Population had been concerned about the problems of 'good human stock' and the 'assimilation difficulties' of black immigrants compared with Europeans (Williams, 1989), but it considered that the movement of colonized migrants, as members of the Commonwealth, posed fewer administrative problems. From the beginning, then, Commonwealth immigrants were seen both as presenting a 'problem' and as a necessary solution to the temporary labour shortage. They were seen primarily as units of labour rather than as people with general or specific welfare needs.

The use of migrant labour, combined with an ideology stressing mothers' presence in the home, meant that married white women were not drawn as fully into the labour market as they had been during the war and as they were in many other western industrialized countries at this time. Nevertheless, many working-class women needed work to supplement or, in the case of widows or lone parents, to replace a male wage. For many white working-class women, the compromise was part-time work, which was not seen as interfering with domestic duties (Wilson, 1977). This also suited employers, as it was low-paid labour that carried no extra costs such as National Insurance or sickness benefits. In different ways, then, compromises were struck in the demand for more labour, but struck in ways which reproduced gender, class and racial inequalities.

As members of the Commonwealth, the new migrants should have been able to exercise their rights as welfare citizens, but different processes of direct and indirect racism served to exclude black people from some of their rights, to marginalize their needs, and to reveal the limited definition of welfare citizenship. One part of this process emerged, ironically, through the notion of 'universalism'. The universalist services that were part of the Beveridge plan – such as the safety-net of National Assistance, the health and education services – incorporated an apparently egalitarian philosophy of treating everyone the same, regardless of origin or status. Not only was this ideal premised upon a particular view of gender relations and family life, it also assumed white, Christian Britishness as the normative structure governing people's needs and expectations. Furthermore, treating people the same often meant failing to recognize the specific needs of some social groups – in the case of new migrants their needs for immediate housing, for information and translation services – or for the positive acknowledgement of differences in cultural and religious traditions.

Universalism in practice often meant uniformity, and for many of those who did not conform, their differences were seen in pathologizing terms. In other areas of provision, the conditions of eligibility were inappropri-ate to black people's immediate experience: for example, in council housing the qualification condition of long-term residency within a local area immediately made such provision inaccessible to new migrants. In this situation black people were forced into the private sector of housing, where, along with employment, racism was at its most overt (subsequently made illegal by the Race Relations Act 1968). In some areas, initially at least, needs were met through informal networks or voluntary groups such as the National Council for Commonwealth Immigrants. In Liverpool in 1948, for example, the Colonial People's Defence Committee organized for the subsistence needs of black seamen who had been denied access to Unemployment Benefit. Perhaps more importantly, though, black workers and their dependants stepped into a situation still heavy with a legacy of suspicion that all 'aliens' were potential scroungers and trouble-makers, and framed by a cost-benefit analysis of immigrant labour: the costs of their social and welfare needs were constantly set against the usefulness of their labour. The sub-sequent debate that accompanied the restriction of (unskilled) Common-wealth immigrants by the Immigration Act 1962 was about the 'drain' on welfare services by black workers and their dependants, even though little empirical evidence existed for the abuse or overuse of provision. In the Immigration Act 1971 the 'sole responsibility' rule restricted the opportunity for lone parents to bring children to live with them unless they could prove they had solely maintained or visited them.

Because of limited incomes and limited access to public-sector housing, black workers and their families often sought accommodation in the declining working-class areas, which were marked not only by poor housing but by lower standards of healthcare and educational services. In relation to schools, their children entered a process that was already operating to control and select children for a hierarchically structured labour market along class and gender lines. These processes took on a racialized and racist dimension. Working-class failure at school had been explained in terms of the inadequacy of working-class culture: this became reformulated to explain black children's under-achievement in terms of the inadequacies of Asian, African or Caribbean culture or family life. One example of this process is illustrated by the situation of many Afro-Caribbean women in the 1950s and 1960s. Many of these women were self-supporting and were recruited to work in full-time, often low-paid jobs with unsocial hours (often in the developing welfare services). In some cases this meant leaving children behind in the Caribbean until there were sufficient resources and accommodation to bring them over, or it meant bringing children into a situation where there was no formal provision for working mothers and in which the separation of mothers from their children and the whole idea of full-time working mothers was antithetical to familial ideology. So, while such women were working under the conditions imposed on them as migrant workers, they were seen at the same time to be failing in terms of the post-war ideals of motherhood. In this way, perceptions of the inadequacies of black family life entered the discourses of welfare professionals, although often in quite contrary or ethnically specific ways: Afro-Caribbean women being stereotyped as domineering and over-assertive, Asian mothers as subjugated and withdrawn. Some evidence of the pathologizing of black families can be found in the evidence that emerged in the 1980s of the disproportionate numbers of black children taken into care (ABSWAP, 1983).

A further example of the pathologizing of black families can be seen in the treatment of black children in the education system. From the beginning of the 1960s the presence of black children in schools became defined as a 'problem', even though the 'problem' was often that they were victims of the direct and indirect racism of teachers and pupils. In 1965 a Department of Education and Science circular suggested schools should have no more than 30 per cent immigrant children and recommended the 'bussing' of surplus black children to other schools. In the 1960s a disproportionate number of Afro-Caribbean schoolchildren were labelled as 'educationally sub-normal' (ESN) and sent to special schools, or were labelled as 'disruptive' and sent to special units (Carby, 1982). Such processes did not go unchallenged. By the early 1970s campaigns and research by black professionals and parents had begun to expose this situation, for example Bernard Coard's book *How the West Indian Child is Made Educationally Sub-Normal in the British School System* (1971). In their book about black women in Britain, Beverley Bryan, Stella Dadzie and Suzanne Scafe describe this process:

As mothers and as workers, we came into daily contact with the
institutions which compounded our experience of racism. We were
the ones who had to take time off to confront teachers and the
education authorities about the miseducation of our children. We
were the ones who battled it out with the housing authorities, the
Social Services, and the DHSS, as we demanded our right to
decent homes and an income above subsistence level.

(Bryan *et al.*, 1985, p.163)

The fact that black and white women in particular found work in the
growing welfare state was significant in two ways. First, as low-paid
workers black people and white women played an important role in
reducing public expenditure costs. Indeed, to some extent the welfare
state, especially the NHS, has continued to depend on the availability
of low-cost labour. A study of a London hospital by Doyal, Hunt and
Mellor (1981) found that 84 per cent of domestics and 82 per cent of
catering workers were from abroad, and that, in spite of the tightening
up of immigration controls, the NHS had still found ways of recruiting
migrant labour. Second, such public service workers also became an
important site of resistance in terms of defending public-sector cutbacks
through their unions from the mid 1970s, and by increasingly challenging the racism and sexism of welfare provision through the development
of anti-racist and anti-sexist strategies, especially in education and
social work in the 1980s.

4.1 CONTRADICTIONS IN WELFARE

This final strand in our discussion about the development of Britain's
welfare state in the post-war period focuses on its contradictory
elements. In this context we return to the ideological assumptions about
family, work and nation and suggest that these have been instrumental
both in conceptualizing the relationship between women and welfare
and in maintaining the contradictions and inconsistencies within that
relationship. For, on the one hand, welfare provision can play a
significant and liberating role in women's lives, but on the other hand it
may also serve to restrict women, to define them in certain ways (as,
for example, wives and mothers) and even to reproduce existing
divisions of class, gender, 'race', disability, age or sexuality. For
example, the creation of Beveridge's 'safety-net' of National Assistance
(later Supplementary Benefit and now Income Support) has provided
an important and necessary alternative to financial dependency on a
man for some women with children. At the same time, this kind of
financial dependency on the state, while giving women freedom from an
oppressive or unreliable relationship, also puts them on the poverty-line
and reproduces existing economic inequalities between men and women
(see **Cochrane, 1993**, on the relationship between female lone parents
and poverty). This contradictory relationship can also be seen in some
aspects of healthcare.

The creation of a National Health Service in 1948 was marked by an improvement in both health and the availability of healthcare. In 1951, for example, infant mortality was half the rate it had been in 1931, and by 1971 it had fallen further. Yet at the same time the class differences in the infant mortality rate actually widened. For example, in 1979 three times as many babies aged between 28 days and one year in Social Class V died as in Social Class I. A similar ratio of disadvantage was found in babies born to mothers whose country of origin was Pakistan (Graham, 1984, pp.50–1). Studies into the distribution of healthcare also found that middle-class people benefited from health provision more than those in the working class (Le Grand, 1982). These sorts of differences can also be found in women's experiences of healthcare. On the one hand, the universal provision of healthcare is particularly important for women. Women use and need healthcare services more often than men; this is not only because they bear children but also because they are usually responsible for the healthcare of their families; in addition, as women live longer than men they are likely in their old age to experience more chronic illness. Yet the way in which health services intervene in women's lives can be restrictive and serve to reproduce existing divisions and inequalities.

Take the example of fertility control. The development and availability of contraceptive and reproductive technologies have undoubtedly provided women with greater control over their lives, but at the same time these have been used by the medical profession as forms of control over women. The Abortion Act 1967, which legalized abortion, was a landmark for women. The Act represented one of a number of liberalizing reforms in the late 1960s, including the legalization of homosexuality between consenting adults over the age of 21 and the easing of the divorce law. Subsequently, over the 1970s and 1980s, the abortion reform was threatened by attempts to restrict its scope (as indeed were both divorce law and the freedom of gay men and lesbians) – especially on its availability to women of over 20 weeks' pregnancy. These threats became one of the focal organizing issues of the Women's Movement under the slogan 'A woman's right to choose'. However, under the Abortion Act, access to abortion within the NHS is still controlled and determined by the medical profession. By contrast, research into the experiences of black and disabled women show they have had to struggle for the right to control their fertility. Studies have shown that such groups were often seen to 'need' *control* through abortion, sterilization or long-term contraceptive injections (Bryan, Dadzie and Scafe, 1985). Research suggests that welfare professionals often take for granted the assumption that disabled women are unable to take on the responsibilities of motherhood (Morris, 1991; Begum, 1992). In the case of women with learning difficulties, such assumptions have led to sterilization without their consent (Williams, 1992).

The signs of strain around such conflicts, tensions and contradictions in the welfare regime became increasingly visible during the 1970s. The

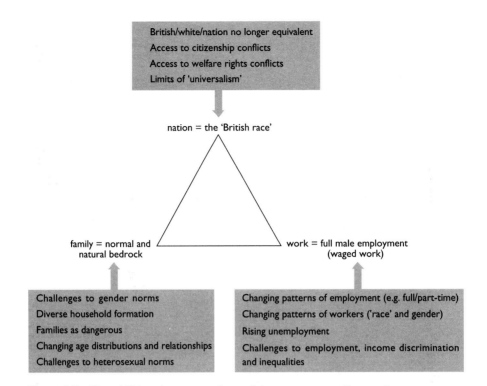

British/white/nation no longer equivalent

Access to citizenship conflicts

Access to welfare rights conflicts

Limits of 'universalism'

nation = the 'British race'

family = normal and
natural bedrock

work = full male employment
(waged work)

Challenges to gender norms

Diverse household formation

Families as dangerous

Changing age distributions and relationships

Challenges to heterosexual norms

Changing patterns of employment (e.g. full/part-time)

Changing patterns of workers ('race' and gender)

Rising unemployment

Challenges to employment, income discrimination
and inequalities

Figure 2.7   Destabilizing the assumptions of the post-war welfare regime

core social assumptions of the Beveridge-inspired welfare system were
under challenge (see Figure 2.7). In various ways, social and economic
changes combined with social and political challenges to destabilize or
'unsettle' (Hughes and Lewis, 1998) these assumptions. By the mid
1970s the welfare state was at the centre of a range of social and
political challenges. Some of these centred on what was provided
(contesting the level and content of benefits and services). Some focused
on who had legitimate access to welfare, questioning processes of
marginalization and exclusion. Still others challenged the conditions
and relationships of social welfare, in particular the inequalities of
power between welfare providers and welfare users. As a result, there
were complicated patterns of popular 'disenchantment' with the welfare
state, around its costs, its benefits, its conditions and its effects.
However, the emergence of a 'crisis' of the welfare state was signalled
most dramatically by changes in economic conditions.

4.2   THE BEGINNING OF THE END?

The British welfare regime had continued to expand up to the mid
1970s, along the intersecting axes of state, market, voluntary sector
and family established in the 1940s. In part this expansion continued
in the 1960s and 1970s in response to the perception of national decline,
out of the conviction that more high-tech healthcare and a well housed
and better educated population would be better equipped to revive

Britain's national fortunes. In part, too, welfare services – and welfare spending – continued to increase in response to the growing pressure from those excluded from the labour market, lone-parent families and the increasing proportion of older people. As the pace of economic expansion began to falter in the late 1960s, and was replaced by recession in the early 1970s, the difficulties of sustaining the pattern of state welfare in its post-war form emerged as a persistent focus of public and political debate.

In 1974 the Labour Party was returned to office on the basis of a counter-crisis programme and the promise of a 'social contract' – a deal between the government and the unions to preserve welfare services in return for restraining demands for wage increases (Panitch, 1976). In the first two years of the Labour government real wages fell as inflation raged and the unions acquiesced to an incomes policy. As the nation's economic plight deteriorated, the government was obliged to seek assistance in the form of a loan from the International Monetary Fund. The form of the loan obliged the government to cut public expenditure on welfare, drastically curtailing capital projects in health and education from 1976 onwards. The Labour government's shift towards austerity welfare policies at a time of rapidly rising unemployment produced a combination of widespread protest against 'the cuts' in various public services and more general disillusionment with Labour's programme.

The Callaghan government's persistence in trying to hold down the wages of some of the lowest paid public-sector employees finally provoked an upsurge of union militancy in what became known as 'the winter of discontent' in 1978–9. The Labour government's attempt to create a social-democratic or 'corporatist' response to the problems exposed by the first major post-war recession was generally judged a failure. The breakdown in the consensus of support for the welfare state in the 1970s reflected the erosion of the underlying assumptions of the post-war welfare regime. Where the Beveridge system had assumed and required full employment for its successful operation, the decline of the British economy created growing numbers of unemployed. Where the system assumed a patriarchal family supported by the family wage, neither the wage nor the family lived up to expectations. Where Beveridge assumed a declining role for means-tested benefits, the combination of growing numbers of unwaged people and the low rates of insured benefits ensured the steady expansion of means-testing. Most significantly, where economic growth had allowed potentially conflicting interests to be reconciled in the post-war consensus, the arrival of recession meant the collapse of the post-war settlement. By the end of the 1970s 'welfare' in Britain became the explicit focal point for a number of conflicts: between taxpayers and welfare scroungers; between ratepayers and 'profligate' local authorities; between rich and poor; between the 'general interest' and 'special interests'; and between citizens and 'aliens' – all increasingly framed by the question of 'what the nation could afford'.

REFERENCES

Abel-Smith, B. and Townsend, P. (1965) *The Poor and the Poorest*, London, Bell and Hyman.

ABSWAP (Association of Black Social Workers and Allied Professionals) (1983) *Black Children in Care*, evidence to House of Commons Social Services Committee, London, ABSWAP.

Alcock, P. (1987) *Poverty and State Support*, London, Longman.

Atkinson, A.B. (1975) *The Economics of Inequality*, Oxford, Oxford University Press.

Begum, N. (1992) 'Disabled women and the feminist agenda', *Feminist Review*, no.40, Spring.

Beveridge, W. (1942) *Social Insurance and Allied Services* (The Beveridge Report), Cmnd 6404, London, HMSO.

Brenton, M. (1985) *The Voluntary Sector in British Social Services*, New York, Longman.

Brett, T., Gilliatt, S. and Pople, A. (1982) 'Planned trade, Labour Party policy and US intervention: the successes and failures of post-war reconstruction', *History Workshop Journal*, no.13.

Bryan, B., Dadzie, S. and Scafe, S. (1985) *The Heart of the Race: Black Women's Lives in Britain*, London, Virago.

Calder, A. (1969) *The People's War*, London, Calder.

Calvocoressi, P. (1987) *World Politics since 1945*, fifth edition, London, Longman.

Carby, H. (1982) 'Schooling in Babylon', in Centre for Contemporary Studies, *The Empire Strikes Back*, London, Hutchinson.

Clarke, J. (ed.) (1993) *A Crisis in Care? Challenges to Social Work*, London, Sage/The Open University. (Book 4 of D311 *Family Life and Social Policy*.)

Coard, B. (1971) *How the West Indian Child is Made Educationally Sub-Normal in the British School System*, London, New Beacon Books.

Cochrane, A. (1993) 'The problem of poverty', in Dallos, R. and McLaughlin, E. (eds) *Social Problems and the Family*, London, Sage/The Open University. (Book 3 of D311 *Family Life and Social Policy*.)

Cohen, S. (1985) 'Anti-semitism, immigration controls and the welfare state', *Critical Social Policy*, no.13, Summer.

Coleman, D.A. (1988) 'Population', in Halsey (1988).

Davin, A. (1978) 'Imperialism and motherhood', *History Workshop Journal*, no.5.

Ditch, J.S. and Morrissey, M.J. (1992) 'Northern Ireland: review and prospects for social policy', *Social Policy and Administration*, vol.26, no.1, March, pp.19–39.

Doyal, L., Hunt, G. and Mellor, J. (1981) 'Your life in their hands: migrant workers in the National Health Service', *Critical Social Policy*, Issue 10.

Esping-Andersen, G. (1990) *The Three Worlds of Welfare Capitalism*, Cambridge, Polity Press.

Finch, J. and Groves, D. (eds) (1983) *A Labour of Love*, London, Routledge and Kegan Paul.

Finlayson, G. (1994) *Citizen, State and Social Welfare in Britain, 1830-1990*, Oxford, Clarendon Press.

Fleming Committee (1944) *Report of the Committee on Public Schools and the General Educational System*, The Hon. Lord Fleming, MC (Chair), London, HMSO.

Galbraith, J.K. (1958) *The Affluent Society*, Harmondsworth, Penguin.

Gordon, P. and Newnham, A. (1985) *Passport to Benefits? Racism and Social Security*, London, Child Poverty Action Group and Runnymede Trust.

Gough, I. (1979) *The Political Economy of the Welfare State*, Basingstoke, Macmillan.

Graham, H. (1984) *Women, Health and the Family*, Brighton, Wheatsheaf.

Hall, C. (1998) 'A family for nation and empire', in Lewis, G. (ed.) *Forming Nation, Framing Welfare*, London, Routledge/The Open University.

Halsey, A.H. (1978) *Change in British Society*, Oxford, Oxford University Press.

Halsey, A.H. (ed.) (1988) *British Social Trends since 1900: A Guide to the Changing Social Structure of Britain*, second edition, Basingstoke, Macmillan.

Harrington, M. (1962) *The Other America: Poverty in the United States*, Harmondsworth, Penguin.

Hayek, F. (1944) *The Road to Serfdom*, London, Routledge and Kegan Paul.

Hills, S.J. (ed.) (1990) *The State of Welfare: The Welfare State in Britain since 1974*, Oxford, Oxford University Press.

Hughes, G. and Lewis, G. (eds) (1998) *Unsettling Welfare: The Reconstruction of Social Policy*, London, Routledge/The Open University.

Jacobs, S. (1985) 'Race, empire and the welfare state: council housing and racism', *Critical Social Policy*, no.13, Summer.

Kilbrandon Committee (1964) *Report of the Committee on Children and Young Persons (Scotland)*, Hon. Lord Kilbrandon (Chair), Cmnd 2306, Edinburgh, HMSO.

Land, H. (1978) 'Who cares for the family?', *Journal of Social Policy*, vol.7, no.3.

Langan, M. and Schwarz, B. (eds) (1985) *Crises in the British State, 1880–1930*, London, Hutchinson.

Le Grand, J. (1982) *The Strategy of Inequality*, London, Allen and Unwin.

Lewis, J. (1999) 'Reviewing the relationship between the voluntary sector and the state in Britain in the 1990s', *Voluntas*, vol.10, no.3.

MacGregor, S. (1981) *The Politics of Poverty*, London, Longman.

Marshall, T.H. (1950) *Citizenship and Social Class*, Cambridge, Cambridge University Press.

Morgan, K.O. (1984) *Labour in Power, 1945–1951*, Oxford, Oxford University Press.

Morris, J. (1991) *Pride Against Prejudice*, London, Virago.

Panitch, L. (1976) *Social Democracy and Industrial Militancy*, Cambridge, Cambridge University Press.

Parker, H. (1983) *The Moral Hazard of Social Benefits*, London, Institute of Economic Affairs.

Parker, J. and Mirlees, C. (1988) 'Welfare', in Halsey (1988).

Riley, D. (1983) *War in the Nursery: Theories of the Child and the Mother*, London, Virago.

Seebohm Committee (1968) *Report of the Committee on Local Authority and Allied Personal Social Services*, F. Seebohm (Chair), Cmnd 3703, London, HMSO.

Seldon, A. (1981) *Whither the Welfare State?*, London, Institute of Economic Affairs.

Sleeman, J.F. (1979) *Resources for the Welfare State: An Economic Introduction*, London, Longman.

Taylor-Gooby, P. (1984) 'The welfare state from the Second World War to the 1980s', in D355 *Social Policy and Social Welfare*, Block 2 'Issues in the study of welfare', pp.1–56, Milton Keynes, The Open University.

Titmuss, R.M. (1958) *Essays on 'the Welfare State'*, London, Unwin.

Westergaard, J. and Resler, H. (1975) *Class in a Capitalist Society*, London, Heinemann.

Williams, F. (1989) *Social Policy: A Critical Introduction*, Cambridge, Polity Press.

Williams, F. (1992) 'Women with learning difficulties are women too', in Langan, M. and Day, L. (eds) *Women, Oppression and Social Work*, London, Routledge.

Wilson, E. (1977) *Women and the Welfare State*, London, Tavistock.

Younghusband, E. (1959) *Report of the Working Party on Social Workers in Local Authority Health and Welfare Services* (The Younghusband Report), London, HMSO.

CHAPTER 3
REMAKING WELFARE: THE BRITISH WELFARE REGIME IN THE 1980s AND 1990s

JOHN CLARKE, MARY LANGAN AND FIONA WILLIAMS

CONTENTS

	INTRODUCTION	72
1	SOWING THE SEEDS OF DISILLUSION	73
2	ROLLING BACK THE STATE?	76
3	TIGHTENING THE NET: WELFARE BENEFITS	79
4	A NEW WELFARE MIX: VARIETIES OF PRIVATIZATION	85
5	FAMILY, NATION AND WORK IN THE NEW RIGHT	91
6	STILL IN DISPUTE: FAMILY, NATION AND WORK AT THE END OF THE CENTURY	94
7	A NEW WELFARE REGIME?	100
	REFERENCES	106

INTRODUCTION

As Chapter 2 showed, the British welfare regime emerged out of the post-war resolution of international and domestic social tensions, and was consolidated in conditions of relative economic expansion and political stability. In the 1960s and early 1970s the welfare state was expanded and modernized in response to the changing demands and needs of a society that, despite the post-war boom, remained vulnerable to the problems of long-term economic decline. At the same time, the welfare state was subjected to a range of challenges and critiques that questioned its role and consequences. These emerged from very different directions. Some pointed to the welfare state's failure to remedy patterns of structural inequality. Others challenged the ways in which welfare policy and practice constructed and reproduced forms of social division and inequality. In particular, the role of welfare in relation to gendered and racialized divisions, and the distinction between able-bodied and disabled people became the focus of significant conflicts (Hughes and Lewis, 1998). Together with user movements, involving disabled people and benefit claimants, such developments produced a wide-ranging and complex set of challenges to, and demands on, the welfare state.

Such challenges intersected in peculiar ways with the shock waves from the international economic recession of the mid 1970s. The oil price rise of 1973, triggering the first worldwide recession since the 1930s, brought the return of mass unemployment throughout the west, eroding what had been for the founders of the welfare state one of its supporting 'pillars'. The combination of slowing growth and rising prices – 'stagflation' – produced intense pressures to curtail public expenditure and wages at a time of growing job losses and increasing poverty. As the problems of economic recession persisted, and even intensified, through the 1980s, the pressures on public provision of welfare provoked both widespread rethinking about the state's role in welfare and the restructuring of welfare regimes throughout the advanced capitalist world. In Britain, the failure of the Labour government's attempts to reconcile the conflicting demands unleashed by the crisis of the mid 1970s through the corporatist mechanism of the social contract was a condition for the emergence of a new Conservative approach dominated by the 'new right'. Their programme, which advocated an enhanced role for market forces and proposed to 'roll back' state intervention in industry and welfare, developed in Britain in parallel with similar 'neo-conservative' and 'free market liberal' policies in the USA. Under Margaret Thatcher and Ronald Reagan these policies came to dominate the 1980s (the experience of the USA is discussed in Chapter 4). There was a concerted effort to change the balance of the mixed economy of welfare – to shift the state from its dominant role and to promote the roles of the market, voluntary and informal sectors in welfare provision.

This chapter focuses primarily on the changes to the British welfare regime that took place during the period of new right political rule: the governments of Margaret Thatcher and John Major that were in power between 1980 and 1997. The chapter also explores the approach of the Labour government (self-defined as 'New Labour') that took office in 1997. This change of political party poses some analytical problems for the study of changing welfare regimes that will be apparent during the chapter. In particular, it poses a difficulty about whether to focus on what appear to be long-term trends or to concentrate on the more detailed comparison of similarities and differences in specific party policies. Giving too much attention to long-term trends risks missing the difference that the (party) politics of welfare may make. In reverse, an over-concentration on party politics and policy may obscure deeper trends in the remaking of social welfare. In this chapter we have tried to foreground the main trends and tendencies in the changing British welfare regime, while signalling some of the more significant political continuities and differences. Even this is a risky process, given that the social policies of the 'new' Labour government are still emerging. Furthermore, at different times the government itself has stressed both its continuities with its predecessors (especially in relation to economic policies and public spending controls) and its differences from them (in combating social exclusion, for example). In the last section of the chapter, we consider the problems of assessing the new welfare regime that has emerged from two decades of remaking.

1   SOWING THE SEEDS OF DISILLUSION

For the transatlantic new right, a principal concern was to reduce the role of the state in the provision of welfare. This was the focus of a sustained ideological campaign which placed a heavy burden of blame on the welfare state for causing economic and moral decline. This campaign began in the early 1970s, but in Britain it became more influential after Margaret Thatcher took over the leadership of the Conservative Party. In this section we shall be concentrating on three central themes in the new right critique of the welfare state: its claims that state welfare had contributed to *deindustrialization*, had created *disincentives*, and had caused *demoralization*. These three 'Ds' link economic, political and moral evaluations of the consequences of state welfare. They claimed to identify conditions that could only be remedied by reductions in public spending and a withdrawal from the state's dominant role in social welfare.

The *deindustrialization* thesis (most strongly advanced by Bacon and Eltis, 1976) claimed that the growth of the state was detrimental to national economic performance and was, indeed, creating the conditions for the structural decline of Britain's manufacturing base. The expansion of the state had these economic effects through a number of interlinked mechanisms. The expansion of the state (or public sector) took resources away from the market sector and industrial production, both in terms of the potential labour force (as state employment grew) and in terms of potential investment (as taxation increased to pay for the expanded state). More indirectly, although people were receiving a wider range of 'social goods' – those provided by the state rather than being purchased in the market-place – wage- and salary-earners were reluctant to take these into account when considering the impact of both taxation and inflation on their purchasing power, and thus demanded higher levels of income to increase their 'real' (i.e. cash) purchasing power. The expansion of state spending had resulted in manufacturing being subjected to a multiple squeeze – by resource competition from the public sector, by rising wage demands and, finally, by rising levels of taxation of corporate profits. The result of these combined pressures was a rapidly declining level of new investment in the manufacturing sector, and this created the prospect of deindustrialization.

These concerns were articulated in the agenda of the new right in the Conservative Party from the mid 1970s. They focused concern about public spending on the costs it imposed on personal, corporate and national economic development and argued for the need to free enterprise from the constraints and inhibitions imposed by what they identified as 'excessive' taxation. Public spending was thus at the forefront of the Conservative agenda for the 1980s; this was paralleled in the USA by the adoption of what has been termed the 'business agenda' during the Republican presidencies of Ronald Reagan (Moody, 1987). There, too, 'big government' was identified as strangling enterprise through excessive taxation and interference in the workings of the market.

The arguments about deindustrialization and economic decline overlap with Conservative claims about disincentives and public spending. Drawing on neo-liberal (or free market) economics, the argument about *disincentives* emerged during the late 1970s and exerted a strong influence on Conservative Party thinking and policy throughout the 1980s. Public spending was held to exert a disincentive effect on people's level of economic activity in two very different ways. First, high levels of personal and corporate taxation were seen as inhibiting enterprise and risk-taking, because both individuals and companies failed to gain the 'just rewards' of their efforts. Thus both individuals and companies would exert themselves to less than maximum levels because of the diminishing returns created by increasing levels of taxation. If the nation's economic performance was to be improved, the enterprising instincts of both individuals and companies had to be liberated from the stifling effect of taxation.

Reducing taxation meant that public spending would have to be reduced, at least if national debt – that is, government borrowing – was not to be increased. The concern about disincentives identified another result of public spending which provided a justification for reducing public spending: the disincentive effect of welfare benefits. Here, it was argued, the level of income that people received through various state benefits cushioned them from the necessity of seeking employment. The generosity of public spending undermined the will to work. Enterprise was thus being stifled by both the source and output of public spending, although through rather different mechanisms. The US economist J.K. Galbraith ironically summed up this economic theory: the rich don't work because they get too little money, while the poor don't work because they get too much. The disincentive effects of public spending were linked, in Conservative arguments, to other inhibiting conse-quences of an overpowerful and over-interfering state: an excess of regulation and officialdom which prevented people and companies getting on with their own business.

Although both deindustrialization and disincentive arguments focus on the economic consequences of public spending, the new right critique of welfare was not limited to the identification of economic malaise, but also pointed to the social and cultural consequences of state welfare. Linked to the inhibition of enterprise was the decline of 'independence' – the ability of people to take responsibility for their own lives. In these terms, the result of state welfare was *demoralization* – the sapping of a once vital national culture through people's expectation that the state would provide. Again, there is an overlap with the arguments about disincentives, in that the expansion and accessibility of state benefits as a substitute for wages were seen as undermining the 'will to work' and as promoting a 'culture of dependency' in which individuals no longer took responsibility for their own lives (see, for example, Davies, 1987; Murray, 1984).

These criticisms of state welfare formed the basis for new right arguments about the need for change – the need, as Margaret Thatcher once put it, to 'shake off the shackles of socialism'. The various new right claims about the effects of state welfare have been hotly contested, and studies of the economic and social consequences of welfare have raised considerable doubt about, and evidence against, many of the core arguments. However, the new right's views had a more substantial political and ideological impact, shifting the way in which the welfare state was publicly thought and talked about. Most decisively, state welfare moved from being discussed as a social, political and economic investment to being treated as a socially dangerous and 'unproductive' economic cost to the nation. New right attention centred on both reducing and changing the role of the state in providing welfare. Some argued that the welfare benefit system needed to be reformed to tighten up eligibility, to reduce the demoralizing effects of excessive benefit levels, and to make the system more 'efficient' by targeting benefits on the 'most needy' (Smart, 1987). More broadly, arguments from the new right stressed the need to break up the state's 'monopoly' of welfare provision, creating enhanced roles for private and voluntary sector alternatives and thereby allowing welfare 'consumers' to exercise greater choice among different welfare providers. In these ways the expanded role of the post-war state in the organization and provision of welfare featured as a central issue on the agenda of the new right in the late 1970s and 1980s, combining arguments from neo-liberal economics with neo-conservative (or traditionalist) moral evaluations of the consequences of state intervention.

2 ROLLING BACK THE STATE?

In discussing the new right's 'roll-back' of the welfare state, it is important, as Mishra (1990) argues, to distinguish a number of different stages in the unfolding of the offensive on welfare, or the distinct levels on which it operated. The first stage was a general ideological attack on welfare, which often had a propagandist or rhetorical character. This was important in creating an anti-welfare climate of opinion, but did not necessarily translate into practicable policy proposals. The second stage was policy as outlined in party conferences or election manifestos: again, this may have fulfilled other purposes (enthusing the party faithful, impressing the media, allaying public fears) rather than acting as a precise indication of what the party might do in government (for example, statements such as 'the NHS is safe in our hands'). Government policy, which may well be far removed from think-tank schemes or manifesto promises, formed the third stage, expressed in Acts of Parliament, policy circulars, financial and other resource commitments, and policy targets or objectives. The final stage was the implementation of government measures enacted in legislation or other executive actions. In general, these may be subject to 'drift', 'resistance' or uneven effects, such that the originally stated aims may not be achieved, or become modified in practice.

From the political agenda established by the new right, and from the hostility expressed towards the inefficiencies, inequities and social and economic consequences of state welfare by senior government figures during the 1980s, it would be reasonable to expect evidence of a shrinking welfare state or declining public spending on welfare. In fact, this is not what we find when considering the patterns of public spending during the 1980s and 1990s. Table 3.1 presents data on welfare spending between 1973/4 and 1995/6, which suggest that patterns of public expenditure on welfare have been remarkably stable. Indeed, the evidence is so at odds with the expectation that one commentator has written: 'Overall, what all this shows is that the welfare state, and indeed welfare itself, is very robust. Over the thirteen years from 1974 to 1987, welfare policy successfully weathered an economic hurricane in the mid 1970s and an ideological blizzard in the 1980s' (Le Grand, 1990, p.350).

A number of reasons have been advanced for this 'robustness' of welfare spending (see Le Grand, 1990; Glennerster, 1998). One is the effect of bureaucratic and professional inertia within the state, such that any attempt to change policy direction significantly will be a much longer

TABLE 3.1   Public expenditure on the welfare state, overall trends, United Kingdom, 1973/4–1995/6*

	Year-on-year increase in welfare spending (%)	Spending on welfare as % of general govern- ment expenditure	Spending on welfare as % of GDP
1973/4		50.3	21.9
1974/5	12.9	50.9	24.9
1975/6	2.6	52.1	25.7
1976/7	3.6	55.3	25.9
1977/8	−4.7	55.8	24.0
1978/9	1.5	53.8	23.7
1979/80	1.2	52.9	23.3
1980/1	1.5	52.6	24.4
1981/2	1.0	52.6	24.8
1982/3	2.2	52.3	24.7
1983/4	4.2	53.8	24.8
1984/5	1.0	53.1	24.5
1985/6	1.3	54.0	23.9
1986/7	4.5	56.0	23.8
1987/8	1.3	56.6	23.0
1988/9	−1.2	57.6	21.8
1989/90	0.8	55.6	21.6
1990/1	3.3	57.2	22.4
1991/2	8.4	60.9	24.7
1992/3	6.6	61.3	26.3
1993/4	3.7	61.6	26.6
1994/5	2.0	61.6	26.1
1995/6	0.7	60.2	25.8

* Calculated from real spending at 1995/6 prices.

Source: Glennerster, 1998, Table 8.1

drawn-out process than might be assumed from the statements of politicians. A second explanation relates to the changing patterns of demography and need. The long-term trend towards a growing population of older people continued during the 1980s and 1990s and brought with it increased demands for welfare benefits and services. Alongside this was the substantial growth in the numbers of people unemployed, which rose sharply at the beginning and end of the 1980s and again in the 1990s. The actual size of the unemployed population and its consequences for welfare costs were made more complicated by frequent changes in government definitions of unemployment and the conditions of eligibility for benefit. Nonetheless, the underlying trend of increased unemployment had a significant impact on patterns of welfare spending during the 1980s and 1990s.

A third explanation involves making distinctions within the broad patterns of welfare spending and looking at the relative fortunes of different welfare programmes. Figure 3.1 shows that the proportions of welfare spending directed to different programmes changed over the period 1973/4 to 1995/6, with some welfare programmes faring better than others during the 1980s and 1990s. Across the period, health and personal social services increased their share of welfare spending slightly, from 18.8 per cent to 22.3 per cent and from 3.6 per cent to 4.8 per cent respectively. The shares of welfare spending of education and housing (including housing benefit) declined from 25.6 per cent to 19.8 per cent and from 17.6 per cent to 8.8 per cent respectively. At the same time, the share taken by social security increased from 34.7 per cent to 44.3 per cent. While changing social and demographic patterns may influence these changes, Glennerster considers whether social divisions may also have had an effect, pointing to arguments about 'pro-poor

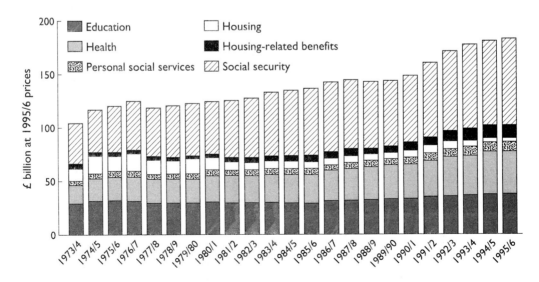

Figure 3.1   Public welfare expenditure by function, United Kingdom, 1973/4–1995/6

Source: Glennerster, 1998, Figure 8.1

policies' (targeting, etc.) or 'middle-class capture' of key services, from which middle-class constituencies reap disproportionate benefit (Glennerster, 1998, pp.322–4; see also Le Grand, 1990; Le Grand and Winter, 1987; and Powell, 1995). Glennerster concludes that, although there is some evidence that targeting increased, there was no 'dramatic' shift towards poor people benefiting more in absolute or relative terms. Similarly, there is no decisive evidence that 'middle-class' welfare services received relative protection. However, what had been the most decisively pro-poor area of welfare (public housing and housing benefit) suffered most in the re-ordering of welfare priorities (see also Pryke, 1998). Perhaps the most significant conclusion drawn by Glennerster in this review of state welfare is that, despite 'pro-poor' targeting of benefits and services, 'the gap between rich and poor grew' as a result of 'the widening of rewards in the labour market and labour market inactivity combined with the decline in benefit levels relative to earnings and tax policy' (Glennerster, 1998, p.235).

Most of these general trends were maintained by the Labour government of 1997, not least because they entered office with a commitment to maintain Conservative public spending limits for the first two years of government. Extra resources were subsequently directed to initiatives and 'modernizing' reforms in education and the NHS. At the same time, the government was seeking to reduce the growth of social security spending, partly by reducing the numbers in receipt of benefit, and partly by encouraging a shift to private pension provision (Department of Social Security, 2000a). We shall return to these issues in later sections.

Although this analysis of the different programmes of the welfare state deals with important issues, it does not capture all the significant changes that have taken place during the 1980s and 1990s. The involvement of the state in welfare means more than determining the overall level of spending or its distribution within particular programmes. There are also important issues about both how – or under what conditions – welfare is provided and about the relationship between the state and the other providers of welfare. These are the subjects of the following two sections.

3 TIGHTENING THE NET: WELFARE BENEFITS

Although it was the Labour government of the mid 1970s that abandoned the full employment 'pillar' of the welfare state, it was not until the 1980s that the 'safety-net' provided by the welfare state for those out of work or otherwise unable to support themselves was significantly tightened (by reducing the value of benefits) and shrunk (by reducing eligibility). Together with a series of measures to deregulate the labour market (the abolition of wages councils, anti-union legislation, significant reductions in protection against unfair dismissal, etc.), these policies resulted in a sharp deterioration in the welfare rights of a substantial section of the population.

Given the new right's view of the disincentive and demoralizing effects of welfare, it is hardly surprising that the benefits system was a major focus of Conservative policy-making during the 1980s and 1990s. They pursued a number of objectives in order to:

- reduce the disincentive and dependency-creating effects of benefits;

- create a more efficient benefits system by 'targeting' benefits at the most needy; and

- encourage moves away from the state as the primary agency of social insurance.

In pursuing these objectives, successive governments made changes to the benefits system, ranging from changes in regulations affecting the conditions of eligibility and payment, through changes in the value of payments, to substantial restructurings of the Supplementary Benefits programme (renamed as Income Support). In many respects, the 'New Labour' government of the late 1990s continued the pursuit of the first two policy objectives for the benefits system. They found themselves engaged in more complex problems about changing the basis of social insurance, particularly for pensions, in pursuit of 'modernizing' the welfare state (Department of Social Security, 2000a; Powell, 1999).

Perhaps the most important single contribution to reducing 'disincentives' were the changes affecting Unemployment Benefit and Income Support in the shift to a 'Job Seeker's Allowance' in 1996. The conditions of eligibility were revised to dissuade 'scroungers', by requiring, for example, that those claiming benefit should prove they were 'genuinely seeking work' and, for some groups of claimants (the young unemployed), that they should attend training schemes or face loss of benefit. Unemployment benefits were made taxable in 1982, thus reducing their value. During the 1980s the overall value of unemployment benefits declined substantially in comparison with average male earnings (Barr and Coulter, 1990). Despite the decline in their relative value, expenditure on such benefits rose because of the rise in the numbers of people unemployed during the first half of the 1980s, a trend repeated at the beginning of the 1990s. The Labour government of 1997 renewed the emphasis on work incentives, constructing what it described as an 'active' benefits system to encourage people to move 'from welfare to work' (Department of Social Security, 2000b). Measures were aimed specifically at young people, the long-term unemployed, disabled people and lone parents in a 'New Deal' programme (Finn, 1998).

The search for greater efficiency in the benefits system focused on the principle of *targeting*. This meant an attempt to move away from 'universal' benefits to more selective and conditional benefits, with an increasing role for 'means-testing' (Deacon and Bradshaw, 1983). This principle was most clearly articulated in the review of social security which reported in 1985 (Department of Health and Social Security, 1985; see Smart, 1987). The resulting legislation reduced the value of SERPS-based pensions; restructured Supplementary Benefit (with particular impact on what were termed 'special needs payments'); replaced Family Income Supplement (paid to low-earning households) with Family Credit; and froze the value of Child Benefit, thus moving family support increasingly away from universal benefits to means-tested ones. Table 3.2 indicates the degree of success achieved by such measures in increasing the proportion of benefit spending channelled through means-tested rather than insurance-based or non-contributory routes. While insurance-based benefits increased by 62 per cent, and non-contributory benefits by 102 per cent over the period from 1974 to 1996, means-tested benefits increased by 609 per cent.

TABLE 3.2   Social security spending, Great Britain (£ billion at 1995/6 prices), 1973/4–1995/6*

	Insurance	Non-con-tributory	Means-tested	Administrat-ive costs	Other	Total social security
1973/4	25.1	8.0	2.5	1.7	1.5	38.7
1979/80	31.1	9.3	4.3	2.0	2.8	49.4
1984/5	35.6	10.4	10.7	2.7	2.1	61.3
1989/90	36.1	10.1	10.1	3.1	2.0	61.4
1990/1	36.1	10.9	10.7	3.2	2.2	63.1
1991/2	39.2	12.1	12.9	3.4	2.3	69.8
1992/3	39.9	13.4	15.9	3.7	2.5	75.4
1993/4	41.2	14.8	17.0	4.0	2.7	79.7
1994/5	40.7	15.2	17.4	3.8	2.8	79.9
1995/6	40.6	16.2	17.6	3.6	2.8	80.8
Growth 1973/4 to 1995/6 (%)						
Overall growth	62	102	609	115	90	109
Average annual rate of growth	2.2	3.3	9.3	3.5	3.0	3.4
Contribution to overall growth	37	19	36	5	3	100

*Excluding Housing Benefit, mortgage interest payments from Supplementary Benefit and Income Support, and previous means-tested rent and rate support in Supplementary Benefit.

Source: Evans, 1998, Table 7.3

One particular feature of the change from Supplementary Benefit to Income Support was the reorganization of the basis of 'special needs payments', available to those facing exceptional hardships or special circumstances which fell outside the normal benefit coverage. In the mid 1960s these had been codified as a set of payments for which claimants could apply, and the discretionary control of them by Supplementary Benefit officers had been reduced. The Social Security Act of 1986 reversed this trend, restoring discretion to officers, establishing a cash-limited budget for such payments, and adding a further twist by requiring most payments to be made on a loan footing. As a result, the amount paid out in such exceptional payments declined rapidly – the combined effect of declining numbers applying for them, a more rigorous refusal of applications (often on the basis that claimants were deemed unable to repay such payments) and the effects of the cash-limited Social Fund itself (see Huby and Whyley, 1996; and Stewart, Stewart and Walker, 1989).

Targeting continued to be a central thread in benefit reforms throughout the 1990s. Its expanded role was legitimated by claims about its economic efficiency and by arguments that it ensured benefits were directed to those 'genuinely in need' (that is, as opposed to 'false' claimants intent on defrauding the system) or to those 'most in need'. Such distinctions – about legitimacy, merit and desert – played an increasingly significant role in both Conservative and New Labour approaches to social security. Both parties argued for reducing eligibility for some groups (for example asylum-seekers, refugees and the 'less severely disabled') through such arguments (see Morris, 1998).

The third objective of social security policy was to reduce dependency on the state. This was interpreted as increasing the availability of alternatives to state-based insurance systems, and governments achieved rather less success here than in relation to the first two objectives. Two major initiatives aimed at transferring sickness insurance and pension insurance to the private sector collapsed in the face of considerable hostility, not least from the private insurance sector itself. The insurance companies found the prospect of establishing universal insurance schemes for both sickness and pensions less than attractive, given that the requirement to insure *all* employees meant covering 'poor risks' (low-waged with low job security) as well as good risks (understood as white-collar and salaried employees). At the end of the 1980s this proposal returned in a more limited form in the encouragement to 'contract out' from SERPS and take out personal pensions. The encouragement took a characteristic double form, with tax relief available for those choosing to transfer to private pensions combined with the declining rewards promised to those staying within the state sector. In the late 1990s, criticisms about this approach and the methods of 'selling' pensions had become a significant public and political concern. New Labour has continued to explore alternatives to the state pension, producing proposals for 'stakeholder pensions' and other second-tier pensions above the basic state pension (Department of

Social Security, 2000a). These will run alongside the growth in occupational pension schemes which dominate the rise in private-sector pension provision. One key long-term objective is to reduce the proportion of gross domestic product spent on pensions (from 5.4 per cent in 1998 to 4.5 per cent in 2000).

Assessing the consequences of benefit policy during this period is a complicated issue. The first, and most notable, feature is the increase in the dependent population as a whole – that is, the number of people in receipt of state benefits. In 1974, 8 per cent of the population of Great Britain were reliant on means-tested benefits; by 1994 this had risen to 20.7 per cent (Evans, 1998). In part, this is the predictable result of trends we have considered earlier, namely increasing numbers of retired people and rising unemployment. But it is also the result of a further trend, sometimes referred to as the 'familialization of poverty'. This is reflected in the dramatic rise in the number of children 'living in poverty' during the 1980s and 1990s. Evans (1998, p.300) estimates that by 1994, around 25 per cent of children lived in households that relied on means-tested benefits – an increase from 6 per cent in 1974. The group most likely to be at risk of poverty shifted during the 1980s from single pensioners to lone-parent families. Given that the vast majority of lone-parent households are headed by females, some commentators have also referred to this trend as the 'feminization of poverty', while other evidence suggests that there has also been a 'racialization of poverty', with increasing numbers of ethnic minority households in poverty (see **Cochrane, 1993**). Studies suggest that, through the 1980s and 1990s, unemployment and economic inactivity were the main sources of increasing poverty (though they are intensified by the effects of gendered and racialized inequalities in employment and earnings). Increases in part-time and low-waged employment also added significantly to the rising numbers living in poverty (Evans, 1998; Piachaud, 1999). These increases took place in a context of significantly widening inequalities, where the incomes of the poorest declined or rose less rapidly than those of higher income groups (see Figure 3.2). The numbers living in poverty and the degree of inequality both increased.

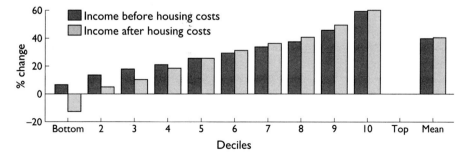

Figure 3.2 Changes in real income by decile group, 1979–1993/4 (including self-employed)

Source: Evans, 1998, Figure 7.14

The attempts to reform the benefits system during the 1980s and 1990s can be judged a partial success *in their own terms*. The supposed disincentive effects of the benefits system were reduced by lowering the 'replacement ratio' (the level of benefits relative to earned income). The various benefits programmes became more 'targeted', reflected in the increased use of means-tested benefits, and there was some growth of private-sector alternatives to state benefits, at least in the field of pensions. However, at the same time both the numbers in poverty and the numbers dependent on state benefits grew, as did the income gap between those dependent on benefits and those in employment. New Labour committed itself to reversing the first of these trends, seeking to move people off benefits through the active promotion of work. In contrast, it has been reluctant to increase benefit levels, arguing that higher benefits are not a solution to poverty.

One further effect of trying to control public spending and reduce the disincentive effects of benefits was that benefits failed to bridge the widening gap between rich and poor (see Stepney, Lynch and Jordan, 1999). The commitment to get people 'off welfare and into work' that was at the centre of New Labour approaches in the late 1990s highlighted a number of policy problems, such as whether:

- national governments wished to, or could, engage in economic management to create the conditions of 'full employment';

- promoting waged work as a policy objective meant that benefit levels for those not in employment would continue to decline;

- the trends towards part-time, low-waged and 'flexible' (or 'insecure') employment in western economies would undermine the capacity of 'work' to provide the living standards or welfare needs of large numbers of people;

- the commitment to reduce benefit dependency could be squared with the commitment to reduce childhood poverty.

The challenge of reducing poverty, following a 25-year period of widening inequality (and its associated social effects – see Wilkinson, 1996), has become a central political and policy issue for the New Labour government. In a careful analysis of policy proposals between 1997 and 1999, Piachaud (1999) argued that the scale of impoverishment created by the late 1990s represented a major problem for a government still concerned to contain public spending on welfare. He indicated that 'between 1979 and 1997 the number of individuals in poverty ... rose from five to fourteen million or one-quarter of the population (Piachaud, 1999, p.154 – see Table 3.3).

TABLE 3.3   Poverty by personal, economic and family status, 1996–7

	Total number	Proportion poor	Number poor
Elderly	9.8m	31%	3.0m
Lone-parent family	4.6m	63%	2.9m
Unemployed	2.9m	78%	2.3m
Adult men	21.1m	20%	4.2m
Adult women	22.2m	24%	5.3m
Children	13.0m	35%	4.5m
All	56.3m	25%	14.1m

Note: poverty is defined as below 50 per cent of average income after housing costs.

Source of data: households below average income 1979 to 1996–7.

Source: Piachaud, 1999, Table 1

Piachaud suggested that, in order to make a significant impact on child poverty, two things needed to happen that went beyond current policies:

> First, there will have to be much more redistribution. Most of those who remain in poverty will be those who cannot work; if they are to keep up, let alone catch up, with the rest of society, then redistribution ... will have to increase.

> Second, there will have to be much greater efforts to tackle the long term causes of poverty. Further reductions in unemployment and tackling the causes of low pay are needed.

> (Piachaud, 1999, p.160)

Whether the increased public spending (and increased taxation) that these two conditions imply can be accommodated within New Labour's vision of 'modernizing the welfare state' is an uncertain political calculation. It is, however, the calculation that is central to how the relation between inequality, inclusion and welfare develops.

4   A NEW WELFARE MIX: VARIETIES OF PRIVATIZATION

We have already noted that one concern of the new right at the beginning of the 1980s was to encourage alternatives to state provision of welfare. This was expressed in terms of claims for the superior performance of non-state institutions in relation to two key values. First, private-sector alternatives were viewed as being more efficient than public-sector ones, as a result of being 'disciplined' by market forces or competition. By comparison, public-sector institutions were viewed as excessively bureaucratic, controlled by administrative or professional interests, and unresponsive to the pressures for efficiency that market-based organizations faced. Second, the existence of alternative sources of welfare – whether market-based or in the voluntary sector – was seen as important in promoting consumer choice and responsiveness. In state welfare provision, public-sector bodies held the position of 'monopoly suppliers'. It was argued that this had the effect of preventing welfare consumers from exercising choice about how their needs were to be met, while the absence of competition meant such public-sector monopolies were under no pressure to be responsive to consumer interests (see, for example, Butcher, 1995; Clarke and Newman, 1997).

The break-up of such monopoly positions was a constant theme of Conservative social policy during the 1980s, and the creation of alternatives has taken a variety of forms. The most obvious one has been the encouragement of 'market forces' in the supply of welfare services. In some aspects of welfare, this has meant fostering private-sector competition directly, for example through tax concessions supporting private medical insurance. Between 1976 and 1990 the numbers of people covered by private medical insurance tripled from 2.2 million to 6.6 million, but then stabilized (Le Grand *et al.*, 1990, p.106; Le Grand and Vizard, 1998, p.98). A related development was the drive to encourage private sources of finance for public service programmes, particularly in the construction and maintenance of buildings and infrastructure. The limited Conservative PFI (Private Finance Initiative) was revised and extended by the 1997 Labour government as part of a wider attempt to promote more public–private partnerships.

A more substantial route to privatization was the requirement for competitive tendering for the provision of public services. Compulsory Competitive Tendering was applied to the NHS and local authority services during the 1980s and 1990s, requiring organizations to put out to tender aspects of service provision (such as cleaning and catering in the NHS, environmental services and leisure facilities for local authorities). Competitive tendering and 'market testing' were extended to areas of central government provision during the 1990s in pursuit of both economy and improved service standards (Walsh, 1995). Market relations were introduced into public housing through the requirement that local authorities allow tenants the 'right to buy', thus moving substantial amounts of the public-sector housing stock (usually the most desirable) into private ownership (Pryke, 1998).

These sorts of changes have fostered a greater involvement of the private sector in the provision of some welfare services. But in many respects they were marginal to the core activities of welfare – education, health and benefits – which became the focus for other reform processes aimed at promoting what have been termed the 'three Es': economy, efficiency and effectiveness (Audit Commission, 1988). One core change was the introduction of market processes into the organization of welfare services. 'Quasi-market' is a term used to refer to the creation of internal trading systems within public-sector organizations: these are intended to mimic the behaviour of real markets by creating internal trading between different sections (Mooney, 1997). The most visible quasi-markets were created in the NHS through the National Health Service and Community Care Act 1989, whereby healthcare-providing organizations (hospitals, ambulance services and so on) were required to price their services (for particular types of operations, for example). 'Purchasers' (either District Health Authorities or GPs, who became 'fund-holders') could then 'shop around' for the best priced service. In this setting both purchasers and providers functioned as trading entities within the internal market of the NHS. The 1997 Labour government retained the distinction between purchasers and providers but proposed more integrated forms of service 'commissioning' to overcome the fragmenting effects of the internal market in the NHS. Service planning and commissioning is being re-organized through primary care groups and trusts (Glendinning *et al.*, 1998). Similar patterns of internal markets were imposed on local authorities for many services which were not put out to competitive tendering. Le Grand and others have developed the concept of quasi-market to cover a variety of ways in which the 'purchaser' and 'provider' roles are being separated in the provision of welfare, such that the major role of the state is intended to become a purchaser rather than provider (Le Grand, 1990; Bartlett *et al.*, 1999). Bartlett *et al.* argue that:

> The Conservative social policy revolution was based on ideological commitments to market principles and the belief that only by introducing them into what was perceived as sluggish, unresponsive bureaucratic apparatuses of the welfare state could efficient services, responsive to consumer choices, be delivered. However, the ideology provided only the framework for a more pragmatic objective: to contain spiralling cost pressures in all sectors of the welfare state.

(Bartlett *et al.*, 1999, p.2)

As Bartlett *et al.* indicate, claims about the intended improvements 'have proved difficult to substantiate' for a range of reasons (p.2; see also Clarke, forthcoming; Pollitt, 1995; and Walsh, 1995). Nevertheless, the structural separation between the public funding and purchasing of services on the one hand and the provision of services on the other has become embedded in a range of welfare areas: education, housing, health and social care. Commercial and voluntary organizations have been encouraged to take on an increased role in service provision.

This shift has contributed to the development of a new 'welfare mix', or what some have called a new 'welfare pluralism' (Rao, 1996). It has disintegrated or fragmented welfare services, producing a much more complex and 'dispersed' organizational structure of welfare provision (Clarke and Newman, 1997), with three significant consequences. The first concerns the increasingly 'residual' role for publicly provided services. This residualized role for the public sector depends on a combination of two sets of conditions: the potential profitability of the service in question (which will determine the extent of private-sector interest) and the availability of private- and voluntary-sector alternatives (which vary between services and between different localities). Competition tends to concentrate provision where expectations of 'profitability' or 'success' are highest (such as prestigious medical centres and teaching hospitals).

The voluntary sector has been drawn into new partnerships with the public sector, but has been reluctant to take on the task of filling gaps in the network of service provision. Where voluntary alternatives were well established, the new model posed few problems, but the spread of voluntary alternatives is by no means complete, either in terms of the range of services or geographically. Some voluntary bodies, particularly those based in minority ethnic communities, have expressed reservations about becoming dependent upon funding from, and subject to scrutiny by, state agencies (Lewis, 1993). Nevertheless, the effect of such trends is that residual public-sector provision will become concentrated on the unprofitable and unattractive services for those defined as 'poor' or 'difficult'.

The second tendency of the new welfare mix is the rise of a 'consumerist' orientation. The stated objective of many of the 1980s and 1990s reforms was to create greater customer responsiveness among public-sector services through the introduction of market forces. The 'quasi-market' rarely involves direct consumer choice over services or service providers. Rather, the interests of consumers are mediated by 'proxy customers': health authorities, primary care bodies and GPs in health services; parents, school governors and headteachers in education; care managers in personal social services, and so on. These 'proxies' are expected to represent the best interests of the customers (Bartlett et al., 1998; Clarke, 1998).

Third, the reorganization of funding, purchasing and providing has been accompanied by a greater concern with 'regulation' or 'inspection'. In theory, the creation of an 'arm's-length' relationship between purchasers and providers should also include an element of regulation or inspection to ensure that the contracted 'provider' is delivering satisfactory standards of service. The 1990s saw a significant expansion of regulatory, inspection and audit agencies, offering new means for central control 'at arm's length' (Hoggett, 1996; Hood et al., 1999). Such developments included new agencies (for example OFSTED, the Office for Standards in Education); new roles for existing inspectorates (for example the SSI, the Social Services Inspectorate); and a particularly significant place for the Audit Commission (Clarke et al., 2000). If anything, these developments were intensified in

New Labour approaches to the co-ordination of public services after 1997, which emphasized the combination of efficiency and improvement that could be driven by external scrutiny (Clarke, Gewirtz and McLaughlin, 2000).

Finally, there is one further tendency in the new welfare mix, where a different meaning of 'private' has been at work. This is the transfer of welfare from the public realm (which includes public, voluntary and commercial sectors) to the private realm of the family. In terms of ideological commitments, this was in line with Conservative views about 'freeing' the family from the state, enabling the restoration of responsibilities to the family which had been appropriated by the state and thereby reinforcing parental responsibility and authority. In practice, it meant the expectation that families will undertake an increased amount of the 'caring' work that is involved in the provision of welfare, particularly in relation to the 'dependent' population of children, people who are sick or have disabilities, and older people (Graham, 1984).

One example may illuminate this transfer from the state to the family. One of the proclaimed successes of the NHS during the 1980s and 1990s was that hospitals were treating more patients than ever before. Leaving aside the phenomenon of lengthening waiting lists, the key to the success was increased 'throughput'. The length of time being spent in hospital by patients was substantially reduced. As a result, recuperative or post-operative care that once took place within the hospital was transferred to the patient's 'private' realm, usually the family. Given the prevailing gender distribution of care within families, this mostly hidden transfer of care responsibilities meant an increase in female domestic labour – the 'labour of love' that is embodied in women's family obligations (Brown and Smith, 1993; Finch, 1989).

Since these forms of welfare work are private in the strongest sense, being hidden within households and kin networks, they cannot be adequately assessed in terms of establishing the social costs of welfare. Elsewhere it is possible to measure patterns of resource inputs and outputs and the shift of resources or activities between sectors, but women's unwaged work is not measurable in this way. In terms of the national economics of the welfare regime, then, it is difficult to estimate the size of, or the shift towards, this form of privatized care. Nonetheless, most studies of particular patterns of care – whether of children, people with disabilities or older people – indicate both that many welfare or care needs are fulfilled through wives, sisters and daughters and that the burdens of care have increased during the 1980s and 1990s (Finch and Mason, 1992; Jane Lewis, 2000; Mayo, 1994).

Such patterns were given increasing official legitimacy through the idea of the importance of 'primary carers'. The 'discovery' of the amount of care provided by and within families during the late 1970s led to the work of women in providing care being dignified through the concept of 'primary carer'. All other forms of care (provided by the state or other agencies) were viewed as the provision of 'secondary' care (see Barclay Committee, 1982). In a speech to the 1977 Conservative Party conference, a future Secretary of State for Social Services, Patrick Jenkin, expressed this view of primary care in a definitive way:

> Quite frankly, I don't think that mothers have the same right to work as fathers do. If the good Lord had intended us to have equal rights to go out to work, he wouldn't have created men and women. These are biological facts ... We hear a lot today about social work – perhaps the most important social work is motherhood.

(quoted in Clarke, Cochrane and Smart, 1987, p.140)

In spite of this eloquent combination of religious, biological and legal justifications for the importance of motherhood, Conservative social and economic policy never quite resolved the issue of working mothers. Although rhetorically committed to the celebration of motherhood, the Conservatives nevertheless oversaw the expansion of women's paid employment during the 1980s and 1990s, including a continuing rise in the numbers of mothers taking on paid work. In part, this reflects the primacy of market forces over family obligations in the Conservative agenda – employers wanted an increasingly 'flexible' labour force, for which women 'returners' proved the best recruiting ground. It also reflects the growing salience of women's earnings, either as sole or joint earner, for maintaining household incomes and living standards (Smart and Silva, 1999). In part, it reflects the absence of any formalized or sustained family policy, either in the form of adequate benefits for child support or of developed childcare facilities. Instead, the pattern of women's 'double shift' (domestic work at home combined with waged labour outside the home) developed on the assumption that their labour time is infinitely flexible and expandable – women are able to fill gaps in the labour market and the work of welfare wherever and whenever they appear (Langan, 1988). The issue was revived by proposals from the Labour government in 1998 to reform the benefits system to enable lone mothers to 'get off benefit and into work' (Smith, 1999). The policy echoed US initiatives around 'welfare to work' that were explicitly directed at lone mothers (see Chapter 4). Such changes proved contro-versial as they appeared to prioritize paid employment over (unpaid) domestic labour in government policy. In many respects, this approach to lone mothers reflected a New Labour view of (paid) work as the preferred solution to problems of poverty, dependence, social exclusion and social disorganization (Clarke and Newman, 1998; Lister, 1998). New Labour's efforts to create an 'active' benefit system aimed to promote 'work for those who can, security for those who can't'.

In this section we have explored the changing conditions under which welfare has been delivered, highlighting the shift away from a central role for the state in the direct provision of services. This involved expanded roles for the private, voluntary and domestic sectors of welfare and a retreat by the state from direct provision. Such changes have been described as producing a new 'mixed economy of welfare' or 'welfare pluralism' (Johnson, 1999; Rao, 1996). Nevertheless, there are reasons for qualifying such descriptions. First, there are several different 'mixed economies': the 'mix' in health is not the same as that in education, which is not the same as that in income support, and so on. Although there is a general tendency towards the reduction of direct provision by the state and towards expanded roles for other sectors, it is not a uniform process. Second, there are continuing problems about how to describe the 'sectoral shifts' in social welfare. Different analysts have categorized the sectors in varying ways. Some distinguish between the public and private (Burchardt and Hills, 1999), or between the state and the independent sector. Others separate out the public, commercial, voluntary and informal sectors (Johnson, 1999), while Wistow *et al.* (1996) identify the same four, but use the term 'private sector' instead of 'commercial'. The simple binary distinction between public and private risks compounding different elements and meanings of the private, such that the private (commercial) sector is elided with the private (domestic) sphere. In a different way, as we saw earlier, there are problems about treating the informal/domestic provision of care or welfare as if it was a sector, comparable to the other organization-based sectors. Third, it is worth remarking that it may be important to distinguish between the public sector and the state in examining the changing welfare mix (Clarke, 1996). While the role of the public sector may have changed in relation to funding, purchasing and providing welfare, the state retains a central role (and power) in setting both the terms of welfare and the balance of roles and sectors in the mixed economy of welfare (see Jessop, 2000). The 'welfare state' has been dis-integrated in terms of its organizational forms, but the central state has retained – and sometimes expanded – its powers of control, direction and regulation (Clarke and Newman, 1997).

5   FAMILY, NATION AND WORK IN THE NEW RIGHT

Here we return to issues about the ideological assumptions that have underpinned, and been articulated in, welfare policy and politics. The focal concerns of family, nation and work discussed in Chapter 2 have continued as central themes in new right ideology. The new right's approach to social welfare reworked the ideological imagery of the traditional family and British culture in ways that stressed their inextricable links to the market and its 'freedoms'. One core theme was the attempt to increase the family's 'responsibility' for the welfare of its members. The family was made responsible for making provision for its own welfare; for exercising choice in the selection of private and/or state welfare provision (schools, healthcare, housing, and so on); and for promoting morality, discipline and the transmission of British cultural values. The move towards making families responsible was visible in the extension of children's financial dependence on their parents through the removal of rights to social security from most 16- and 17-year-olds. It was also reflected in the emphasis on parental responsibility for the discipline of their children in the Criminal Justice Act 1991 and the

Crime and Disorder Act 1998. This notion of parental responsibility also extended to attempts to restore specifically *paternal* responsibility. The Child Support Act 1991 aimed to minimize state support for female lone parents through pursuing 'errant' fathers to enforce their financial responsibility for their children.

These moves were not only favoured by the new right, but they also overlapped with demands by some parts of the feminist movement to encourage the greater involvement of men in responsibilities for both childcare and financial maintenance. However, what marks a difference is that within new right discourse the shifts were associated with the identification of female lone parents as central to the growth of a 'dependency culture' (see also **Cochrane, 1993**). This gained particular currency in the writings of Charles Murray (1984; 1990), who suggested that welfare benefits in the USA and Britain had created an 'underclass' characterized by high rates of female-headed families, illegitimacy, poverty, crime and unemployment. He proposed shifting the dependency of mothers away from the state and on to breadwinner fathers. Along with others in the new right, Murray viewed the ethics of male wage-earning and family responsibility as inextricably linked: 'Young men who don't work don't make good marriage material. Often they don't get married at all; when they do, they don't have the ability to fill their traditional role. In either case, too many of them remain barbarians' (Murray, 1990, p.23).

Community care policies, as we have seen, stressed the mobilization of 'families, friends and neighbours' in providing support for older people (Griffiths, 1988; Brown and Smith, 1993). These policies, as Janet Finch (1989, p.125) has pointed out, worked not so much with a model of an independent nuclear family as with the assumed existence of a spatially separated, but nevertheless interdependent, extended family where members may call on female relatives for care. The Conservative attempt to devalorize 'non-traditional' relationships and ways of living was visible in Section 28 of the Local Government Act 1988, which prohibited local authorities from promoting homosexuality as a 'pretended family relationship', as well as in the restrictions placed on access to *in vitro* fertilization (Evans, 1989).

The ideological strategy of the new right in the 1980s aimed to make the traditional family a vital link between moral principles and cultural life on the one side, and market principles and economic life on the other. But the cultural values that the family was asked to defend derive from its days of high imperialism and, as such, were essentially British, white and Christian (Hall, 1998). The assertion of British (or, more specifically, English) culture by the new right was developed as a way of affirming the national interest. The national interest was seen by the new right to be the reassertion of the freedom of the market, underpinning the revival of Britain as a major competitor in the world economy. However, this assertion of British/English culture required the minimizing, in the name of national interest, of the influence of 'other cultures'. One consequence of this was the development of a new form of *cultural essentialism*, which emphasized the inevitability of cultural differences between nations/peoples as a means of asserting the unity of 'British identity' (Gail Lewis, 2000). Although this ideological project was neither as consensual nor coherent as it appeared, nevertheless it became a key theme in some new right politicians' resistance to European Union membership. The process was clearly visible in the educational debate and education policy of the 1990s. In a collection of essays entitled *Anti-Racism: An Assault on Education and Value* (Palmer, 1986), new right educationalists argued that anti-racist initiatives in schooling contributed to a lowering of standards and constituted an assault on the traditional British values in education. Moves to reduce the influence of anti-discriminatory practice in favour of the restoration of 'British' cultural values could be seen in the Education Act 1988. This also demonstrated the way in which notions of the family are seen as holding together the values of both work and nationhood through state welfare provision. The Act introduced a core curriculum and testing explicitly addressed to the needs of employers. It also emphasized the need for the teaching of traditional morality and British cultural values (as against anti-racist and anti-sexist teaching). Finally, it represented the role of the family as consumers, shopping wisely in the market-place for education to fit the needs of its children. The Act also included the right for parents to choose education appropriate to their own 'culture'. In 1990 a ruling from the Secretary of State for Education said that parental choice included the right of white parents to withdraw their children from schools with a large proportion of Asian children, and that this choice overrode the race relations law. In support of this ruling, Fred Naylor of the Parental Alliance for Choice in Education stated: 'The Secretary of State has now cleared up the matter. It has nothing to do with race but with culture' (*The Observer*, 22 April 1990). Figure 3.3 summarizes the key themes of new right ideological assumptions of family, nation and work.

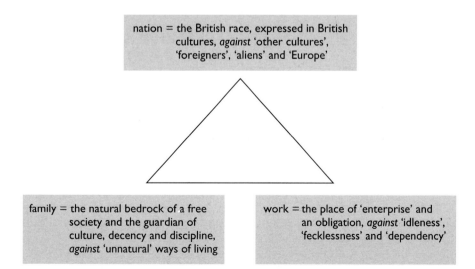

Figure 3.3   Structuring assumptions of new right approaches to welfare

6 STILL IN DISPUTE: FAMILY, NATION AND WORK AT THE END OF THE CENTURY

Whilst the new right's reworking of family, nation and work can be seen as a particularly aggressive combination of economic liberalism and social (or cultural) conservatism, it has also to be seen as a defensive strategy to resist the perceived threats and challenges to inequalities in these three areas. For what also marked the 1980s was a growing awareness of, and struggles against, 'race' and gender inequalities. Such inequalities became the focus of social action in increasingly diverse political forms: acts of rebellion (riots against racism in Brixton in 1981); institutionalized equal opportunities and anti-racist and anti-sexist strategies; voluntary self-help (such as black women's refuges); or religious fundamentalism and opposition to fundamentalism (for example Southall Black Sisters, 1990).

Within the field of welfare, the development of local authority equal opportunities programmes in the areas of gender, 'race', disability and sexual orientation was significant. Such programmes addressed issues of access to employment, the training of employees and the delivery of services, as well as acknowledging diversity of family and cultural experience, revealing previously hidden areas of, for example, racism, sexism, heterosexism and ableism, and legitimizing these as areas for concern and action. However, such initiatives were sometimes tokenistic or, more importantly, developed within the context of the shifting balance of power between central and local government. They also were the target of an ideological counter-attack by the new right, in which 'special needs' were redefined as 'special privileges' or 'special pleading' by particular interests.

Nevertheless, the development of movements based on 'identity' gave rise to a better appreciation of the complex and interrelated formations of social power in society. This development was accompanied by a more thorough-going set of critiques of, and demands about, the social relations of welfare – attacking the hierarchical relations between the providers and users of welfare services. In particular, many groups representing people with disabilities, learning difficulties and psychological distress began to analyse their situation as a particular form of compounded oppression. They identified themselves as marginalized and oppressed by the institutions of society, a process that is compounded by the creation of dependency by welfare professionals. Their demands therefore included not only rights in relation to employment, education, marriage, sexuality, motherhood and so on, but also rights *within* welfare provision, including access to information, accountability and representation.

Similar sorts of demands around the right to self-help alternatives and access to professional knowledge also emerged from the women's health movement (especially the setting up of 'well woman' clinics) and the women's refuge movement for women escaping domestic violence (see also **Foreman and Dallos, 1993**). In some ways this focus of user-led movements overlapped with new right discourses within health, education and personal social services which emphasized consumer sovereignty and consumer choice. Some of the arguments also overlapped, for example in the critique of welfare professionals, power and control. However, there were key differences: the user-led movements also operated within overlapping discourses of democracy and oppression; the language was of rights, representation and citizenship, and of discrimination. Furthermore, their demands usually included the provision of universally available specialist services – '[the] provision of free counselling for all; [the] provision of refuge, planned and under the control of survivors of psychiatry, adequate funding for non-medical community services, especially crisis intervention' (Survivors Speak Out, 1987). On the other hand, consumer sovereignty and consumer choice were framed within the individualistic market (or quasi-market) model advocated by the new right, in which the consumer's power lies in the exercise of choice from a range of services presented by welfare agencies, and where accountability is not tied to user representation (Clarke and Newman, 1997).

Optimistically, it is possible to see the introduction of concepts like consumer sovereignty, accountability and quality control as the openings through which user movements could begin to push for their demands. Pessimistically, it could be seen as a displacement of more fundamental concerns over resources, funding and structured inequalities. In the early 1980s the left and feminist critiques of welfare as statist, authoritarian and bureaucratic were seen by some to have contributed to the conditions for the new right's restructuring of the welfare state (Hall and Jacques, 1983). Yet by the 1990s the new right's advocacy of consumer sovereignty, professional accountability, the identification of differentiated needs and the concern with quality and standards can be seen to have given an impetus for the new constituencies of welfare to demand, though not necessarily to achieve, more far-reaching and radical reforms of welfare provision. Similar cross-cutting pressures were also visible in New Labour proposals to 'modernize' the welfare state. Some of the arguments for modernization derived from challenges by users and excluded, marginalized or oppressed social groups. Nevertheless, the dominant tendencies of the reform proposals emphasized managerialist and centralized forms of power, while also insisting on the 'responsibility' of individuals, families and communities to produce welfare for themselves. The process of redrawing the relationship between citizens, welfare and the state remains a central and contested axis of welfare politics at the beginning of the twenty-first century (Clarke, Gewirtz and McLaughlin, 2000; Hughes, 1998).

While the new right sought to reinscribe values of the traditional family, of traditional British culture and the work ethic, the social conditions of these three elements have themselves changed, placing further strains on the new right's project. Some of the changes in relation to the organization of paid work have already been outlined. In the UK there was an increase in the number of people working in low-paid, part-time, casual and sub-contracted work. The inequalities between this group – often women, lone parents and black and minority ethnic workers – and those in full-time, constant, skilled or professional work widened. This was exacerbated by the decreasing availability of public benefits or provisions (such as housing, transport, etc.) to this group. The tightening of benefits, changes in social security, labour law and workforce programmes all played a role in directing and controlling labour into the acceptance of low-paid, flexible work (Lister, 1990; Deakin and Wilkinson, 1992).

It became increasingly evident that changes in the organization of work, in demographic change and in the role of women had exposed the inadequacies of the post-war social security and insurance system. But it is also clear that the reforms in social security, while supporting the changes in the nature of work, simply intensified inequalities in new ways (see Deakin and Wilkinson, 1992). This twin failure may lead to further debate about an alternative system based on a universal principle of a basic wage but incorporating a recognition of diverse needs – for example, the role of women (and men) in caring for children or older people (see Lister, 2000). Indeed, New Labour took up the unfinished business of benefit reform, aiming to realign the relationship between welfare and work in ways that would enable most citizens to be 'independent' through being in paid employment. The reforms were intended to provide 'work for those who can, security for those who cannot'. Borrowing from the USA (in terms of policies and language), the 1997 Labour government proposed a 'new deal' to get welfare claimants 'back to work'. Critics suggested that the proposals undervalued unpaid work in caring, and that the supposed 'security' for those who could not work was undermined by a consistent refusal to increase benefit levels (Lister, 1998).

In relation to the family, one contradictory element was the tension between the reality of diversification of family forms and policies which reinforced a specific patriarchal family form. This diversification was marked by a shift away from the male-breadwinner nuclear family held to be the administrative norm in the post-war social security reforms, to an increase in divorce, remarriage, lone (predominantly female) parents, older women living on their own, and wives and mothers in paid, often full-time work (Smart and Silva, 1999; see also **Dallos and Sapsford, 1993**). It is important to say that the changes were not the same across all social groups: for example, Afro-Caribbean women commonly worked in full-time jobs throughout the post-war period. The changes in paid work were not accompanied by wholesale changes in attitudes about, and behaviour in, the division of domestic labour (Land, 1999b).

Issues about the relationship between the family and welfare remained central to the reconstruction of the welfare state during the 1990s (Smart, 1997). While Conservative approaches were dominated by an emphasis on the normative value of the 'traditional family', Labour views tended to be more ambiguous. While often asserting the importance of a strong family life as the 'bedrock of a decent society', New Labour also appeared to include *diverse* forms of household organization alongside the conventional family form. In government after 1997, this ambivalence about norm versus diversity tended to be resolved in favour of the 'conventional' (Land, 1999a). In setting up the National Family and Parenting Institute, New Labour reinforced the view of the importance of the family, while leaving the question of 'family or families' a subject of continuing dispute.

There has been some partial and uneven acknowledgement within social policy of the greater cultural diversification of family forms and the effects of ethnocentric, pathologizing and racist responses from service providers (Dominelli, 1988). There was also an articulation through the gay and lesbian movements of alternatives to the heterosexism of the nuclear family which subsequently found support in legal judgements in UK, US and European courts. This is one setting where the dynamics of 'family' and 'nation' intersect. More generally, the issue of 'nation' reveals a tension similar to that of 'family' in the opening up of geographical and cultural borders on the one hand, and the efforts to impose national and cultural border controls on the other. The breaking-up and shifting of national boundaries in Eastern Europe and the former Soviet Union, together with moves to closer integration within Europe, were contrasted with assertions within Britain about the uniqueness of British/English cultural traditions and the need to preserve them. Such assertions were made both in the context of being, or the threat of becoming, 'European' and in the context of Britain as a multi-racial society. They were reflected in the tightening up of the implementation of the nationality and immigration laws and in the approach to refugees and asylum-seekers (see Morris, 1998). Such moves had a knock-on effect on black users of welfare services, because controls operated through public agencies such as colleges, DSS offices and housing departments often served to throw suspicion indiscriminately on black users. At the same time, the murder of the black teenager Stephen Lawrence became a highly visible fulcrum in efforts to address and challenge patterns of racism embedded in the public institutions of British society. The Macpherson inquiry into the Metropolitan Police's handling of the Lawrence murder investigation addressed 'institutional racism' and recommended urgent action on its eradication not just from the police service but from the whole range of public services (highlighting education in particular). The report and its aftermath provoked intense public and organizational conflicts that testified to the continuing struggle over the meaning of Britishness (McLaughlin and Murji, 2000).

A second element in this tension around 'nation' lies in the greater awareness of the international dimensions of problems such as poverty and ill-health. The international flows of capital and labour, the growth of the multinationals and the internationalization of the market all limit the extent to which national welfare policies can solve their own social problems, just as Europeanization limits the legitimation of such policies. In other words, internationally based political strategies and social policies became increasingly significant developments. At the same time, any shift towards harmonization of social policies within the EU would have very uneven outcomes. For example, the adoption of the European Social Chapter has implications for social rights through the recognition of the rights of 'vulnerable groups' and its demands for equal treatment for men and women and gay men and lesbians. It also has significant consequences for the rights of part-time workers, and for working parents (providing for parental leave). Yet the Social Chapter makes little reference to racism and the needs of immigrant workers. Its protective employment provisions only apply to EU nationals, and any moves towards harmonization may lead to a strengthening of those policies and procedures by which Europe's racialized and migrant communities are denied rights. These include a tightening of immigration controls and restrictions on asylum-seekers, circumscribed or restricted access to social security, housing, health and education provision, and denial of the right to family reunion, or to nationality (Arnott, 1990).

These examples of changes in work, family and nation illustrate the ways in which discourses around these areas are subject to contradictory pressures as the social and material conditions of family life, nation and work themselves change. While these changing conditions provide opportunities to challenge forms of inequality and power within society, they also give rise to processes which strengthen and reinforce these forms of inequality. These changes represented some countervailing influences on the new right's attempt to articulate a coherent and traditional project of the relationship between family, nation and work. In addition, this model faced challenges, not only in terms of the realities of people's lives, but in terms of alternative discourses rooted in theories of oppression and liberatory and anti-discriminatory strategies. In relation to welfare policies, concepts of the individual, choice and freedom have created a space for the elaboration of concepts of democratic, civil and welfare rights by those who use welfare services.

In pursuing a 'Third Way', New Labour straddled some of these changes, challenges and conflicts. Proponents of Third Way modernization argued that a new politics made it possible to transcend apparently irreconcilable principles – going beyond 'left or right', 'state or market', or 'freedom or equality' to a new synthesis (Blair, 1998; Giddens, 1998). Critics were less persuaded, many arguing that New Labour was prone to settling such tensions in favour of the market, business interests and traditional morality, rather than pursuing an agenda to promote a more equal, more diverse and more internationalist 'modern Britain' (see, for example, some of the discussions in Hay, 1999; Powell, 1999).

In relation to the three core ideological themes of family, work and nation, New Labour's view of modernization has been partial, uneven and ambiguous. They have articulated a view of the family as the 'bedrock of a decent society', vital to individual, communal and national well-being. Despite recognizing the existence of diverse household forms, official views tended to revert to asserting the merits of the conventional family. The creation in 1999 of a National Family and Parenting Institute revealed a commitment to improving parenting and the quality of family life, but at 'arm's length' from government to avoid accusations of a 'nanny state'. 'Work' emerged as the centre-piece of New Labour's view of a modernized society. Work, in the form of waged work, was the route to independence, personal well-being, the creation of good role models for young people, and the reduction of social security spending. Work defined the core relationships between the citizen and society – the fulfilment of responsibilities or obligations (as opposed to claiming rights). For some critics, this celebration of waged work risked devaluing other forms of labour (performed by carers, for example) and devalued the social status and support for those unable to work (Lister, 1998). Finally, New Labour's view of a 'modern Britain' resisted some of the narrow new right views of the British (English) people surrounded and embattled by dangerous 'others'. Constitutional changes affecting the governance of Scotland, Northern Ireland and Wales moved the UK to a more devolved, and more multinational, nation. A more European-oriented set of economic, social and political alignments (albeit cautious and uneven) challenged some of the 'little Englander' views of the nation and its place in the world. Internally, New Labour seemed more at ease with a view of Britain as 'diverse', made up of different traditions, cultures and communities – though without wanting to address the inequalities associated with patterns of difference. However, this more expansive view of nation coexisted with a fierce defence of national borders and national citizenship in relation to migrants in the form of refugees and asylum-seekers. Such groups met an increasingly hostile (and inefficient) legal process, with reduced forms of welfare support and a climate of intense political hostility. In these different ways, then, New Labour tried to reconcile or resolve the different patterns of change and challenge – the different possible routes to being 'modern'. In the process, it was possible to see deep continuities with both neo-liberal and neo-conservative ideologies (around the economy and work, and around authority, morality and responsibility), coinciding with elements of social democratic and 'equal opportunities' ideologies (see, for example, Clarke and Newman, 1998; Hay, 1999; Mouffe, 1998). These ambiguities – or unresolved tensions – are summarized in Figure 3.4.

The significance of such political developments, reflected also in welfare campaigns and struggles, points to the complexities of social power and inequalities. People's lives and their needs and demands for welfare provision are constituted, articulated and structured by a diversity of identities and inequalities. It is these diverse identities and needs which the new social movements and the user movements in welfare have begun to articulate. In so doing they have exposed the 'false universalism' of the Beveridge welfare state. Yet one of the tensions that still remains unresolved is how to develop universal welfare

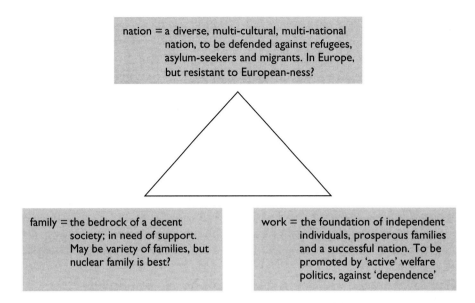

Figure 3.4   The ambiguities of New Labour's assumptions of family, nation and work

policies that are neither monolithic nor uniform but which are able to meet the diversity and difference of people's welfare needs in forms that do not reproduce difference in unequal ways. This tension – between universalism and difference – is not just peculiar to welfare; it is one of the central issues in the development of social, political and cultural life, nationally and internationally, at the beginning of the twenty-first century.

7   A NEW WELFARE REGIME?

The changes to the British welfare regime have been the subject of intense debate and discussion, with arguments about the scale and pace of change, and controversies about how best to describe the main directions of change. To some extent, these arguments reflect the inevitable problems of analysing processes of change that are still in progress. Social policy is having to address what Esping-Andersen (1996) calls 'welfare states in transition', rather than simply classify and compare different (relatively static) welfare systems. As a result, different approaches tend to foreground either continuity or change in the British regime, as we shall see. But the conflicting arguments also reflect different evaluations of both the starting-point (the post-war welfare system or 'welfare state') and the main trends of the last twenty years. In this concluding section we will look at three areas of debate about changes in the British welfare system that exemplify some of these issues.

The first set of arguments focus on the extent to which the British welfare system has been remade, so that it is no longer appropriate to talk of a 'welfare state'. Some social policy analysts have stressed the relative continuities of welfare provision in the UK, particularly the level and patterns of public spending on welfare. Glennerster and Hills (1998, p.1) argue that, contrary to the image of a 'continuous "rolling back" of cherished institutions', their study reveals that 'reports of the death of the welfare state have, like Mark Twain's, been greatly exaggerated'. They point to shifts within public spending on welfare (between services and recipients), to a context of rising expectations and demands, and to the expanded role for non-state sources of welfare as significant features of the last two decades of the twentieth century. Nevertheless, they conclude that welfare institutions have been surprisingly robust and that the dominant trend has been 'welfare with the lid on' – the containment of welfare spending rather than the transformation of welfare (Glennerster, 1998).

This analysis contrasts with other studies that have viewed the changes of the 1980s and 1990s as dismantling core features of the welfare state. Such arguments tend to treat the evidence about public spending on welfare more negatively – as reflecting a refusal to increase public spending in the face of rising need resulting from unemployment, poverty, ageing and illness. However, some arguments about the 'end of the welfare state' tend to point to other dimensions of 'welfare statism' that have been challenged or displaced. Some have stressed the 'dis-integration' of the welfare state as a process in which the state tries to absolve itself of social responsibilities – transferring them to other agencies (private enterprise, voluntary bodies, new partnerships, individuals and families). For example, Bauman (1998) points to how 'the new poor' have been made more responsible for their plight, and become more socially and politically marginalized as the state withdraws support. Some analysts have argued that the remaking of the welfare state coincided with the abandonment of key social and political objectives – around the promotion of social equality and integration. In particular, the 'containment' of welfare spending accompanied the rapid intensification of social inequalities during the 1980s and 1990s, marking a withdrawal from redistributive social policies (Dean and Melrose, 1998; Jones and Novak, 1999).

A second cluster of arguments concerns what has happened to the welfare state as a set of institutions, organizations and processes. Most analysts agree that significant changes have occurred in what some refer to as the organization or delivery of welfare. Instead, disagreements tend to focus on how to describe the main trends of reorganization. Some have stressed the centrality of the shift to markets, market-like mechanisms or 'quasi-markets', suggesting that they constitute what Bartlett et al. (1999) have described as 'a revolution in social policy' that seems unlikely to be displaced by New Labour approaches to the organization of welfare services. Other have foregrounded the 'new welfare pluralism' (Rao, 1996) or the new 'mixed economies of welfare' (Johnson, 1999). For these authors, market-like processes that co-ordinate purchasing/commissioning functions with providers are secondary to the shifting mix of welfare provision, in particular the move away from public sector provision. Still others have described a 'system shift' in the delivery of welfare. They point to a movement from an old 'public administration'-based system to a 'new set of practices and values, based upon a new language of welfare delivery which emphasises efficiency and value for money, competition and markets, consumerism and customer care' (Butcher, 1995, p.161). Finally, some have argued that the core element that crosses these different organizational shifts – and has an impact beyond the delivery systems of welfare – is the shift to a managerial state. In this view, the structures, cultures and processes of the state have been aligned around managerial power, ways of calculating and forms of control (Clarke and Newman, 1997; Newman, 1998). Although the analyses differ, these concerns testify to changes in the form of the welfare state. They suggest that it may no longer be appropriate to use the phrase 'welfare state' because of the shifts away from a relatively integrated set of political, policy and provision structures, systems and processes.

To some extent these arguments about structures, systems and processes overlap with the third area of conflicting analyses, concerning the relationship between the welfare state (or welfare system) and citizens. For some, the recent developments mark a distinctive move away from bureaucratic and professional paternalism in which citizens were treated as passively grateful recipients of the state's generosity. This view appears in a variety of political evaluations that range from those that stress the value of 'consumerism' and individual choice, through 'Third Way' pluralists to those associated with 'user' movement views. These have been challenged by arguments about the limited nature of 'consumer power' in welfare. They have also been criticized by those who consider that citizen rights provide a stronger base for welfare claims than consumer rights (see the discussions in Butcher, 1995; Clarke and Newman, 1997; Clarke, 1998; Edgell, Hetherington and Warde, 1996; Giddens, 1998 and 2000; Rao, 1996). At the same time, there are other views of the welfare state/citizen relationship that stress how the state has diminished citizenship rights and made them more contingent. For some, the state both exercises more power over its citizens (or at least 'troublesome' sections of them), while transferring 'responsibilities' to them for their own well-being and good behaviour. Dwyer's (1998) discussion of 'conditional citizenship' highlights the ways in which citizens are expected to perform 'responsibly' in order to be eligible for welfare benefits and services. Jones and Novak (1999) have argued that a 'disciplinary state' has been constructed in which policing, surveillance and imprisonment are combined with more authoritarian welfare provision to control poor people (see also Pantazis, 1999).

It is not our aim here to settle these complicated arguments. What is important is that they highlight different aspects of the remaking of the British welfare regime, and indicate how hard it is to treat those changes as a one-dimensional and one-directional process. We think it is useful to treat these changes as affecting three key terms – welfare, state and citizenship – and the relationships between them. Rather than treating the welfare state as a single identifiable entity, we need to explore how welfare, the state and citizens were constructed and connected, and how those constructions and connections have changed. This approach avoids some of the problems of treating the welfare state as if it were a commonly understood object whose core features all perspectives could agree on as a point of departure. On the contrary, the welfare state needs to be seen as a social and political construction – a powerful image about collective identity, collective interest and collective provision.

What 'welfare' means now – in terms of policy objectives and the content of benefits and services – is not the same as it did in the mid 1970s. Some of its ambitions and scale have been diminished. Some of it has been made more conditional, while increasing responsibility has been placed on citizens to promote and preserve their own well-being. Some aspects of welfare have new objectives, with employment, economic growth and competitiveness having become more explicit aims of social policy. Neo-liberal economic and social imperatives have played a significant role in the remaking of welfare benefits and services. Claims about 'welfare to work' or 'promoting independence' have reinstated social policy objectives that date back to the Poor Law. At the same time, some welfare services and systems have become increasingly 'targeted' on those groups defined as the poorest, the most needy or the genuinely deserving, becoming less supportive – and even punitive – to those who fall outside these classifications. Those who are poor, marginalized or excluded are vulnerable to demands that they behave responsibly (as the precondition of inclusion) and to forms of surveillance and criminalization.

The state has changed, even though arguments continue about what the main tendencies are. Various terms have been coined to describe these changes in the state: the 'hollowed out state'; the 'congested state'; the 'contract state'; the 'fragmented state' and the 'managerial state' (Clarke and Newman, 1997). One line of argument concerns whether the state has shrunk, or been 'rolled back'. It is clear that there has been a withdrawal from much direct provision of services, particularly in the field of social care. However, the state remains the dominant provider of education, healthcare and income maintenance. More importantly, the state has retained – or perhaps even enhanced – its role in directing and co-ordinating the mixed economies of welfare, even where services are being provided through contracted or 'arm's length' agencies (Hoggett, 1996). It has also expanded processes of scrutiny – inspection, evaluation and audit – over provider organizations. There are processes of devolution (both geographic and political) and decentralization (typically to 'local management'). But these combine, in contradictory ways, with increasingly centralized control – through resources, the specification of service content and standards, and the evaluation of performance. The creation of new modes of control – the use of contracts, managerial power, patterns of regulation and audit –

indicate how the state might have both 'shrunk' (in organizational size) and extended its reach and power.

Finally, citizenship has also changed in complex ways. It has been the focus of conflicting political struggles: between the effort to expand access to citizenship (or to change 'second-class citizens' into first-class ones) and the attempts to narrow such access (particularly to migrants of all kinds, from Commonwealth citizens to asylum-seekers). On a second axis, the last two decades have seen the drive to reinvent citizens as 'consumers' of public services, thereby disconnecting 'consumers' from 'taxpayers', and juxtaposing them against the 'scroungers', 'benefit frauds' and those 'not genuinely in need' who abuse the welfare system. Consumerism responds to the claims that people have different needs for welfare, echoing the attack on the 'false universalism' of the old welfare system made by new social movements and user groups. However, it does so by reducing differences to individualized – and potentially idiosyncratic – wants. In the process, consumerism ignores the inequalities of resources and power associated with social differences. Citizenship has thus become both more and less differentiated. Increasingly, there is a new universalism, based on what Fraser (1997) has called the 'universal breadwinner' model. For British social policy, this model implies that men and women, black and white, able-bodied and disabled alike, are all entitled – and expected – to strive to support themselves (Clarke and Newman, 1998; Lister, 1998). At the same time, other elements of social policy construct and reproduce critical social divisions, not least in the continued gendering of parenting, care and domestic labour. 'Difference' tends to appear and disappear in social policy: 'gender-blind' or 'race-blind' language often obscures real social differences that have profound consequences.

In other respects, citizenship, and its entitlements to welfare, has also become more fragile and conditional, with the onus on the citizen fulfilling his or her 'obligations and responsibilities'. These range from striving to be employed, through being a good parent and taking responsibility for one's own health, to being a good neighbour. If there has been a process of 'rising expectations' in terms of what citizens hoped for from the welfare state, this has been echoed in the increasing expectations that the state has of its citizens. Citizenship, then, remains a focus for conflicting and contradictory processes that seek to realign the relationship between the state and the people through the composition of what Morris (1998) calls 'legitimate membership of the welfare community'.

Drawing out these different dimensions of the remaking of the welfare state highlights three important issues. First, it is difficult to find a satisfactory one-dimensional designation of the changes to the welfare state because the changes are about more than one thing. Some address the objectives, content and character of welfare; others the role, scale and form of the state, while others engage the composition, rights and relationships of citizenship. Second, it is hard to produce a satisfactory synoptic overview of these changes because they are uneven, contradictory and contested – there is no single trend or direction of change. Third, it is hard to produce a definitive account of the remaking of the welfare state because these processes are continuing ones. The last two decades have seen a constant ferment of innovation and initiatives, reform and modernization, abolition and adaptation as successive governments have tried to remake the British welfare regime. Different struggles have taken place within and through social welfare – about public spending, the state, citizenship, economic and social objectives – and these struggles continue. The New Labour government of 1997 was as energetic as its Conservative predecessors in its pursuit of a new welfare system. It combined many of the same obsessions (about public spending, creating responsible and independent citizens, promoting economic competitiveness) with new strands of its own (reducing social exclusion, rebuilding communities, working in partnership).

So what sort of transition has the British welfare regime been engaged in? In part, answering this question depends on whether it is possible to provide a clear statement of what sort of regime was constructed in the post-war period. The British welfare system has always been a difficult case for comparative social policy studies because of its lack of fit with most typologies of welfare states or regimes. For example, in Esping-Andersen's three forms of 'welfare capitalism' (recall the discussion in Chapter 1) Britain was viewed as combining features of the 'liberal' welfare model (market-centred, limited decommodification and limited redistribution) with some elements of the social democratic (Scandinavian) model (relatively strong universalism) in an uncomfortable hybrid. It could be argued that the last twenty years have seen the regime move towards a more liberal – or possibly neo-liberal – model, learning lessons from the USA in particular. The emphasis here would be on a reduced role for the state, the expansion of market relations, a greater emphasis on individual freedom/responsibility and a more explicit pursuit of 'economic' objectives in social policy. While this may be true of many labour-market and income maintenance-related elements of social policy, it is less convincing in relation to many welfare services, where all sorts of familialist, patriarchal and socially conservative (or traditionalist) trends have been visible. Added to this is the impact of membership of the European Union on employment, welfare and human rights issues – through which more corporatist approaches to economic and social policy have been encountered. It may be that the British welfare regime is in transition from one peculiar hybrid to another. The post-war regime combined 'liberal' and 'social democratic' elements around a powerful cluster of assumptions about the conventional family, the racialized (white) nation and the (able-bodied, male) breadwinner at work. The emerging regime appears to combine strong neo-liberal principles with more residual social democratic concerns (overlaid by occasional corporatist influences from the EU). These are organized around the uneasy 'modern' versions of family, nation and work. Poised between US and European 'models' of welfare, Britain's welfare system is likely to remain 'in transition' for some time.

REFERENCES

Arnott, H. (1990) 'Fortress Europe', *Poverty*, no.75.

Audit Commission (1988) *The Competitive Council*, London, The Audit Commission for Local Authorities in England and Wales.

Bacon, R. and Eltis, W. (1976) *Britain's Economic Problem: Too Few Producers*, Basingstoke, Macmillan.

Barclay Committee (1982) *The Future of Social Work*, London, Tavistock.

Barr, N. and Coulter, F. (1990) 'Social security: solution or problem?', in Hills (1990).

Bartlett, W., Roberts, J. and Le Grand, J. (eds) (1999) *A Revolution in Social Policy: Quasi-market Reforms in the 1990s*, Bristol, The Policy Press.

Bauman, Z. (1998) *Work, Consumerism and the New Poor*, Buckingham, Open University Press.

Blair, T. (1998) *The Third Way,* London, Fabian Society.

Brown, H. and Smith, H. (1993) 'Women caring for people: the mismatch between rhetoric and women's reality', *Policy and Politics*, vol.21, no.3, pp.185–93.

Burchardt, T. and Hills, J. (1999) 'Public expenditure and the public/private mix', in Powell, M. (ed.) *New Labour, New Welfare State?*, Bristol, The Policy Press.

Butcher, T. (1995) *Delivering Welfare*, Buckingham, Open University Press.

Clarke, J. (1996) 'The problem of the state after the welfare state', in May, M., Bransdon, E. and Craig, G. (eds) *Social Policy Review 8*, London, Social Policy Association.

Clarke, J. (1998) 'Consumerism', in Hughes, G. (ed.) *Imagining Welfare Futures*, London, Routledge/The Open University.

Clarke, J. (forthcoming) 'Making a difference? Markets and the reform of public services', in Schröter, E. and Wollmann, H. (eds) *Public Service Reform in Britain and Germany*, Basingstoke, Palgrave.

Clarke, J. and Newman, J. (1997) *The Managerial State: Power, Politics and Ideology in the Remaking of Social Welfare*, London, Sage.

Clarke, J. and Newman, J. (1998) 'A modern British people? New Labour and the remaking of social welfare', paper presented to conference on 'Discourse analysis and social research', Denmark, September.

Clarke, J., Cochrane, A. and Smart, C. (1987) *Ideologies of Welfare*, London, Hutchinson.

Clarke, J., Gewirtz, S. and McLaughlin, E. (eds) (2000) *New Managerialism, New Welfare?*, London, Sage.

Clarke, J., Gewirtz, S., Hughes, G. and Humphrey, J. (2000) 'Guarding the public interest? The rise of audit', in Clarke, J., Gewirtz, S. and McLaughlin, E. (2000).

Cochrane, A. (1993) 'The problem of poverty', in Dallos, R. and McLaughlin, E. (eds) *Social Problems and the Family*, London, Sage/The Open University.

Dallos, R. and Sapsford, R. (1993) 'Patterns of diversity and lived realities', in Muncie, J. *et al.* (eds) *Understanding the Family*, London, Sage/The Open University.

Davies, S. (1987) 'Towards the remoralization of society', in Loney *et al.* (1987).

Deacon, A. and Bradshaw, J. (1983) *Reserved for the Poor: The Means-Test in British Social Policy*, Oxford, Martin Robertson.

Deakin, S. and Wilkinson, F. (1992) 'Social policy and economic efficiency: the deregulation of the labour market in Britain', *Critical Social Policy*, vol.33.

Dean, H. and Melrose, M. (1998) *Poverty, Riches and Social Exclusion*, London, Routledge.

Department of Health and Social Security (1985) *Reform of Social Security*, vols 1–3, Cmnd 9517/8/9 (Green Paper), London, HMSO.

Department of Social Security (DSS) (2000a) *The Changing Welfare State: Pensioner Incomes*, London, Department of Social Security.

Department of Social Security (DSS) (2000b) *The Changing Welfare State: Social Security Spending*, London, Department of Social Security.

Dominelli, L. (1988) *Anti-Racist Social Work*, Basingstoke, Macmillan.

Dwyer, P. (1998) 'Conditional citizens? Welfare rights and responsibilities in the late 1990s', *Critical Social Policy*, vol.18, no.4, pp.493–518.

Edgell, S., Hetherington, K. and Warde, A. (eds) (1996) *Consumption Matters*, Oxford, Blackwell/The Sociological Review.

Esping-Andersen, G. (1990) *The Three Worlds of Welfare Capitalism*, Cambridge, Polity Press.

Esping-Andersen, G. (ed.) (1996) *Welfare States in Transition*, London, Sage/UNRISD.

Evans, D. (1989) 'Section 28: law, myth and paradox', *Critical Social Policy*, vol.27.

Evans, M. (1998) 'Social security: dismantling the pyramids?', in Glennerster and Hills (1998).

Finch, J. (1989) *Family Obligations and Social Change*, Cambridge, Polity Press.

Finch, J. and Mason, J. (1992) *Negotiating Family Obligations*, London, Routledge.

Finn, D. (1998) 'Labour's 'New Deal' for the unemployed and the stricter benefit regime', in Bransdon, E., Dean, H. and Woods, R. (eds) *Social Policy Review 10*, London, Social Policy Association.

Foreman, S. and Dallos, R. (1993) 'Domestic violence', in Dallos, R. and McLaughlin, E. (eds) *Social Problems and the Family*, London, Sage/The Open University.

Fraser, N. (1997) 'After the family wage: a postindustrial thought experiment', in *Justice Interruptus: Critical Reflections on the "Postsocialist" Condition*, London, Routledge.

Giddens, A. (1998) *The Third Way*, Cambridge, Polity Press.

Giddens, A. (2000) *The Third Way and its Critics,* Cambridge, Polity Press.

Glendinning, C., Rummery, K. and Clarke, R. (1998) 'From collaboration to commissioning: developing relationships between primary health and social services', *British Medical Journal*, no.7151, pp.122–5.

Glennerster, H. (1998) 'Welfare with the lid on', in Glennerster and Hills (1998).

Glennerster, H. and Hills, J. (eds) (1998) *The State of Welfare*, second edition, Oxford, Oxford University Press.

Graham, H. (1984) *Women, Health and the Family*, Brighton, Wheatsheaf.

Griffiths, R. (1988) *Community Care: Agenda for Action. A Report to the Secretary of State for Social Services*, London, HMSO.

Hall, C. (1998) 'A family for nation and empire', in Lewis, G. (ed.) *Forming Nation, Framing Welfare*, London, Sage/The Open University.

Hall, S. and Jacques, M. (1983) *The Politics of Thatcherism*, London, Lawrence and Wishart.

Hay, C. (1999) *The Political Economy of New Labour*, Manchester, Manchester University Press.

Hills, J. (ed.) (1990) *The State of Welfare: The Welfare State in Britain since 1974*, Oxford, Oxford University Press.

Hoggett, P. (1996) 'New modes of control in the public service', *Public Administration*, vol.74, pp.9–32.

Hood, C., Scott, C., Jones, G. and Travers, T. (1999) *Regulation Inside Government: Waste-watchers, Quality-police and Sleaze-busters*, Oxford, Oxford University Press.

Huby, M. and Whyley, C. (1996) 'Take-up and the Social Fund', *Journal of Social Policy*, vol.25, no.1, pp.1–18.

Hughes, G. (ed.) (1998) *Imagining Welfare Futures*, London, Routledge/ The Open University.

Hughes, G. and Lewis, G. (eds) (1998) *Unsettling Welfare: The Reconstruction of Social Policy*, London, Routledge/The Open University.

Jessop, B. (2000) 'Governance failure', in Stoker, G. (ed.) *The New Politics of British Local Governance*, Basingstoke, Macmillan.

Johnson, N. (ed.) (1999) *Mixed Economies of Welfare: A Comparative Approach*, London, Prentice Hall Europe.

Jones, C. and Novak, J. (1999) *Poverty, Welfare and the Disciplinary State*, London, Routledge.

Land, H. (1999a) 'New Labour, new families?', in Dean, H. and Woods, R. (eds) *Social Policy Review 11*, London, Social Policy Association.

Land, H. (1999b) 'The changing worlds of work and families', in Watson and Doyal (1999).

Langan, M. (1988) 'Women under Thatcherism', in Alcock, P. and Lee, P. (eds) *Thatcherism and the Future of Welfare*, Papers in Social and Urban Policy, no.1, Sheffield Polytechnic.

Le Grand, J. (1990) 'The state of welfare', in Hills (1990).

Le Grand, J. and Winter, D. (1987) 'The middle classes and the welfare state under Conservative and Labour governments', *Journal of Public Policy*, vol.6, pp.399–430.

Le Grand, J. and Vizard, P. (1998) 'The National Health Service: crisis, change or continuity?', in Glennerster and Hills (1998).

Le Grand, J., Winter, D. and Woolley, F. (1990) 'The National Health Service: safe in whose hands?', in Hills (1990).

Lewis, G. (2000) 'Discursive histories, the pursuit of multi culturalism and social policy', in Lewis, G., Gewirtz, S. and Clarke, J. (eds) *Rethinking Social Policy,* London, Sage.

Lewis, J. (1993) 'Developing the mixed economy of care: emerging issues for voluntary organisations', *Journal of Social Policy*, vol.22, no.2, pp.173–92.

Lewis, J. (2000) 'Gender and welfare regimes', in Lewis, G., Gewirtz, S. and Clarke, J. (eds) *Rethinking Social Policy*, London, Sage.

Lister, R. (1990) 'Social security', in McCarthy, M. (ed.) *The New Politics of Welfare: An Agenda for the 1990s?*, Basingstoke, Macmillan.

Lister, R. (1998) 'From equality to social exclusion: New Labour and the welfare state', *Critical Social Policy*, vol.18, no.2, pp.215–26.

Lister, R. (2000) 'Gender and the analysis of social policy', in Lewis, G., Gewirtz, S. and Clarke, J. (eds) *Rethinking Social Policy*, London, Sage/ The Open University.

Loney, M. *et al.* (eds) (1987) *The State or the Market: Politics and Welfare in Contemporary Britain*, London, Sage/The Open University.

Mayo, M. (1994) *Communities and Caring: The Mixed Economy of Welfare*, Basingstoke, Macmillan.

McLaughlin, E. and Murji, K. (2000) 'The news media and racist violence', in May, M., Page, R. and Bransdon, E. (eds) *Understanding Social Problems: Issues in Social Policy*, Oxford, Blackwell.

Miliband, R. *et al.* (eds) (1987) *Socialist Register 1987*, London, Merlin.

Mishra, M. (1990) *The Welfare State in Capitalist Society: Policies of Retrenchment and Maintenance in Europe, North America and Australia*, Hemel Hempstead, Harvester Wheatsheaf.

Moody, K. (1987) 'Reagan, the business agenda and the collapse of labour', in Miliband *et al.* (1987).

Mooney, G. (1997) 'Quasi-markets and the mixed economy of welfare', in Lavalette, M. and Pratt, A. (eds) *Social Policy: A Conceptual and Theoretical Introduction*, London, Sage.

Morris, L. (1998) 'Legitimate membership of the welfare community', in Langan, M. (ed.) *Welfare: Needs, Rights and Risks*, London, Routledge/ The Open University.

Mouffe, C. (1998) 'The radical centre: a politics without adversary', *Soundings*, vol.9, pp.11–23.

Murray, C. (1984) *Losing Ground: American Social Policy, 1950–1980*, New York, Basic Books.

Murray, C. (1990) *The Emerging British Underclass*, London, Institute of Economic Affairs.

Newman, J. (1998) 'Managerialism and social welfare', in Hughes, G. and Lewis, G. (eds) *Unsetling Welfare*, London, Routledge/The Open University.

Palmer, F. (1986) *Anti-Racism: An Assault on Education and Value*, Nottingham, Sherwood Press.

Pantazis, C. (1999) 'The criminalization of female poverty', in Watson and Doyal (1999).

Piachaud, D. (1999) 'Progress on poverty', *New Economy*, Institute for Public Policy Research, pp.154–60.

Pollitt, C. (1995) 'Justification by works or by faith? Evaluating the new public management', *Evaluation*, vol.1, no.2, pp.135–54.

Powell, M. (1995) 'The strategy of equality revisited', *Journal of Social Policy,* vol.24, no.2, pp.163–85.

Powell, M. (ed.) (1999) *New Labour, New Welfare State?*, Bristol, The Policy Press.

Pryke, M. (1998) 'Thinking social policy into social housing', in Hughes and Lewis (1998).

Rao, N. (1996) *Towards Welfare Pluralism*, Aldershot, Dartmouth Publishing Company.

Smart, C. (1987) 'Securing the family? Rhetoric and policy in the field of social security', in Loney *et al.* (1987).

Smart, C. (1997) 'Wishful thinking or harmful tinkering? Sociological reflections on family policy', *Journal of Social Policy*, vol.26, no.3, pp.301–21.

Smart, C. and Silva, E. (eds) (1999) *The New Family?*, London, Sage.

Smith, S. (1999) 'Arguing against cuts in lone-parent benefits', *Critical Social Policy*, vol.19, no.3, pp.313–34.

Southall Black Sisters (1990) *Against the Grain*, London, Southall Black Sisters.

Stepney, P., Lynch, R. and Jordan, B. (1999) 'Poverty, exclusion and New Labour', *Critical Social Policy*, vol.19, no.1, pp.109–28.

Stewart, G., Stewart, J. and Walker, C. (1989) *The Social Fund,* London, Association of County Councils.

Survivors Speak Out (1987) *Report of the First National Conference of Users of Psychiatric Services*, London, Survivors Speak Out.

Walsh, K. (1995) *Public Services and Market Mechanisms: Competition, Contracting and the New Public Management,* Basingstoke, MacMillan.

Watson, S. and Doyal, L. (eds) (1999) *Engendering Social Policy*, Buckingham, Open University Press.

Wilkinson, R. (1996) *Unhealthy Societies: The Afflictions of Inequality*, London, Routledge.

Wistow, G., Knapp, M., Hardy, B., Forder, J., Kendall, J. and Manning, R. (1996) *Social Care Markets: Progress and Prospects*, Buckingham, Open University Press.

CHAPTER 4
US WELFARE: VARIATIONS ON THE LIBERAL REGIME

JOHN CLARKE

CONTENTS

INTRODUCTION   114

1   CONSTRUCTING US WELFARE: FROM NEW DEAL
    TO GREAT SOCIETY   114
1.1   THE NEW DEAL   114
1.2   THE GREAT SOCIETY: FIGHTING THE WAR AGAINST POVERTY? 120

2   LAUNCHING THE WAR ON WELFARE:
    THE NEW RIGHT IN THE 1980s   125
2.1   THE PROBLEM OF THE STATE   127
2.2   THE PROBLEM OF DEPENDENCY   130
2.3   THE PROBLEM OF THE UNDERCLASS   132

3   CLASS, 'RACE' AND GENDER IN THE POLITICS OF
    WELFARE   135

4   THE END OF WELFARE?   137
4.1   HEALTHCARE: THE FAILURE OF REFORM   137
4.2   ENDING 'WELFARE AS WE KNOW IT'   140
4.3   THE END OF THE US WELFARE STATE?   144

5   WHAT FUTURE FOR THE LIBERAL WELFARE
    REGIME?   146

    REFERENCES   148

INTRODUCTION

The USA has always stood out as a different – or even 'exceptional' – case in the comparative study of welfare systems. From a western European standpoint, it has often been treated as a 'laggard', arriving late to the creation of national welfare systems, or as a 'deviant' case, drawing attention to the particular formulation of the USA's divergent political, social and institutional formations. More recently, however, US and European studies have challenged both the 'laggard' and the 'deviant' views of the USA (e.g. Amenta, 1998; Esping-Andersen, 1990; Skocpol, 1992). The development of systematic comparisons and the creation of typologies such as Esping-Andersen's 'three worlds' of welfare capitalism have repositioned US welfare within a range of welfare systems, rather than merely emphasizing its difference from an assumed European norm. At the same time, developments in the US welfare system (not least the development of 'workfare') have made the USA more visible in its political conflicts over the future of welfare. Reference is often made to the 'US model' and its implications for the development of British and other European welfare systems.

This chapter explores the development of the US welfare system. We examine two core periods in the construction and enlargement of US welfare policy (the 1930s and the 1960s), and then look at the 'anti-welfare' backlash of the new right and the 'end of welfare' proclaimed in the 1990s. Although the US welfare system has been cast as a prime example of a 'liberal welfare regime' in Esping-Andersen's typology, this chapter suggests that US welfare has been shaped by a more complex set of social and political forces than this might imply. We also see how 'liberalism' has been a shifting and contested category within the USA. Finally, we trace some of the conflicts that have produced a very different US welfare system for the beginning of the twenty-first century.

I   CONSTRUCTING US WELFARE: FROM NEW DEAL TO GREAT SOCIETY

Rather than trying to provide a complete history of the development of welfare policy in the United States, we will focus on two periods of major welfare reform and innovation: the 1930s and the 1960s. These two periods feature in most accounts of US welfare as formative periods in which major structural developments in the organization and provision of welfare took place. These periods acquired a political significance that gave them a central place in later conflicts over welfare in the USA.

1.1   THE NEW DEAL

Prior to the 1930s, welfare in the USA was organized and delivered at local level, through the states and cities and through voluntary and philanthropic agencies. The only national system of welfare was the

Civil War Veterans' pension organized by the federal government (Amenta and Skocpol, 1989; Skocpol, 1992). There were also limited forms of welfare support provided by corporations to their employees, including healthcare, housing and education. Such provision tended to cover only some groups of white-collar and skilled blue-collar workers (see Brandes, 1976; on the wider role of corporations, see Trachtenberg, 1982). The economic depression of the 1930s exposed the limitations of this patchwork pattern of welfare. The scale of unemployment and the resulting poverty rapidly outran the ability of philanthropic and local state arrangements to cope. This failure of welfare provoked substantial social movements among the poor and unemployed, who demanded public intervention to remedy unemployment and relieve poverty (Piven and Cloward, 1993).

The Roosevelt Administration's 'New Deal' combined temporary measures to remedy unemployment through public works schemes supported by federal funds, with longer-term programmes establishing more systematic and more rigorously administered welfare benefits. Amenta (1998) has described this as the creation of a 'work and relief state' rather than a 'welfare state', as a way of emphasizing the central role of employment-creation measures in the New Deal initiatives:

> The program that absorbed the greatest amount of both public spending and public attention was the 'Works Program' – public employment mainly though the Works Progress Administration (WPA). Its priority was so great that it was brought before Congress ahead of the Economic Security Act, as the security bill was initially called.
>
> (Amenta, 1998, p.81)

The creation of the Works Program in 1933 (providing work in public schemes for the unemployed) was followed by the Social Security Act of 1935, which provided the foundation for the subsequent structure of US welfare benefits. The Act created a system of social insurance to provide benefits for old age, alongside federal support for state schemes for unemployment insurance. It was later extended in respect of survivors (widows and their dependants), sickness and disability. In August 1935, upon signing the Social Security Act, Roosevelt claimed that: 'Today a hope of many years' standing is fulfilled ... We can never insure 100 per cent of the population against 100 per cent of the hazards and vicissitudes of life, but we have tried to frame a law which will give some measure of protection to the average citizen and to his family against the loss of a job and against poverty-ridden old age' (quoted in Alsop, 1982, p.127). Like insurance schemes elsewhere, the Social Security Act's central principle was the accumulation of a record of insurance contributions through employment. A great number of occupations, including many of those in which black people and female workers were concentrated such as agriculture and domestic work, were excluded from the scheme. Other occupations involved levels of pay too low to qualify for insurance payments and benefits, again disproportionately affecting both white women and black workers (Quadagno, 1994, pp.20–4).

Collective or socialized, rather than individual, insurance had been established as a core principle of welfare provision in European welfare regimes much earlier. Until the advent of the Social Security Act, demands for its introduction into the USA had been consistently resisted by politicians and employers' organizations on the grounds that it would undermine the workings of the labour market and the incentives to individuals to make provision for their own welfare (Skocpol and Ikenberry, 1983). However, the scale of the social dislocation created by the Depression – and the threat of social disorder associated with it – led to a willingness to supplement the fragmentary patterns of local public and philanthropic assistance, and gave the idea of a more integrated and national system of social insurance a greater political legitimacy (Piven and Cloward, 1993). In adopting an insurance model, Roosevelt sought to maintain proper incentives to work, and his New Deal embodied three core principles:

1 That social insurance should not be directed at the elimination of all hardship, but only be concerned with a limited range of specified risks (unemployment, ill health, old age and widowhood) that were not voluntary conditions.

2 That workers should see the connection between their income, their insurance payments and the benefits they would eventually receive, avoiding expectations of high benefit levels and maintaining work incentives.

3 That the scheme should be clearly distinguished from public assistance, such that its benefits were seen to be 'earned' as a right through a contribution record rather than collected as a stigmatizing and means-tested relief from the public purse or private charity (see Katz, 1986, pp.236–7).

The Committee on Economic Security, which oversaw the development of social security, was concerned that the development of new welfare measures should not blur the line between insurance-based provision and 'public assistance' (the locally provided, means-tested support for those in poverty). In the end only two of the New Deal reforms threatened to blur this distinction. One was the decision to pay old-age pensions immediately to those who had no contribution record, but this was a temporary arrangement intended to last only until the scheme was fully established. Subsequently, a means test for people who were not insured was reintroduced.

The second measure that threatened to blur the distinction between insurance-based provision and 'public assistance' was the creation of ADC (Aid to Dependent Children) in the 1935 Act, which allowed the federal government to contribute to the costs of states' programmes for benefits to poverty-struck families for the maintenance of children. ADC was derived from the 'mothers' pensions' programmes that a number of states had developed, between 1911 and 1930, to provide some assistance to widowed or deserted mothers with young children. Amenta (1998, p.63) notes that 'these programs were staffed mainly by middle class women, and most included strict rules of eligibility', and also that their practices were highly socially selective. He cites a 1931 study which showed that, of the mothers receiving such pensions, 'about 82 per cent were widows, and only about 3 per cent of recipients were African-American. In some states, such as Louisiana and Mississippi, there were no black recipients' (p.70). The mothers' pensions and the ADC programmes were constructed around two core assumptions: that families were normally supported by a 'family wage' (earned by a man), and that mothers would normally be at home, looking after children. This 'maternalist' view of women and welfare was central to the development of US welfare policies (see Gordon, 1994; Koven and Michel, 1993). Gordon points to the impact of these structuring assumptions on single mothers within welfare:

> The structure of ADC arose from a maternalism shared by women and men, its practice 'assigned' to women. Women welfare reformers, working in this female sphere, accepted a family-wage system. In the nineteenth century and earlier, the poor, women as well as men, had often crusaded for a family wage as a means of rescuing children from labor, lessening women's drudgery, and forcing concessions from capital – as well as confirming men's privileged positions ... Long after the family wage was doomed, welfare experts tried to contrive a magical assistance program that would somehow shore it up. The result often placed single mothers in a double bind: already victimized by the failure of the family-wage system, the charity of the public assistance system added to their disadvantages – such as low wages and responsibility for children – by emphasizing domesticity as the only maternal virtue.
>
> (Gordon, 1994, pp.290–1)

ADC's funding from the federal government moved public assistance part way towards being a national scheme, although its administration remained at local level (see Gordon, 1994; Koven and Michel, 1993; and the discussion of changing entitlements in Bussiere, 1997, chapters 3 and 4). The scheme allowed a very substantial extension of the partial pattern of mothers' pensions, tripling the numbers of children covered by 1940 (Amenta, 1998, p.146). ADC became the paradigm within which the complex inter-relationship between welfare, 'race', class and gender in the USA took place. Where social insurance was earnings-related, ADC was available if the candidate's family passed a series of 'tests'. Gordon describes three key tests, beginning with the means test:

> To establish need a client had to be not only without income but also without resources, including property or services ... which might stave off poverty and help a temporarily reduced client

regain position. Cash savings were not allowed ... The means test was ongoing. If a resource was gained, in kind as well as cash, it had to be reported and the stipend reduced proportionately.

Closely related to the means test was ... the 'work test' which operated in contradictory ways for ADC recipients. The rules banned paid employment unless the earnings were reported and then deducted from a stipend; but the stipends were beneath subsistence and caseworkers knew that their clients had to supplement their incomes somehow.

ADC was unique among all welfare programs in its subjection of applicants to a morals test. The most frequent measurement of a 'suitable home' was sexual behaviours. The presence of a man in the house, or the birth of an illegitimate child, made the home unsuitable. These provisions also permitted racist policies. For example, black–white relationships were particularly likely to make a child's home declared unsuitable. The search for these 'moral' infractions produced intense supervision and invasions of privacy.

(Gordon, 1994, p.298)

The 'suitable home' provision drew on well-established and often racially coded assumptions about 'moral fitness' that had developed during the administration of mothers' pensions schemes:

'Moral fitness' was encoded with Anglo-Saxon biases – for temperance, nuclear-family households, American cooking ... [W]ide discretion was ordinarily delegated to administrators and social workers – most of whom were white and middle class. Discretion allowed for the imposition of Anglo-Saxon criteria, as well as for racial exclusion where uplift was seen as either undesirable or impossible. Discretion meant, for example, that black mothers, barred from eligibility in some southern states, were elsewhere denied entitlement by policy managers. Further, both law and discretion invited pension agencies to police their clients regularly to enforce fitness: evidence of smoking, lack of church attendance, poor hygiene, male boarders.

(Mink, 1991, p.110)

THE LIMITATIONS OF THE 'SEMI-WELFARE' STATE

For the United States, the New Deal was a small and partial revolution – the founding of what Katz (1986) calls a 'semi-welfare state'. Although it maintained the formal separation between federal and state or city administration of different aspects of welfare, it nevertheless changed the balance between national and local through the development of some national schemes and the greater use of federal funding to support the delivery of locally based welfare. It laid the foundation for a nationally co-ordinated system of social insurance, with benefits and entitlements for limited categories of the population. The creation of an insurance system aligned the USA with other western societies in the decommodification of limited welfare rights in relation to unemployment, old age, disability and ill health. Because of the insurance principle, however, the benefits of this decommodification were limited to those with a record of contributions earned through employment. For those who were included within the insurance system, the New Deal represented a considerable step forward. However, the combination of social insurance with the preservation of local systems of public assistance created a 'two tier' welfare state in which those outside the insurance system had to prove both need and moral worth in order to receive assistance. This categorization of those entitled to welfare reflected the wider structures of the inequality of American society. Amenta summarizes some of the major effects of welfare in the form of public works and benefits:

> Though not denied WPA [Works Progress Administration] work, women received it at a much lower rate than men and lower than one would expect given women's representation in the labor force ... In 1940, for instance, women constituted one-fourth of the private labor force, but in 1939 they constituted only 13.1 per cent of WPA's certified labor force ... WPA women, moreover, were clustered in the Division of Service and Professional Projects ... The most significant welfare project, in turn, was the [sex-segregated] sewing project, which produced garments and household items ... ADC was the policy-makers' preferred program for women without husband-breadwinners in the home. The OASI [Old-Age and Survivors Insurance] program wrote its age and gender expectations explicitly into the legislation ... The benefit of the primary beneficiary's wife was set at one-half of his benefit. She was entitled to it only if she remained married to the 'primary', however. Widows could receive benefits, too, only if they did not remarry.
>
> (Amenta, 1998, pp.156–7)

If the New Deal reproduced some core assumptions about gender, work and family roles, it also intersected in complex ways with racialized structures in the USA. Amenta suggests that black workers were strongly represented in WPA works programs, but that this possibly reflected their disproportionately high levels of unemployment by comparison with white workers. He also argues that they 'did less well in other New Deal programs', even where these represented an advance over preceding schemes. Black workers also lost out through the exclusion of agricultural and domestic work from the insurance systems for old-age and unemployment insurance, since 'in the 1930s, two-thirds of African Americans were working in these occupations' (Amenta, 1998, p.159). Quadagno (1994) argues that this structuring of social security reflected a political alliance between the Roosevelt Administration and Democrat congressmen in the southern states (where black people were geographically concentrated but politically disenfranchised).

> Because of southern opposition, agricultural workers and domestic servants – most black men and women – were left out of the core programs of the Social Security Act. Instead they were relegated to the social-assistance programs, where local welfare authorities could determine benefit levels and set eligibility rules ... Southerners would simply not allow the federal government to dictate standards or set benefit levels. They sought control over any social program that might threaten white domination, so precariously balanced on cotton production.
>
> (Quadagno, 1994, pp.21–2)

However partial the changes wrought by the New Deal, they dominated the pattern of US welfare through to the 1960s and created the conditions from which the subsequent wave of welfare reform developed. In particular, they established within the welfare regime the distinction between insurance-based benefits and public assistance that later overshadowed the politics of welfare in the USA. The distinction had ramifications for benefit levels, the conditions of access and eligibility and for decisions on who were the 'primary beneficiaries' of the different types of welfare. Gordon has argued that:

> Symbolically and practically, welfare differentiation created two arenas of social citizenship: federal and local. White men were usually covered by federal provision, women and minority men by locally controlled programs. The federal programs have higher standards, more generous stipends, a bigger tax base to support them – and dignity. State programs are far more vulnerable to political attacks, declining tax bases and interstate competition.
>
> (Gordon, 1994, p.294)

1.2 THE GREAT SOCIETY: FIGHTING THE WAR AGAINST POVERTY?

The 'Great Society' programmes of welfare reform are associated with the Kennedy and Johnson presidencies of the 1960s. Katz presents a summary of the pressures to reform welfare that indicates how traditional concerns about welfare intersected with social and political change in the early 1960s:

> Racial conflict, urban riots, militant welfare clients and increased out-of-wedlock births among black women impelled a search for new ways to preserve social order and discipline. Unemployment induced by technology, functional illiteracy, or inadequate education; fear of Soviet competition; new manpower theories; and the

realization that welfare regulations discouraged work, all encouraged the use of welfare policy to shape and regulate labor markets. The increased Democratic dependence on the votes of urban blacks insured the continued use of welfare as a source of political mobilization, and the shock and outrage aroused by the rediscovery of poverty, hunger and malnutrition in the early 1960s spurred the improvement and extension of social welfare to relieve human suffering. To these conventional uses of welfare, the civil rights movement added a new element: for the first time, social welfare policy became one strategy for attacking the consequences of racism in America.

(Katz, 1986, pp.251–2)

As Katz suggests, the Civil Rights movement, including its attacks on existing patterns of welfare, was a particularly significant force in demanding change. Movement activists combined with anti-poverty workers in challenging the 'suitable home' provisions of the ADC scheme, which many states had used as a racially exclusionary mechanism (Bell, 1965). Such alliances focused political attention on the urgent need for welfare reform and helped to shape some of the policies that increased the resources of the poorest families through food stamp, nutritional and health programmes (West, 1981). Piven and Cloward argue that welfare reform emerged out of the wider impact of the Civil Rights movement – as 'a political response to political disorder':

> The welfare explosion occurred during several years of the greatest domestic disorder since the 1930s – perhaps the greatest in our history. It was concurrent with the turmoil produced by the civil rights struggle, with widespread and destructive rioting in the cities and with the formation of a militant grass-roots movement of the poor dedicated to the combating of welfare restrictions. Not least, the welfare rise was also concurrent with the enactment of a series of ghetto-placating federal programs (such as the antipoverty program) which, among other things, hired thousands of poor people, social workers and lawyers who, it subsequently turned out, greatly stimulated people to apply for relief and obtain it.

(Piven and Cloward, 1993, p.198)

Specific programmes developed during this period targeted particular aspects of social life in poor communities such as juvenile delinquency, civil rights, job training and education. One of the most salient features of these initiatives was that they stressed that community programmes should develop the 'maximum feasible participation' of the residents (Title II of the Economic Opportunity Act). This emphasis, on the need for programmes to be carried out *by* the community rather than *for* the community, identified state and city politicians and welfare agencies as part of the problem to be overcome (Marris and Rein, 1967).

The Office of Economic Opportunity (OEO) was set up in 1964 through the Economic Opportunity Act, which allowed federal money to be channelled directly to community groups. This attempt to make funding usurp existing power structures was very quickly curtailed, with political resistance leading to restrictions on the OEO's ability to fund community groups directly (Quadagno, 1994). The programme was ended in 1974, when the Nixon Administration closed the OEO and transferred its responsibilities to other government departments. The OEO was a key element in a wider 'war on poverty', conceived in the Kennedy Administration and carried through by Johnson.

Beginning with the Public Welfare Amendments of 1962 and ending with the Social Security Amendments of 1974, the period saw a major restructuring and expansion of US welfare. Between 1965 and 1972, federal spending on welfare rose from $75 billion to $185 billion, rising from 7.7 per cent of the USA's gross national product in 1960 to 16 per cent by 1974. This expansion had three main features:

1   an increase in the numbers of those eligible for welfare services and benefits;

2   a change in the balance between services and benefits; and

3   a shift in the relationship between social security and public assistance.

The reforms expanded the numbers of people eligible for welfare services and benefits. There was a reduction in the racially discriminatory administration of welfare programmes, particularly in the change of ADC to AFDC (Aid to Families with Dependent Children). Between 1960 and 1970, AFDC was granted to an additional 800,000 families – an increase of 107 per cent, of which 71 per cent occurred between 1964 and 1968 (Piven and Cloward, 1993, pp.183, 187). Less visibly, but numerically more significant, there was a withdrawal or reduction of means-testing across a range of welfare services, which turned them from a conditional entitlement into an unconditional right. This change in the access criteria had some effect in destigmatizing public services and affected their ethos, turning them away from a focus on assessing, investigating and supervising the poor towards seeing these services as means of promoting greater social integration and participation. Handler suggests that these changes reflected a political intersection of civil rights and legal rights:

> The Democratic Party courted African Americans, and along with the civil rights revolution, there was a legal rights revolution. The federal courts and welfare rights activists forced open the ADC gates. Welfare became a 'right', and in streamed the previously excluded – women of color, divorced, separated, deserted, and, increasingly, never married.

(Handler, 1995, p.28)

The reforms also pushed welfare provision towards a greater emphasis on the provision of services (for example healthcare, housing and access to legal services) rather than on direct cash payments. A variety of initiatives provided 'matching funding' from the federal government to states' social service schemes and provided funding for the purchase of service from private sources (including voluntary and not-for-profit agencies as well as commercial providers). Between 1964 and 1974, federal spending on 'in-kind' programmes increased from 3 per cent to 20 per cent of social welfare costs (Katz, 1986, p.265). The most significant of these developments related to public housing, nutritional programmes (particularly the provision of food stamps to poor families) and health services.

Nevertheless, the policy responses to these social problems were dominated by a view of poverty which saw it as the result of 'blocked opportunities'. Poverty was not seen as the result of structured economic inequality, but as the inadvertent effect of historically created barriers which inhibited people from taking advantage of the opportunities that the USA presented to its citizens. Theories of 'cultural deficit' or 'cultural deprivation' among the poor played a leading role in shaping the policy responses (Katz, 1989). As a consequence, policy initiatives such as the Office of Economic Opportunity (OEO) (employment) and Operation Headstart (education) were designed to overcome barriers to participation in the opportunity structures of the USA by enhancing the skills and capacities of the poor.

Health services became a particular focus of attention. The costs of healthcare (either directly for services or indirectly through private insurance) had effectively excluded many Americans. At the same time, however, the costs of socializing healthcare were thought politically prohibitive, and the proposal was forcefully resisted by the health and insurance industry lobby groups. What emerged instead was a package of measures which aimed to subsidize health costs among those in need. The Medicare and Medicaid programmes introduced in 1965 provided public funding for health costs among eligible groups, but the two schemes reproduced the different logics of social security and public assistance:

> Though adopted together, Medicare and Medicaid reflected sharply different traditions. Medicare was buoyed by popular approval and the acknowledged dignity of Social Security; Medicaid was burdened by the stigma of public assistance. While Medicare had uniform national standards for eligibility and benefits, Medicaid left states to decide how extensive their programs would be. Medicare allowed the physician to charge above what the programme would pay; Medicaid did not and participation among physicians was far more limited. The objective of Medicaid was to allow the poor to buy into the 'mainstream' of medicine, but neither the federal government nor the states were willing to spend the money that would have been required.

(Starr, 1982, p.370)

SOCIAL SECURITY VS PUBLIC ASSISTANCE

This split approach to the funding of health costs reflected the continuing distinction between social security and public assistance in US welfare. The two programmes remained at the core of US welfare policy and spending, and played a major role in its expansion during the 1960s and early 1970s. In relation to public assistance, AFDC played the leading role, with the numbers covered by the scheme increasing from 3.1 million in 1960 to 4.3 million in 1965, 6.1 million in 1969 and 10.8 million in 1974 (Patterson, 1981, p.171). Popular challenges to entitlement restrictions and federal and state relaxations of conditions caused an increase both in the numbers of families eligible and the rate of take-up among those eligible.

Despite the dramatic increase in AFDC assistance, it was social security that grew most in the period, partly through demographic trends affecting the numbers eligible for insured benefits, particularly the elderly. But, as Katz argues, its demography was less significant than its social and political base:

> Social security cut across class lines. Like public education, it offered at least as much to the middle classes as to the poor. Its constituency, therefore, was broad, articulate, effective and, above all, respectable. In 1970, social security payments to the elderly, $30.3 billion, were about ten times higher than federal payments for AFDC, $2.5 billion. By 1975, the gap had widened: social security cost $64.7 billion and AFDC, $5.1 billion. Throughout the late 1970s and early 1980s the disparities increased even more: in 1984, social security spending, which was indexed to inflation, had mushroomed to $180.9 billion while AFDC, which was not, had risen only to $8.3 billion.

(Katz, 1986, p.267)

Social security emerged as the dominant feature of US welfare, combining income benefits for the elderly, disabled people and the unemployed with the insurance of health costs for eligible groups. The value of social security benefits was enhanced throughout the late 1960s and 1970s, which saw benefits increased by more than the cost of inflation and welfare extended to the 'non-poor'. Presidents Nixon and Carter both attempted to push welfare towards a closer integration of insurance and assistance-based schemes through proposals for a guaranteed family income. Katz argues that these attempts at welfare reform failed because they threatened the underlying distinction between the deserving and undeserving poor – a distinction that was embodied in the split between insurance and assistance (Katz, 1986, p.269; see also Quadagno, 1994, chapter 5). As we shall see in section 2, this distinction between the programmes was to be a major issue in the politics of welfare in the 1980s.

Before leaving this period, however, it is worth noting some wider issues in relation to the reconstruction of US welfare. Although this account has focused on the domestic conditions of reform and expansion, the pattern is shared more widely by western capitalist societies. From the early 1960s to the mid 1970s, welfare state spending increased considerably in most major western societies. This appears to be associated with the peak of the long post-war boom in the world economy and with a greater role for the state in both social and economic planning.

TABLE 4.1   Social expenditure as a percentage of gross national product

	1960	1981
United States	10.9	20.8
United Kingdom	13.9	23.7
West Germany	20.5	31.5
Sweden	14.5	33.4

Source: Organization for Economic Co-operation and Development (OECD), 1985

During this period US welfare spending grew faster than that of many other countries, such as West Germany and the UK (see Table 4.1), although from a much smaller base. While the USA participated in the general growth in welfare spending, the shape of its reforms and the nature of the welfare regime created were distinctively American.

2   LAUNCHING THE WAR ON WELFARE: THE NEW RIGHT IN THE 1980S

Welfare came to play a central role in the new right's agenda for the reconstruction of the USA in the 1980s. The issue of 'welfare' encompassed a variety of themes about the economy, the state, the family, 'race' and gender that were essential to the new right's diagnosis of the USA's fall from grace and its prescription for a return to greatness. Just as the period of welfare expansion is one that the USA shared with other western societies, so too the period of welfare backlash and retrenchment is one that links the USA to other societies, with Britain an obvious example. Whereas the long post-war boom underpinned welfare expansion, so the onset of world recession, from the mid 1970s, provided a starting-point for challenges to expanded welfare states. This was posed as an apparently simple question of economics: 'can we afford welfare?' But such questions are never quite so simple: they draw our attention to how economic and political crises are *represented*. Such crises have to be identified, their causes explained and their remedies defined. The apparently simple question 'can we afford welfare?' was itself part of the changing ideological framework. It evoked a definition of social welfare as an 'unproductive' cost on national economies, which made them less competitive. In the 1960s welfare had been, at least partly, viewed as an expenditure necessary to modernize societies and make them more competitive, as well as more harmonious and more socially just. This shift is not simply the rise of an 'economic view' of social policy (in place of a 'social' or 'political' view); it was a move to a distinctive type of economic view (neo-liberal or neo-classical) and calculation of the 'problem' of public spending.

While the USA shared some common features with other societies during the 1980s, the particular trajectory that emerged was the product of domestic political forces and alliances; at the heart of this was the reshaping of the right in US politics. An alliance, composed of different social and ideological groupings, came to dominate the Republican Party and supported the Reagan presidency (Saloma, 1984). This alliance included neo-liberals, neo-conservatives and the radical right. Neo-liberalism provided an economic rationale for change, identifying an over-regulatory, over-interfering and over-taxing state as a major cause of the USA's declining competitiveness; individual and corporate 'enterprise' needed to be liberated from the state. Neo-conservatism provided a political rationale for change, arguing that the 'elite liberalism' of the 1960s and 1970s had gone too far, producing an over-extended state and a collapse of political and moral leadership. In particular, elite liberalism had sponsored relativism, disorder and dependency in domestic policy; instead, the USA needed to return to simpler, and more 'popular', virtues and values, including 'family values'. The radical or far right (itself a messy confederation of religious fundamentalists, moral majoritarians, anti-Communists, and racist or white supremacist groupings) provided a moral rationale for change. They argued that the liberalism of the 1960s had undermined fundamental American values, denied fundamental American freedoms (for example, through enforced desegregation of schooling) and created a moral vacuum. These three streams of ideology coincide in their hostility to elite or corporate 'liberalism':

> The three tributaries are aligned in a view of a generalised sense of crisis of American values, for which corporate liberalism is held responsible. Whether in infringing freedoms, corrupting values, being soft on communism, promoting cultural diversity or undermining the family – the liberalism of the 1960s and 1970s stands at the heart of the new right's demonology. Within this it is possible to see how different elements of their agendas intersect. The rhetorical power of individual freedoms derives from the intersections of economic liberalism's revival of classical political economy's insistence of the free market rights of the

individual to dispose of his (very rarely her) goods and abilities with neo-conservatism's concern to reassert individualism as the centre-piece of American political culture and evangelical fundamentalism's commitment to the rights and responsibilities of the individual.

(Clarke, 1991, p.128)

This alliance of unstable and potentially divergent interests and agendas contained sufficient focal points of agreement – or at least overlap – to hold them together in their support for Reaganite republicanism. Welfare was an absolutely central focus for this alliance. The 'costs of welfare' turned out to be economic, political and moral, and the different participants in the alliance were united in their commitment to turn back the rising tide of welfare. One way of making sense of this complex assault on welfare in the USA is to distinguish a set of core 'problems' defined by the new right: the problem of the state, the problem of dependency, and the problem of the underclass.

2.1   THE PROBLEM OF THE STATE

The expansion of welfare in the 1960s and early 1970s had taken an increasing share of an expanding federal budget. For the new right, the growth of the state had had a range of significant political, economic and social consequences. At the heart of the political problem was the fear of 'ungovernability'. The process of expansion was seen to have created a spiral of rising expectations and demands, as new social groups made new social claims on government. This issue was the focus of a study by the Trilateral Commission, formed in 1973, to foster co-operation between the regions of Western Europe, North America and Japan. The Commission was a private body, bringing together corporate representatives (from industry, finance and the media, particularly) with lawyers, politicians and senior government officials. The Commission's 1975 report, *The Crisis of Democracy* (Crozier, Huntington and Watanuki, 1975), argued that the 'rising expectations' of the post-war period threatened to destabilize the social and political order. They suggested that the mobilization of previously passive or acquiescent social groups created the potential for 'the disintegration of civil society, the breakdown of social discipline, the debility of leaders and the alienation of citizens' (Crozier, Huntington and Watanuki, 1975, p.2). Both the concerns and the proposed solutions of this report foreshadowed key features of new right politics and policies. In particular, the Commission's work underpinned the new right's obsession with 'rolling back the state' and reducing the scale and scope of government.

The expanded state was also identified as an economic problem by the new right. They claimed that it promoted economic decline and de-industrialization by diverting resources from the productive to the unproductive sectors of the economy. It was paid for by taxation, or 'legalized robbery' as some new right proponents preferred to call it, and as a consequence had a disincentive effect on the spirit of enterprise, encouraging people to rely on welfare instead of seeking work. These neo-liberal economics of welfare created a logic of reduced public spending on welfare: reduced taxation was necessary to encourage the rich to be more enterprising, while reduced welfare spending was necessary to make the poor more enterprising.

At the same time state employees were identified as a distinct social and political 'interest', with a stake in maintaining or expanding welfare programmes. New right analysts argued that public employees had to be counted among the 'beneficiaries' of public spending. Public employees had an interest in the maintenance and growth of the state both in terms of keeping their employment and in terms of their development of professional or bureaucratic empires. The hostility towards (public) bureaucracies is visible in the following quotation:

> Bureaucracies themselves should be assumed to be noxious, authoritarian parasites on society, with a tendency to augment their own size and power and to cultivate a parasitical clientele in all classes of society ... People must be taught to start calling for a roll-back of the bureaucracy, where nothing will be lost but strangling regulation and where the gains will always take the form of liberty, productivity and jobs.
>
> (Simon, 1979, p.235)

Drawing on Djilas's (1957) analyses of the social organization of communist regimes, the new right identified public employees as a 'new class' (see the discussions in Ehrenreich, 1987, and Hunter, 1981). The designation of public employees as a 'class' made a link between their material interests (the continuation of state-sponsored employment) and their engagement in wider political and ideological commitments in favour of greater state intervention: 'social engineering' and the promotion of 'liberal values'. Liberal values in this context meant a mixture of 'system blaming' views of disadvantage (rather than promoting individual responsibility), a commitment to rights and equalities at the expense of individual freedom, and a degree of 'cultural relativism' rather than moral absolutes. Allen Hunter (1981, p.126) argued that the new right attack on the 'Great Society' programmes demonstrated an 'anger directed at the bureaucrats and professionals who administered these programs. It was these liberals who led the advance towards cultural nihilism and who disdained and walked over the traditionalists of the silent majority'. One of the effects of these arguments was to produce significant cut-backs in public sector spending during the Reagan presidencies in an assault on 'waste and fraud':

> When Ronald Reagan was elected president, he promised to roll back the welfare state. His 1981 Omnibus Budget Reconciliation Act eliminated the entire public service jobs program, removed 400,000 individuals from the food stamp program, and reduced or

eliminated welfare and Medicaid benefits for the working poor. It also eliminated the minimum benefit for low-income Social Security, ended the modest death benefit, and phased out the benefits for older children of deceased workers ... In addition, residents of public housing were required to pay 30 per cent of their income toward rent instead of 25 per cent.

(Quadagno, 1994, p.162)

Such reductions intersected in a complex way with wider politics in the USA. One critical dimension was that the growth of welfare agencies from the mid 1960s had been one of the main routes for both employment and career development for women and black men. Joel Krieger argues that this gave a particular set of social consequences to the apparently gender- and race-blind language of cost-cutting or 'downsizing' in public services:

Between 1969 and 1980 the social welfare economy (both government and private contract work) accounted for 39 per cent of all new jobs for women, for black women it accounted for fully 58 per cent of the jobs gained during this period. As a result, women, blacks, and especially black women have been disproportionately harmed by the reductions in force (RIFs) mandated by the cuts.

(Krieger, 1987, p.192)

So, the expansion of welfare in the 1960s and 1970s affected poverty not only through the services and benefits provided but also by providing employment routes for those most vulnerable to poverty (black women in particular). The subsequent restructuring of welfare in the 1980s had reciprocal effects, not merely on the level and nature of benefits and services, but also on patterns of employment and unemployment (Malveaux, 1987). At the same time, of course, cuts in welfare spending also affected the provision of services and benefits.

Beginning with the Omnibus Budget Reconciliation Act (OBRA) of 1981 mentioned above, a variety of government-imposed measures throughout the 1980s reduced eligibility for benefits, reduced levels of provision, transferred costs to states from the federal government and promoted both 'availability for work' tests and 'workfare' programmes. Such programmes made benefits conditional on either taking part in public works schemes or attending work training (Handler, 1995, chapters 3 and 4). Such measures tended to affect women with dependent children, which is of considerable significance given the growth in the number of lone-parent households headed by women (Sidel, 1992). The changing consequences of the politics of welfare, combined with wider social and economic changes (particularly the growth of unemployment), can be seen in Table 4.2 (Ginsburg, 1991, p.104). This shows both the reduction in family poverty effected by changes in the 1960s and 1970s and the subsequent increases during the 1980s.

TABLE 4.2 Percentage of families below and just above the poverty line in the USA

	All families	White	Black	Hispanic	Lone-mother
Below the poverty line					
1960	18.5	15.2	48.1	n/a	n/a
1970	9.7	7.7	27.9	n/a	32.7
1980	9.2	6.9	27.8	20.3	30.4
1986	11.4	9.1	28.7	25.5	34.0
Within 125% of the poverty line					
1986	15.3	12.7	35.8	n/a	40.8

Note: n/a = not available

Source: US Bureau of the Census, 1987, Tables 746, 749

At the same time, tax cuts in the early years of the first Reagan presidency promoted a widening gap between rich and poor (Phillips, 1990; Ginsburg, 1991, p.103). Between 1980 and 1984, changes in income tax policy and increases in social security taxes left families who had a net income of below $10,000 a year with a net $95 loss; by contrast, families with a $75,000–$100,000 income gained $403. Those with an income above $200,000 gained $17,403 (Katz, 1986, p.288). At least in broad terms, the new right agenda for welfare got off to a flying start, driving reductions in both taxation and welfare spending. However, the agenda was never simply an economic matter. It was also concerned with the social consequences of welfare, and here the distinction between social security and public assistance had a central role to play.

2.2   THE PROBLEM OF DEPENDENCY

For the new right, the major mistake of welfare expansion in the 1960s and 1970s was its effect on the poor. Social security programmes, for the main part, could be seen as promoting independence by virtue of earning the benefits one received. Public assistance (AFDC in particular) was represented as undermining independence and creating 'demoralization' among the poor. As Katz (1995, p.73) indicates, 'Conservatives placed the blame on welfare and government social programs which, they argued, had demoralized the poor by eroding incentives to work, undermining family stability and nurturing a self-perpetuating culture of dependence'. The basic components of this view are familiar:

giving people welfare stops them trying to help themselves, makes them dependent on the benefits they receive, and undermines the will to self-improvement. In relation to AFDC, new right commentators pointed to the growth of lone-parent families, arguing that the existence of AFDC meant that men could father children without taking financial responsibility. At the same time, women were freed from the responsibility of trying to keep men in the household and in employment. It was claimed that the existence of the benefit created 'perverse incentives' that led to inappropriate behaviour being rewarded.

Public assistance and AFDC in particular were the focus of new right attacks and became equated with 'welfare' in a way that social security was not. Charles Murray's *Losing Ground* (1984) was a huge and apparently well-documented survey on the impact of welfare on employment, family life and achievement among black people in the USA. It was significant in its own right and influential far beyond the USA in its critique of welfare and in the way it linked welfare to the emergence of an 'underclass'. Murray used four key indicators to demonstrate the demoralizing effects of poverty programmes:

1 labour force participation (very low for young black males);

2 illegitimate births (very high for young black females);

3 the number of lone-parent families (very high among black people); and

4 the number of homicide victims (very high among young black males).

These indices, Murray argued, described a section of the population that had become demoralized and dependent. His core argument was that these declining fortunes of black people reflected the impact of the Great Society welfare reforms, which had increased access to welfare benefits. In the process, the distinction between the 'deserving' and 'undeserving' poor was destroyed, and 'status rewards' previously attached to striving for mobility and self-improvement were removed. Murray put forward two main propositions about the effect of welfare programs. First, 'status was withdrawn from the low-income independent working family, with disastrous consequences for the quality of life of such families; and [second] status was withdrawn from the behaviors that engendered an escape from poverty' (Murray, 1984, p.179). The status rewards system had been undermined by 'elite liberal' thinking which engaged in 'system blaming' rather than encouraging people to take responsibility for themselves. Murray concluded that this disastrous tale demonstrated the failure of 'elite liberalism' and the necessity of aligning welfare policy more closely with 'popular wisdom':

> The popular wisdom is characterized by hostility to welfare (it makes people lazy), towards lenient judges (they encourage crime), and towards socially conscious schools (too busy bussing kids to teach them how to read). The popular wisdom disapproves of

favoritism towards blacks and of too many written in rights for minorities of all sorts. It says that the government is meddling far too much in things that are none of its business.

(Murray, 1984, p.146)

Murray's study has been subject to a wide range of criticisms which suggest that his claims about the relationship between welfare policy and its effects cannot be sustained (e.g. Handler, 1995; Morris, 1994). However, the quotation above suggests that its empirical truth was rather less significant than its political and ideological reverberations. Murray's description of 'popular wisdom' bears a striking similarity to the new right's social and political agenda. Indeed, the new right has consistently presented itself as able to speak for the 'silent majority' and to represent 'common sense'. In particular, Murray's argument was constructed around a distinctively new right premise about the relation between 'race' and welfare. He used statistical comparison about the fortunes of black and white people in the USA as the basis for his arguments about poverty, despite the fact that there were twice as many white people living in poverty as black. Claiming that there is no usable data about the poor, he insisted that black people provide a satisfactory 'proxy' for poor people. The effect of this device was to construct an elision between the categories of 'poor' and 'black' and to tell the story of black America only from the standpoint of welfare. Such constructions were endemic to the new right's attack on welfare, to the extent that many commentators argued that 'welfare' became simply a synonym for 'race' in US politics during the 1980s (see, for example, Mink, 1998, and Quadagno, 1994). The culmination of this connection was to be found in the idea of the 'underclass'.

2.3   THE PROBLEM OF THE UNDERCLASS

Murray's analysis linked with wider discussions about the supposed emergence of an urban 'underclass'. This category was constructed in the 1970s and 1980s to designate a group of people supposedly living a semi-detached existence from the rest of the society. They were marked by their disengagement from normal patterns of behaviour in employment and family life and by their engagement in criminal and anti-social activities (on the development of this label, see Gans, 1995, chapter 2). Murray's contribution to the development and popularization of this idea has been to link it explicitly to the perverse and demoralizing effects of welfare policy. One archetypal description of the underclass identified four different components:

(a) the passive poor, usually long term welfare recipients;

(b) the hostile street criminals who terrorize most cities, and who are often school dropouts and drug addicts;

(c) the hustlers, who, like street criminals, may not be poor and who earn their livelihood in an underground economy, but rarely commit violent crimes;

(d) the traumatized drunks, drifters, homeless, shopping bag ladies
and released mental patients who frequently roam or collapse on
city streets.

(Auletta, 1982, p.xvi)

The underclass has proved to be an enormously powerful social image,
although its empirical basis and forms of explanation are considerably
more shaky (see Morris, 1994). Nevertheless, it is an image which
'captured' the public discourse on poverty in the USA, as Katz
indicates:

> Why, at this moment in American history, have so many commen-
> tators eagerly, often unreflectively, appropriated underclass as a
> shorthand for describing the population of inner cities? One reason
> is that underclass is not really a sociological term but a convenient
> metaphor for use in commentaries on inner-city crises. As a
> metaphor, underclass evokes three widely shared perceptions:
> novelty, complexity and danger. Conditions within inner cities are
> unprecedented; they cannot be reduced to a single factor; and they
> menace the rest of us.

(Katz, 1995, p.63)

What the term provided was a stark and striking image of urban
collapse and urban fear, inscribing a profound distinction between the
'we' who belong to the mainstream and the dangerous 'other'. The
underclass, claimed the new right, was the outcome of the misguided
reforms of the 1960s that have undermined authority, values and
respectability and substituted lawlessness, immorality and dependency
in their place. The underclass also repeats the elision of 'race' and
welfare, for the underclass is above all identified as a black underclass.
The visibility of 'race' in this context owes much to the shifting patterns
of urbanization and suburbanization of the 1960s and 1970s in which a
growing black population in the cities coincided with 'white flight' to
the suburbs.

The complex mixture of the metaphors of a 'dependency culture' and
the 'underclass' in the new right's demonology of welfare underpinned
the retreat from welfare spending in the 1980s. It supported the
toughening up of welfare eligibility and conditions and a greater
concern with the use of welfare as a way of controlling the poor.
Handler (1995) describes the concerns of welfare reformers to change
the morality and social behaviours of the poor in relation to work,
education, parenting and forms of 'social deviancy' through making
welfare more conditional. In the 1980s, welfare came under attack at
all levels – federal, state and city – through budget-trimming practices
and changing regulations (Gans, 1995, chapter 5). This attack was
concentrated on public assistance rather than social security, reflecting
their different political constituencies. Social security was concentrated
in middle-class and skilled working-class sections of the population
who, it was argued, would align themselves with the new political trend

against the 'poor'. One significant exception to the general protection of social security involved benefits paid to disabled people under the Social Security Act. Congress amended the Act in 1980 to require a periodic review of all cases, which the Reagan Administration accelerated. Katz notes that, between March 1981 and April 1982, 400,000 cases were reviewed, from which 190,948 cases were ruled ineligible (Katz, 1986, p.286). The major assault, however, was on public assistance and social service programmes:

> By 1983, under complex, new regulations, 408,000 people had lost their eligibility for AFDC and 299,000 had lost their benefits ... Through these reductions federal and state governments saved $1.1 billion in fiscal 1983. Other regulations restricted eligibility for food stamps and sliced $2 billion out of the program's $12 billion budget ... Spending on Medicaid dropped 3 per cent in fiscal year 1982 ... The social services block grant to the states was chopped by 20 per cent in 1981.
>
> (Katz, 1986, p.287)

The cumulative effect of these and other changes is shown in alterations in spending as a result of government action on a number of programmes between 1982 and 1985 (see Table 4.3).

TABLE 4.3   Reductions in spending on selected welfare programmes, 1982–5

Welfare programme	Reduction (%)
AFDC	12.7
Food stamps	12.6
Child nutrition	27.7
Housing assistance	4.4
Low income energy assistance	8.3

Source: Katz, 1986, p.288

These changes set the tone for welfare in the 1980s. Although the Reagan Administrations did not 'abolish the welfare state', as some of the new right ideologists would have wished, its programmes, staffing and resourcing were significantly diminished – albeit selectively – by 1990. The brunt of the 'war on welfare' was borne by the poorest – those dependent on public assistance programmes rather than social insurance.

3   CLASS, 'RACE' AND GENDER IN THE POLITICS OF WELFARE

One simple way of reviewing the effect of the politics of welfare in the 1980s is to state that differentials widened. In class terms, the gap between rich and poor (whether working or non-working) grew substantially. Katz (1995, p.87) argues that 'the rise in ghetto poverty ... is not an isolated event. Rather it is the most visible instance of growing income inequality in America'. In gender terms, although women's share of employment and their average wage in proportion to the average male wage increased, so too did their share of poverty. Some analysts referred to this process as the 'feminization of poverty'. In terms of 'race', the income of the average black family stood at 56.1 per cent of that of the average white family – the lowest proportion since the early 1960s (Phillips, 1990, p.207).

In some ways, it is tempting to leave it at these bare statements. After all, such trends seem to reflect accurately the class, gender and racial politics of the new right. Yet to do so would be to treat class, gender and 'race' as separate dimensions of inequality when in fact it is their interconnectedness that is most significant. What happens when one looks at these interconnections? Working-class women suffered more from the Reagan years than did middle-class women, but in either case being lone parents exacerbated the situation. Among black households, the gap between upper and lower income groups widened considerably, partly as a result of the emergence of a small black middle class and two-earner households, and partly as a result of the disproportionate impact of unemployment and welfare benefits cuts on the lower income section. Here, too, woman-headed households meant increased poverty. Gender, class and 'race' intersected in complex ways in what Phillips (1990) has called the 'politics of rich and poor' in the 1980s.

But such politics are not just about the distribution of income and wealth, significant though they are. They are also about the ideologies which both shape and legitimate such patterns of inequality – providing the normative judgements of worthiness and blame (see Gordon, 1994). Welfare policy is not just a matter of benefits and services and the administrative principles of their distribution, but also concerns the social assumptions that underpin and motivate those principles. It is here that the politics of rich and poor, and the politics of class, 'race' and gender meet. Above all, the 1980s saw a political challenge to gains that had been made in the 1960s and 1970s in US welfare, and to the ideologies that had driven and supported those gains. The 1980s featured a 'class politics' of reverse redistribution, which challenged the tenuous notions of social justice created in the 1960s. Neo-liberal 'trickle down' theories of wealth creation claimed that, rather than trying to distribute income more evenly, it was economically more effective to concentrate wealth. The rich would then spend their wealth, enabling it to make its way through the circuits of the economy and, eventually, pass into the hands of the poor through either employment or philanthropy. The evidence suggests that it got held up somewhere on the way.

The politics of the 'gender backlash' are more complicated. The moral majority's reassertion of family values and visions of feminine domesticity coincided with a continuing rise in women's employment and (small) improvements in women's earnings relative to men's. At the same time, at least some versions of women's 'independence' carried greater penalties. The decline of welfare support of all kinds to families with children ensured that lone-parent households faced the prospect of poverty, and since the vast majority of these were headed by females, the feminization of poverty proceeded apace (Sidel, 1992). Along with these changes was the emergence of an increasingly punitive public and political view of 'welfare mothers' (Gordon, 1994; Mink, 1998; Withorn, 1998). The attack on AFDC and the metaphor of the underclass combined in identifying lone women parents as a major cause of social ills. Supposedly unable or unwilling to keep a man, and unable or unwilling to make sure he kept a job to support his family, the 'welfare mother' was identified as the root cause of moral collapse in the present generation (the feckless man she failed to domesticate) and in the future generation (young men without a role model because she couldn't keep her man). While such arguments are travesties of lone-parent family life, they provided effective images to justify transferring blame away from wider social, economic and political circumstances onto an easier target.

As we have already seen, the 'welfare mother' and the underclass combined a distinctive pattern of racial and gender politics. In the eyes of the new right, welfare policy, not racism, had produced the increasing dislocation of the black population from the 'American way of life'. Since black Americans had so signally failed to take advantage of the opportunities that America presented, they now had only themselves (or their mothers) to blame. At the same time, the new right argued strenuously against the gains made in the 1960s in the form of equality initiatives, legal rights and affirmative action, claiming that such developments interfered with the natural workings of the 'free market' and individual freedom (see also Bussiere, 1997).

In the 1980s, economic arguments for dismantling welfare benefits and services, protective and social legislation, and welfare as a source of black and female employment combined with a political culture that was intensely hostile to the 'liberalism' of the 1960s. This combination restored some of the class, gender and racial inequalities that seemed to be essential for the 'American way of life' to flourish again. By the beginning of the 1990s, the levels of personal, economic and social dislocation that accompanied the new right's reconstruction had led to a degree of disenchantment. George Bush, the apparent inheritor of the Reagan years, was denied a second term of office in the 1992 presidential elections. The return of a Democratic President posed new problems about the shape of the politics of welfare in the 1990s.

4   THE END OF WELFARE?

The politics of social welfare in the 1990s centred on two main issues: the organization of healthcare and the provision of public assistance (which became popularly identified as 'welfare'). Changes in these two areas resulted in a major retreat from ideas of a 'welfare state' in the United States at the end of the twentieth century. This section explores the politics of healthcare reform and the proclaimed 'end of welfare', before looking at the implications of these changes for the relationship between the state and social welfare in the USA.

4.1   HEALTHCARE: THE FAILURE OF REFORM

The election of President Clinton in 1992 re-opened a public discussion about the organization, coverage and cost of healthcare provision in the USA. A complex and costly system had historically excluded many Americans or, at best, provided them with minimal coverage and services. Economic uncertainty in the 1980s and 1990s led to many more American citizens becoming anxious about the security of their healthcare arrangements. Many of these citizens had been covered by health insurance schemes arranged by their employers, and widespread job losses (particularly in white-collar and middle-class occupations) threatened both the insurance arrangements and the citizens' sense of health security.

The problem of rising costs appeared at the centre of the US healthcare crisis. In this respect, the crisis was similar to those facing healthcare systems in other western societies: all have faced fiscal problems in the context of rising demand, changing demographics (with increasingly elderly populations) and the rising costs of medical technologies and services. What was different in the USA was the organizational setting of these problems, with direct public provision forming only a very small part of healthcare. Most provision had been arranged through private (for-profit and not-for-profit) organizations, with payment for services being financed though a variety of routes. The balance of funding had shifted from the 1930s pattern of direct payments by users, supplemented by public assistance for the poor through non-profit mutual insurance schemes organized by hospitals, such as Blue Shield and Blue Cross, to a situation that was dominated by employment-based health insurance plans. By 1983, 58 per cent of Americans were covered by employment-based schemes, 12 per cent were covered by Medicare and 8 per cent were covered by Medicaid; 15 per cent of Americans had no health cover (Staples, 1989, Table 1). Not surprisingly, the distribution of health insurance followed the familiar patterns of employment stratification, reproducing labour market disadvantages in terms of 'race', gender and class inequalities.

The welfare cuts made in the 1980s affected both Medicare and Medicaid coverage. Tighter limits were introduced on the insurance-based Medicare coverage (typically involving the transfer of costs from the insurance scheme to the patients themselves). Echoing the restrictions on other aspects of public assistance, Medicaid payments became even more stringently restricted, and had the effect of discouraging health providers from accepting Medicaid patients. The changes in the eligibility criteria and increased administrative complexities meant that around 60 per cent of the poor were either not eligible for or not receiving Medicaid by the late 1980s (Ginsburg, 1991, p.131).

Healthcare was provided through a complex of institutions, ranging from for-profit organizations, through not-for-profit organizations, to public hospitals. Two particular changes affected this mix of provision. One was the growth of Health Maintenance Organizations (HMOs), which offered healthcare packages on the basis of an annual fee (which employers could pay or contribute towards). The HMOs either provided healthcare services themselves or contracted with other service providers. By the late 1980s, HMOs covered about 12 per cent of the population (Ginsburg, 1991, p.129). The second major development was the growth of 'for-profit' hospitals and health provision. This involved both an increase in and a greater variety of private sector provision (including some HMOs), and the growing 'incorporation' of healthcare as the basis of major corporate organizations such as Humana and AMI. Wohl (1984) coined the phrase 'the medical–industrial complex' to describe this trend towards the corporate domination of healthcare provision. It was a trend that seemed likely to create a tripartite division of healthcare, with the corporate sector 'creaming off' the most profitable patients, a second layer of not-for-profit or smaller for-profit hospitals taking all but the uninsured, and the bulk of the Medicaid patients remaining in an increasingly residualized public hospital system (Ginsburg, 1991, p.129).

This complex network posed major problems for attempts to control medical costs. For the most part, the system was driven by the power of the medical profession, which has resisted attempts to 'socialize' the costs of healthcare through any form of national health insurance since the 1940s. One result of the complexity of the system was that no alternative concentrations of power existed to check the power of the medical profession, given that payment for healthcare was fragmented between state and federal governments, insurance schemes, employers (paying workers' health insurance) and private individuals. The 1980s, however, saw the beginnings of a rather more concerted attempt to challenge the institutional dominance of the medical profession. There was a variety of federal attempts to impose bureaucratic means of limiting medical costs (Bjorkman, 1989). These moves were paralleled by pressure from both insurance companies and employers for greater cost containment. The growth of corporate healthcare provision suggests a third source of financial pressure: the corporations' desire to rationalize costs and increase profits. Wohl (1984) and Starr (1982) have both argued that this corporate pressure, and the ability of the corporations to exercise greater control over doctors who are employees rather than independent professionals, may be the most significant long-term development in cost containment.

President Clinton took up the issue of healthcare reform in 1993, establishing a task force headed by the First Lady, Hillary Rodham Clinton. He equated the need for 'health security' with the conditions that led to the creation of 'social security' in the New Deal:

> It is hard to believe that there was once a time – even in this century – when retirement was nearly synonymous with poverty, and older Americans died in our streets. That is unthinkable today because over half a century ago Americans had the courage to change – to create a social security system that ensures that no Americans will be forgotten in their later years. I believe that forty years from now our grandchildren will also find it unthinkable that there was a time in our country when hard-working families lost their homes and savings simply because their child fell ill, or lost their health coverage when they changed jobs. Yet our grandchildren will only find such things unthinkable if we have the courage to change today.

(President Clinton, quoted in Skocpol, 1997, p.2)

The solution developed by the presidential task force aimed for a 'middle way' between a nationalized (or state-provided) healthcare system and an extension of individually arranged (or 'free-market') health insurance. The aim was to produce a system that would ensure healthcare insurance for all American citizens, preserve a degree of individual choice, and use the power of the state to regulate and drive down costs.

Although healthcare reform was a popular issue, the task force's proposals came to nothing and were abandoned in September 1994. Many reasons have been advanced for the failure of the Clinton reforms: some point to poor political tactics; some emphasize a widespread public mistrust of government; and others stress the powerful and effective lobbying campaigns of medical, insurance and employer interest groups likely to be adversely affected by the reforms. Skocpol's (1997) analysis of the reform process highlighted some other political issues. She argued that the reform proposals fell victim to their identification by the Republican right as an extension of 'big government', creating more 'bureaucracy' and 'government interference', limiting 'individual freedom' and threatening the quality of the 'best health care in the world' (Skocpol, 1997, p.178). These attacks undermined public and political enthusiasm for healthcare reform.

Skocpol links these right-wing challenges to the Clinton plan to a wider view of political dynamics in the post-Reagan period. Drawing on Brinkley's (1994) analysis of 'Reagan's revenge', she explores the paradoxes of a new Democratic politics framed by neo-conservative and neo-liberal ideologies. 'Reagan's revenge' was the distinctive combination of anti-government politics, tax cut promises (at least in personal and corporate taxation) and a large budget deficit (requiring 'fiscal conservatism' in government to control or reduce it). Skocpol suggests that the Clinton healthcare reforms were trapped in these conflicting legacies. Clinton represented a new, 'fiscally conservative' style of Democratic politics (trying to break the image of 'tax and spend liberalism'). The healthcare reforms, indeed, were planned to be fiscally neutral, requiring no new government funding. The Clinton plan also avoided creating either a nationalized (state-provided) health system or a nationalized (state-administered) health insurance system. Paradoxically, the public were sceptical about promised reforms that involved no new expenditure while fearing the threatened expansion of government bureaucracy and regulation.

The political and ideological paradoxes surrounding the role of government in promoting forms of social welfare created an impact that went beyond the failure of the healthcare reform proposals; the health and social consequences of that failure were significant. So, too, were the implications for other areas of social welfare as the new Democratic conservatism of the Clinton presidency encountered the revival of the Republican right: an encounter that resulted in a competition between a Democratic president and a Republican Congress to bring about 'the end of welfare' (Piven, 1998a).

4.2   ENDING 'WELFARE AS WE KNOW IT'

The popular and political distinction between 'entitlements' (social security) and 'welfare' (Aid to Families with Dependent Children, or AFDC) continued its central role in conflicts over social policy in the 1990s (for the significance of the distinction, see Gordon, 1994, pp.287–95). Welfare remained a primary target for neo-conservative and neo-liberal attacks from within the Republican Party, and from lobby groups and think tanks beyond the party. The most dramatic policy change, however, was President Clinton's commitment in 1992 to 'end welfare as we know it' by bringing about reforms that would 'time-limit' welfare and get people 'off welfare and off to work' (quoted in Piven, 1998a, p.21). This commitment was fulfilled in 1996 when the President signed the Personal Responsibility and Work Opportunity Act. Boris summarizes its main dimensions as follows:

> This act ended any entitlement to welfare by replacing AFDC with Temporary Assistance for Needy Families (TANF), including time limits and work rules. Under its rules, states needed one quarter of the caseloads to be 'working' by fall 1997 or face loss of federal funds. Recipients are eligible for federal benefits for a lifetime maximum of two years. Block grants allow the states to create their own programs and devise more restrictions. Many states actually adopted shorter time limits and stricter work require-ments than the federal law; some refused to treat new migrants to their state the same as longterm residents; some instituted a family cap – no additional monies can go to a child born to a

mother already receiving welfare ... States that lower illegitimate
births without increasing abortion will receive a monetary bonus.
Teenagers have to live with parents, relatives, or in a designated
facility and attend school.

(Boris, 1998, pp.30–1)

The Personal Responsibility Act (PRA) of 1996 dramatically
transformed the character of welfare and the status of welfare
recipients. The Act's preamble redefined the purposes of welfare as
follows:

1   to provide assistance to needy families so that children may be
    cared for in their own homes or in the homes of relatives;

2   to end the dependence of needy parents on government benefits
    by promoting job preparation, work and marriage;

3   to prevent and reduce the incidence of out-of-wedlock preg-
    nancies and establish annual numerical goals for preventing
    and reducing the incidence of these pregnancies; and

4   to encourage the formation and maintenance of two-parent
    families.

(quoted in Mink, 1998, p.66)

There were three significant features of the policy changes brought in
through the Personal Responsibility Act. First, it placed a premium on
the idea of work rather than welfare as the basis of personal and
familial independence. It drew on schemes such as Wisconsin's 'Welfare
to Work' program that had been developed to reduce welfare rolls and
encourage or enforce employment-seeking among welfare mothers.
However, neither the federal government nor individual states were
obliged to find or provide employment for claimants. 'Personal responsibility' had a strict interpretation in the Act: a maximum of two years'
welfare benefit may be claimed in any one period (and was subject to a
five-year lifetime limit). Frances Fox Piven has drawn out the economic
and political dynamic of welfare reform and its attempt to drive a shift
from welfare to work:

> The logic of the new welfare policies from this point of view is
> simply to eliminate the possibility of a welfare-to-work tradeoff for
> many women and to worsen the terms of the welfare option for
> many others ... When welfare is no longer an option, however, or
> when the terms worsen because benefits fall or harassment
> increases, or when stigma intensifies, more women will inevitably
> work.
>
> (Piven, 1998b, pp.68–9)

Piven argues that welfare reform has driven more women into low-paid
and insecure work – either in paid employment or in forms of
'community service' (that themselves often displace workers from public

service employment). Such enforced work also tends to drive down wage levels in other low or lowish paid employment. As Handler (1995, p.42) points out, these employment changes (both reflected in and reinforced by welfare policy) are not only about wage levels: 'Not only is there the spread of low wage jobs, but the nature of work is shifting from a full-time job for a single employer to various forms of "contingent" work. Many workers are employed in part-time, temporary, contract, or other types of flexible work arrangements that lack job security'. This is particularly true of the 'community service' jobs that welfare recipients are obliged to take if they cannot find other employment. Boris argues that the racialized processes of work and welfare combine to reproduce patterns of work for black women:

> Welfare reform has envisioned compensating some women to care for the children of other recipients who would participate in workfare or employment. It would create, as NWRO [National Welfare Rights Organisation] activists insisted, 'a new form of slavery: institutionalized, partially self-employed nannies' ... We are left with an overdetermined identification, deeply rooted in American politics, economy, and culture, that signifies degradation, disparagement and disgust, a low status that prefigures low income: the association of welfare with African American women, and black women with domestic labor ... Substituting work outside the home for family labor, workfare denies value to the labor that poor women already perform for their families and demands that they leave their children as a condition of welfare.

(Boris, 1998, pp.40–1)

A number of policy analysts have argued that 'welfare mothers' have been subjected to oscillating interpretations of their role and responsibilities (Boris, 1998; Gordon, 1994; Handler, 1995; Mink, 1998). In the early twentieth century, 'maternalist' policies, such as mothers' pensions and ADC (Aid to Dependent Children), were introduced to support poor women in the task of raising children. Other policies subsequently emphasized the mothers' responsibility to go out to work in order to provide for their children. The Personal Responsibility Act announced that the *primary* obligation of poor mothers was to find employment (a legal requirement that distinguishes them from non-poor mothers). As Bussiere argues, this placed poor mothers in a doubly vulnerable position:

> On the one hand, welfare recipients have been largely stripped of the particularistic protections of a maternalist ideology that has historically acknowledged the special needs and vulnerabilities of women and children. On the other hand, they have been denied the universalistic principle of a constitutionally sanctioned 'natural right' to subsistence.

(Bussiere, 1997, pp.168–9)

The second significant feature of the Personal Responsibility Act was its explicit commitment to the 'formation and maintenance' of two-parent families. Marriage was put forward as the only legitimate alternative to employment for poor mothers, and the traditional patriarchal norms of family formation were to be both encouraged and enforced by the states through welfare conditions (Mink, 1998, chapter 3). The Act marked a significant moment in the conflict over 'family values' in the USA, embodying the backlash against household diversity, lone parenthood and aspects of greater economic independence for women. The triumph of 'family values' involves the re-normalization and re-naturalization of the patriarchal family form – and makes it an explicit policy objective (see Stacey, 1998). The Personal Responsibility Act created a combination of incentives, demands and powers that engaged the states in policing the morality of their poorest citizens.

This leads us to the third significant element of the 'end of welfare': the Personal Responsibility Act redefined the relationships between the federal government, states and citizens. It broke the link between the federal government and citizens in need of welfare by shifting funding for AFDC to block grants to the states, thus undoing the welfare relationship established in the New Deal. At the same time, the Act gave states greater 'flexibility' in the implementation of welfare reform. Mink summarized the new possibilities as follows:

> The Personal Responsibility Act responded to some degree by authorizing states henceforth to be more restrictive than the law requires. Various 'state options' restore state discretion: to compel mothers to work outside the home sooner than the federal law requires; to establish stricter time limits than the federal law requires; to strip families of cash benefits where mothers do not identify biological fathers; to withhold benefits to children born to mothers while enrolled on welfare; to sanction recipient families that include adults under age fifty-one who do not have and are not seeking a high school diploma; to declare all noncitizens ineligible for assistance; to require drug tests of recipients; to cut benefits to mothers whose children are truant; to treat new state residents under the welfare rules of their former state; and to provide no cash benefits at all.
>
> (Mink, 1998, p.62)

The effect has been to create a substantial geographical unevenness in the conditions for, and administration of, welfare across the United States. The Personal Responsibility Act did indeed mark 'the end of welfare as we know it'. It represented the culmination of neo-conservative and neo-liberal attacks on 'welfare' that had been building since the late 1970s. The ideological segregation and demonization of 'welfare mothers' as a cause of the USA's social and economic problems thus resulted in their disentitlement, stigmatization and subjection to new forms of moral surveillance and economic discipline. Even this outcome, however, failed to satisfy the 'reforming' drive of neo-conservatives and neo-liberals. For neo-liberals, the fact that government remained in the 'business' of welfare at all was a problem. They would rather have seen the 'needy' and the 'philanthropists' settle matters within civil society without government interference (Tanner, 1996), and the urge to reform social policy began to take welfare politics beyond the soft target of AFDC.

4.3   THE END OF THE US WELFARE STATE?

Many studies of the politics of welfare in the USA have pointed to the disproportionate scale and intensity of the attacks on 'welfare'. As Frances Fox Piven (1998a, p.22) points out, AFDC 'is in fact a relatively small program. Fewer than five million adults are on the rolls and the program costs are modest, to say the least, amounting to about 1 per cent of the federal budget'. One reason for the focus on AFDC is that it has symbolized vital political issues, providing a focal point on which conflicts over 'race' and gender, family formation, and the role of the state have crystallized. At the same time, it may be that AFDC was a focal point because it offered a relatively 'easy target' for attacks on broader aspects of social policy. It was certainly a focus for neo-liberal and neo-conservative frustrations about how resistant the state was to being 'rolled back'. As Table 4.4 indicates, the 1980s and 1990s attacks on public spending on welfare curtailed or retrenched such spending, but did not drive it downwards. In part, this reflects the relative struggle of the large social insurance programs, as well as attempts to restore or overturn budget cuts (Clarke and Piven, 2001). The apparent stability of spending, however, conceals significant shifts in the conditions, eligibility and provision of specific programs.

TABLE 4.4   Social welfare expenditure as a percentage of gross domestic product, 1965–95

1965	1970	1975	1980	1985	1990	1995
11.0	14.3	18.2	18.1	17.8	18.5	20.9

Source: *US Social Security Bulletin*, Annual Statistical Supplement, 1999, Table 3A.1

In the 1990s, however, aspects of state welfare provision in the USA, beyond AFDC and other forms of public assistance, came under attack. Social security, and its pension provisions in particular, appeared increasingly vulnerable to neo-conservative and neo-liberal challenges. This marked a distinctive shift in a political culture in which social security had been seen as insulated against the 'welfare backlash' or retrenchment politics. Its insurance-based, universalist model of entitlement and widespread popular support (reflecting the distribution of benefits to working- and middle-class recipients) seemed to have protected these programmes. As Skocpol suggests, the attacks on social security were intended to undermine these sources of support:

> Conservatives who are opposed to large governmental programs of social provision understand well that Social Security is hard to cut back as long as it has middle-class support. It is therefore not incidental that contemporary conservative tactics for shrinking Social Security take the form of efforts, first, to convince young middle-class employees that Social Security is a 'bad deal' for them economically, that they would be better off to turn to private investments for retirement ... Conservatives propose to 'save' Social Security by trimming it back into a program targeted especially on the most needy elderly ... If middle-class Americans can be removed from the system, it would soon turn into one more welfare program for the poor, and could easily be cut back even further in the future.
>
> (Skocpol, 1995, p.7)

Skocpol's comments address one of the central tensions in the politics of social policy. The most popular welfare programmes are those that are universalist (benefiting most, if not all, citizens as of right). Such programmes tend to be well financed because of this popular support. By contrast, programmes that are 'targeted' on people identified as 'the poorest' or 'in greatest need' tend to be conditional, grudging and subject to cut-backs or even removal (as in the case of AFDC). If social security lost its universalism, it too would become vulnerable to the 'anti-welfare' politics of retrenchment.

Critics of social security deployed a variety of tactics during the 1990s. A central theme was the threat of an impending 'entitlement crisis', in which the growing cost of social security would bankrupt the programme or impose unreasonable taxes on those in employment to pay for a growing retired population (Quadagno, 1998, p.108). In part, this theme involved an attempt to create an inter-generational politics, setting the working population against a retired population depicted as 'greedy geezers', unreasonably insisting on their entitlements. Alongside these claims about the increasing costs of the programme was an argument that the privatization of pensions would allow greater individual choice and flexibility, as well as the potential to improve the returns through investment strategies (Quadagno, 1998, p.111). The privatization argument had been launched by neo-liberal think tanks such as the Cato Institute in the mid 1980s, and had become a central theme of public debates about pensions by the late 1990s (for example, Ferrara and Tanner, 1998). But the growing volatility and threatened collapse of global financial markets undercut some of the public and political enthusiasm for privatization: investing for one's own future looked an unexpectedly risky strategy. At the time of writing, the future of social security is still being contested. Although its critics have challenged its popular legitimacy, it continues as the centrepiece of US social policy provision. Nevertheless, it is difficult to see the 1990s as representing anything other than a retreat from social welfare as a collective national concern. The failed attempt to construct an inclusive healthcare system, the abandonment of 'welfare' (in the sense of public assistance) and the intensifying assault on social security together constitute a significant shift away from the possibility of an 'American Welfare State'. Although welfare states have experienced reform, retrenchment and a range of political challenges in most western capitalist societies, the United States has continued to provide a distinctive case. The retreat from social welfare has gone further and faster in the USA than elsewhere. As Jill Quadagno (1998, p.113) suggests, 'the US appears to be on the verge of becoming a welfare-state leader in undoing the core programs of the New Deal and moving toward privatization of income security in old age – a new form of American exceptionalism'.

5   WHAT FUTURE FOR THE LIBERAL WELFARE REGIME?

For the comparative study of social policy, there are three significant issues to be drawn out from the changing forms of social welfare in the USA. The first concerns how we think about the relationship between social policy and the social relations of class, 'race' and gender. Studying the USA reveals the need to pay attention to the way class, 'race' and gender have specific national formations. 'Race' – or what Omi and Winant (1986) call 'racial formations' – is not a universal or naturally occurring phenomenon. Rather, we need to think about the ways in which forms of social division and inequality are racialized – produced as 'race' – and how the processes and forms of racialization vary from society to society (and historically) (Lewis, 1998). Racial formation has a specific American form – in terms of how US society is racialized, in terms of the political salience of racial distinctions, and in terms of how 'race' is articulated with other social divisions – of gender and class in particular. The USA's social formation has been distinctive in a number of ways, particularly around dimensions of 'race' and ethnicity. Its history combines a 'settler' society (including the repression of Native American groups) and a 'slave holder' society (including the forced insertion of black Africans into the American economy and social relations). The effects of these structures on economic, social and political development in the USA have been profound – not least in their intersection with the politics, ideologies and policies of social welfare. As we have seen in this chapter, it is not just a question of how social policy reproduces or remedies social inequalities of class, 'race' and gender; social welfare is profoundly implicated in producing and constructing those divisions.

Second, the changing politics and policies of social welfare in the USA raise issues about the value and limitations of typologies of welfare states and welfare regimes. The designation of the US welfare system as an example of a 'liberal' regime (following Esping-Andersen) was a categorization that highlighted two particular features of the 1960s/1970s form of US welfare. Its relatively low 'decommodification' of welfare (and thus its domination by market relations), and the relatively low and highly conditional value of its welfare provisions were 'exemplary' features of a liberal welfare regime. While there are arguments about whether this was an accurate assessment of the US welfare regime (for example, Amenta, 1998, pp.149–61), the dynamics of the US welfare regime at the beginning of the twenty-first century pose new analytic problems. Are the changes merely accentuating the main features of a liberal welfare regime? It could be argued that the 'end of welfare', the shift towards 'workfare', and the reduced role of government represent a more fully developed liberal welfare regime.

While a strong case can be made for viewing these changes as the intensification of a 'liberal' welfare regime, such an analysis may underestimate other features of the emerging welfare system in the USA. One problem is that the emphasis in the Esping-Andersen typology on state/market distinctions emphasizes liberal (or neo-liberal) political ideology. Yet some of the key elements of US welfare politics and policy of the last thirty years have been conservative (or neo-conservative) forces. The concern with morality, authority, discipline and the reproduction of inequalities are central to US conservatism (see, for example, Lo and Schwarz, 1998). Treating the politics of welfare in the USA as being profoundly shaped by (neo-)liberal *and* (neo-)conservative ideology makes the changing relationships between state, market *and family* more visible, and enables more attention to be given to the complex of inequalities and divisions that make up the US social formation.

Another problem in viewing US changes as the intensification of a 'liberal' welfare regime is that Esping-Andersen's approach to the US welfare system may rest on too narrow a view of social spending, welfare and the state. The regulation or management of poor people by the state in the USA has involved more than 'welfare'. For poor men, in particular, the US system has been a 'penal state' rather than a 'welfare state'. The USA has the highest proportion of the adult male population in prison (and under other penal controls) of any developed capitalist society. By 1995, the USA had one and a half million adult men in prison and a further three and a half million under other forms of penal control outside prison (Christie, 1996, p.11; see also Morley and Petras, 1998). In some sense, the prison system in the USA provides poor men access to minimal provisions of health and education. However, such high levels of incarceration form a means of containing (or 'warehousing') potentially troublesome – or merely 'surplus' – sections of the population. They also make a significant contribution to the USA's much-praised low rates of male unemployment. This distinctive combination of reduced public welfare, punitive workfare and penal regulation has led some authors to talk of the emergence of a 'penal state' or a 'disciplinary state' (Jones and Novak, 1999). Certainly such patterns of state spending and intervention suggest that we should be wary of taking too narrow a view of social policy (Stenson, 2000).

While both these issues (political-ideological forces and the range of state intervention) raise questions about how to characterize the US welfare system, the third and perhaps most significant question is how to link typologies and the dynamics of change. This last point has implications for the relationships between the 'US model' and political debates about welfare in the UK and elsewhere in Europe. Arguments about the future of welfare are often constructed around choices between the 'European model' (usually referring to the corporatism of France and Germany) and the 'American model' (usually meaning the 'liberal' regime). The UK is often viewed as caught between these two models, or as being a 'hybrid' of different forms. But the American model is not static – the shape and implications of the 'liberal' welfare model are changing dramatically (under neo-liberal leadership). The retreat from public provision, the enforcement of personal responsibility and personal morality, the model of workfare, the attack on 'big government' and public spending, and the promotion of private sector 'solutions' have all moved the US and the international frameworks for thinking about social welfare. The 'American model' to which European welfare states may aspire – or which they may be urged to adopt – is itself moving even further away from the social compromises of European corporatism. The UK may turn out to be the transmission belt that connects the American model (in all its neo-liberal force) to the future of social policy in Europe (King and Wickham-Jones, 1999; Peck, 1998).

REFERENCES

Alsop, J. (1982) *FDR 1882–1945: The Life and Times of Franklin D. Roosevelt*, London, Thames & Hudson.

Amenta, E. (1998) *Bold Relief: Institutional Politics and the Origins of Modern American Social Policy*, Princeton, NJ, Princeton University Press.

Amenta, E. and Skocpol, T. (1989) 'Taking exception: explaining the distinctiveness of American public policies in the last century', in Castles, F.G. (ed.) *The Comparative History of Public Policy*, Cambridge, Polity Press.

Auletta, K. (1982) *The Underclass*, New York, Random House.

Bell, W. (1965) *Aid to Dependent Children*, New York, Columbia University Press.

Bjorkman, J.W. (1989) 'Politicizing medicine and medicalizing politics: physician power in the US', in Freddi, G. and Bjorkman, J.W. (eds) *Controlling Medical Professionals*, London, Sage.

Boris, E. (1998) 'When work is slavery', *Social Justice*, vol.25, no.1, pp.28–46.

Brandes, S.D. (1976) *American Welfare Capitalism 1880–1940*, Chicago, University of Chicago Press.

Brinkley, A. (1994) 'Reagan's revenge: as invented by Howard Jarvis', *New York Times Magazine,* 19 June, pp.36–7.

Bussiere, E. (1997) *(Dis)Entitling the Poor: The Warren Court, Welfare Rights and the American Political Tradition*, University Park, PA, Pennsylvania University Press.

Christie, N. (1996) 'Crime and civilization', *New Internationalist*, no.282, pp.10–12.

Clarke, J. (1991) *New Times and Old Enemies: Essays on Cultural Studies and America*, London, HarperCollins.

Clarke, J. and Piven, F.F. (2001) 'An American welfare state?', in Alcock, P. and Craig, G. (eds) *International Social Policy*, Basingstoke, Palgrave.

Crozier, M., Huntington, S.P. and Watanuki, J. (1975) *The Crisis of Democracy: The Trilateral Commission Task Force Report No.8*, New York, New York University Press.

Djilas, M. (1957) *The New Class*, London, Unwin.

Ehrenreich, B. (1987) 'The new right attack on social welfare', in Block, F. *et al.* (eds) *The Mean Season: The Attack on the Welfare State*, New York, Pantheon.

Esping-Andersen, G. (1990) *The Three Worlds of Welfare Capitalism*, Cambridge, Polity Press.

Ferrara, P.J. and Tanner, M.D. (1998) *Common Cents, Common Dreams: A Layman's Guide to Social Security Privatization*, Washington DC, The Cato Institute.

Gans, H.J. (1995) *The War Against The Poor*, New York, Basic Books.

Ginsburg, N. (1991) *Divisions of Welfare*, London, Sage.

Gordon, L. (1994) *Pitied But Not Entitled: Single Mothers and the History of Welfare, 1890–1935*, New York, The Free Press.

Handler, J. (1995) *The Poverty of Welfare Reform*, New Haven, Yale University Press.

Hunter, A. (1981) 'The ideology of the new right', in Union for Radical Political Economy, *Crisis in the Public Sector*, New York, Monthly Review Press.

Jones, C. and Novak, T. (1999) *Poverty, Welfare and the Disciplinary State*, London, Routledge.

Katz, J. (1986) *In the Shadow of the Poorhouse: A Social History of Welfare in America*, New York, Basic Books.

Katz, J. (1989) *The Undeserving Poor*, New York, Pantheon.

Katz, J. (1995) *Improving Poor People*, Princeton, Princeton University Press.

King, D. and Wickham-Jones, M. (1999) 'Bridging the Atlantic: the Democratic (Party) origins of Welfare to Work', in Powell, M. (ed.) *New Labour, New Welfare?*, Bristol, The Policy Press.

Koven, S. and Michel, S. (eds) (1993) *Mothers of a New World: Maternalist Politics and the Origins of Welfare States*, New York, Routledge.

Krieger, J. (1987) 'Social policy in the age of Reagan and Thatcher', in Miliband, R. *et al.* (eds) *Socialist Register 1987*, London, Merlin Press.

Lewis, G. (1998) 'Welfare and the social construction of "race"', in Saraga, E. (ed.) *Embodying the Social*, London, Routledge/The Open University.

Lo, C.Y.H. and Schwartz, M. (eds) (1998) *Social Policy and the Conservative Agenda*, Oxford, Blackwell.

Malveaux, J. (1987) 'The political economy of black women', in Davis, M. *et al.* (eds) *The Year Left 2*, London, Verso.

Marris, P. and Rein, M. (1967) *Dilemmas of Social Reform: Poverty and Community Action in the United States*, London, Routledge & Kegan Paul.

Mink, G. (1991) 'The lady and the tramp: gender and race in the formation of American welfare', in Gordon, L. (ed.) *Women, Welfare and the State*, Madison, University of Wisconsin Press.

Mink, G. (1998) *Welfare's End*, Ithaca, Cornell University Press.

Morley, M. and Petras, J. (1998) 'Wealth and poverty in the national economy: the domestic foundations of Clinton's global policy', in Lo and Schwartz (1998).

Morris, L. (1994) *Dangerous Classes: The Underclass and Social Citizenship*, London, Routledge.

Murray, C. (1984) *Losing Ground: American Social Policy, 1950–80*, New York, Basic Books.

Omi, M. and Winant, H. (1986) *Racial Formation in the United States*, New York, Routledge.

Patterson, J.T. (1981) *America's Struggle Against Poverty*, Cambridge, Mass., Harvard University Press.

Peck, J. (1998) 'Workforce in the sun: politics, representation and method in US welfare-to-work strategies', *Political Geography*, vol.17, no.5, pp.55–66.

Phillips, K. (1990) *The Politics of Rich and Poor*, New York, HarperCollins.

Piven, F.F. (1998a) 'Welfare and electoral politics', in Lo and Schwartz (1998).

Piven, F.F. (1998b) 'Welfare and work', *Social Justice*, vol.25, no.1, pp.67–81.

Piven, F.F. and Cloward, R. (1993) *Regulating the Poor: The Functions of Public Welfare*, New York, Vintage Books (2nd edn).

Quadagno, J. (1994) *The Color of Welfare: How Racism Undermined the War on Poverty*, New York and Oxford, Oxford University Press.

Quadagno, J. (1998) 'Social security policy and the entitlement debate – the new American exceptionalism', in Lo and Schwartz (1998).

Saloma, J.S. (1984) *Ominous Politics: The New Conservative Labyrinth*, New York, Hill & Wang.

Sidel, R. (1992) *Women and Children Last*, New York, Penguin (2nd edn).

Simon, W.E. (1979) *A Time for Truth*, New York, Berkeley Books.

Skocpol, T. (1992) *Protecting Soldiers and Mothers: The Political Origins of Social Security in the United States*, Cambridge, MA, The Belknap Press of Harvard University Press.

Skocpol, T. (1995*) Social Policy in the United States: Future Possibilities in Historical Perspective*, Princeton, Princeton University Press.

Skocpol, T. (1997) *Boomerang: Health Care Reform and the Turn Against Government*, New York, W.W. Norton and Company (2nd edn).

Skocpol, T. and Ikenberry, J. (1983) 'The political formation of the welfare state. An historical and comparative perspective', in Tomasson, R.F. (ed.) *Comparative Social Research*, no.6, London, Jai Press.

Stacey, J. (1998) 'The right family values', in Lo and Schwartz (1998).

Staples, C. (1989) 'The politics of employment–based insurance in the United States', *International Journal of Health Services*, vol.19, no.3.

Starr, P. (1982) *The Social Transformation of American Medicine*, New York, Basic Books.

Stenson, K. (2000) 'Crime control, social policy and liberalism', in Lewis, G., Gewirtz, S. and Clarke, J. (eds) *Rethinking Social Policy*, London, Sage/The Open University.

Tanner, M. (1996) *The End of Welfare: Fighting Poverty in the Civil Society*, Washington DC, The Cato Institute.

Trachtenberg, A. (1982) *The Incorporation of America*, New York, Hill and Wang.

US Bureau of the Census (1987) *Statistical Abstract of the United States*, Washington DC, Department of Commerce.

West, G. (1981) *The National Welfare Rights Movement: The Social Protest of Poor Women*, New York, Praeger.

Withorn, A. (1998) 'Fulfilling fears and fantasies: the role of welfare in right-wing social thought and strategy', in Ansell, A. (ed.) *Reweaving the Right*, Boston, Westview.

Wohl, S. (1984) *The Medical-Industrial Complex*, New York, Harmony Books.

CHAPTER 5
GERMANY: A CONSERVATIVE REGIME IN CRISIS?

LYNNE POOLE

CONTENTS

	INTRODUCTION	154
I	GERMANY AS A CONSERVATIVE WELFARE REGIME	156
2	THE SOCIAL RELATIONS OF WEST GERMAN WELFARE: 1949–1975	159
2.1	CLASS DIVISIONS AND 'INSTITUTIONALIZED CLASS SOLIDARITY'	159
2.2	GENDERED RELATIONS OF WELFARE: WOMEN'S CITIZENSHIP AND THE FAMILY	160
2.3	RACIALIZED WELFARE AND PROCESSES OF INCLUSION/ EXCLUSION	164
3	THE UNSETTLING OF WEST GERMAN WELFARE: 1975–1990	167
3.1	PUSHING FROM WITHIN AND WITHOUT	167
3.2	THE IMPACT OF UNIFICATION	169
4	EXCLUSIONS AND INEQUALITIES IN THE CONTEXT OF UNIFICATION: 1990–2000	173
4.1	UNEMPLOYMENT AND INCOME INEQUALITY	174
4.2	GENDER DYNAMICS AND THE UNEVEN EFFECTS OF UNIFICATION	176
4.3	WELFARE, 'RACE' AND RACIALIZATION IN THE POST-UNIFICATION PERIOD	179
4.4	EASTENERS MEET WESTERNERS	186
5	A FUTURE FOR THE GERMAN MODEL?	187
	REFERENCES	188

INTRODUCTION

In Esping-Andersen's typology, the German system of welfare is characterised as a conservative–corporate regime (Esping-Andersen, 1990, p.26). This characterisation is based on the distinctive features of the welfare programmes and social policies of the old Federal Republic of Germany (FRG, or West Germany). The conservative principles of West Germany's welfare system were enshrined in the constitution, known as the Basic Law, which was introduced in 1949 following the division of Germany into two separate states. As well as guaranteeing individual liberties, limiting the powers of the central state and giving considerable autonomy to the various Federal states (the *Länder*), the new constitution reproduced many of the features of the old Bismarckian or Imperial welfare state. Embedded within it was a conservative definition of social rights and obligations, including those relating to welfare benefits and the primacy of the family. Although there was some variation between the *Länder* in the ways in which social services were provided, the constitution ensured that the key elements of the welfare state were uniformly applied throughout the Federal Republic. In 1990 these elements were extended to the whole of Germany by the Treaty of Monetary, Economic and Social Union and the formal Act of Unification. The latter united Germany as an expanded Federal Republic and extended the West German constitution and West German laws, including welfare and social legislation, throughout the former German Democratic Republic (GDR, or East Germany).

The conservative nature of Germany's welfare regime is apparent not only in its basis in law, but in the centrality given to what might be viewed as its five key 'organizing principles', all of which are interconnected and mutually reinforcing:

- First, the welfare regime is employment-centred with a social insurance system at its heart. Crucially, this serves to secure the maintenance of status differentials, which according to Esping-Andersen (1990) is a defining characteristic of a conservative welfare regime.

- Second, the German welfare regime is corporatist, meaning that various interest groups are incorporated into policy making and administrative processes and into the delivery of welfare. This inclusion is in the interests of coalition building, incremental change and the maintenance of social stability.

- Third, there is a commitment to the principle of subsidiarity, which has its roots in Catholic social ethics. This is reflected in the belief in the family as the provider of 'first resort' (i.e. if the family can do it, the state should not intervene). In addition, administrative responsibility and decision making is devolved to the lowest level possible, with a clear division of legislative competencies between the Central State (the *Bund*) and the *Länder*. The centrality of the principle of subsidiarity to Germany's welfare regime reflects the key role that Catholic thinking has played in its development.

- Fourth, the regime is patriarchal, centring on a male breadwinner model of the family. Again, this aspect of the regime can be seen to reflect the influence of the Church and its commitment to the maintenance of traditional family forms.

- Fifth, the regime is based upon an exclusive conceptualisation of German citizenship. This was initially rooted in the idea that German nationhood is derived from blood ties or descent (*jus sanguinis*) rather than from place of birth (*jus soli*), although as we shall see, this conceptualisation of German citizenship appears to have begun to shift in recent years.

West Germany's welfare system had been heralded as one of the most stable in the world, and a model for those nations emerging from the ruins of state socialism to emulate. In part, this stability can be seen to have arisen from the basic common ground that existed between the main political forces in West Germany in the post-war period: both of the two main parties – the Christian Democratic Union (CDU) and the Social Democratic Party of Germany (SPD) were broadly supportive of social reformism. For the CDU this was rooted in Catholic social ethics, whereas for the SPD it was founded upon a commitment to social justice and social democracy (Lawson, 1996). This broad consensus made possible the development of the West German Social State (*Sozialstaat*). The concept of the *Sozialstaat* was enshrined in the Basic Law and refers to the state's legal social responsibilities towards its citizens, albeit modified by the principle of subsidiarity. The principles of the *Sozialstaat* are reflected in a range of state social commitments and responsibilities, based on legally defined rights (*Rechstaat*) (Clasen and Freeman, 1994). As we shall see, this rights-based system has provided relatively high levels of benefits and health care.

However, in this chapter it is argued that the conservative welfare regime of the unified Germany, although based on the apparently durable West German model, may be facing a crisis – one that is rooted in a series of challenges to its organising principles. Some of these are new challenges created by the unification of East and West Germany, in particular by the huge transfers of resources required to facilitate East German transformation and protect the population from the worst effects of restructuring. Others are challenges arising out of economic, social, demographic and political pressures that pre-date unification but that may have been exacerbated by it. In addition, critical commentators, most notably feminists (Langan and Ostner, 1991; Lewis, 1992; Orloff, 1993; Sainsbury, 1996) but also those writing from Marxist (O'Connor, 1973, 1987; Gough, 1979) and anti-racist perspectives (Williams, 1995), have highlighted the gendered, class/status-reinforcing and racialized nature of western welfare regimes in general, and the uneven and differentiated nature of social policy in the FRG in particular (Offe, 1991; Ginsburg, 1992; Ostner, 1993). Such arguments raise further crucial questions about whether the West German model is one for other societies to follow.

This chapter, therefore, has two main concerns. The first is to examine the different experiences and outcomes of the German welfare system for different social groups. The second is to chart the various destabilising pressures that have emerged since 1975 and have contributed to the 'unsettling' of this apparently hitherto durable regime. We will begin by briefly explaining the key features that define the German welfare regime as conservative, before examining in more detail the unevenness of outcome and the inclusions and exclusions generated by it in the period up to the mid-1970s. We will then focus on the pressures on the West German welfare system prior to unification, the impact of unification, the processes of welfare reconstruction that accompanied it and the consequences of that reconstruction for key sections of the population. The chapter concludes with a brief discussion of the future of the German welfare regime and the system's potential for adapting to recent challenges.

1 GERMANY AS A CONSERVATIVE WELFARE REGIME

At the heart of Germany's conservative model of welfare is the system of social insurance (*Socialversicherung*). In practice, this involves employers and employees paying social insurance contributions that are differentiated in relation to wage income. In times of sickness, unemployment, accident, injury and old age, benefits are paid in such a way as to reflect the level of contributions and hence are strictly proportional to former earnings: this is known as the equivalence principle. Social insurance cover is compulsory for all employed people working eighteen hours or more, with the exception of tenured public-sector employees and the self-employed. Given the near universal coverage of male workers prior to unification, this system worked to compensate for market failures while reinforcing the incentive structure and maintaining status divisions through its income maintenance mechanisms (Clasen, 1994). The corporatist nature of the system is reflected in the fact that the insurance-based schemes are administered by trade unions and employers organized into private corporations (Wilson, 1993, p.143). This has resulted in a decentralized social insurance system that is distanced from both *Bund* and *Länder* bureaucracies. While state regulated, the system of devolved administration ensures provision within the boundaries of conservative and Catholic thinking, guided by the general principle of subsidiarity and the male breadwinner model of the family in particular.

The principle of subsidiarity is also clearly reflected in the provision of welfare services and Social Assistance provision. In relation to service development and provision, responsibility is 'placed at the lowest level possible, ascending step by step through higher levels only when necessary' (Tester, 1994, p.252). Clearly rooted in Catholic social ethics (Spicker, 1991), subsidiarity ensures that responsibility for the provision of welfare services falls to the lowest appropriate level of social organization, thus creating a hierarchy of providers. Individuals and their families are required, wherever possible, to make provision for themselves. In the event that they are unable to support themselves, community, private sector and voluntary sector provision is accessed. Subsidiarity has resulted in a large voluntary sector in the provision of welfare services, with a significant role for the churches as welfare providers (Jarre, 1991). Voluntary providers (who are grouped into denominational and non-denominational associations) get access to state grants, church funding and fees from insurance funds where appropriate. Insurance funds also help to finance private provision. Where provision at these levels is inadequate, individuals and families can then seek assistance from the local state. The federal state is the provider of last resort. However, unlike in the UK where state support is viewed as a residual benefit, in Germany, state support is a guaranteed right, although individuals can only make claims on it where the provisions of lower levels of social organization have been exhausted (Jarre, 1991). This guaranteed right to state support is enshrined in the concept of the Social State (*Sozialstaat*) within the constitution.

Social Assistance (*Sozialhilfe*) can be seen as almost entirely separate from social insurance provision, leading some commentators to refer to the German model as a 'dual system' of income maintenance (Wilson, 1993). Social Assistance, funded by the *Länder*, is available to those who are not insured *and* to those whose insurance cover, as a result of insufficient contributions, yields lower levels of benefits than Social Assistance provision. This latter group can choose to claim Social Assistance in place of social insurance benefits. Like welfare services, Social Assistance is subject to the principle of subsidiarity insofar as it is discretionary and paid out only if an applicant can show that 'neither their own resources nor those of the family are adequate to meet minimum needs' (Wilson, 1993, p.142). However, unlike the provision of services, the role of statutory Social Assistance bodies in the payment of cash benefits is *not* subsidiary to voluntary welfare associations (Jarre, 1991). Nevertheless, this general application of the principle of subsidiarity institutionalises dependency for certain sections of the population, for example those young people whose parents have the means to support them (Wilson, 1993, p.154). Once eligibility has been established, Social Assistance benefits are paid at relatively generous rates (compared to the UK, for example) in line with the recommendations of the German Association for Public and Private Relief. This Association is corporatist in nature and includes representatives of religious and voluntary organizations as well as employees who collectively set benefit levels in such a way as to ensure a 'dignified existence' in accordance with the Basic Law. These rates are not binding on the *Länder* but tend to be broadly adhered to (Wilson, 1993, p.148).

While the concept of the 'dual system' continues to capture the essence of the income maintenance system in the unified Germany, recent developments have presented a challenge, not least to the provision of Social Assistance (see section 4.1). They have also 'unsettled' the fourth organizing principle of German welfare that centres around a traditional model of the family, with a clearly demarcated, gendered division of labour and a commitment to social stability. In this vision the patriarchal family is seen as the cornerstone of society, whereby a male breadwinner role is complimented by female economic dependence and primary responsibility for homemaking, child-rearing and caregiving. Given the post-war dominance of this family form and the support given to the concept of the family wage, public Social Assistance is designed to play a residual role at the local level. The centrality of Catholic thinking and the principle of subsidiarity in particular are apparent in these respects, with the family constructed as the provider of first resort. It should also be noted that in relation to social insurance, married women are reliant on benefits derived from their husbands' contribution records. A high proportion of women are thus highly economically dependent on their husbands – in terms of their 'family wage' or for a share of their benefits. Indeed, working mothers are encouraged to exit the labour market through a system of compensation from tax revenues. Universal child benefit, maternity payments, child-rearing benefits for parents who are either non-working or part time, child-rearing leave and child tax allowances are used to encourage marriage and motherhood (Ostner, 1997). Through such mechanisms the state has attempted to reinforce traditional ideas about the family.

Finally, underpinning Germany's welfare regime is its exclusive conception of German citizenship, although, as we shall see later in this chapter, German definitions of nationhood currently appear to be in a state of flux. From the late 1950s West Germany actively recruited labour migrants into industry. However, different groups of people entering West Germany did not necessarily enjoy equal rights to welfare benefits and services on arrival. A hierarchy of entitlement had been constructed on the basis of perceived racial and ethnic identity. This granted automatic citizenship to all those deemed to be ethnic Germans, while denying those constructed as 'other' official recognition as citizens, irrespective of residency. However, as we shall see, because key aspects of welfare citizenship in Germany stem from employment, economic migrants to Germany have had access to some social rights that were not so easily accessible to migrants in other countries (like the UK). West Germany's exclusive conception of national citizenship was initially rooted in the idea that German nationhood is derived from blood ties or descent rather than from place of birth. This had, in part, been legitimated by West Germany's 1949 constitutional commitment to achieve national unification and to return the German diaspora, scattered across Eastern Europe and the Soviet Union in the aftermath of the second world war, to Germany. Prior to the 1870 unification of Germany, Germans were defined by language and culture. As we shall see in section 4.3.3, culture has once again become significant in redefinitions of German citizenship since 'reunification' in 1990 and place of birth may also be taking on a new significance.

Having identified the key features of Germany's conservative welfare regime, section 2 of this chapter considers its consequences for the social relations of welfare. More specifically, we look at the ways in which the regime has produced divisions along three main axes of differentiation – class, gender and 'race'. The focus in this section is on the period between the introduction of the West German constitution in 1949, which marked the establishment of the conservative welfare regime, and the start of its 'unsettling' in the mid-1970s.

2 THE SOCIAL RELATIONS OF WEST GERMAN WELFARE: 1949–1975

2.1 CLASS DIVISIONS AND 'INSTITUTIONALIZED CLASS SOLIDARITY'

Several commentators have emphasized the role of organized labour in helping to extend social insurance to most sections of the workforce (Esping-Andersen, 1990; Clasen and Freeman, 1994). It is suggested that as a consequence, West German income maintenance benefits were relatively generous, serving to cushion any person's exit from the labour market (Esping-Andersen 1990, p.52). To use Esping-Andersen's terminology, West Germany was a relatively decommodified regime, meaning that aged, sick and unemployed workers were not forced to offer their labour as a commodity (see Chapter 1). However, it is crucial to note the uneven character of benefit levels and cover resulting from the status-reinforcing, and hence differentiated, nature of the social insurance system. Because benefits were proportional to contributions, inequalities of income inside the labour market were also reproduced outside of it – in old age and periods of sickness and unemployment (Wilson, 1993). On average, for blue collar workers, benefits replaced only 40 per cent of their waged income compared to a 60 per cent 'benefit replacement rate' for white collar workers, largely as a result of variations in social insurance contributions (Clasen, 1994). In addition, geographical redistribution between richer and poorer *Länder* was also given low priority, leading to the overall reinforcement of spatial inequalities and divisions. Therefore, in general, the West German welfare regime did not seek to significantly redistribute resources other than across the lifecycle.

However, it is possible to identify *some* redistributive policies within the West German system. For example, the policy of married couples' tax splitting divided total household income between adults for tax purposes. This resulted in a lower household tax bill as each individual was given their own tax allowance. Fiscal welfare policies such as this may have supported the male breadwinner model of single earner families, but crucially they also supported low paid households (Clasen 1994). In the period prior to reunification this resulted in around 11 per cent of the population living in poverty in 1985, a proportion that compared favourably with the UK (Wilson, 1993, p.150). However, this figure tells us little about the distribution of poverty, which varied significantly both across households and in relation to the divisions of marital status, age, occupation, gender and 'race'. For example, Ginsburg (1993, p.178) has shown that post-unification poverty levels differed across family types, with lone parent and elderly families doing relatively badly. Furthermore, on the margins of the labour market, low-waged, low-skilled, poorly unionised work dominated, carrying with it a high risk of unemployment and irregular work, and poor worker protection (Lawson, 1996). As explored below, this type of work was highly racialized. This example illustrates how poverty was unevenly felt across different groups of workers.

Despite these inequalities and in view of the fact that, relatively speaking, workers got generous benefits even at the lower end of the earnings spectrum, the system's corporatist social and labour pro-grammes were designed to regulate conflict and maintain social peace (Lawson, 1996). Offe (1991) refers to this as 'institutionalized class solidarity'. In addition, because under the social insurance system contributions were directly linked to the size of benefits, social insurance was not generally perceived by the middle classes as a system of taxation to support the poor and thus to be resisted; on the contrary, it was widely supported. This institutionalization of middle-class loyalty had arguably been at least in part responsible for the stability of the West German welfare system prior to unification.

2.2 GENDERED RELATIONS OF WELFARE: WOMEN'S CITIZENSHIP AND THE FAMILY

A number of social policy commentators have been critical of traditional comparative frameworks insofar as they fail to consider either the way gender relations affect social policy or the way social policy affects gender relations (Langan and Ostner, 1991; Lewis, 1992; Orloff, 1993; Sainsbury, 1996). In particular, these frameworks are seen to elevate social class as an explanation of welfare regime development, so that the extent to which a welfare regime is dependent on gendered social relations outside of the political or economic-productive spheres is not sufficiently explored.

In contrast, Langan and Ostner's approach (1991) recognizes the significance of the relationship between paid and unpaid work and welfare, and seeks to assess which, if any, of the European welfare regimes can be said to be 'women-friendly'. In their framework, the West German welfare regime was characterized as Bismarckian. According to Langan and Ostner, this model emphasized the importance of capitalist development and the creation of wealth while at the same time relying on the traditional family to help maintain the status quo. As we have seen, the principle of subsidiarity was central, which in essence meant family first, state last. It was underpinned by the morality and traditions of the Catholic Church, which structured dominant welfare discourses. Women's roles as carers and homemakers were essentialized – seen as part of a natural, gendered division of labour ordained by God. This meant that within the 'family first' model, it was women who were the main providers of informal welfare. Moreover the traditional patriarchal family was constructed as a tool for maintaining social stability, and hence a cornerstone of West German society. This gave rise to a male citizenship model in which men had full entitlements as a result of their paid employment, but women were principally reliant on their male partners. In this framework West Germany can be seen as a highly gendered welfare regime.

Similarly, the work of Lewis (1992) has been illuminating insofar as it highlights the degree to which the male breadwinner model has been modified in west European societies. Her three-model framework characterized the West German welfare system as constructed around a strong male-breadwinner model, at the heart of which was a commitment to treat women primarily as wives and mothers. While the state would not over-provide to the extent of undermining the male role, it would step in if necessary. In this model women's participation in the labour market was seen as detrimental to the family and child welfare – in West Germany this was written into the Constitution. Indeed, even after the 1957 reform of family law it remained the case that women were expected to contribute housework and mothering. As a result, until 1977 employment was only an option for women if it was deemed by the *male* head of household not to interfere with these responsibilities (Ostner, 1993). Furthermore, in the 1950s and 60s there was a government and trade union backed campaign against two wage (or dual breadwinner) households (Rueschmeyer, 1993). The tendency for organized male labour to fight to retain the gains made by men over women, despite this resulting in the disadvantaging of women, is evident here. The trade union movement in Western Europe has traditionally fought for the retention of what has been termed the family wage – a concept that is based on the assumption of a gendered division of labour within the home and a lower rate of pay for many women in the labour market (Bryson, 1992). These factors go some way to explaining the slow rate of growth of women's labour market participation and continued wage discrimination in West Germany (Lawson, 1996) – even after the EU-led Equal Treatment legislation was passed in 1976.

These normative assumptions also shaped social insurance, meaning that women were incorporated into the social insurance system in largely subordinated ways; through the general 'contribution nexus', either independently, as single women, or as dependants in the case of married women; and through low premiums attached to care and child-rearing functions (Liebfried and Ostner, 1991). Women were treated on the basis of their family role first and foremost, either as a dependent spouse or mother, their entitlement based on their status as wives first, mothers second and women last (Ostner, 1993). In contrast men were dealt with as individual workers.

Fiscal welfare also reinforced the male breadwinner norm – the example used earlier of married couples' tax splitting illustrates how the state supported the male breadwinner model of single earner families with its focus on household as opposed to individualized incomes (Clasen, 1994). It is well documented that household income is not necessarily shared equally (Pahl, 1989), so the effects of such policies were unevenly felt by women leading to the feminization of poverty in West Germany and female marginalization (Liebfried and Ostner, 1991). Even in old age, women pensioners were generally at greater risk of falling below the Social Assistance level than their male counterparts (Clasen, 1994). Poverty in old age was also largely a female issue rooted in women's dependence on benefits derived from their male partner's contribution record.

Even after the 1979 EC directive on equal treatment for men and women in relation to social security, some groups of women, for example those who were divorced, remained more at risk of poverty than men *across* the lifecycle, though particularly in old age. Indeed, even if benefits had been equally distributed, women would still have been socially dependent on men, making long-term stable marriage the best insurance for women (Liebfried and Ostner, 1991). As was noted in section 2.1, efforts to address social justice in the Federal Republic were mainly based on redistribution across the life cycle. This meant that little attention was paid to the injustice and inequality that may have arisen out of social dependence and a lack of individualisation for women. The approach was one of 'society first', the assumption being that it was possible to act in the interests of society as a whole. This assumption was based on the questionable notion of a national interest arising out of the assumed homogeneity of the population. Hence, the needs of individual groups, particularly those on the margins, were secondary to those of the system (Jones, 1985, cited in Liebfried and Ostner, 1991). Therefore, 'corrections' in relation to inequalities took place only at the margins, as opposed to more radical structural reforms.

Women's entry into paid employment tended to be in part-time work in the secondary labour market, and then only after the children had gone to school. In addition, women gleaned little support from statutory services with regard to their ascribed duties. The principle of subsidiarity ensured that the services that did exist were largely provided by the voluntary and commercial sectors, or church-based associations and offered little in the way of childcare assistance (Tester 1994, King and Chamberlayne, 1996). The example of single mothers illustrates the problem for some sections of the female population in particular. A lack of childcare provision made working difficult, yet because they were judged to be unavailable for work, single mothers were not eligible for social insurance benefits. Consequently, their dependence on discretionary Social Assistance benefits, set at the national minimum level, meant that single mothers, especially those with little or no access to material help from their wider family, were more likely to be in poverty than their married counterparts. Indeed,

Lewis (1997) claims that around 25 per cent of West German lone mothers between the ages of 20 and 55 were living in poverty in 1984. Moreover, where kindergarten facilities did exist, short opening hours assumed 'immobile women' as the norm (Ostner, 1993). This reflected the emphasis upon the essentialist nature of female child-rearing and informal caring, enabling Liebfried and Ostner (1991) to claim that West Germany was built on an 'ancillary culture of care' with women at the centre. All of these normative prescriptions then fitted with Catholic and conservative priorities and the social construction of a clearly demarcated, highly gendered, public–private divide.

The strong male breadwinner model meant that the system was not only status reinforcing for men but also women. People were imagined as a set of groupings and then treated differently on that basis. This centred on highly gendered norms and assumptions and went against universal provision and equality. Deviants from the norm lost out significantly (Ostner, 1993). For example, mothers who had never married were relatively worse off given the lack of tax benefits and flat-rate child payments. Family policy focused on the maintenance of the institution of marriage in particular, with child support coming way down the list, the assumption being that family ties and obligations would result in children being provided for (Lawson, 1996). This obviously created real problems for lone mothers who had the dilemma of how to balance childcare with economic independence. Ostner (1997) suggests that, in order to participate in paid employment, divorced and widowed lone mothers had to rely on their extensive parental leave entitlements and benefits, the granting of preferential treatment in relation to the scarce supply of Local Authority childcare places, support from the child's father and, if necessary, from her own parents in line with the principle of subsidiarity. Unmarried lone mothers were exempted from reliance on their parents and prioritized in terms of childcare places in order to facilitate their participation in paid employment. This example further illustrates the differentiated experience of women in relation to the West German system of welfare.

In sum, the West German state clearly played a central role in sustaining certain forms of the family – in particular the patriarchal nuclear family with women in a nurturing, home-based role and men acting as the family breadwinner – wherever it could. In addition, it played a role in sustaining the distinction between paid and unpaid work and the different status of each. The unpaid work of women encouraged by the state thus fed into their dependence. West Germany was therefore a particularist rather than a universalist welfare state (Liebfried and Ostner, 1991; Ostner 1998) where social policies incorporated social norms, were culture bound, and were closely linked to society's history and traditions, not least those associated with the Catholic Church. And, as we shall see, positive gains for women in West Germany over the last 20 years have not been sufficient to offset the male breadwinner model, though it has been modified making it easier for diverse family forms and single parents, while still encouraging marriage and motherhood as the preferred option (Lewis, 1992).

2.3   RACIALIZED WELFARE AND PROCESSES OF INCLUSION/EXCLUSION

The notion that to be a West German citizen one must be of German descent meant that successive Federal governments constructed the Federal Republic as 'not a country of immigration' in official discourse. (Faist, 1995; Ginsburg, 1992; Joppke, 1999). This is despite the fact that actual levels of immigration between 1950 and 1993 created a net migration balance of 12.6 million, and accounted for 80 per cent of the country's population growth (Joppke, 1999, p.62). Historically there were three ways into West Germany: being of German blood; claiming asylum; or gaining entry as a 'guest-worker'. Not all of these categories of people were viewed in the same way, nor were they treated equally. The next section explores the experiences of guest-workers in particular.

2.3.1   GUEST-WORKERS: THE EARLY YEARS

West Germany adopted an instrumentalist approach to migrants after the early 1950s (Hudson and Williams, 1999), recruiting them as a temporary labour supply to participate in a highly segregated and racialized labour market. The 'guestworker' system was built around a network of recruitment agencies established in southern Europe, northern Africa and the former Yugoslavia in particular, and bilateral recruitment agreements with foreign governments (Ginsburg, 1992). This system of granting temporary residency reflected the interests of the trade unions insofar as it avoided subjecting German workers to wage and job competition through horizontal job segregation (Faist, 1995). Moreover, the 'guestworker' system enabled the upgrading of West German workers to better jobs and thus securer employment and improved welfare benefits (Lawson, 1996). The preferences for cheap foreign labour of some employers were also met by the 'guestworker' system (Faist, 1995).

Legally, 'guestworkers' who came to the Federal Republic enjoyed extensive constitutional rights often positively interpreted and enforced by the courts (Joppke, 1999). This was partly a result of the 1949 Constitution, which elevated the rights of the individual above those of the state. 'Guestworkers' were, therefore, granted basic rights in line with all others who resided in West Germany. Article 6, for example, protected the family and marriage, and as such it was difficult to prevent the family reunification of migrant workers, even after the system of recruitment had ended in 1973 and despite campaigns against liberalizing the system in the 1980s. In spite of the political rhetoric and a lack of *specific* rights, the legal process protected foreigners, who could claim rights under the *general* provisions of the Constitution. Joppke notes that, 'Migrant rights, especially the right to stay, were pushed through by independent courts, invoking the extensive human-rights catalogue of the Basic Law. Once the permanent-residence right of 'guestworkers' was secured, family unification was one avenue along which immigration continued after the oil crisis' (Joppke, 1999, p.99). This also meant that 'guestworkers' enjoyed access to a range of welfare services and benefits, leading some to claim that the West German system of welfare was nationality blind. Indeed, the argument that rights were attached to residency, even if temporary, holds some water (Joppke, 1999). However, notions of West German welfare citizenship are arguably more complex and need to be viewed in the context of the employment basis of income maintenance provision in particular within the conservative–corporate regime. Because 'guestworkers' were, by their very nature, employed – their resident status was dependent upon them being legally employed (Faist, 1995) – they could not legitimately be denied work-related welfare and were thus granted access to equal welfare rights at least in law. This leads Faist to conclude that once migrant workers had been working and resident for more than five years 'their claims to social rights are about equal to those of German citizens' (Faist, 1995, p.227).

Notwithstanding this position, 'guestworkers' were not treated equally in practice. On the contrary they were marginalized and discriminated against through racist practices. For example, 'foreigners' experienced discrimination in the allocation of rented houses and were still excluded from certain leisure facilities as late as the 1980s (Ginsburg, 1992). Moreover, 1969 legislation, still in force today, actually allows overt discrimination against 'foreigners' in the labour market (Ginsburg, 1992). As Faist notes, 'German citizens and migrants are given priority over non-EC migrants such as Turks ... when it comes to filling job vacancies' (Faist, 1995). This helps to explain the fact that 'guestworkers' were (and continue to be) overwhelmingly on the margins of the labour market, filling the most unattractive positions, with a significant proportion officially in poverty (Clasen, 1994). Legal discrimination also existed in relation to social service entitlement and provision (Faist, 1995, p.228).

The construction of migrants as a temporary 'other' had the effect of excluding and marginalizing 'guestworkers', for example by reducing the number of work opportunities open to them, and by delegitimizing their interests and needs. Processes of racialization, discrimination and racism exacerbated the exclusion and marginalization of these 'guestworkers' (Hudson and Williams, 1999) and account in part for the fact that 'guestworkers' and other 'foreigners', even those of the second and third generations, were denied political citizenship rights, including the right to vote (Lawson, 1996; Faist, 1995), though some concessions were granted for local elections after 1980 at the discretion of the local authorities (Ginsburg, 1992). In contrast, these rights *were* granted to EU citizens, making a clear distinction between Germans and EU citizens on the one hand, and 'guests' and non-EU 'foreigners' on the other. As Castles argues, 'Foreigners enjoy all basic rights, except the basic rights of freedom of assembly, freedom of association, freedom of movement, and free choice of occupation, place of work and place of education, and protection from extradition abroad' (Castles, 1984, p.77 cited in Ginsburg, 1992, pp.81–82). This is also despite the fact that reforms in the 1970s began to change the status of 'guestworkers' (redefined as 'foreigners' after the suspension of guestworker arrangements in 1973) and reconceptualize them as more permanent members of West German society. For example, in 1978 a 'permanence regulation' was introduced that allowed the discretionary distribution of unrestricted residence permits under certain conditions. However, it did not have the status of law and was weakened by the discretionary principle and subsidiarity, both of which meant that there was a diversity of interpretation and an unevenness of application across the *Länder* – in part depending on the local party in power (Joppke, 1999). In public discourse, policies and in people's minds, 'guestworkers' were separated out from the general population and stigmatized as 'other'. This may well have served to legitimize the xenophobic reactions of some sections of society across both the Federal Republic and the unified Germany throughout the 1980s and 90s.

2.3.2   THE DIFFERENTIATED EXPERIENCES OF 'FOREIGNERS'

At this juncture it is crucial to note that, notwithstanding the exclusions and examples of discrimination explored above, there was no universal experience for all 'incomers'. This is illuminated when we consider two separate cases: that of different groups of 'guestworkers' and the experiences of ethnic Germans who sought entry into West Germany. Taking the case of 'guestworkers' first, it is clearly the case that some groups, for example Turks, have been the specific targets of racist attacks and racial discrimination (Ireland, 1997). In addition, on coming to Germany, women's ability to achieve a certain standard of living and residency status has often been tied to their dependency upon breadwinner husbands. Should they separate from or divorce their husbands they are at increased risk of poverty and/or benefit dependency. This is especially the case in periods of high unemployment, as experienced by Germany in periods throughout the 1980s and 90s, but may also be the result of both gender and racial discrimination within the labour market (Kofman and Sales, 1992). Taking the second case of those claiming rights to citizenship based on their German ethnicity (relatively small numbers by more recent standards), Kymlicka argues:

> Membership in the German nation is determined by descent, not culture. As a result, ethnic Germans who have lived their whole lives in Russia, and who do not speak a word of German, are automatically entitled to German citizenship, while ethnic Turks who have lived their whole lives in Germany and so are completely assimilated to German culture are not allowed to gain citizenship ... Such descent-based approaches to national membership have obvious racist overtones and are manifestly unjust.
>
> *(Kymlicka, 1995a, p.23, cited in Hudson and Williams, 1999)*

The situation for asylum seekers whose numbers have also grown significantly throughout the 1980s and 90s, is different again and will be discussed in section 4.3.2.

In summary, there were clear tensions between the granting of 'guestworker' rights and the withholding of citizenship in the Federal Republic, and between the provision of benefits and services (at least formally) and the ongoing dominance of notions of ethnocultural citizenship, with no provision for dual citizenship. As Joppke notes, 'Before reunification, a liberal foreigner-rights regime had co-existed with an ultra-restrictive citizenship regime' (Joppke, 1999, p.200).

To conclude this first half of the chapter, the West German approach, based principally on a close relationship between work, welfare and notions of German nationhood, served to exclude certain sections of the population and include others largely in subordinated ways. However, while a diversity of experience in relation to different groups of women and 'foreigners' has been illustrated throughout the chapter so far, it is nevertheless the case that for both women and 'guestworkers' as a whole, social insurance benefit criteria often presented a problem, and as a result there was a disproportionate risk of dependency on the less legitimate system of Social Assistance.

3 THE UNSETTLING OF WEST GERMAN WELFARE: 1975–1990

The West German model of welfare became unsettled in the period after 1975 as a result of economic, demographic and social pressures from within West German society. Political shifts, marked by the election of the first Kohl government in 1982, were also to have an impact upon the shape of social welfare provision. In addition, the progress of the EU project, alongside German unification, threw up other challenges. This section of the chapter looks firstly at the internally and externally generated pressures that were placed on the West German welfare system and the drive for EU convergence, before going on to explore the unification process and its outcomes.

3.1 PUSHING FROM WITHIN AND WITHOUT

With recession biting in 1975 after the oil shocks, the control of public expenditure became a priority in West Germany. This led to a steady fall in social spending, as a proportion of GDP, and this continued until unification in 1990 (Lawson, 1996). In addition, the 'demographic time-bomb', resulting from the falling birth-rate and the growth in numbers of people living to an older age, was identified as increasing the demand on the social security system, and fears surfaced about the ability of old-age pension and health insurance funds to cope (Lawson, 1996). Moreover, women were increasingly joining the labour market, albeit largely on unequal terms with men (Nickel, 1998). While the patriarchal nuclear family continued to dominate, numbers of single parents increased slowly and a diversification of household forms became apparent. These developments challenged the conservative assumptions that were at the heart of the West German model.

In addition, men were increasingly at risk of unemployment, particularly those working in the shrinking industrial sector, but also those racial and ethnic minorities who were vulnerable to largely legal processes of discrimination. Periods of recession had been in evidence throughout the 1980s and these continued into the 1990s. In part this was a reflection of global changes, including the growth of international trade and the movement of finance and capital, which in turn had an impact upon the supply of industrial employment, economic growth rates and the participation rates of male workers in particular. Esping-Andersen (1996, p.256) captures some of these key developments when he notes that, 'a nation's growth today requires economic openness which, in turn, entails tougher competition and greater vulnerability to international trade, finance and capital movements. Governments' freedom to conduct fiscal and monetary policy "at will" is therefore more constrained'. As we shall see in section 4.1, unemployment continued to be a critical issue *across* the unified Germany throughout the 1990s, with unification intensifying the effects of global forces.

'New' poverty relating to increasing unemployment among those who had traditionally enjoyed stable and permanant work and, consequently, the growing polarisation of what came to be termed the 2/3–1/3 society (referring to the notion of a two-thirds middle class and one-third marginalized, no-longer-working class division of the West German population) were increasingly identified as problems. This led to a questioning of the role of social welfare in society and the system's ability to cope. In this same period, the Kohl governments instituted a series of policy shifts as well as benefit cuts.

For many commentators the election of Kohl represented a sea change (*Wendepolitik*) in terms of the perceived relationship between welfare and the economy. Efficiency and economy were elevated as key principles of social policy, giving rise to a renewed emphasis on community, self help and individual responsibility, all commensurate with the principle of subsidiarity (Clasen and Freeman, 1994). The welfare state was increasingly characterized as a 'social hammock' (Hauser, 1995) that created welfare dependency and undermined incentives to work. This argument was used to legitimize welfare cuts and reforms in the interests of maintaining the 'market-conforming' nature of the West German welfare regime. Labour-market solutions, for example re-training programmes, were increasingly used in an attempt to reduce reliance on Social Assistance (Lawson, 1996; Wilson, 1993). However, where this involved female claimants, there were clear tensions with traditional ideas about the family. On the one hand, the low levels of childcare services, the raising of care allowances in this period and the moral expectation that mothers should be at home caring for their children, worked to keep *married* women in the private sphere. However, in contrast, lone mothers who were dependent on Social Assistance benefits were encouraged to seek paid employment once their children had reached the age of three, and benefits were no longer sufficient to support a woman and her children in the absence of a male family wage or some other family support. Clearly the impact of such policy developments in relation to Social Assistance was differentiated in accordance with marital status in particular. This may help to explain the low levels of female labour market participation in West Germany in general (standing at only 50.3 per cent of women of working age actually in work as late as 1986 (Wilson, 1993, p.146)), combined with the high percentage of lone mothers in paid employment – over 75 per cent in 1982, with the majority of those working full-time (Chamberlayne, 1994).

A complex picture is also in evidence when we consider Social Assistance provision for non-citizens including asylum seekers. The perceived problems of Social Assistance dependency resulted in cuts to asylum seeker benefits of about 25 per cent by the early 1990s (Wilson, 1993, p.149). This example serves to illustrate how ideas about 'race' and nation cut across class in West Germany with the effect of undermining the principle of 'dignified existence' for some categories of claimants but not others. Indeed, as noted above, from the early 1970s the 'guestworker' system came under more systematic scrutiny, and the government negotiated the termination of bilateral agreements and explored the possibilities of repatriation in a bid to stem unemployment. This had the effect of encouraging migrant workers to seek permanent residence status and, therefore, raised a whole set of issues around who got welfare in the Federal Republic, something that is discussed more fully in section 4.3.1.

Externally, the progress of the EU's convergence project created new challenges for the German model. Plans for European Economic and Monetary Union (EMU) placed constraints on public spending in all participating member states (see Chapter 8 in this volume), prompting the 1996 Savings Package in West Germany (Gissendanner, 1998). In addition, throughout the 1980s and 1990s the EU increasingly demanded harmonization around the principle of individualized social protection, which raised the question of women's unequal entitlements both in West Germany and in the whole of Germany after unification (Nickel, 1998). Indeed the range of demands placed on Germany, as on other member states, by the EU were often contradictory, requiring policy changes that would cost money on the one hand, while encouraging governments to work towards a low level of public debt in preparation for meeting EMU convergence criteria on the other (Mangen, 1998).

The West German welfare system, then, was already under pressure by the end of the 1980s and this was to be compounded by German unification in 1990.

3.2   THE IMPACT OF UNIFICATION

In order to explore the unification process and its impact on German society, it is necessary to begin by briefly examining the model of welfare that existed in the GDR. Only by highlighting the main structures and principles of the East German welfare system, and their impact on different sections of the population, can we understand the implications of using West Germany's constitutional structure and principles as a framework for the reform of Germany as a whole.

3.2.1   THE EAST GERMAN MODEL OF WELFARE

After the second world war the East German government, led by the Communist Party, proclaimed a policy of extensive state provision and the distribution of resources in accordance with need (Mishra, 1977). This system of welfare was to be supplemented by across-the-board price subsidies for all basic necessities – including food, heating, housing and transport. However, the implementation of these policies in the GDR fell far short of the rhetoric (Deacon, 1992). In practice the welfare model that emerged centred on the right to work: not only was work constructed as a right to be provided for everyone, regardless of gender, but everyone had a duty to work. Indeed, this was enshrined in the GDR's constitution.

For those who were out of work for reasons other than sickness and disability, no system of unemployment insurance or transfers existed. The majority of state welfare services and benefits – including medical services, crèche facilities and childcare benefits and housing – were provided free or in exchange for nominal payments (Deacon, 1992). The Party-State apparatus used work enterprises as a way of channelling state welfare (and scarce consumer goods) to workers and as a way of tying welfare eligibility to work performance (Deacon, 1992). For enterprise managers it was an important tool for attracting and keeping labour in order to ensure production plan fulfilment. Therefore, as in the Federal Republic, welfare was linked to work (albeit in rather different ways) and not universalist. However, unlike the Federal Republic, women as well as men needed to be in paid work to gain welfare entitlement. Welfare was conditional on work and not an alternative to it. As a consequence of this, the vast majority of women were economically active. By 1988, women's participation rates as a percentage of the total workforce stood at 49.9 per cent in the GDR, compared to 39.7 per cent in the Federal Republic, with many western women working part-time (Holmes, 1997), an option not open to their eastern counterparts. Moreover, in the GDR, 91 per cent of women were in work, compared to 55 per cent in the Federal Republic (Einhorn, 1993).

Under state socialism, dominant ideas about the natural role of women as homemakers, mothers and caregivers were retained, but with a limited view of women's liberation – based around their participation in economic activity – bolted on (Poole, 2000; Kolinsky, 1998; Einhorn, 1993). The underplaying of 'non-economic elements in women's op-pression' (Molyneaux, 1981, p.19) within official discourse meant that, in the 'private' sphere, women were expected to reproduce the next generation of workers, supported by pro-natalist state policies that included: the outlawing of abortion until 1972; the provision of state family benefits and services (representing up to 80 per cent of the cost of child-rearing by the 1960s); and the allocation of paid time off for women to meet their domestic responsibilities (Ostner, 1998). This model was modified in the 1970s, largely in response to falling birth rates (Ferree, 1994). Both fathers and grandparents were granted parental leave in order to assist women, and abortion laws were relaxed to enable women to plan child-rearing in line with their other responsibilities (Rueschmeyer, 1993). Moreover, the East German state granted women one paid 'household day' per month to assist them in *their* domestic work (Einhorn, 1993). Space precludes any detailed discussion of the reasons for this, suffice to say that the post-war system of production in eastern Europe depended on ever-increasing supplies of cheap labour (see Smith and Thompson, 1992).

However, the closed nature of the Eastern Bloc, the difficulties in raising productivity levels through the introduction of technology and the problem for women of shouldering the double burden of paid and unpaid work, with its consequent impact on the birth rate, meant that the system was inherently time limited: it was to run into terminal crisis as the supply of workers stagnated. Dennis (1998) explains how, by the late 1960s, the birth rate in the Democratic Republic fell to one of the lowest in the world and, by 1971, the population was failing to reproduce itself. The extent to which this was perceived by the State-Party apparatus to be a significant problem is reflected in the introduction of a number of family policies designed to help women to combine work and child-rearing commitments. In addition to those already mentioned, these included the introduction of a baby year in 1976, additional holidays for employed mothers with children under 16, and increased benefits and access to loans. In sharp contrast to West Germany, these policies were designed to propel women into the labour force (King and Chamberlayne, 1996) while still leaving primary responsibility for any domestic work in the hands of women (Dannenburg, 1992, cited in Kolinsky, 1998, p13). Gender divisions were therefore reinforced both inside the home and out as women's 'double burden' meant that they were unable to compete with men in the public sphere on equal terms. Women earned 76–84 per cent of male earnings by the late 1980s. And, while this gap was not as wide as that between men and women in West Germany, which stood at 65–70 per cent, it was significant (Einhorn, 1993, p.122). Wage equality was principally due to acute horizontal and vertical occupational segregation. Women suffered disadvantage in terms of work chances and were disproportionately exposed to poor work conditions (Einhorn, 1993). But crucially, they also tended to be concentrated in particular employment sectors: textiles and light industries, including consumer goods production, and the service sector.

To summarize, despite an ideology of universalism and comprehensiveness the reality of state socialist social policy was one of work-based welfare in which economic policy and production targets were elevated above the needs of the population. Where welfare programmes served to ensure social order and social reproduction, this was bound up with the needs of an economic and political system that required a disciplined workforce and increasing supplies of workers. For example, the welfare measures introduced in 1976, and outlined above, did not distinguish between lone parents (divorced, widowed and single) and cohabiting or married mothers. The *type* of family formation was essentially less important than increasing the birth rate and enabling women to combine work and child-rearing, which is what the policies were principally designed to do. While there were very basic guarantees, there was not the material means of meeting anything more than a minimum for the majority. Social provision simply was not afforded the priority status required for that. However, it is important to recognize the advantages of the old system, which included a low cost of living, a high degree of security in general and job security in particular, a relatively high level of wage equalization and a guaranteed level of social protection for the huge majority, albeit at a very modest level.

3.2.2   THE FALL OF THE GDR AND GERMAN UNIFICATION

The wall was breached on 9th November 1989 under the slogan 'we are one people'. By the beginning of 1990 both Russia, under the leadership of Gorbachev, and the West German government had accepted the principle of German unification. Unification presented a series of challenges in terms of the economy, social structures, political systems, models of welfare and cultural practices, requiring more than eastern economic renewal and the integration of the five new Länder.

Kohl chose the option of extending West Germany's Basic Law, as opposed to rewriting the constitution, a legal alternative that offered the potential for a reconceptualization of German society and interests. Hence, it was the structure and principles of the West German state that provided the constitutional framework for unification. This marked the shape of things to come – a very unequal 'partnership' with minimal change in relation to West German institutions and practices, in the hope of securing long-term stability and western dominance. From the West German perspective, unification was perceived as a temporary blip from normality. Following the rapid transformation of all aspects of state socialist society, including its institutions, political processes and economy, supported by huge cash and investment transfers from West to East in the short to medium term, the former East German *Länder* would join the Western *Länder* on the path of stability it had mapped out in the post-war period. In short, unification saw the imposition of the western legal and institutional order of liberal market capitalism over night with the expectation that within two years stability and growth would be restored. This approach to transformation has been termed 'shock therapy' (Padgett, 1992).

Unification shook the basic relations and principles of the Federal Republic in a number of ways. Firstly, Federal power was increased as a result of the financial dependency of the five new *Länder* (Gissendanner, 1998). This threatened to increasingly centralize decision making and thus unsettle the balance of power as the *Bund* propped up the East financially. The extent of the transfer of resources from West to East is hotly contested, although there is clear agreement that the scale of the subsidy has been and continues to be enormous. Clasen and Freeman (1994) claim that in 1991 alone Deutsch Mark 93 billion, out of a total Federal government budget of DM 412 billion, was spent on meeting the *direct* costs of unification. Indeed some forecasts have suggested that such enormous annual transfers will be required well into the twenty first century. Berentsen (1999) claims that by the end of the 1990s more than $515,000 million dollars of net public fund transfers had been shifted eastwards. This figure includes large investments and consumption components, but excludes those transfers that have been reimbursed, for example by the EU, and those from private investors.

Secondly, tensions between the *Länder* and Federal State, and among the different *Länder* themselves, became more apparent. Unification also shook the relations and bargaining processes that had been institutionalized since 1949 (Sturm, 1992). The increase in the number of relatively poorer *Länder* within the Federation threatened to create new alliances and struggles around the issue of who would foot the growing bill for unification. The Basic Law made the state responsible for pursuing equalization of living standards and opportunities across *Länder* (Gissendanner, 1998), so unification with the Eastern *Länder* threatened to disadvantage poor western regions and increase the costs to the better off regions unless central government stepped in. As it turned out, *Länder* resistance to carrying the financial burden of unification put pressure on the Federal government's budgets as they were forced to foot the lion's share of the unification bill.

In addition, the Federal State constructed West Germany's model of welfare – the conservative–corporate system – as the norm to be institutionalized *throughout* the newly unified *Länder*. At the level of social policy, this created further problems given the very distinct nature of the two models that had existed prior to unification. With no reopening of the welfare debates of the 1980s, the imposition of the West German model on the East created newly constituted exclusions and an intensification of many inequalities. The West German government seemed to believe that it was possible to impose western welfare, its normative assumptions and culturally specific frameworks, on East Germany. This position was shown to be immediately problematic.

4 EXCLUSIONS AND INEQUALITIES IN THE CONTEXT OF UNIFICATION: 1990–2000

This section explores the impact of unification in relation to unemployment and income inequality, gender relations and outcomes, and racial divisions, before going on to examine the problems of bringing together West and East German populations who had been effectively isolated from one another for 40 years.

4.1   UNEMPLOYMENT AND INCOME INEQUALITY

Those in employment in the former East Germany have, on the whole, done well in terms of wages. Trade unions in the West saw low wages in the East as a threat to their workers and hence supported wage harmonization. By 1995 average wages in the East were up to 75 per cent of those in the West (Hauser, 1995). However, given the workings of the social insurance system, many East German workers are not fully covered and are thus forced into Social Assistance dependency in times of economic inactivity.

Shock therapy, the approach used to facilitate the rapid restructuring of the East German economic, political and administrative systems, facilitated a massive decline in production and a process of deindustrialization (Ganssmann, 1993). The impact on employment levels in the region was immediate and enormous (Roesler, 1991). By August 1993 the *official* unemployment rate in the East was significantly greater than in the West – up to 15.4 per cent, excluding those forced into early retirement, those not claiming benefit, the underemployed and those participating in work schemes (Mangen, 1994). This rate helps to explain the high levels of migration of East German men to the former Western *Länder* in search of work. However, it is important to note that the impact of mass unemployment was uneven. Some sections of the male workforce ran a greater risk of losing their jobs than others, depending on skill and education levels and the sector in which they were employed (Ganssmann, 1993). Those 'foreign' workers recruited by the East German government from the late 1970s onwards who had not been repatriated post-1989 were also particularly vulnerable to unemployment. Moreover, the impact of economic restructuring varied across the different regions of the GDR (Roesler, 1991).

It is also crucial to note that East German women were about twice as likely as their male counterparts to be unemployed (Mangan, 1994). In fact, Kolinsky (1998a) claims that as the 1990s progressed the relative position of women worsened so that by 1995 they accounted for about 65 per cent of the unemployed. Perhaps more alarmingly, women accounted for 75 per cent of the long-term unemployed and only 38 per cent of new recruits (Flockton, 1998). Being over-represented in the long-term unemployment figures also meant that women in general, and lone mothers in particular, were more likely to be dependent on Social Assistance and thus at greater risk of having to live in poverty (Kolinsky, 1998). Despite women fighting to keep their employment (Nickel, 1998), the end of the East German system, and consequently work-based childcare services, facilitated women's movement out of the labour market (Rueschmeyer, 1993). This was in part due to their over-representation in service and welfare employment, but also a result of their assumed responsibilities in the private sphere, not least in relation to childcare. The gendered nature of West German policy discourses, on the ascendancy in the East after unification, can be seen to have contributed to women's falling participation rates (Roesler,

1991) and the growing trend for families in the East to rely on potential male breadwinners commuting to the West to work while married women were confined to the home (Einhorn, 1993). Taking a further example, that of older women, the evidence indicates that they were increasingly encouraged into early retirement on the grounds that they were too old to retrain. The enforcement of early retirement policy has, however, been highly gendered (Einhorn, 1993). The future for women very much depends, not only on developments in the welfare system, but also on those relating to hiring and firing practices, and on the potential for a diversification of work opportunities that would give at least some groups of women new chances. As it stands, the employment sectors they dominate – from child-care facilities to textiles (Einhorn, 1993) – have been and continue to be most at risk: women are the first to be fired and last to be hired.

Relatively high levels of long-term unemployment were also a feature in the former Western *Länder* after unification. Hauser (1995) claims that by 1993 the official unemployment rate had reached 8.1 per cent in the former West Germany and that long-term unemployment accounted for 26 per cent of that. This was an outcome of increased competition and economic downturn in the main, but the collapse of East European markets had also been significant in terms of the decline in demand for German goods (Hauser, 1995).

Together, these developments in the former Eastern and Western *Länder* resulted in social insurance schemes amassing large deficits (Mangen, 1994) and thus becoming increasingly reliant on Federal subsidies. Furthermore, the system of Social Assistance came under strain, not least from those who were long-term unemployed, those without a contribution record sufficient to grant insurance cover and those unable to work as a result of other commitments and a lack of publicly funded support. This meant an increased reliance on Social Assistance. Indeed, claims in the Western *Länder* alone climbed from 1.6 per cent of the population in 1970 to 4.7 per cent in 1992 (Hauser, 1995).

Both unification and unemployment in the West have, then, placed increased pressures on the *Länder*-funded system of Social Assistance, and this has resulted in cuts. These cuts, introduced in 1994, were legitimized as a tool for tackling the disincentives to work that reliance on means-tested benefits was said to create (Mangen, 1994). While poverty rates remained fairly constant in the West throughout the early 1990s – though rising steadily in the East along with income differentials during the same period – increased evidence of poverty from the mid-1990s onwards in the West can be explained in terms of rising unemployment, the inadequacy and inflexibility of the 'dual system' and the problems of including a more diverse set of family forms where women are more likely to be seeking work. But, in part, these outcomes have also resulted from a severe underestimation of the costs of unification and the duration of the transition process. Indeed the German government was forced to use the Solidarity Pact of 1992 to introduce a temporary solidarity surcharge of 7.5 per cent on income tax (Mangan, 1994) to help meet these costs. Employer social insurance contributions and taxes were also increased, impacting on employees to a greater extent than employers (Clasen, 1997), and as noted above, benefit cuts were implemented in 1994. These represented the most extensive cuts in the post-war period affecting a whole spectrum of people but especially the poorest sections of the population, including asylum seekers and refugees (Lawson, 1996). A toughening of attitudes towards the 'undeserving' poor, and especially 'foreigners', was evident in public debates – with a renewed emphasis on behavioural explanations of poverty and fighting welfare fraud (Lawson, 1996). Xenophobic activities also increased in the post-unification period, particularly in the former Eastern *Länder* where unemployment and poverty were most marked and 'foreigners' were being 'distributed' by the Federal government, despite a lack of services and infrastructural support.

However, notwithstanding these challenges, over half of all households in the East saw improvements in their real income two years after unification, and only one in seven was worse off, in no small part due to the improvements in the wage and benefit systems of the East (Mangan, 1994). However, this general picture hides the growth of inequalities and the uneven impact of processes of marginalization. According to Lawson (1996), policy developments since 1975 have disproportionately benefited the better off, especially those with property and incomes from entrepreneurial activity. Where the burden of unification has fallen on contributors to the social insurance system the impact has also been uneven. According to Hauser, 'the contribution rates applied to income from wages increased progressively from 26.5 per cent in 1970, to 32.4 per cent in 1980 and to 38.9 per cent in 1994, half of which is borne by employers.' (Hauser, 1995, p.47). Certain groups who do not pay, for example civil servants and the very well off, and who are protected by an income ceiling for contribution levies, are advantaged (Mangen, 1998). These inequities have resulted in a widening of the 2/3–1/3 society. The productive core maintained and strengthened their hold, but increased inequality and exclusion has resulted for those at the bottom of the social ladder (Lawson, 1996) with an increasing proportion of the population reliant on Social Assistance.

4.2 GENDER DYNAMICS AND THE UNEVEN EFFECTS OF UNIFICATION

Processes of unification and the tendency towards the wholesale export of the West German system to the East had particular implications for women across Germany. Despite some similarities in the experiences of women in the West and the East, most notably their provision of informal care, albeit within diverse frameworks of service provision and cash transfers (Tester, 1994; Kolinsky, 1998b), a number of key differences can be identified.

Firstly, while employment was the principal basis of welfare under both regimes, historically western women have not generally been expected to be included in it (Kolinsky, 1992). In the GDR subsidies and work-related welfare propelled *all* able-bodied women into the labour market, whereas West German benefits provided incentives for married women in particular to remain in the home (King and Chamberlayne, 1996). In turn women in the East were more economically independent than their West German counterparts (Nickel, 1998).

Secondly, in the West the state was subsidiary with the expectation that marriage-based patriarchal families would ensure the care of children, the home and the financial maintenance of the family unit. In contrast, the East German state existed as the 'generalized father', weakening the public-private distinction so dominant in the west (Ostner, 1993). Divorce was unproblematic to the East German state, which worked principally to maintain reproduction and production. How that was done was less of a concern for the regime, giving rise to an early tolerance of diverse household and family forms, including those headed by lone mothers, and in sharp contrast to constructions of the 'normal family' found in the West (Kolinsky, 1998b). This has implications for particular types of families who may now be more at risk of exclusion and discrimination. For example, the fact that the unified Germany does not view lone mothers as a separate and single issue to be placed on the public agenda (Ostner, 1997, p.23) has meant that no specific policies for lone-parent families have been developed, putting this group at risk of marginalization. Kolinsky (1998b) points to the high rates of poverty among east German single parents, who are overwhelmingly mothers – 19 per cent in the mid 1990s. These statistics reflect not only lower wages but assumptions about normal family forms and the structuring of the welfare system around them. Moreover, so long as lone mothers continue to be constructed as morally problematic, the law and social policy will continue to reflect this. Notwithstanding these obstacles to equal treatment for lone mothers, the move towards a family policy based on the needs of children (Ostner, 1997) coupled with the ongoing discomfort with abortion expressed in public discourse, may improve the prospects for this group of women in the more medium term.

Thirdly, East German women enjoyed reproductive rights far outweighing those of Western women (Einhorn, 1993). Abortion was technically illegal in West Germany, except in very specific, limited circumstances, defined and regulated by the medical profession (Rueschmeyer, 1993). In contrast it had been legal up until the first trimester in the East since 1972 (Ferree, 1994). In practice this has been one of the few policies that has not been harmonized through an imposition of Western laws. After much struggle and debate, a 1992 Constitutional Court ruling decriminalized abortion in the West in line with Eastern norms. However, the ruling embodied religious and moral overtones insofar as abortion had to be accompanied by pro-life counselling, leading to claims from East German feminists that, even in a western democracy, decisions were made by a handful of powerful men (Ferree, 1994).

Clearly then, the structure of welfare and dominant discursive practices positioned women in the two regimes in very different ways in relation to work, childcare, family and men. Both regimes were highly gendered but in very different ways. The Western system centred on a strong male breadwinner model paralleled by strong family obligations for women. The East German system embodied a weak male breadwinner model and weak family obligation with a substantial role for the state, though such a system does not equate to that in Sweden (see Chapter 6) since women in East Germany were given very little choice about their participation in paid work, and had virtually no option of part-time work (Ostner, 1998). The dilemma then has been whether to reinforce western gender relations in the West and export them to the East, and/or whether to individualize entitlement as in the East German model (Chamberlayne, 1994). Some changes to the western system would seem inevitable given the slow diversification of the 'normal' family form and the incorporation of more diverse East German lifestyles, which parallel changes to the labour market and evidence of new poverty. Indeed, throughout the 1980s and 1990s Western women's benefits and choices have improved: they have been granted increased leave with a 70 per cent replacement rate for three years and an option to return to work; pension rights have been developed for mothers (Kolinsky, 1992); caring has been recognized in terms of social insurance contributions; and from 1996 parents have been able to choose child benefit or tax allowance depending on the level of their incomes (Mangen, 1998). However, these changes have arguably served to reinforce, as opposed to challenge, traditional gender roles insofar as the recognition of caring, for example, encourages and provides incentives for women to continue these roles rather than seek a more equitable restructuring of responsibilities within the private sphere (Ostner, 1993). For women in the East these policy developments have meant a rise in the value of their benefits. However, this has been offset to a large extent by a decrease in the range of benefits available to them and by their new exclusion from the labour market, thus effectively closing down their choices. Perhaps the decreasing marriage and birth rates among East German women between 1989–94 can be explained by these changing conditions of increased unemployment and decreased family benefits, which make dependent homemaker status a risky business, especially in the context of increased male uncertainties (Adler, 1997).

In sum, there remains little choice for many eastern women who are increasingly marginalized in the labour market and have limited expectations of reversing the situation in the light of limited childcare services. Indeed, Roesler (1991) claims that, while in the former East Germany 80 per cent of children had nursery places, 94 per cent could access a kindergarten, and 82 per cent made use of after school care by the 1980s, in contrast the figures for the former West Germany were 2,

79, and 4 per cent respectively. Even if there is the political will, the financing of a major expansion of facilities is unlikely in the shorter term. A more likely outcome involves the spread of the female home-maker model from the former West Germany into the former Eastern *Länder*, particularly in the light of the unemployment issues discussed in section 4.1.

For some sections of the female population, most notably single parents, there is enormous pressure to continue in paid employment if they are to avoid a life of extreme poverty. For these women, moving into the labour market may depend on their being able to access informal help, from their own mothers in particular. With older women moving out of the labour market themselves as a result of government policy, the withdrawal of opportunities for older women may become increasingly bound up with the maintenance of opportunities for others, especially given the unified Germany's attitude to publicly funded childcare services. In contrast, married women in the East may *enjoy* the option of non-labour market participation, at least in the short term (Liebfried and Ostner, 1991; Corrin, 1992; Rai et al, 1992; Einhorn, 1993; Rueschmeyer, 1993), but if it becomes the *only* option they may become less amenable.

It would appear from the preceding analysis that as a result of unification, different groups of women have lost out to different extents and in different ways. Men too have lost out, particularly though not exclusively those from the former Eastern *Länder*. But again there is no universal experience even for East German men. There are import-ant variations between different groups of workers within the unified Germany, depending on education and skill level but also the type of work an individual does. As Buckley (1997) notes, albeit with reference to the former Soviet Republics, ' "Men" and "women" are not homogen-ous categories. There are thus variations among women and men and overlapping tendencies between them. Alongside general paths, one can find exceptions, alongside apparent certainties are ambiguities' (Buckley, 1997, p.8). So variations exist both within and across social groupings. This complexity has been illustrated here with particular reference to the differential impact of unemployment across East and West and between different groups of women including lone mothers, wives and older women. Indeed a similar level of complexity is in evidence when we consider the case of racialized and ethnic minority groups.

4.3   WELFARE, 'RACE' AND RACIALIZATION IN THE POST-UNIFICATION PERIOD

The 1980s has seen a number of discursive shifts in German society. These shifts and the policy developments that grew out of them were the result of a combination of factors: political and ideological change, new and intensified economic pressures, the growing influence of the EU and the impact of the collapse of state socialism in the East, not least the huge growth in population movements, asylum seeking and the 'return' of ethnic Germans. In order to explore the significance of these discursive shifts and subsequent policy developments, the processes of inclusion and exclusion at work and the impact on different groups of people, it is necessary to examine how ideas about German nationhood and the discourses of immigration have evolved since the mid 1970s.

4.3.1 CHANGES TO THE 'GUEST-WORKER' SYSTEM PRIOR TO UNIFICATION

As has already been noted, between the 1950s and mid-1970s there was a substantial migration of 'guestworkers' into West Germany. However, principally as a reaction to economic downturn and the growing threat of unemployment, the Federal government introduced a number of reforms that restricted further migration – not least through the ending of 'Guestworker' recruitment in 1973 and the introduction of tougher immigration controls thereafter – while at the same time securing the position of long-settled 'guestworkers' (Ginsburg, 1992).

After 1973, 'guestworkers' were encouraged to accept voluntary repatriation, often with some monetary incentives. Indeed in 1990 Germany formally cancelled contracts with governments who supplied 'guestworkers' and this was followed by further voluntary repatriation efforts (Roesler, 1991). But, this process also had the rather paradoxical effect of prompting migrant workers to seek permanent residence status and family reunification (Faist, 1995; Ginsburg, 1992). Consequently Germany faced the problem of how to adjust to the permanent settlement of migrant workers after a long period of denying immigration. However, the process of change and acceptance of a less homogenous German nation was not assisted by the fact that after 1973 the term 'guestworker' was replaced by 'foreigner' (*Auslander*). Although formally (i.e. in terms of state definitions) this term applies to all foreigners, in popular usage it was not usually applied to white people from Northern Europe and North America (Ginsburg, 1992) and thus clearly signified a continued distinction between different groups of non-Germans on the basis of 'race'.

Nevertheless in 1991 a new Foreigner Law was finally implemented. The law acknowledged that most 'foreigners' had been resident in the former West Germany for over ten years and that many had been born there. The government could not undo or deny that reality and forced repatriation was a non-starter, given Germany's past on the one hand and the practical problems of implementing such a policy on the other. As a result 'foreigners' were granted specific, legally defined rights.

Some of these developments – permanent residency, family reunification rights and the granting of specific legal rights to settled 'foreigners' – seem to indicate that already, by the early 1980s there had been an 'unsettling' of the arrangements of the post-1949 period and perhaps even a shift away from citizenship on the basis of *jus sanguinis* to at least a partial recognition of *jus soli*. But, the unfinished nature of these shifts is also clearly evident: in a 1997 speech dedicated to the 'European Year Against Racism' Federal President Roman Herzog spoke of 'guest rights' even for those born in Germany who were not deemed to be of German blood (Checkel, 1999). Moreover, the 1991 Foreigner Law was paralleled by claims that the 'guestworker' system was historically specific, a one-off policy not to be repeated in the future. Indeed, since the suspension of the 'guest-worker' system, unattractive positions of employment have been filled by contract workers with a much more limited set of rights – a clear signal that Germany does not wish to repeat the experiences of that earlier period (Faist, 1995) while at one and the same time continuing to allow business to reap the benefits of a flexible reserve army of labour that was marginalized in a segregated and highly racialized secondary labour market. Such developments were coupled with a commitment to limit, or where possible prevent, future immigration of non-Germans from outside of the EU. It is to this that we shall now turn.

4.3.2   ASYLUM POLICY

West Germany's Basic Law gave all those seeking asylum, including those who had been refused admission into a third 'safe' country, the right of entry and legal-constitutional protection. This made the Federal Republic the only country in the world to grant free entry to all (Joppke, 1999, p.85).

The *Länder* had legal responsibilities to house and provide social welfare benefits for asylum seekers who were distributed across the western regions (and, after unification, the former East). Those granted asylum were given work permits and encouraged to find employment. However, while this approach may have resulted in the welfare claims of asylum seekers being constructed as legitimate in the longer term, given their growing contribution record and the close links between work and welfare in conservative welfare regimes (Esping-Andersen, 1996), initially new arrivals were to be reliant on the more stigmatized Social Assistance provisions of the local German state. Given that this aspect of the income maintenance system was subject to local discretion, some *Länder* interpreted their responsibilities in such a way as to provide only benefits in kind. Moreover, in some cases, they housed asylum seekers in camps as a disincentive to would-be settlers (Joppke, 1999). This also had the effect of making the experiences of asylum seekers rather geographically uneven. There were also clear differences in the opportunities afforded to different sections of this population. For example, according to Marshall (1992), those who could speak the language were more likely to find work. There was little targeted help for those who could not and as a result they were more likely to be excluded from labour market participation.

THE GROWTH OF ASYLUM

Throughout the 1980s there had been a steady increase in the numbers seeking asylum in Germany. This same period had seen the rise of the neo-liberal project under the leadership of Kohl and a growing concern about the economy and Germany's place in Europe and the world. These factors help to explain why a more open debate at the Federal level between different parties was in evidence throughout the 1980s and into the 1990s. Distinctions between different types of 'incomers' grew in importance for certain racist groups who made very rigid distinctions between those who were imagined to be ethnic Germans of pure blood and those who were not. These distinctions also became more apparent in party political discourses. For example, Joppke (1999) notes the growing racialization in public discourse about who is German speaking and European (and thus deserving of help) on the one hand, and who is of Turkish, Asian or African origin and could not/should not be assimilated on the other. He highlights the importance of perceptions that increasing numbers 'stand at a greater distance from' German culture (Joppke, 1999, p.79). Similarly, Faist (1995) highlights the ongoing debate between the conservative parties (the Christian Democratic Union and the Christian Social Union) and the Social Democratic Party in this period, and the pressure on the latter to waiver on the issue of asylum given arguments of cultural difference, welfare abuse and economic competition forwarded by the former. He also highlights the general relevance of religion here, and Islam in particular, and the potential threat it was perceived to pose to support for the Christian parties.

Therefore, since the early 1980s, despite the fact that they did not engage in the border screening practised by other EU member states, successive German governments made clear pronouncements about the 'problem' posed by 'foreigners' and 'bogus' asylum seekers, fuelling xenophobic and racist activities in the years that followed. Policies also changed. For example the Federal courts increasingly interpreted the definition of a refugee using narrow criteria and drawing in particular on the concept of 'objective persecution', so that asylum seekers' subjective experiences (e.g. feelings of fear) were given less weight than the state's supposedly objective definition of 'real' risk of persecution. The impact of such a development is highlighted by Joppke who writes that, 'The concept of objective persecution has allowed the federal courts to reject 95 per cent of all asylum claims since the mid-1980s' (Joppke, 1999, p.90).

However, perhaps surprisingly, the rejection of the vast majority of asylum applications did not result in mass deportations. Joppke claims a figure of about 1–2 per cent (Joppke, 1999, p.90), in part explained by the legacy of Germany's Nazi past. Indeed, it is a further paradox that, just as the ending of the guestworker system led to increased numbers seeking permanent residence rather than a fall in 'foreigner' numbers perhaps as expected, so the tightening of asylum conditionality led to increased numbers staying on in Germany illegally. The problem of future illegal settlement was, however, tackled more assertively in the period after unification.

From 1989 onwards there was a huge growth in entries into West Germany and later the unified Germany (Joppke, 1999; Faist, 1995). As noted above, the 1949 Constitution embodied a commitment to the national unification of all German people. So with the demise of state socialism in Central and Eastern Europe 'Ethnic Germans' (*Aussiedler*) were free to travel back to their 'homeland'. Furthermore, the collapse of the Soviet-style social system created a wave of asylum seekers, fleeing war, unrest and persecution and seeking entry into Germany. The number of new applicants in 1990 stood at 193,063, and in 1992 alone 438,191 asylum seekers sought refuge (Joppke, 1999, p.90).

However, it was not just this growth in transborder migration that precipitated renewed and increased debate about the issue of immigration; broader changes at the national and international level were also significant. Unemployment on the one hand and welfare state retrenchment on the other were particularly important in fuelling concern about the growing numbers of asylum seekers competing for scarce resources with those excluded from the labour market (Faist, 1995). These pressures intensified after unification. With significant numbers of Germans from the former GDR moving westwards in search of work and the dispersal of asylum seekers into the former Eastern *Länder* (in line with the Unification Treaty), there was conflict between 'ethnic Germans' and 'non-Germans' over resources, jobs and so on, sometimes erupting into violence. In addition, the economic pressures brought to bear by the EU on its member states in preparation for EMU were becoming ever more evident (Gissendanner, 1998) and the trend was towards greater harmonization in the political sphere, not least in relation to immigration control.

ASYLUM POLICY AND THE EUROPEAN UNION

The threat 'foreigners' were perceived to pose to the German nation must be seen in the context of increasing European integration and the discursive distinctions made between European and non-European migrants at the regional level, but also in relation to the similar concerns expressed by other member states about migration, particularly from outside the European Union. Throughout the late 1980s, but particularly in the early 1990s, co-operation in relation to preventing 'others' moving through other nation states in order to get to the society of choice was increasingly seen as a priority. The concept of 'fortress Europe' has been used to capture the processes by which internal controls within the EU and across member states have been relaxed while at the same time external controls have been introduced or strengthened in parallel with increased internal surveillance (Kofman and Sales, 1992), particularly after 1992.

In order to understand the policy developments at the European level it is useful to explore briefly their context. At the level of global economy and international change, concerns have been expressed that the employment of immigrant labour might undermine pay and conditions for indigenous labour, and thereby threaten 'social cohesion'. This has been one dimension of the more general debate on social dumping. With the development of the Single European Market, competitive pressures from low-cost producers within the EU, where social security, wages and employment conditions are relatively poor, are perceived to be a threat to more advanced EU member states. In response the EU has proposed directives relating to the extension of minimum standards. Moreover, it has committed member states to co-operate in combating drug trafficking, international crime and terrorism as well as the control of immigration. A number of agreements have resulted from this commitment.

At the Dublin Convention it was agreed that asylum applications should be dealt with by the first EU state that an applicant enters, and the Schengen Group, formed in 1985 in response to the lack of common immigration and asylum policy among member states, called for a common approach on strategies for reinforcing and strengthening external borders, visa policy and asylum seekers (Baldwin-Edwards, 1991). While this Group was outside of EU structures and institutions, representing an inter-governmental initiative whose decisions are not legally binding and cannot be forced upon all EU members, it has claimed some success. For example, restrictions have been strengthened as a result of informal agreements across member nations and the Schengen Agreement of 1990 in particular, which came into force in 1995 (Baldwin-Edwards, 1991; Kofman and Sales, 1992).

These developments have affected German immigration policy making in quite significant ways. Given the unevenness of immigration policy across member states and Germany's relatively liberal approach to asylum seekers in particular, there was much concern that the rest of Europe would 'offload' their applicants onto Germany (Joppke, 1999). The answer, then, lay in Germany finding ways to shift towards the EU 'norm'. This was arguably made easier in the light of the Dublin and Schengen Agreements, which helped to legitimize shifts in German national immigration policy. The 1991 Foreigner Law also helped insofar as it narrowed acceptance criteria. But a further 'asylum-compromise' at the national level allowed Germany to reject asylum seekers deemed to be fraudulent at its borders (in line with the rest of Europe), and put an end to asylum seekers arriving through other 'safe' states. This decision, ruled constitutional by the Federal Court in 1996, had the effect of curtailing asylum seeking massively from 1994 onwards (Joppke, 1999). However, while it effectively guarded against the possibility of the future illegal settling of applicants who had been denied asylum, it still left the 'problem' of those who had already settled in Germany illegally.

It was, then, essentially the EU that helped Germany to bring its policy in line with the rest of Europe, though this should be understood in conjunction with the shift in discursive practices at the national level, which helped to frame the asylum debate and shape the experiences of those seeking entry into Germany on the grounds of persecution.

4.3.3 ETHNIC GERMANS AND SHIFTING CONCEPTIONS OF GERMAN CITIZENSHIP

In contrast to the experiences of asylum seekers (and to a lesser extent foreign workers and their families), the experience of ethnic Germans from eastern Europe has been one of full citizenship rights granted upon arrival. Moreover, those deemed to be of German origin (*Aussiedler*) are also able to access the whole range of social citizenship rights and special integration programmes (for example skills and language training) (Heinelt, 1993 cited in Faist, 1995, p.221). However, while *Aussiedler* have formal rights, many find it difficult to get into the mainstream labour force. The hostility towards them is reflected in the tightening up of entry rules for 'ethnic Germans' in parallel with those for asylum seekers. For example, 'ethnic Germans' coming to Germany now have to demonstrate a connection to German culture and must apply for admission prior to arrival at the border. This is probably the result of numbers expected to attempt entry, especially from the East, but also reflects the increased support for right-wing parties on the immigration ticket (Marshall, 1992).

At the same time, naturalization laws were relaxed between 1990 and 1995 (Hudson and Williams, 1999) resulting in the relative elevation of residence criteria. Both the tightening up of entry rules for 'ethnic Germans' and the relaxation of the naturalization laws may reflect a further shift away from narrow conceptions of German citizenship based on *jus sanguinis* begun in the early 1980s (see section 4.3.1, above). However, the extent to which this represents a phasing out of 'ethnic German' priority status is much less clear. The impact on those from outside of the Union is also not necessarily a positive one. Indeed, even where residency is elevated and rights granted on that basis, those deemed to be non-Germans are still constructed as 'aliens' or 'other', as opposed to 'citizens-in-waiting' (Checkel, 1999). Moreover, in the last ten years the foreign population has become more disadvantaged (see Lawson, 1996, p.46). For example, the unemployment rate of 'foreigners' is 'more than double that of German citizens' (Faist, 1995, p.231), although it should be noted that the reasons for this are likely to be multiple – not just legal discrimination and racist practises but also factors relating to the restructuring of the economy (Wilson, 1993; Faist, 1995, p.232). In addition dependence on Social Assistance has increased, though benefit rates have fallen (Wilson, 1993; Faist, 1995).

The future for 'foreigners' in Germany depends in part on the actions of 'foreigners' themselves and more liberal forces in society. Some groups have become active in the churches, which have taken up their cause calling for a shift towards a full recognition of *jus soli* as a basis for German citizenship (Checkel, 1999). Trade unions are also increasingly supporting the liberalization of citizenship and naturalization laws. This is in part a result of more 'non-Germans' who have long been settled or were born in Germany now being established in unionized employment (Checkel, 1999).

As noted and illustrated above, the experience of entering and settling in Germany is differentiated according to how you are perceived – as an ethnic German, an asylum seeker, or a foreigner. Moreover, that experience is also differentiated according to 'racial'/ethnic identity and gender, as the examples of female migrants and Turks illustrate. Yet whichever grouping we consider, the picture is generally one of second class citizenship. As Kofman and Sales note, 'While the experience of black and ethnic minority women in Europe is extremely diverse, varying, for example, according to ethnic background, the state in which they are settled, legal status, social class, generation and political situation, they share, nevertheless, common experiences that make possible some generalizations as a starting point for analysis' (Kofman and Sales, 1992). Given the range of incomers – 'ethnic Germans', asylum seekers and the families of former 'guestworkers' – and Germany's history on immigration, the challenges Germany has faced are perhaps rather more complex than elsewhere in Europe. However, there is still one more layer to add – that of the specific challenge presented by the unification of East and West Germans themselves.

4.4   EASTENERS MEET WESTERNERS

The emerging relations between East Germans (*Ossis*) and West Germans (*Wessis*) have not always been positive. In the context of unemployment, housing shortages and growing poverty levels, there appears to have been a reluctance on the part of certain sections of the population, especially the younger generation, to share the fruits of economic success, despite endorsing the principle of 'one people' when the Wall fell (Merkl, 1992). Socio-cultural issues have also been important here. Horschelmann (1997) looks at the impact of unification on identity formations and the construction of essentialized 'same'/ 'other' dichotomies in Germany. He argues that these arise from claims about the different social character of the two regimes over the forty year period of separation. Stereotypes of *Ossis* and *Wessis*, often created and reinforced by contemporary media discourses, have served to problematize East Germans as a barbaric 'them' in contrast to a civilized western 'us'. For example, news programmes have devoted disproportionate attention to fascism in the East, assuming homogeneity and paying little attention to the diversity of experiences in the five *Länder*. These discourses have also challenged the official line that Germany is socially homogenous by suggesting something rather different (Hudson and Williams, 1999). Eastern perceptions of German nationhood, which may differ significantly to West German ideas, have also worked to unsettle traditional western notions of what it means to be a German.

Horschelmann (1997) also claims that gendered discourses are at work in the unified Germany. For example, he suggests that the socialist working mother has been constructed as a 'bad' mother. Media representations of 'natural' motherhood as being in opposition to 'socialist' motherhood undermine the efforts of women from the former

Eastern *Länder* to retain a degree of economic independence and an attachment to old forms and norms (Kolinsky, 1998). Of course, the extent to which the majority of the German people accept such constructions is questionable, but it is clear that socio-cultural differences arising out of the two very different paths of development followed by the two Germanies are likely to remain important (Dunbar and Bresser, 1997).

In sum, social unification has been less clear cut than monetary, economic and political unification (Kolinsky, 1998b). Throughout the 1980s, but from 1990 in particular, the problem of exclusions and inequalities around the social dimensions of class, gender and 'race' have perhaps become more visible. They have certainly been reconstituted through the process of unification. Class, gender and racial cleavages work together to shape the lives of men and women in Germany often in complex ways, as the examples used throughout this chapter have illustrated. But before turning to consider the future of the German model it is also crucial to emphasize that people are not just victims of structural change – they are agents in and of themselves. Men and women from majority and minority groups within Germany have, and continue to struggle against, disadvantage and discrimination and, in the case of the population of the former GDR, fight to retain the limited gains they have made since 1949.

5   A FUTURE FOR THE GERMAN MODEL?

Looking at the experience of German unification perhaps highlights the positive aspects of the 'rich uncle' approach to societal transformation, not least the improvements in standards of living in the old GDR, which have far outstripped those achieved elsewhere in the former Eastern Bloc (Offe, 1996; Berentsen, 1999). However, notwithstanding this point, the unevenness of the gains and the new exclusions and challenges arising out of the process remain significant, not just for those of the former GDR but also for those who have lived for forty years in the West German *Länder*. Whether the West German model of social policy can address these issues effectively, and rise to the new demands placed upon it is open to question.

Some commentators have expressed a degree of pessimism about the stability of the German model, arguing that the social insurance system is outdated, its normative, patriarchal basis – excluding those who have transgressed traditional roles – and its employment-orientation no longer reflecting the patterns of work in Western Europe (Offe, 1994). Similarly those on the political right are sceptical about its durability as a system, albeit for very different reasons. Arguments are emerging in Germany about the costly nature of the regime, its recent tendency towards deficit, and its detrimental implications for the competitiveness of the German economy. It is also yet to be seen how the confessional mix of the unified Germany, with the preponderance of Protestantism in the East, will affect a welfare regime that is so deeply rooted in Catholic social ethics.

In contrast, while recognizing the challenges that face the German social insurance system, others have argued that the structures and institutions of the post-war German welfare settlement have shown themselves to be highly durable. While the Kohl governments re-emphasised self-reliance and implemented selective cuts and austerity measures as well as more significant policy changes, these developments were in line with the basic principles of the system (Clasen and Gould, 1995). They, therefore, argue that the social insurance system is capable of adapting to change and, moreover, is incredibly difficult to restructure in any radical way. Two examples in particular illustrate this: the recent recognition of non-waged forms of work (childcare in particular); and the 1995/6 expansion of social insurance to include long-term care insurance. Indeed other commentators agree that claims of crisis are exaggerated (Hauser, 1995) and that continuity is the most likely scenario (Pierson, 1996). Such a conclusion – that the German welfare state is 'tradition-bound' – does not, however, bode well for significant sections of the population, perhaps most notably women.

REFERENCES

Adler, M.A. (1997) 'Social change and declines in marriage and fertility in Eastern Germany', *Journal of Marriage and the Family*, vol.59, pp.37–49.

Baldwin-Edwards, M. (1991) 'Immigration after 1992', *Policy and Politics*, vol.19, no.3, pp.199–211.

Berentsen, W.H. (1999) 'Socioeconomic development of Eastern Germany, 1989–1998: a comparative perspective', *Post-Soviet Geography and Economics*, vol.40, no.1, pp.27–43.

Bryson, L. (1992) *Welfare and The State: Who Benefits?*, Basingstoke, Macmillan.

Buckley, M. (1997) *Post-Soviet Women: from the Baltic to Central Asia*, Cambridge, Cambridge University Press.

Chamberlayne, P. (1994) 'Women and social policy', in Clasen, J. and Freeman, R. (eds) *Social Policy in Germany*, Hemel Hempstead, Harvester Wheatsheaf.

Checkel, J.T. (1999) 'Norms, institutions and national identity in contemporary Europe', *International Studies Quarterly*, vol.43, pp.83–114.

Clasen J. (1997) 'Social Insurance in Germany – dismantling or reconstruction', in Clasen J. (ed.) *Social Insurance in Europe*, Bristol, Policy Press.

Clasen, J. and Gould, A. (1995) 'Stability and change in welfare states: Germany and Sweden in the 1990s', *Policy and Politics*, vol.23, no.3, pp.183–201.

Clasen, J. and Freeman, R. (1994) (eds) *Social Policy in Germany*, Hemel Hempstead, Harvester Wheatsheaf.

Clasen, J. (1994) 'Social security – the core of the German employment-centred Social State', in Clasen, J. and Freeman, R. (eds) *Social Policy in Germany*, Hemel Hempstead, Harvester Wheatsheaf.

Corden, A. and Duffy, K. (1998) 'Human dignity and social exclusion', in Sykes, R. and Alcock, P. (eds) *Developments in European Social Policy: Convergence and Diversity*, Cambridge, Polity Press.

Corrin, C. (1992) *Superwomen and the Double Burden*, London, Scarlett Press.

Daly, M. (1997) 'Welfare states under pressure', *Journal of European Social Policy*, vol.7, no.2, pp.129–46.

Dalton, R.J. (1992) 'Two German electorates', in Smith, G. *et al.* (eds) *Developments in German Politics*, Basingstoke, Macmillan.

Deacon, B. (1992) *Social Policy in Eastern Europe: Past, Present and Future*, London, Sage.

Dennis, M. (1998) 'Family policy and family function in the German Democratic Republic', in Kolinsky, E. (ed.) *Social Transformation and the Family in Post-Communist Germany*, Basingstoke, Macmillan.

Dunbar, R.L. and Bresser, R.K.F. (1997) 'Appreciating cultural differences: the case of German Reunification', in *Administration and Society*, vol.29, no.4, pp.440–470.

Einhorn, B. (1993) *Cinderella Goes to Market: Citizenship, Gender and Women's Movements in East Central Europe*, London, Verso.

Esping-Andersen, G. (1990) *The Three Worlds of Welfare Capitalism*, Cambridge, Polity Press.

Esping-Andersen, G. (1996) 'Welfare states without work: the impasse of labour shedding and familialism in continental European social policy', in Esping-Andersen (ed.) *Welfare States in Transition*, London, Sage.

Faist, T. (1995) 'Ethnicization and racialization of welfare state politics in Germany', in *Ethnic and Racial Studies*, vol.18, no.2, pp.219–50.

Ferree, M.M. (1994) 'The time of chaos was the best: feminist mobilization and demobilisation in East Germany', in *Gender and Society*, vol.8, no.4, pp.597–623.

Flockton, C. (1998) 'Economic transformation and income change', in Kolinsky, E. (ed.) *Social Transformation and the Family in Post-Communist Germany*, Basingstoke, Macmillan.

Ganssmann, H. (1993) 'After unification: problems facing the German welfare state', in *Journal of European Social Policy*, vol.3, no.2, pp.79–90.

Ginsburg, N. (1992) *Divisions of Welfare*, London, Sage.

Ginsburg, N (1993) 'Sweden: the social democratic case', in Cochrane, A. and Clarke, J. (eds) *Comparing Welfare States*, London, Sage.

Ginsburg, N. (1994) 'Ethnic minorities and social policy', in Clasen, J. and Freeman, R. (eds) *Social Policy in Germany*, Hemel Hempstead, Harvester Wheatsheaf.

Gissendanner, S. (1998) 'German social policy after the integration of East Germany', in Sykes, R. and Alcock, P. (eds) *Developments in European Social Policy: Convergence and Diversity*, Cambridge, Polity Press.

Gough, I. (1979) *The Political Economy of the Welfare State*, Basingstoke, Macmillan.

Hauser, R. (1995) 'Problems of the German welfare state after unification', in *Oxford Review of Economic Policy*, vol.11, no.3, pp.44–58.

Holmes, L. (1997) *Post-Communism: An Introduction*, Cambridge, Polity Press.

Horschelmmann, K. (1997) 'Watching the East: constructions of 'otherness' in TV representations of East Germany', in *Applied Geography*, vol.17, no.4, pp.385–96.

Hudson, R. and Williams, A.M. (eds) (1999) *Divided Europe: Society and Territory,* London, Sage.

Hughes, G. and Lewis, G. (eds) (1998) *Unsettling Welfare*, London, Sage.

Ireland, P. (1997) 'Socialism, unification policy and the rise of racism in Eastern Germany', in *International Migration Review,* vol.XXXI, no.3, Fall, pp.541–68.

Jarre, D. (1991) 'Subsidiarity in social services provision in Germany', in *Social Policy and Administration*, vol.25, no.3, pp.211–17.

Joppke, C. (1999) *Immigration and the Nation-State*, Oxford, Oxford University Press.

King, A. and Chamberlayne, P. (1996) 'Comparing the informal sphere: public and private relations of welfare in East and West Germany', in Sociology, vol.30, no.4, pp.741–61.

Kofman, E. and Sales, R. (1992) 'Towards Fortress Europe', in *Women's Studies International Forum*, vol.15, no.1, pp.29–39.

Kolinsky, E. (1992) 'Women in the new Germany: the east-west divide', in Smith, G. *et al.* (eds) *Developments in German Politics*, Basingstoke, Macmillan.

Kolinsky, E. (1998a) 'Recasting biographies: women and the family', in Kolinsky, E. (ed.) *Social Transformation and the Family in Post-Communist Germany*, Basingstoke, Macmillan.

Kolinsky, E. (ed.) (1998b) *Social Transformation and the Family in Post-Communist Germany*, Basingstoke, Macmillan.

Langan, M. and Ostner, I. (1991) 'Gender and welfare', in Room, G. (ed.) *Towards a European Welfare State?*, Bristol, SAUS.

Lawson, R. (1996) 'Germany: maintaining the middle way', in Taylor-Gooby, P. and George, V. (eds) *European Social Policy*, Basingstoke, Macmillan.

Leibfried, S. and Ostner, I. (1991) 'The particularism of West German welfare capitalism: the case of women's social security', in Adler, M. (ed.) *The Sociology of Social Security*, Edinburgh, Edinburgh University Press.

Lewis, J. (ed.) (1997) *Lone Mothers in European Welfare Regimes; Shifting Policy Logics,* London, Jessica Kingsley.

Lewis, J. (1992) 'Gender and the development of welfare regimes', in *Journal of European Social Policy*, vol.2, no.3, pp.159–73.

Mangen, S. (1994) 'The impact of unification', in Clasen, J. and Freeman, R. (eds) *Social Policy in Germany*, Hemel Hempstead, Harvester Wheatsheaf.

Mangen, S. (1998) 'Social protection and family transformation: speculations on the German agenda', in Kolinsky, E. (ed.) *Social Transformation and the Family in Post-Communist Germany*, Basingstoke, Macmillan.

Marshall, B. (1992) 'German migration policies', in Smith, G. *et al.* (eds) *Developments in German Politics*, Basingstoke, Macmillan.

Merkl, P.H. (1992) 'A new German identity', in Smith, G. *et al.* (eds) *Developments in German Politics*, Basingstoke, Macmillan.

Mishra, R. (1977) *Society and Social Policy: Theoretical Perspectives on Welfare*, London, Macmillan.

Mishra, R. (1981) *Society and Social Policy: Theories and Practises of Social Welfare*, Basingstoke, Macmillan.

Molyneux, M. (1985) 'Family reform in socialist states: the hidden agenda', in *Feminist Review*, no.21, Winter 1985.

Molyneux, M. (1981) 'Socialist societies old and new: progress towards women's emancipation', in *Feminist Review,* no.8, Summer 1981.

Nickel, H.M. (1998) 'Women and women's policies in East and West Germany, 1945–1990', in Kolinsky, E. (ed.) *Social Transformation and the Family in Post-Communist Germany*, Basingstoke, Macmillan.

O'Connor, J. (1973) *The Fiscal Crisis of the State*, London, St. James Press.

O'Connor, J. (1987) *The Meaning of Crisis: A Theoretical Introduction*, Oxford, Blackwell.

Offe, C. (1991) 'Smooth consolidation in the West German welfare state: structural changes, fiscal policies and population politics', in Piven, F.F. (ed.) *Labour Parties in Post-Industrial Societies*, Cambridge, Polity Press.

Offe, C. (1994) 'A non-productivist design for social policies', in Ferris, J. and Page, R. (eds) *Social Policy in Transition*, Aldershot, Avebury.

Offe. C. (1996) *Varieties of Transition*, Cambridge, Polity.

Orloff, A.S. (1993) 'Gender and social rights of citizenship: the comparative analysis of gender relations and welfare states', in *American Sociological Review*, vol.58, no.3, pp.303–28.

Ostner, I. (1993) 'Slow motion: women, work and the family in Germany', in Lewis, J. (ed.) *Women and Social Policies in Europe: Work, Family and the State*, Aldershot, Edward Elgar.

Ostner, I. (1997) 'Lone mothers in Germany before and after unification', in Lewis, J. (ed.) *Lone Mothers in European Welfare Regimes: Shifting Policy Logics,* London, Jessica Kingsley.

Ostner, I. (1998) 'Gender, family and the welfare state – Germany before and after unification', in Kolinsky, E. (ed.) *Social Transformation and the Family in Post-Communist Germany*, Basingstoke, Macmillan.

Padgett, S. (1992) 'The new German economy', in Smith, G. *et al.* (eds) *Developments in German Politics*, Basingstoke, Macmillan.

Pahl, J. (1989) *Money and Marriage*, Basingstoke, Macmillan.

Pierson, C. (1991) *Beyond the Welfare State?*, Cambridge, Polity.

Pierson, P. (1996) 'The new politics of the welfare state', in *World Politics*, vol.48, pp.143–79.

Poole, L. (2000) 'New approaches to comparative social policy: the changing face of Central and East European welfare', in Lewis, G., Gewirtz, S. and Clarke, J. (eds) *Rethinking Social Policy,* London, Routledge.

Rai, S., Pilkington, H. and Phizaklea, A. (1992) *Women in the Face of Change*, London, Routledge.

Roesler, J. (1991) 'Mass unemployment in Eastern Germany: recent trends and responses by workers and policy makers', in *Journal of European Social Policy*, vol.1, no.2, pp.129–36.

Rueschemeyer, M. (1993) 'Women in East Germany: from state socialism to capitalist welfare state', in Moghadem, V.M. (ed.) *Democratic Reform and the Position of Women in Transitional Economies*, Oxford, Clarendon.

Ruspini, E. (1998) 'Women and poverty dynamics: the case of Germany and Britain', in *Journal of European Social Policy,* vol.8, no.4, pp.291–316.

Sainsbury, D. (1996) *Gender, Inequality and Welfare States*, Cambridge, Cambridge University Press.

Smith, G. (1992a) 'The nature of the unified state', in Smith, G. *et al.* (eds) *Developments in German Politics*, Basingstoke, Macmillan.

Smith C. and Thompson, P. (1992) *Labour in Transition: The Labour Process in Eastern Europe and China*, London, Routledge.

Spicker, P. (1991) 'The principle of subsidiarity', in *Journal of European Social Policy*, vol.1, no.1, pp.3–14.

Sturm, R. (1992) 'Government at the centre', in Smith, G. *et al.* (eds) *Developments in German Politics*, Basingstoke, Macmillan.

Sykes, R. (1998) 'Studying European social policy – issues and perspective', in Sykes, R. and Alcock, P. (eds) *Developments in European Social Policy: Convergence and Diversity*, Cambridge, Polity Press.

Tester, S. (1994) 'Implications of subsidiarity for the care of older people in Germany', in *Social Policy and Administration*, vol.28, no.3, pp.251–62.

Therborn, G. (1987) 'Welfare states and capitalist markets', in *Acta Sociologica*, no.30, pp.237–54.

Titmuss, R. (1974) *Social Policy: An Introduction*, London, George Allen and Unwin.

Williams, F. (1995) 'Race/ethnicity, gender and class in welfare states: a framework for comparative analysis', in *Social Politics,* Summer 1995, pp.127–59.

Wilson, M. (1993) 'The German welfare state: a conservative regime in crisis?', in Cochrane, A. and Clarke, J. (eds) *Comparing Welfare States: Britain in an International Context* (1st edn), London, Sage.

CHAPTER 6
SWEDEN: THE SOCIAL DEMOCRATIC CASE

NORMAN GINSBURG

CONTENTS

1	THE SOCIAL DEMOCRATIC CONTEXT	196
1.1	CONTRASTING PERSPECTIVES	196
1.2	THE DEVELOPMENT OF THE MODERN WELFARE STATE	197
1.3	SOCIAL EXPENDITURE AND TAXATION	199
2	SOCIAL SECURITY POLICIES AND OUTCOMES	200
2.1	INCOME INEQUALITY AND POVERTY	200
2.2	OLD-AGE PENSIONS	202
2.3	SOCIAL ASSISTANCE	204
2.4	UNEMPLOYMENT	205
2.5	ACTIVE LABOUR-MARKET POLICIES	206
2.6	UNEMPLOYMENT BENEFITS	208
3	RACE, ETHNICITY AND MIGRATION	209
3.1	IMMIGRATION AND RACE	210
3.2	RACE, ETHNICITY AND SOCIAL POLICIES	211
4	FAMILY POLICIES	213
4.1	FAMILY-POLICY REFORM	213
4.2	LONE-MOTHER FAMILIES	215
4.3	PARENTAL LEAVE AND DAYCARE	216
4.4	THE NEW PATRIARCHY?	217
5	CONCLUSION: ADAPTING TO THE EU AND GLOBALIZATION	218
	REFERENCES	220

I   THE SOCIAL DEMOCRATIC CONTEXT

For supporters and detractors alike, Sweden is almost invariably portrayed as having one of the most expansive and progressively redistributive welfare states under capitalism. It is frequently used as the clearest example of what has been called the social democratic model or welfare regime (Esping-Andersen, 1990; see also p.12 in Chapter 1 of this book). The reasons for this are evident: since the 1970s Sweden has spent a greater proportion of its national income on welfare benefits and services than any other capitalist state, with a concomitant emphasis on direct public provision and universal accessibility and participation. The welfare state in Sweden has been explicitly committed to mitigating class and gender inequalities and the result of this has been that inequalities in disposable income and in access to decent services meeting essential material needs have been significantly less than in most other western countries. From the 1930s until the late 1980s labour-market, industrial and economic policies were also successfully geared to maintaining 'full employment' so that Sweden maintained exceptionally low levels of official unemployment until the late 1980s. In the 1990s the Swedish welfare state has come under exceptional pressure with much higher levels of unemployment, tougher restraints on social expenditure, increasing racial tension and some widening of inequalities. In section 1 we examine the construction and consolidation of the social democratic welfare state in Sweden. This is followed in section 2 by a more detailed account of the social security benefits system and an examination of its impact on income inequality and poverty, by paying particular attention to old-age pensions, unemployment and labour-market programmes. Section 3 looks at the emergence of Sweden as a multi-ethnic society, and focuses on institutional racism and anti-discrimination measures. In section 4 we examine the extensive development of family policies in Sweden, looking particularly on their impact on women. Finally, we reflect briefly on the continuing impact of globalization and European integration on Swedish social policy.

1.1   CONTRASTING PERSPECTIVES

Although Sweden is commonly viewed as epitomising the social democratic welfare regime, there is some debate about the accuracy of the 'social democratic' label for the Swedish welfare state. Social democrats and socialists such as Esping-Andersen and Korpi (1984) argue that the development of Swedish social policy has been driven since the late 1800s by the political struggle and pressures of the organized working class, led by the trade union federation (LO) and the Social Democratic Party (SAP). They argue that the Swedish regime is not only social democratic in terms of outcomes, but also in terms of its class base and its close relationship to the social-democratic political party. This is borne out by the fact that, despite periods out of government in each of the past three decades, the SAP has dominated political life in Sweden from the early 1930s up to the present. Equally important is the fact that for several decades over 80 per cent of Swedish workers have been organized in trade unions, compared to around 30 per cent currently in Germany and Britain.

Pluralists, on the other hand, stress the extent to which a social democratic gloss has frequently been placed on incremental changes resulting from a more diffuse set of political pressures. According to Heclo and Madsen (1987, p.44), 'retrospective rationalizations of critical choices in different policy areas frequently transform instances of muddling-through into part of a grand design for Swedish social solidarity'. Instead of identifying a class basis for the Swedish welfare state, they emphasize the importance of other interest groups and movements (as discussed by Therborn (1989), for example). Some have gone further to argue that social policy has been shaped by the demands of Sweden's middle and agrarian classes as much as those of the working class. Baldwin (1990, p.30) suggests that 'the ability of the Scandinavian welfare states to cater to the middle classes as success-fully as to workers has been the secret of their success'. There is little doubt that the longevity and strength of the SAP hegemony owes much to its adeptness and pragmatism in attracting the support of farmers – in the 1930s in particular – and the middle classes, particularly since the 1950s. This was certainly true of the 1990s where the perception of a broad swathe of the electorate was that the SAP remained the most coherent force available for government: while the SAP lost 9 per cent of its vote in the 1998 election, most of the lost votes went to the Left Party (formerly the Communists), a central element of whose platform is the defence of the welfare state.

These are important debates which give different interpretations of the political basis of Sweden's welfare system. Both sides, however, agree on the universalistic nature of the system itself and stress the import-ance of the historical roots of the settlement that underlie it. There is no one turning-point from which the modern welfare state in Sweden can be said to have begun: policy history in Sweden is a story of gradualism, a slow but fairly inexorable development of social policy, reflecting a long tradition of compromise and coalition in a modern political history unpunctuated by war or major upheaval.

1.2   THE DEVELOPMENT OF THE MODERN WELFARE STATE

The clearest moment of ideological shift towards the welfare state in Sweden occurred in the 1930s when the SAP for the most part abandoned both Marxist and neo-classical or deflationary economic policies in favour of Keynesian counter-cyclical economic policies (such as public works and food price subsidies). The 1930s witnessed what Korpi (1978, p.84) has described as an historic compromise between capital and labour, in which private capital was guaranteed economic freedom (particularly from the threat of nationalization) and labour the full protection of a welfare state. The emotive phrase, 'the People's

Home', was coined by the SAP leader, Per Albin Hansson, in 1928; still widely used, the term came to synonymize the establishment of the welfare society, a society characterized by 'equality, concern, cooperation and helpfulness' (Korpi, 1978, p.84). 'The people' signalled the party's intention to move beyond an emphasis on the needs of the working class; 'home' implied the re-creation of a 'sharing, just community on a national basis ... a person would not take more than his or her share, but neither would anyone stand outside the system of community provision' (Heclo and Madsen, 1987, p.158).

There was in fact only modest growth of the welfare state in the 1940s and 1950s, albeit largely on a universalist and progressive class-redistribution basis. The 1960s and 1970s, however, saw rapid expansion of welfare benefits and services on a more class-neutral distributional basis, solidifying middle-class commitment to the welfare state. During the 1960s, pressure also built up on the leadership of the SAP to renew the socialist commitment to equality of outcome in terms of both class and gender. This was inspired by the 'rediscovery of poverty' within the welfare state, the student movement, the rebirth of feminism and other radical, new social movements. In 1969, the party issued a policy document that called for increased social equality, arguing that this was the primary issue faced by the labour movement. This 'equality movement', underpinned by the left and the women's movement, had a considerable impact on SAP ideology and policy-making in the 1970s, manifested above all perhaps in the introduction of sharply progressive income tax in 1971. It led to a great expansion of services and staffing within the welfare state with some modest success in improving equality of outcome.

The looming problems of stagflation, unemployment and growing union militancy from the late 1960s prompted governments to adopt a stout, Keynesian defence of the welfare state until the 1980s, keeping unemployment relatively low. Sweden's response to the fiscal crisis of the state and recession in the 1970s was significantly different from most other capitalist welfare states: the welfare state was consolidated and even expanded – in such areas as pre-school child care – in the 1980s.

However, the early 1980s witnessed the beginning of a distinct shift in the economic and social policy discourse in governing and industrial circles towards what was dubbed a new 'Third Way' in economic and social policy. This was neither traditionally Keynesian nor overtly neo-liberal. The influence of the Keynesian-oriented trade union federation waned as Swedish multinationals struggled to remain globally competitive. The SAP governments of the 1980s gradually moved towards more stringent anti-inflationary measures, involving social-expenditure restraint, demunicipalization of services and cuts in direct taxation. Macroeconomic mismanagement, continuing industrial uncompetitiveness and another world recession succeeded in creating a dramatic stagflationary, economic crisis in the early 1990s (Hirst, 1999, pp.90–1, Pontusson, 1994, pp.36–7). Between 1990 and 1993, Gross

Domestic Product (GDP) declined by 5 per cent and unemployment quadrupled, remaining at unprecedented levels for the rest of the decade.

In 1990 the SAP government abandoned promised extensions of parental-leave insurance and the public day-care programme, and embarked on cuts in other welfare entitlements. This was perhaps the most significant turning-point since the 1930s. In the 1990s the growth of social expenditure was modestly reversed: there were restrictive changes to sickness and unemployment benefits and pensions. Income inequality and poverty increased. Charges for primary care, prescriptions and municipal services also rose significantly, while public services such as hospitals shed labour. In 1995 Sweden joined the European Union (EU), after a narrow victory in a referendum where women and manual workers predominated amongst the 'no' voters. The latter feared that the convergence of macroeconomic and social policies, implied particularly by monetary union, would inevitably undermine the welfare state structurally. In contrast, the Swedish employers' organization, who were most enthusiastic for EU entry, looked forward to just such an outcome. In the late 1990s the economy staged a recovery with strong economic growth and low inflation. The government modestly loosened social expenditure restrictions, hand in hand with an announcement of significant cuts in both income and corporation tax. Social policy is shaped more than ever by the roller coaster of the economic cycle and, perhaps, in the future by Brussels and the European Central Bank.

1.3 SOCIAL EXPENDITURE AND TAXATION

Sweden has had the highest level of public social expenditure amongst western states over the past two decades. In 1995 public social expenditure in Sweden accounted for 33.0 per cent of Gross Domestic Product (GDP) compared to 22.4 per cent in the UK, 15.8 per cent in the US and 27.1 per cent in Germany (Adema, 1999, Table 2). Social expenditure as defined by the Organization for Economic Co-operation and Development (OECD) here includes publicly provided benefits and services such as housing, health care, social services and labour market measures, but does not include education spending. It was not until the end of the 1970s that Sweden could claim to be one of the highest spenders on social welfare among the 24 leading industrial states in the OECD. Up to the 1960s Sweden's welfare effort had been average; the most significant increase in the proportion of national economic resources devoted to social spending took place through the 1960s, 1970s and into the 1980s. The years 1975–81 saw a particularly rapid increase in social spending, as the Swedish government protected and expanded the welfare state during the global recessions engendered by the oil price rises. This reflected a continuing commitment to progressive Keynesian economic policies by both the social democratic and centre-right coalition governments of the time. The proportion of economic resources devoted to social spending rose to record levels in the deeper recession of the early 1990s (Adema, 1999, Table 7). However, increasingly stringent measures to contain social expenditure are having a long-term impact, evident perhaps in a sharp fall in public social expenditure as a proportion of GDP in the mid 1990s as the economy boomed once again.

It is hardly surprising that in order to fund the welfare state, levels of personal and indirect taxation are comparatively high in Sweden, though corporate taxation has been reduced significantly in the 1990s. It is also important to note that when the taxation of public social benefits and services as well as the charges made to consumers are taken into account, net direct public social expenditure (the size of the welfare effort) is reduced, down to only 25.4 per cent of GDP in 1995. This compares with 22.5 per cent in the UK, 17.5 per cent in the US and 25.9 per cent in Germany (Adema, 1999). These figures suggest that the Swedish government is adept at 'clawing back' cash from welfare beneficiaries and consumers through the tax system. This is a reminder that there may be more of a convergence between states in effective public social spending than has been implied in the recent vogue for divergence analysis prompted by Esping-Andersen (1990).

2 SOCIAL SECURITY POLICIES AND OUTCOMES

2.1 INCOME INEQUALITY AND POVERTY

An important measure of the extent to which an economy and a welfare state achieve fairness or social justice is the degree of inequality between incomes. The 'market income' or 'gross income' of a household is that derived from the market *before* the welfare state intervenes: gross salaries, wages, income from self-employment, property income and so on. The 'net income' or 'disposable income' of a household is the cash income received once taxation and social security benefits have been taken into account. Economists have devised indices for measuring the degree of income inequality amongst households, taking account of the different sizes of households (called equivalent household income). Table 6.1 uses one of these indices, the Gini coefficient index, to show the degrees of income inequality before and after taxes and benefits – the bigger the number, the greater the degree of inequality. The data indicate, perhaps surprisingly, that market incomes are more unequal in Sweden than in the US and Germany. However, after taxes and benefits are taken into account, disposable incomes are much more equally distributed in Sweden than in the US and Germany. The tax system and, more significantly, the pensions and social security benefits system in Sweden succeeded in achieving more than a 50 per cent reduction in the inequality index in 1995, compared with 35 per cent and 25 per cent in Germany and the US respectively. Such data illustrates very clearly one of the key differences between the social democratic model in Sweden, the conservative Bismarkian model in Germany and the liberal model in the US.

TABLE 6.1 Changes in income inequality, as measured by the Gini Coefficient, before and after taxes and transfer (benefits)

	Before taxes and transfers	After taxes and transfers	% changes due to taxes and transfers
Sweden, 1995	48.7	23.0	−52.9
% changes, 1975–95	17.2	-1.0	
Germany, 1994	43.6	28.2	−35.3
% changes, 1984–94	1.2	6.4	
United States, 1995	45.5	34.4	−24.5
% changes, 1974–95	13.1	10.0	

Source: Burniaux et al., 1998, Table 3.2

Table 6.1 also suggests that inequalities in market incomes have increased most markedly in Sweden with the US not far behind in recent decades. Increasing inequality of market incomes has been almost universal in the western world in the 1980s and 1990s. This can be almost entirely accounted for by the widening or increasing 'dispersion' of wages and salaries, a seemingly global trend. Nevertheless, the final outcomes in terms of disposable income inequality are increasingly diverse. The most significant reductions in Swedish disposable income inequality occurred in the early 1970s in the wake of the 'equality debate' and subsequent tax reforms. From the mid 1970s to the mid 1980s disposable income inequality continued to fall though more slowly as the professional and middle classes gained more tax breaks (Ginsburg, 1992, p.35). From the mid 1980s to the mid 1990s, disposable income inequality had risen back to the level of the mid 1970s. It is tempting to suggest that these changes in the income distribution reflect the broad changes in policy we discussed in section 1, with the earlier period (mid 1970s to mid 1980s) influenced by continuing equality pressures, and the more recent period (mid 1980s to mid 1990s) reflecting a modest shift towards competitive liberalism.

Poverty is another important parameter for assessing the performance of a welfare system. One widely used definition of relative poverty is the proportion of individuals with an income less than half the median. Table 6.2 suggests that the poverty rate in Sweden remained fairly stable from the mid 1970s to the mid 1990s. Following a similar trend to that for disposable income inequality across the whole society, there was a modest fall in poverty from the mid 1970s to the mid 1980s, and a comparable increase since then through to the mid 1990s. The most glaring comparison is with the US where, on this measure, the poverty rate remains almost three times that of Sweden. This is another vivid statistical illustration of the enormous difference between the social democratic and the liberal traditions. Although directly comparable data is not available, there is clear evidence that relative poverty in the UK has leapt from near Swedish levels in the 1970s to levels approaching that of the US in the 1990s. The limited comparable data for Germany suggests that re-unification has had specific effects (see Chapter 5 for a fuller discussion of this).

TABLE 6.2 Trends in poverty, as measured by percentage of individuals with incomes below 50 per cent of the median

	Mid 1970s	Mid 1980s	Mid 1990s
Sweden, 1975, 1983, 1995	6.6	6.0	6.4
Germany, 1978, 1984, 1994	6.5	6.2	9.1
US, 1974, 1985, 1995	15.5	18.3	17.1

Source: Burniaux et al., 1998, Tables 5.1 and 5.7

Despite the comparatively equitable income distribution and low level of poverty in Sweden, as elsewhere poverty and low income affect particular social groups such as old people, unemployed people and lone parents differentially. In section 2.2, we examine the positions of old people, in section 2.3, social assistance claimants and, finally, in section 2.4, unemployed people in the income maintenance system to throw light on how Swedish social policy can both reduce and reinforce social divisions of class, 'race' and gender.

2.2   OLD-AGE PENSIONS

As might be expected in a social democratic system, the incomes of old people come overwhelmingly from state pension schemes. In Sweden these give a comparatively very high level of replacement of earnings. There are two compulsory statutory pension schemes: a basic flat-rate payment and the contributory earnings-related scheme (ATP), which supplements it. Both schemes are funded on a 'pay-as-you-go' basis; hence, they are not financed from an invested fund, but are paid for out of contributions from current employers and employees. All citizens and long-term residents are entitled to the basic pension, but full ATP requires a thirty-year history of contributions. There is also a supplement to the basic pension to compensate those with low or no ATP. For the great majority of retired people, the statutory pension schemes provide or replace about 65 per cent of pre-retirement gross salary, though these pensions are themselves subject to taxation. As a top-up to the statutory schemes, 90 per cent of workers are now covered by one of four negotiated occupational pension schemes covering different groups of workers; these provide up to another 10 per cent of replacement income (Ståhlberg, 1995, p.2).

The movement for the ATP helped to forge the integration of the white collar unions into Swedish social democracy during the 1950s. The SAP thereby managed to extend its support amongst the growing ranks of 'the new middle strata' and give them a material stake in the welfare state (Stephens, 1979, p.179). After a long and furious conflict (one of the most significant debates in the history of the Swedish welfare state), the ATP was passed by a single parliamentary vote in 1959 (see Heclo, 1974). This was a victory for the ideal of a universal, state-earnings-related pension as advocated by the SAP and the trade union movement, and against the notion of state-regulated occupational and/ or private pensions, as advocated by the centre-right parties. However, as Ståhlberg (1997, p.50, and 1995, p.12) shows, the ATP has benefited the professional and managerial middle classes more than the blue and white collar working class. A reform in 1999 indexed ATP to wages, which, with other adjustments, was intended to achieve a more socially just outcome.

One way of assessing the impact of the pensions system is to use a 'replacement ratio': this considers the incomes of 'elderly' households as a proportion of the incomes of 'late middle age' households. Data from the OECD (1998b) give replacement ratios in terms of the disposable income of all households with the head aged 67 relative to that of households with the head aged 55. The ratio for Sweden is almost 80 per cent, compared to less than 70 per cent in the UK (the lowest among a sample of eight western states). In Sweden approximately 90 per cent of elderly households' income comes from public transfers (pensions and other benefits), but in the UK it is considerably less than half. This means that UK pensioners are much more dependent on private sources of income such as occupational pensions and earnings. Data on poverty amongst old people in Sweden indicates that the build-up of ATP since the 1960s has had a substantial impact. In 1992 only 6.3 per cent of people in Swedish households headed by an over-65-year-old were poor after taxes, pensions and benefits were taken into account in comparison to 13.4 per cent in 1975. Contrast this with the US, for instance, where over 20 per cent of elderly households were poor in 1994 (Burniaux *et al.*, 1998).

The lower wages and more intermittent working lives of both women and ethnic minorities inevitably result in lower pensions in retirement. This can only be inferred from data on the position of ethnic minorities in the labour market (see section 2.4). In respect of gender, Ståhlberg suggests that in 1990 'men received almost 70 per cent more in pension than women. Two-thirds of men had a negotiated pension ... but only 44 per cent of women' (Ståhlberg, 1997, p.14). These differences have, nevertheless, decreased over time since increases in women's paid employment from the 1960s have come into effect. Ståhlberg (1997, p.15) shows that the pension scheme rules regarding part-time and intermittent working generally disadvantage women. The 1999 pension reform is expected to reduce some of these disadvantages, especially for working-class women, particularly by introducing pension contribution credits for parents looking after young children. Thus, incomes in old age in Sweden continue to reflect divisions of class, 'race' and gender, but they are mitigated to a much greater extent than in most states.

2.3   SOCIAL ASSISTANCE

In common with many other EU states, but unlike the UK, means-tested social assistance in Sweden is administered by local authority social services departments as part of the social work system. The scheme was known as 'poor relief' until 1956 when it was reformed and renamed 'social assistance'; in 1982 it was reformed once again and renamed 'Socialbidrag' (SB – Social Benefit). Until the 1990s the proportion of individuals receiving SB fluctuated at around 5 per cent of the population. With higher rates of long-term employment and increasing numbers of refugees and asylum seekers in the 1990s, the proportion of the population receiving SB rose to an unprecedented peak of 8.5 per cent in 1997 (Statistics Sweden, 1999). The costs of SB doubled in four years in the mid 1990s, prompting significant real cuts in the levels of benefit paid by the local authorities. While there are national guidelines for the levels of benefit, rates of payment are determined locally and are sometimes paid at well below the guidelines (Gould, 1996, p.81). In 1997, the guideline benefit level for a single person was just under 20 per cent of the average wage for a full-time blue collar worker. Most SB claims are short-term: less than 10 per cent of recipients live on benefit for more than a year. In 1992 SB accounted for 6.7 per cent of social security spending in Sweden, a 46 per cent increase on 1980 but a comparatively modest proportion, particularly when compared with the liberal welfare states.

Until the 1970s most claimants were elderly or poor families. Since the 1980s recipients have been more likely to be single, young and often childless. The improvement of pensions and family benefits has not benefited the latter groups so much. This is confirmed by data on poverty rates once taxes and benefits are taken into account, which show that in 1992 over 18 per cent of people in households headed by an under-30-year-old were poor in Sweden, compared to less than 10 per cent in 1975 (Burniaux et al., 1998). The gender profile of SB recipients has remained relatively stable over the past two decades with roughly equal proportions of men and women recipients; in 1998 51.2 per cent of adult recipients were women, compared to 48.2 per cent in 1980. Social workers cite unemployment, mental and/or physical illness and alcohol/drug problems as factors in claims for SB. Ethnic minorities are more likely to receive SB because of their differential vulnerability to unemployment and their failure sometimes to fulfil eligibility criteria for mainstream benefits covering sickness, old age, unemployment and disability. It could be argued that the social assistance system combined with labour market measures (see section 2.5) function both to discipline and maintain people on the margins who are in and out of the labour market, with apparently quite a disparate social composition – young post-materialists or drop-outs, older long-term unemployed single people, ethnic minorities and others who have slipped through the social insurance system.

2.4   UNEMPLOYMENT

Until the recession of the 1990s standardized unemployment (on the internationally accepted International Labour Office (ILO) definition) in post-war Sweden averaged 2 per cent, and was exceptionally low in comparison to other western societies (Ginsburg, 1992). This was a hallmark of the social democratic model and one reason was the continuous growth of public sector employment in the developing welfare services. The 1990s, nonetheless, witnessed a dramatic change as unemployment rates increased sharply and stayed around 10 per cent from 1993 to 1997, falling back to 7 per cent in 1999. Unemployment in the mid 1990s was close to the EU average and to the post-reunification German level, but more than double the rate in the US. Official figures as headlined within Sweden, however, are based on the Labour Force Survey (which does not include full-time students looking for work) and reduce the official unemployment rate in the 1990s by about 1.5 to 2 per cent compared to the standardized ILO definition (Thoursie, 1998, p.85). However when the number of people participating in labour market programmes is included (around 4.5 per cent of the labour force), the headline figure rises to over 12 per cent for 1993 and it remained at this level for four years through the mid 1990s. According to the Swedish Institute (1998, p.2), 'the increase in registered unemployment was less than the decline in employment ... because many people who lost their jobs entered labour market programs, became students or began collecting disability pensions.' So, while in the 1970s and 1980s, structural unemployment was to some extent soaked up by the continued expansion of employment in the public services, in the 1990s official unemployment has been masked by the considerable numbers making an exit from the labour market through early retirement and incapacity benefits. The apparent abrupt end of 'full employment' is such a recent phenomenon in Sweden that it is too early to judge its effect on the social democratic model, but it clearly puts enormous stress on its long-term sustainability.

The sudden emergence of mass unemployment in the 1990s has, of course, affected some social groups more than others. Swedish unemployment statistics are not racialized, making it impossible to quantify precisely the extent to which visible minorities have been differentially affected, but it is clear that they have experienced much higher levels of unemployment. Foreign nationals make up around 5 per cent of the labour force in Sweden, with a rate of unemployment around three times the overall level both before and during the recent slump (Swedish Institute, 1999a, p.1). Hence, in 1998 over 20 per cent of foreign nationals were unemployed. Given that about half of the foreign nationals are from other Nordic countries, it seems reasonable to assume that the more visible minority ethnic groups will have experienced even higher levels of unemployment. Furthermore, Clasen, Gould and Vincent (1997, p.7) report much higher levels of unemployment among young people, particularly the 10 per cent of school leavers without academic certification. Before the 1990s official unemployment amongst Swedish women was low, but always higher than the level for men (Ginsburg, 1992). In the early 1990s, as unemployment surged, the unemployment rate for men exceeded that for women, as industrial employers shed male workers, particularly in the construction and manufacturing sectors. However, the number of public employees was also being cut back to the levels of the 1970s with the loss of over 160,000 jobs between 1990 and 1997, a process which disproportionately affected women who work predominately in the public services. Hence, from the mid 1990s, the unemployment rates for men and women converged quite closely (Thoursie, 1998). Comparing unemployment levels between men and women is problematic, as hidden unemployment is much higher among women, even in Sweden with its comparatively high levels of female paid employment. Given the dramatic fall in women's employment in the public services in the 1990s, it is not surprising that women have been in the vanguard of movements to defend the welfare state, to fight for a shorter working week, and to resist neo-liberal policy pressures emanating from Swedish employers and the EU.

2.5   ACTIVE LABOUR-MARKET POLICIES

A celebrated feature of the Swedish welfare model has been its 'active labour market' policy, designed in explicit Keynesian, social democratic terms to counter technological unemployment by retraining and redeploying human capital. In the 1940s the Labour Market Board (AMS) was established as a quango managed by employers' organizations and trade unions to deliver the policy. The AMS smoothed the way for the restructuring of Swedish industry and its labour force, particularly in the 1960s and 1970s, presiding over a range of measures. First, the employment service matched unemployed people to vacancies on a national basis and paid substantial mobility and relocation grants. The latter often took the form of serious financial inducements to facilitate workers' migration to the booming industries of the south (sometimes reluctantly and with the resultant break-up of established communities). Secondly, there were AMS training schemes organized in training centres and schools. Thirdly, AMS oversaw job-creation measures including relief-work projects, temporary employment subsidies and recruitment subsidies. Finally, there were extensive special measures for people with learning difficulties or physical disabilities, often involving the subsidizing of wages in the open labour market. The expenditure on these programmes in the 1980s amounted to nearly 2 per cent of GDP, the highest level of such spending in the

OECD. While the extensive provision of sheltered workshops for disabled people remains intact, the advent of mass unemployment in the 1990s has understandably created something of a crisis for the AMS as it has been forced to adapt to the more 'flexible', post-industrial labour market. The entire concept of the active labour market policy has been called into question, not least by the employers who withdrew from the AMS Board in 1991. In practice, the emphasis has moved away from more costly public-sector job creation schemes and conventional occupational training towards generic work experience, work preparation, business start-up and Information and Communication Technology (ICT) courses. Some of the activity in training and support for unemployed people has been taken over by the municipalities. By the late 1990s the AMS had lost much of its legitimacy, because for the unions and the left it symbolized the failure to maintain full employment, while for employers and the right it was an inefficient anachronism. Yet during the unemployment crisis of the 1990s AMS programmes and complementary municipal measures proved reasonably popular with unemployed people and reached out to enormous numbers, as much as 7 per cent of the labour force. In the mid/late 1990s labour-market policy (excluding cash benefits) continued to command around 2 per cent of GDP and 5 per cent of central government spending (Swedish Institute, 1999b). This suggests that the proportion of national economic resources devoted to labour-market measures has not increased in response to mass unemployment, but it has certainly not withered either.

From the 1960s women were keenly recruited into paid employment, not least through the active labour market measures. The proportion of the labour force who are women rose dramatically from then until the 1980s. In 1960 the proportion was around the OECD average of 34 per cent; by 1987 it had reached 48 per cent, the highest level in the western world, which was sustained through the 1990s. By the 1990s over 80 per cent of women were in the labour market, and their labour-market participation rate was almost as high as that for men. The proportion of women in part-time paid employment has been comparatively high, fluctuating around 40 to 42 per cent of the total number of women employees in the 1990s. An important feature of women's position in the Swedish labour market has been their vertical and horizontal occupational segregation. Compared to other states, women are much less prominent in 'unskilled' factory work in the private sector and extremely prominent in public sector employment in the welfare state. From 1965 to 1985 Esping-Andersen (1990, p.202) notes that 'women accounted for 87 per cent of total health-education-welfare employment growth in Sweden'. He concludes that those two decades saw the upgrading of women's employment from 'junk-jobs' in private industry to higher status and better paid jobs in the welfare state. This has resulted, however, in increased horizontal occupational segregation by gender with women increasingly concentrated in clerical and welfare work. In this respect, when compared to the US and Germany, 'Sweden emerges as the most gender-segregated among the three countries.

More than half of the women are locked into typical female jobs, while very few women have penetrated the sanctuaries of male dominance. Post-industrialization in Sweden only augments the problem' (Esping-Andersen (1990, p.212).

It would seem therefore that women in Sweden have not been used as substitutes for male workers in industry. They have been the beneficiaries in paid employment terms of the expansion of welfare services in the 1960s and 1970s as part of counter-cyclical Keynesian economic policies. Positive discrimination in active labour-market measures, sex-equality legislation and belated trade union pressure had some success in improving women's wages and salaries relative to men in the 1970s and 1980s, but differentials stabilized in the 1990s. Such pressures had less effect in mitigating horizontal and vertical occupational segregation. The level of part-time paid employment of women, much of it in low-paid service sector jobs, may also reflect the marginalization of women workers. As much as 40 per cent of the women in the labour market with children under seven in reality take parental leave. As Cousins (1999, pp.80–1) notes, 'the distinctive nature of Sweden in this respect is that mothers with young children are paid to take leave to care for their families and are counted as being in the active labour force'. This phenomenon and the high level of part-time paid employment of women (much of it low-paid service sector jobs) reflect modern aspects of the marginalization of women workers in Sweden.

2.6   UNEMPLOYMENT BENEFITS

Earnings-related unemployment insurance benefit (UIB) is administered by 40 voluntary societies under the control of the trade unions, and is financed by government, employers and trade union contributions. In 1998 the government set up a society to cater for non-union members, who had previously only been eligible for a flat-rate insurance benefit. Contribution levels vary from one society to another, so that members more likely to experience unemployment pay higher contributions. The UIB societies have been seen by the unions since the nineteenth century as an important means of recruiting and keeping members. UIB covers around three-quarters of unemployed people; the remainder are dependent on social assistance.

With the growth in unemployment and the pressure to restrain social expenditure, the UIB system came under severe strain in the 1990s. Policy reform became something of a political football between the parties, the employers and the unions. The right have been pushing to cut benefit levels and restrict eligibility, while the left have been defending benefit levels and pressing for improved coverage. By the late 1990s the outcome was some modest but significant tightening in UIB eligibility and a cut in the proportion of previous income received from 90 per cent to 80 per cent. UIB is now paid for up to twelve months at 80 per cent of previous income up to a ceiling of around £45 per day. In 1996, a government commission proposed to cut this figure to 75 per cent but the labour movement forced the government to stick at 80 per cent. In 1993 a five-day waiting period was introduced and in 1998 the minimum number of months worked within the previous twelve-month period was increased to six, compared with four in 1993.

There is now much more pressure on unemployed people to participate in AMS schemes and to demonstrate availability for work. Since 1996 UIB can be withdrawn for 60 days if a claimant refuses a job or training offer (an increase from 20 days in the early 1990s). The incentive to participate in AMS schemes is perhaps sustained above all because it enables the re-establishment of entitlement to UIB. Hence, a three-year benefit duration limit has been introduced. The system still remains much more generous and less disciplinary than 'workfare' or the Job Seeker's Allowance in Britain. According to an OECD (1998a, Table 5.2) study, in 1995 the net replacement of previous income for an unemployed person (previously on an average factory worker's wage) with a spouse and two children was 85 per cent in Sweden compared with 59 per cent in the US and 67 per cent in the UK (before the abolition of unemployment benefit). Replacement of income for those eligible for UIB is among the highest in the world.

3   RACE, ETHNICITY AND MIGRATION

The Swedish people are widely described as having one language, one (Lutheran) religious tradition and a common culture and history, without recently being colonialists or being colonized. Native Finns, Lapps, Jews and Gypsies form long-established, relatively small ethnic minority communities. Prior to the 1930s, Sweden experienced large-scale emigration, especially from poorer, rural areas, to countries such as the United States. In the 1930s the Social Democratic ideology of the People's Home and expansionary socio-economic policies were legitimated in part by their intention to reverse the falling birth rate. The fear of national population decline mingled with 'a mild sort of nationalism', according to Gunnar Myrdal (1938, p.204), the influential social democratic sociologist. Writing for an American audience in 1938, he was highly ambiguous on the question of whether immigration would be part of a solution to 'the population question' (Myrdal, 1939, p.203). In the same context, he also wrote that 'we are just as much, and even more, interested in the physical, intellectual and moral quality of the population as in its quantity. Now at least in Sweden with its homogeneous population, quality does not depend on racial differences' (Myrdal, 1940, p.203). Myrdal later became a very significant advocate of liberal race relations reform in the US. Here in the Swedish context he was hinting at a social eugenic attitude to race and immigration, which was then a significant element of social democratic ideology both in Sweden and elsewhere. The implementation of social eugenic policy in Sweden came under public scrutiny in the mid 1990s when a victim of forced sterilization sought compensation. It emerged that the government had been pursuing a programme of sterilizing women considered to be 'inferior' or of 'poor or mixed racial quality'. This meant 'people with learning difficulties, those from poor families or those not of Nordic blood stock' (Haydon, 1997). The programme lasted from 1935 to 1976, the numbers peaking in 1946, and involved at least 60,000 women. Such women were rounded up in Institutes for Misled and Morally Neglected Children, with their personal stories becoming public in recent times as they have been released into the community. This example of government-sponsored ethnic cleansing and the implicit repression of women's sexual behaviour was not, of course, unique to Sweden, though it may seem more shocking in the context of the social democratic welfare state. Particularly before the Nazi regime took social eugenicism to greater extremes, such measures were a common, if unpublicized, feature of social policy in the west. In Britain under the poor law up to at least the 1940s, unmarried mothers could be labelled as 'feckless' and irresponsible, legitimating the removal of their children, forced sterilization and/or incarceration in an asylum. Similar processes took place in the US (Ginsburg, 1992, pp.123–4).

3.1 IMMIGRATION AND RACE

From the mid 1950s to the late 1960s several hundred thousand migrant workers came to Sweden, mostly from Finland but also from Yugoslavia, Greece, Turkey and Italy. Finnish workers gained the right of unhindered entry to Sweden in 1954, when Iceland, Denmark, Norway, Finland and Sweden established the Nordic free labour market. Swedish offices for the collective recruitment of workers were established in Ankara, Athens, Rome and Belgrade. However, from 1967 onwards, due to declining demand for labour, concern about the impact on national identity and the increasing participation of married women in the labour force, the government used existing immigration laws to limit, increasingly severely, the number of non-Nordic immigrants. The recruitment offices were closed down by the end of the 1960s, except the Yugoslav one, which closed in 1977. By the mid 1970s, as elsewhere in northern Europe, a formidable immigration control system had been established, allowing entry to a regulated number of Finns, relatives of established immigrants and political refugees, but nobody else. This policy was consolidated into Immigration Policy Acts of 1975 and 1976. According to Hammar (1984, p.29), in the day-to-day practice of immigration control at the borders, immigration officers have been instructed since 1976 to identify non-Nordic people by their physical appearance, clearly an explicit form of institutional racism. The legitimation of immigration control is presented in terms of enabling 'underemployed national groups to have access to the labour market' (Widgren, 1982, p.151) and 'the protection of the Swedish labour market' (Hammar, 1984, p.28). Yet these considerations emerged *before* the modest increases in unemployment in the 1970s, and could equally well have applied in the 1950s, for example, to the recruitment of women. Another official argument for immigration control made in the late 1960s was that 'if the number of resident immigrants became too large it would become impossible to guarantee them a reasonable standard of living' (Hammar, 1984, p.41).

Non-Nordic immigration since 1974 has consisted partly of relatives of already-settled immigrant workers, but mostly of refugees and asylum seekers from many different parts of the world. Sweden has been comparatively generous in accepting the latter. In the 1990s, for example, Sweden received a comparatively large number of refugees, particularly from the former Yugoslavia and from Iraq. A peak number of 37,500 were admitted in 1993, but numbers have been firmly restricted since then, not exceeding 13,000 even during 1999 with the war in Kosovo. Sweden has long been a preferred destination for asylum seekers because it gives foreigners comparatively open access to the welfare state and to Swedish citizenship, which can be sought after five years' residence. By the late 1990s, approximately 20 per cent of Swedish residents had a non-Swedish ethnic background, either being born abroad or having at least one parent born abroad. While it is impossible to be at all precise, possibly up to half this number are not of Nordic origin, of whom the great majority are not Western European. Visible minority communities of Caribbean, African and South Asian origin are small, but Sweden can now be regarded as a highly multi-ethnic society. The sudden emergence of mass unemployment in the early 1990s affected minority ethnic communities particularly adversely. Refugee migrants, particularly in the 1990s, have found the labour market and the housing market increasingly exclusionary. Many have been ghettoized on housing estates in the suburbs of the big cities. Instead of being acknowledged as net contributors to the costs of the welfare state as they had been in the 1970s, immigrants and former immigrants were seen as net beneficiaries, over-dependent on the welfare state. In this context the early 1990s witnessed an upsurge in racist activity, unprecedented in modern Swedish history (Larsson, 1991; Deland, 1997; Jederlund, 1998). Racist violence on the streets, in schools and against immigrant hostels increased sharply. From the mid-1990s the recovery of the labour market and anti-racist measures (see section 3.2) and activity contributed to a waning of extreme racist pressures.

3.2 RACE, ETHNICITY AND SOCIAL POLICIES

Up to the mid 1960s, there were no positive social policy measures specifically directed towards migrant workers and their families, who it was assumed would assimilate with the support of the universal welfare state. Between 1964 and 1974 a long process of public discussion and consultation took place in the media and in parliament on whether the assimilationist ideology should continue or whether multi-culturalism should be adopted. The Immigration Policy Act of 1975, which closed the doors to non-Nordic workers, adopted a less strongly assimilationist policy towards Sweden's immigrant and minority ethnic communities. The policy had three goals: equality of living standards, cultural freedom of choice, and political solidarity between the indigenous Swedes and ethnic minorities. Government promoted ethnic minority political, social and cultural organizations and activities, including – on a limited scale – bilingualism in schools, and in 1976 foreigners with at least three years' residence were given the vote in local and regional elections. In 1986 legislation against racial discrimination in employment was passed, enforced by the office of the Ombudsman Against Ethnic Discrimination (DO). In 1994 anti-discrimination law was extended beyond the workplace and the powers of the DO were strengthened. Employers are now required to demonstrate that those hired are the best qualified, but demands for Swedish qualifications are routinely made in order to exclude minority ethnic applicants (Jederlund, 1998). The DO is dealing with a rapidly increasing flow of formal complaints (reaching a thousand in 1999, including cases of alleged discrimination in public and private services such as housing and education). In 1998 a new government agency, the Integration Office within the Ministry of Culture, was set up to revitalize and develop 'integration policy'. This is said to mark a shift in emphasis beyond the assimilation of minority ethnic groups towards more active promotion of multi-culturalism addressing the ethnic majority's attitudes. A new programme of grants to around 30 different national minority ethnic associations has been introduced as part of this initiative.

Castles and Miller (1998) have proposed a useful typology of Western states. This puts Sweden among the 'classical countries of immigration' which have adopted a 'multicultural model' of assimilationist settlement, a category which also includes Canada, Australia and the US. This regime type is contrasted with the quasi-assimilationist, postcolonial regimes in France, Britain and the Netherlands, and with the guestworker, exclusionary regimes in Germany, Austria and Switzerland. These 'race regimes' are obviously rooted in historical, cultural discourses surrounding national identity, for example, the ethnic German identity reconstructed in the Cold War context, the postcolonial, Anglocentric identity in Britain, and a secure yet internationalist monoculture in Sweden. Certainly the Swedish regime has been comparatively liberal in facilitating the naturalization of settled migrants and has explicitly sought the incorporation and assimilation of minority ethnic communities into Swedish society and the welfare state, modified by some multicultural awareness. However, the economic strains of the 1990s have exposed the tensions between the multi-ethnic reality and the monocultural tradition, leaving the minority ethnic communities increasingly exposed to direct, indirect and structural processes of racism within the labour market and the welfare state.

4   FAMILY POLICIES

4.1   FAMILY-POLICY REFORM

Sweden is well known for its pioneering, interventionist and liberal (as opposed to conservative) family policies, reflecting widely held, long-established values amongst the population. For example, the legal status of illegitimacy was abolished in 1917, liberal divorce reform was introduced in 1920, homosexuality was decriminalized in 1944 and compulsory sex and birth control education was introduced in schools in 1956. Historically, public support for lone mothers and their children has been comparatively generous, and cohabitation has been treated relatively tolerantly. Compared to most other Western states, defenders of a traditional patriarchal view of marriage and the family as an almost sacrosanct private institution have had much less influence. The origins of these liberal values lie deep in Sweden's cultural and socio-economic history, particularly perhaps in its liberal Protestantism and the absence of a conservative Catholic tradition.

The instigation of the People's Home and social democratic Keynesianism in the 1930s was accompanied by a significant wave of reform in family policy. The predominant influence upon the policy-making discourse from the 1930s through to the 1960s was 'population policy', the concern with the declining population size linked to fears of the extinction of the nation. Sweden's birth rate was the lowest in Europe before the war, and the need for positive pronatalist measures was widely accepted, alongside support for birth control to ensure that 'every child should be a wanted child'. Most of the measures adopted in the 1930s were concerned with supporting poor families, including providing free maternity care in public clinics, special public housing schemes for large families, rent rebates according to family size, child tax allowances, marriage loans, guaranteed maintenance for some lone mothers and employment protection for mothers. The effects of the reforms on the birth rate are debatable; it stabilized as elsewhere during the mid 1930s, although this was probably linked more to economic recovery and the fall in unemployment than the family policy reforms.

Socialist and feminist pressures for measures to facilitate women's entry into paid employment were unsuccessful, although married women and mothers were not actively deterred from paid employment as they were in many other countries. In 1948, universal child benefit was introduced, and in the 1950s, statutory provision of birth control and family-planning advice by the health service and statutory maternity leave were implemented. Notably absent from this list is liberal abortion reform, and day care/nursery education for the under sevens (primary school in Sweden starts at the age of seven), both of which represented too much of a challenge to traditional ideology. Policy discourse from the 1920s to the late 1950s was dominated by notions of women's primary roles as mothers and housewives, sustained by the male breadwinner's family wage. Therefore, until the early 1960s, Swedish women made up a smaller proportion of the labour force than the OECD average (Ginsburg 1992, p.203), reflecting also the absence of a war-time mobilization of women workers due to Sweden's neutrality.

A second wave of family policy reform began in the mid 1960s. Pronatalism remained on the agenda and family poverty was also of growing concern, with the rediscovery of family poverty, particularly amongst lone mothers. Of much greater significance than these two factors were the growing demand for women's participation in paid employment and the emergence of second-wave feminism. In the tight labour markets of the 1960s it became quite clear that the LO, the powerful blue collar trade union federation, advocated the recruitment of women into the labour force rather than migrant workers. Fearful that women would be used as cheap labour to undermine the male breadwinner's family wage, the LO strongly supported sex-equality measures in the workplace. Second-wave feminism manifested itself both within the SAP and beyond in radical, liberal and socialist feminist organizations and pressure groups (Jenson and Mahon, 1993; Scott, 1982). This movement advocated the break-up of the sexual division of labour and of patriarchal power in the home, and promoted equal opportunities and affirmative action policies in the welfare state, political representation and employment. All these pressures contributed to what was called the 'sex-role equality' movement, one element of the wider movement for social equality of outcome in the welfare state, which radicalized the Social Democrats in the 1960s. Thus, second-wave feminism had a more profound impact on social policy in Sweden than in most other western states. A number of inter-related factors account for this: the liberal family-policy tradition, the comparatively significant presence of women in the labour market from the 1970s on, and the comparative openness of Swedish social democracy to feminist ideas.

Among the policy reforms ensuing from the sex-role equality movement were liberal abortion law reform (1975), extensive statutory parental leave and universal provision of pre-school child care services (see section 4.3). Workers with pre-school children were given the right to work part time (six hours a day) without loss of status. Probably most significant of all, in 1971 the implementation of mandatory independent taxation for men and women made it much more financially advantageous to a household for a woman to have a paid job than had been the case before (Hobson et al., 1995, p.5). This second wave of family policy reform made a contribution, entirely unquantifiable, to two phenomena associated with the 1970s and 1980s: a significant increase in the birth rate and a sharp increase in women's paid employment. By the late 1980s Sweden had one of the highest birth rates among the OECD countries and women's 'economic activity' was also among the highest in the OECD; 80 per cent of working age women were in the labour force, compared to around 85 per cent of men, a level more or less sustained through the 1990s. In sections 4.2 and 4.3, we look at two important aspects of family policy in a little more detail: the treatment of lone-mother families and the provision of parental leave and day-care for children.

4.2 LONE-MOTHER FAMILIES

The case of lone mothers provides a good illustration of both the achievements and the limitations of family policy in contemporary Sweden. OECD (1998b) data indicate that the proportion of lone-parent households (of which around 90 per cent are headed by lone mothers) rose gradually over the post-war period until the 1980s when it reached 20 per cent. More recently, the figure has declined slightly, and the proportions of lone-parent families in the US and UK have overtaken Swedish levels. National data on living standards suggests that in 1991 only 15 per cent of families in Sweden had a lone parent (Hobson and Takahashi, 1997). This discrepancy may be explained in part by the increasing phenomena of parents cohabiting part time and of joint parenting, where a child lives partly with the father and partly with the mother. Whatever the diverse and complex realities, the most striking fact about contemporary lone-motherhood in Sweden has been the low and declining level of poverty amongst lone-mother households. Less than 4 per cent of Swedish lone-mother households were poor in the early 1990s, compared with almost 60 per cent in the US. Although the proportion of lone mothers with paid employment was a little higher in Sweden in comparison to the US, the key difference was that, on average, Swedish lone parents earned much higher wages and salaries, and also derived a significantly greater proportion of their income from benefits and from paternal maintenance (Lewis, 1997). As Hobson and Takahashi (1997, p.133) observe, lone mothers in Sweden have not 'been targeted as a problem group in policy debates ... a discourse on the decline of the traditional family has little resonance in Sweden in contrast to the situation in Britain and the United States'. There appears to be an important cultural difference here, again reflecting the particularity of Swedish family policy discourse, as we discussed above.

Although there is no guaranteed minimum income for lone parents, 'advanced maintenance payments' were introduced in 1937 and subsequently have been considerably improved. These index-linked, flat-rate payments are about one and a half times the rate of child benefit, but 'payment is conditional on the custodial parent assisting in efforts to establish paternity' (Kindlund, 1988, p.89) so that not all lone-mother families receive it. Lone mothers who choose not to reveal the identity of the father can still be denied financial compensation for the absence of a parent, and in that respect, remain unequal with other families. Another significant element of the Swedish policy discourse on lone mothers is that they have always been expected to support themselves and their children through paid employment. Hence, in the era of women's domesticity in the 1950s and 1960s, lone mothers were considered quite differently from mothers in two-parent families. In 1968 85 per cent of lone mothers had paid employment compared with only 45 per cent of married mothers (Hobson and Takahashi, 1997, p.134). The explosive growth of paid employment amongst married mothers in the 1970s and 1980s eradicated much of this difference. Lone mothers also benefited from the universal family policy reforms, particularly the development of pre-school childcare services. Nevertheless, many lone mothers continue to shoulder the triple burden of full-time work, childcaring and the absence of paternal income and/or support. The economic restructuring and mass unemployment of the 1990s appear to have had a differentially adverse impact on lone mothers; unemployment among lone mothers rose from 4 per cent in 1985 to 12 per cent in 1995 (Hobson and Takahashi, 1997, p.136). The future for lone mothers is intimately connected with the uncertain future of the labour market and social expenditure as a whole. Lone-mother families in Sweden probably remain more generously supported by the welfare state than in any other country in the world, but they are far from equal with two-parent families.

4.3 PARENTAL LEAVE AND DAYCARE

The growth of women's paid employment from the 1960s onwards and the rise of the sex-equality and women's movements have made a striking impact on policy concerning the parenting and care of children, particularly pre-school children. By the early 1980s over 80 per cent of Swedish mothers of pre-school children were in paid employment. Policy had developed in two directions: first, it gave parents very substantial statutory rights to paid leave to care for children, and second, there was greatly increased public investment in day care. Parental leave and benefit (replacing maternity leave and benefit) became part of the social insurance system in 1974, since when it has been extended and adjusted (see Hobson *et al.*, 1995, pp.14–18). As of 1998, parents were, together, entitled to 360 days leave at 80 per cent of salary up to the child's eighth birthday. Parents can decide how to share this leave between them, but a minimum of 30 days has to be taken by each parent – the so-called 'daddy month'. By the 1990s, fathers were using about 10 per cent of parental insurance benefits. Another 90 days' leave on a fixed rate allowance is also available; parents not in paid employment receive this allowance for 450 days. Mothers are also entitled to 50 days' pregnancy leave on parental benefit. Fathers are entitled to 10 days' leave on parental benefit when a child is born with a take-up rate of 80 per cent. Furthermore, either parent can take up to 60 days' leave (with benefits) per year per child to care for a sick child. In 1996 31 per cent of the latter was used by fathers.

A very significant sexual division of labour in parenting clearly remains and this is reflected in the take-up of parental leave. This is in part a reflection of the considerable disparity in earnings between mothers and fathers. Hence, 'the kinds of decisions families make around the uses of parental leave, child sick days, and the day-to-day organization of care, that is mainly women's work, cannot be divorced from their position in the labour market and vice versa' (Hobson *et al.*, 1995, p.18). Nevertheless, Swedish policy still goes much further than almost any other welfare state in facilitating and supporting both parents in juggling working life with parenting.

Public provision and funding of daycare for children, both after school for older children and pre-school for the under sevens, has probably been the most significant new development in the Swedish welfare state in the last three decades. Up to the early 1970s, pre-school children were largely cared for privately by mothers, relatives, nannies or childminders; a small minority attended nurseries or nursery schools. A major investment in pre-school and after-school care began in the 1970s, so that, by 1998, virtually all six-year-olds were attending pre-school classes, the majority of seven to nine-year-olds were attending after-school leisure centres and 73 per cent of children aged one to five were enrolled in publicly provided pre-school child care. Around 80 per cent of the latter is provided in 'pre-schools', which are open all year round and in the evenings. The bulk of the cost is shared between local and central government: parents pay a modest, means-tested fee per hour. The other form of public provision is 'family day-care', which is provided by salaried, municipal childminders in their own homes, and is more common in rural areas and small towns. The proportion of children in family day care has been in decline in recent years as pre-schools have become the norm. The demand for public day-care has consistently outstripped the supply as local authorities have tried to keep up. Parliament passed legislation in 1985 decreeing that all children over 18 months old should have access to publicly provided day-care, but the target date of implementation in 1991 was not met, prompting unprecedented levels of investment in new day-care facilities. In 1995 local authorities were given a duty to provide childcare 'without undue delay for all children requiring it' and this aim appears to have been met. However, it seems to have been achieved to some extent at the expense of the much increased numbers of unemployed people, whose children are largely excluded from public childcare. Also excluded are children with a parent looking after a younger sibling at home (Swedish Institute, 1999c, p.3). Such features suggest that the provision of day-care is driven principally by labour market considerations, with the needs of children and parent carers as secondary. Nonetheless, the fulfilment of much of the sex-equality agenda for social policy established in 1970s is, especially in a comparative perspective, an impressive testimony to the modernization and adaptation of the People's Home and the social democratic heritage.

4.4 THE NEW PATRIARCHY?

Comparative analysis of family and gender policies puts Sweden firmly in the 'dual breadwinner' (Lewis, 1993) or 'parent-worker' (Hobson, 1995) regime categories for reasons that are readily apparent from the examples above. Hernes (1987) sees Scandinavian welfare corporatism

as a reconstitution of patriarchy in male-dominated corporate institutions, upon which women are particularly dependent. Women are
much more reliant on the welfare state for paid employment than men,
and their daily lives depend much more directly on the services and
benefits of the welfare state than do men's lives, because women still
carry the greater burden of unpaid domestic and caring work. Borchorst
and Siim (1987, p.154) also suggest that, as a result of the substantial
gains for women from the development of the welfare state, patriarchal
power is now maintained by 'the institutionalization of women's dual
roles as mothers and workers', which has left men free to consolidate
their power in public and private corporate institutions. The
Scandinavian welfare state has thus had a contradictory impact for
women. On the one hand, it is comparatively 'woman friendly' having
partially swept away traditional patriarchal assumptions about the
primacy of women's unpaid domestic work. On the other, it has
established newer forms of patriarchal dependence for women in
partnership with the welfare state as both employer and provider
(Hobson *et al.*, 1995, p.3).

5   CONCLUSION: ADAPTING TO THE EU AND GLOBALIZATION

This brief and selective review of Swedish social policy suggests that
the social democratic model remains very much intact, but that it has
been adjusted and adapted in response to pressures, which came to a
head in the economic and unemployment crises of the early 1990s. The
source of these pressures can be traced to a withdrawal of support for
the 'Swedish model' by big business, which in turn is linked to the
phenomenon of economic globalization: the growth of transnational
corporations, trade and capital markets. From the late 1970s, Sweden's
increasingly transnational industries were moving abroad to escape the
fetters and costs of the Swedish model, while foreign investors shied
away for the same reasons. During the 1980s Swedish business
embraced more insistently the twin discourses of global competitiveness
and neo-liberalism, and were strongly supportive of the European single
market and Swedish entry to the EU, and the deregulation of capital
and labour markets. The Employers' Federation sought 'a diminished
role for organized labour and the state, as a counter-hegemonic project'
(Clement, 1994, p.375). In 1990, in an act of great symbolism, the
employers withdrew from the national wage-bargaining structures
dating back to the 1930s. The pressure reached something of a political
climax with the election of a coalition government of the four 'bourgeois'
parties in 1991. Neo-liberal influence was successful in inaugurating
some modest restrictions in the extent of the welfare state (as discussed
above) and above all in securing Sweden's entry into the EU in 1995.
However, neo-liberal strategy was also undermined by the sudden and
dramatic rise in unemployment and the economic recession, which
increased needs and demands for welfare state protection. Hence, the

Social Democrats were restored to government in 1994 with a proportion of the vote that equalled those achieved in the golden age. However, in the next election in 1998, their vote slumped to the lowest proportion since the 1920s forcing the SAP into a loose coalition with the Greens and with the Left Party who doubled their vote to 12 per cent on a platform of robust defence of the welfare state. As elsewhere in Western Europe, the neo-liberal momentum built up in the 1980s has been stalled by the revival of social democracy since the mid 1990s.

Although globalization is conventionally associated with the increasing size and velocity of transnational flows of goods, services and finance, it can also be seen to incorporate increasing transnational flows of people through migration and of ideas, for example, about universal human rights. In some of these respects Sweden can claim to have adjusted to globalization comparatively progressively and successfully, for example in terms of the rights of women parents and asylum seekers, as well as in its renewed efforts to maintain a tolerant, multi-ethnic civil society. It could be suggested, nonetheless, that the impact of EU membership has been most widely seen as distilling the problems of globalization for Sweden. The EU, particularly its convergence criteria for monetary union, is held to be responsible in part for the erosion of Swedish welfare as perceived by supporters of the Swedish model (Gould, 1999). The harmonization of economic policies seems to be leading to a harmonization of social policies, which would mean a further reduction in the generosity and universalism of the welfare state. Yet social policy harmonization is a long way off, and may even have slipped off the EU agenda altogether in the late 1990s, while the economic and political future of a small country like Sweden outside the EU seems fraught with risks and uncertainties. Back in the crisis of the early 1990s, Rudolf Meidner (1994, p.344), one of the architects of post war social democratic economic policy, asked whether the Swedish model could survive the onslaught of neo-liberalism and EU entry. His answer was that Sweden within the EU 'can choose to preserve the main components of its own model' and that any dismantling would be 'a question of *political* choice rather than one of economic necessity'. As the new century opens, such a choice has certainly not been made. Hence, that keen advocate of corporate neo-liberalism, *The Economist,* can continue to bemoan the lack of affordability of Sweden's 'bloated' welfare state in the long term and suggest that the Swedish model is 'heading into a cul-de-sac' (Smiley, 1999, p.9). Certainly, Sweden's ranking in terms of GDP per head has fallen from fifth to fifteenth within the OECD over the last two decades, but as *The Economist* is forced to admit, 'Sweden is still a remarkably comfortable, steady, decent, peaceful and egalitarian sort of country' (Smiley, 1999, p.10).

The 1990s witnessed some apparent trade offs, which seem likely to continue to shape policy discourse and outcomes in the future. The development of the welfare state has been contained and restructured, even reversed in some respects in the name of making the economy, particularly the labour market, more competitive. At the same time, some degree of economic growth and affluence has been sacrificed in order to preserve the universal welfare state, which achieves comparatively egalitarian outcomes in terms of social divisions of class, gender and possibly even 'race'.

REFERENCES

Adema, W. (1999) *Net Social Expenditure: Labour Market and Social Policy – Occasional Paper, No.39*, Paris, OECD.

Baldwin, P. (1990) *The Politics of Social Solidarity*, Cambridge, Cambridge University Press.

Borchorst, A. and Siim, B. (1987) 'Women and the advanced welfare state – a new kind of patriarchal power?', in Sassoon, A. (ed.) *Women and The State*, London, Hutchinson.

Burniaux, J-M., Dang, T-T., Fore, D., Förster, M., Mira d'Ercole, M. and Oxley, H. (1998) *Income Distribution and Poverty in Selected OECD Countries: Economics Department Working Papers No.189*, Paris, OECD.

Castles, S. and Miller, M. (1998) *The Age of Migration*, Basingstoke, Macmillan.

Clasen, J., Gould, A. and Vincent, J. (1998) *Voices Within and Without: Responses to Long Term Unemployment in Germany, Sweden and Britain*, Bristol, Policy Press.

Clement, W. (1994) 'Exploring the limits of social democracy: regime change in Sweden', in Clement, W. and Mahon, R. (eds) *Swedish Social Democracy: A Model in Transition*, Toronto, Canadian Scholars' Press.

Cousins, C. (1999) *Society, Work and Welfare in Europe*, Basingstoke, Macmillan.

Deland, M. (1997) 'The cultural racism of Sweden', *Race and Class*, vol.39, no.1, pp.51–60.

Esping-Andersen, G. and Korpi, W. (1984) 'Social policy as class politics in post-war capitalism', in Goldthorpe, J. (ed.) *Order and Conflict in Contemporary Capitalism*, Oxford, Oxford University Press.

Esping-Andersen, G. (1990) *Three Worlds of Welfare Capitalism*, Cambridge, Polity Press.

Freedland, J. (1997) 'Master race of the Left', *The Guardian: The Week*, 30 August, pp.1–2.

Ginsburg, N. (1992) *Divisions of Welfare*, London, Sage.

Gould, A. (1996) 'Sweden: the last bastion of social democracy', in George, V. and Taylor-Gooby, P. (eds) *European Welfare Policy: Squaring the Welfare Circle*, Basingstoke, Macmillan.

Gould, A. (1999) 'The erosion of the welfare state: Swedish social policy and the EU', *European Journal of Social Policy*, vol.9, no.2, pp.165–74.

Hammar, T. (1984) 'Sweden', in Hammar, T. (ed.) *European Immigration Policy*, Cambridge, Cambridge University Press.

Haydon, S. (1997) 'Sweden admits to racial purification', *The Independent*, 25 August, p.10.

Heclo, H. (1984) *Modern Social Politics in Britain and Sweden*, New Haven, Yale University Press.

Heclo, H. and Madsen, H. (1987) *Policy and Politics in Sweden*, Philadelphia, Temple University Press.

Hernes, H. (1987) 'Women and the welfare state: the transition from private to public dependence', in Sassoon, A. (ed.) *Women and the State*, London, Hutchinson.

Hirst, P. (1999) 'Globalization and social democracy', in Gamble, A. and Wright, T. (eds) *The New Social Democracy*, Oxford, Blackwell.

Hobson, B. (1995) 'Remaking the boundaries of women's citizenship and the dilemma of dependency', in Kauppinen, K. and Gordon, T. (eds) *Unsolved Dilemmas: Women, Work and the Family in the United States, Europe and the Soviet Union*, Aldershot, Ashgate.

Hobson, B., Johansson, S., Olah, L. and Sutton, C. (1995) 'Gender and the Swedish welfare state', in Brundson, E. and May, M. (eds) *Swedish Welfare: Policy and Provision*, London, Social Policy Association.

Hobson, B. and Takahashi, M. (1997) 'The parent-worker model: lone mothers in Sweden', in Lewis, J. (ed.) *Lone Mothers in European Welfare Regimes*, London, Jessica Kingsley.

Jederlund, L. (1998) 'From immigration policy to integration policy', *Current Sweden*, no.422, Swedish Institute, www.si.se, accessed January 2001.

Jenson, J. and Mahon, R. (1993) 'Representing solidarity: class, gender and the crisis in Social-Democratic Sweden', *New Left Review*, No.201, pp.76–100.

Kindlund, S. (1988) 'Sweden', in Kahn, A. and Kamerman, S. (eds) *Child Support: Cross Cultural Studies*, Newbury Park (CA), Sage.

Korpi, W. (1978) *The Working Class in Welfare Capitalism*, London, Routledge.

Larsson, S. (1991) 'Swedish racism: the democratic way', *Race and Class*, vol.32, no.3.

Lewis, J. (1993) 'Introduction', in Lewis, J. (ed.) *Women and Social Policies in Europe*, Aldershot, Edward Elgar.

Lewis, J. (1997) 'Introduction', in Lewis, J. (ed.) *Lone Mothers in European Welfare Regimes*, London, Jessica Kingsley.

Meidner, R. (1994) 'The rise and fall of the Swedish model', in Clement, W. and Mahon, R. (eds) *Swedish Social Democracy: A Model in Transition*, Toronto, Canadian Scholars' Press.

Myrdal, G. (1938) 'Population problems and policies', *Annals of the American Academy of Political and Social Science*, vol.197, March.

Myrdal, G. (1940) *Population and Democracy*, Cambridge (MA), Harvard University Press.

OECD (1998a) *Background Documents, The Caring World: National Achievements – Tables and Charts*, DEELSA/ELSA/MIN(98)2/ANN, Paris, Organization for Economic Cooperation and Development.

OECD (1998b) *Background Documents, The Caring World: An Analysis – Tables and Charts*, DEELSA/ELSA/MIN(98)3/ANN, Paris, Organization for Economic Cooperation and Development.

Pontusson, J. (1994) 'Sweden: after the golden age', in Anderson, P. and Camiller, P. (eds) *Mapping the West European Left*, London, Verso.

Scott, H. (1982) *Sweden's 'Right to be Human'*, London, Allison and Busby.

Smiley, X. (1999) 'The Nordic Countries Survey', *The Economist*, Supplement, 23 January.

Ståhlberg, A-C. (1995) 'The Swedish pension system: past, present and future' in Brundson, E. and May, M. (eds) *Swedish Welfare: Policy and Provision*, London, Social Policy Association.

Ståhlberg, A-C. (1997) 'Sweden: on the way from standard to basic security?', in Clasen, J. (ed.) *Social Insurance in Europe*, Bristol, Policy Press.

Statistics Sweden (1999) *Sweden in Figures 2000*, http://www.scb.se/scbeng/svsiffror/svsiffroreng.htm

Stephens, J. (1979) *The Transition from Capitalism to Socialism*, London, Macmillan.

Swedish Institute (1998) *The Swedish Economy, Fact Sheets on Sweden*, Svenska Institutet.

Swedish Institute (1999a) *Immigrants in Sweden, Fact Sheets on Sweden*, Svenska Institutet.

Swedish Institute (1999b) *Swedish Labour Market Policy, Fact Sheets on Sweden*, Svenska Institutet.

Swedish Institute (1999c) *Childcare in Sweden, Fact Sheets on Sweden*, Svenska Institutet.

Therborn, G. (1989) '"Pillarization" and "popular movements"', in Castles, F. (ed.) *The Comparative History of Public Policy*, Cambridge, Polity Press.

Thoursie, A. (1998) 'Sweden', in *Trends*, no.30, European Employment Observatory for the European Commission, Berlin, Institute for Applied Socio-Economics.

Widgren, J. (1982) 'The status of immigrant workers in Sweden', in Thomas, E-J. (ed.) *Immigrant Workers in Europe: Their Legal Status*, Paris, The Unesco Press.

CHAPTER 7
IRELAND: FROM CATHOLIC CORPORATISM TO SOCIAL PARTNERSHIP

EUGENE McLAUGHLIN

CONTENTS

	INTRODUCTION	224
	THE DEFINING FEATURES OF CATHOLIC CORPORATISM: THE ORIGINAL 'THIRD WAY'?	224
1	CATHOLIC CORPORATIST SETTLEMENT, 1922–45	227
1.1	CHURCH AND STATE	227
1.2	THE IDEOLOGY OF 'MOTHER IRELAND'	229
2	TOWARDS A POST-WAR WELFARE STATE?	232
2.1	THE CHANGING NATURE OF THE STATE'S ECONOMIC POLICIES	232
2.2	SOCIAL CHANGES	234
2.3	THE CHANGING POSITION OF THE CATHOLIC CHURCH	234
3	THE IMPACT OF POST-WAR SHIFTS IN SOCIAL EXPENDITURE	235
3.1	EMPLOYMENT	236
3.2	TAXATION	236
3.3	WELFARE EXPENDITURE OUTCOMES	237
4	SOCIAL PARTNERSHIP: THE BASIS FOR A NEW WELFARE SETTLEMENT	239
4.1	SOCIAL PARTNERSHIP	240
4.2	SOCIAL INCLUSION AND THE NATIONAL ANTI-POVERTY STRATEGY	242
5	THE OTHER SIDE OF PARTNERSHIP: WOMEN, WELFARE AND CITIZENSHIP	244
5.1	DISCRIMINATION IN THE LABOUR MARKET	245
5.2	REFORM, REACTION AND FURTHER REFORM	246
5.3	CONTRACEPTION	247
5.4	ABORTION	248
5.5	DIVORCE	251
5.6	THE FUTURE OF THE IRISH FAMILY	252
6	CONCLUSION	255
	REFERENCES	256

INTRODUCTION

There is general agreement that the Republic of Ireland (hereafter referred to as Ireland) poses a challenge to conventional definitions of a welfare state. Esping-Andersen's (1990) formulation of a 'Catholic corporatist' welfare regime provides a useful conceptual starting-point for Irish social policy debates, particularly on the gendering of welfare relations. However, two points need to be borne in mind. First, Ireland's social policy history cannot be divorced from its colonial experience. And second, waves of globalization, on-going European integration and post-colonial socio-cultural transformations are constructing a 'cross-cutting' welfare regime of increasing complexity. The stance taken in this chapter is that, although there is no once-and-for-all correct classification of Ireland's welfare regime, 'partnership' is the recurring theme linking the various stages of Irish social welfare development.

This chapter begins by briefly exploring the historical evolution of social policy in Ireland between 1922 (when independence was gained) and the end of the Second World War. This period witnessed the construction of an integral Catholic nation state with the teachings and practices of the Church governing many aspects of social policy. As a consequence, the state viewed social welfare as being primarily the responsibility of the family and voluntary – that is, Church – organizations. The chapter then looks at the shifts in the 1970s and 1980s towards an institutional form of welfare. The exact nature of the state's involvement and social security and expenditure outcomes are examined. It is argued that, despite the dramatic increases in state welfare expenditure, Catholic social teaching still played a considerable role in ideologically shaping the contours of social policy in Ireland during this period. It is not until the late 1990s and the formation of the 'Celtic Tiger' economy that we witness the institutionalization of a 'social partnership' approach and the foregrounding of strategies to tackle social exclusion and marginalization. By examining how social policies have operated in Ireland we are provided with one of the clearest examples of how Catholic corporatism can severely restrict women's economic, social and reproductive rights. However, before discussing the specifics of the Irish case, it is necessary to relate the general features of this welfare regime.

THE DEFINING FEATURES OF CATHOLIC CORPORATISM: THE ORIGINAL 'THIRD WAY'?

In the late nineteenth century and the first decades of the twentieth, the Catholic Church enunciated a set of corporatist principles which it believed should guide social and political matters in Catholic countries. Catholic corporatism was a conservative response to 'a world that was growing more liberal and democratic, more urban and industrial, and more secular and scientific' (Hynes, 1990, p.55). It was also propagated as a 'Third Way' between the extremes of free market capitalism and communism. Catholic social thinkers favoured a social and moral order based on small-scale capitalism, family property, small businesses and farms. These social thinkers wanted to ensure that the political and civic culture of Catholic nations was also imbued with a Catholic ethos. Central to their vision of the world were the principles of subsidiarity, family solidarity and social consensus.

In response to the emergence of strong nation states, a 1931 Papal Encyclical, *Quadragesimo Anno*, espoused the principle of subsidiarity as a means of circumscribing state encroachment on voluntary welfare and charity arrangements (Grogan, 1978). The state was viewed as a functional necessity – an integrating force in society which had the important role of ensuring social order. However, it should refrain from intervening in economic and social affairs unless either the national interest or social equilibrium was threatened. The Encyclical stated that: 'It is an injustice and at the same time a great evil and disturbance of right order to assign to a greater and higher association what lesser and subordinate organizations can do' (quoted in Whyte, 1980, p.67). Welfare services should be delivered by voluntary organizations, the appropriate role for the state being to oversee and facilitate their activities.

Catholic social teaching stressed that the family was the 'first and vital cell of society'. It 'knitted' society together and the institution of marriage 'knitted' families and communities together. The family was the carrier of Catholic social values and the link between past, present and future (Coman, 1977). Since it predated the state, the latter had no right to interfere with it as long as it fulfilled its responsibilities and cared for the welfare of its members. The function of the state and voluntary organizations was to protect the family so that it could carry out its reproductive, socialization and welfare obligations. And, as Peillon has noted:

> In defending the family unit and independence of voluntary organizations, the Church was seeking to consolidate its own authority and influence. By means of voluntary associations the Church can dominate such spheres of activity as health and social services. Further, it is in a position to exercise greater influence on a family which has not been integrated into a state-controlled, welfare framework, and is therefore dependent on the state. Thus, the bitter opposition between Church and state can be seen as the clash of rival notions of the place of the family in society, and an expression of the Church's determination, by keeping the state at bay, to hold its ground in those areas where it has always maintained a preponderant influence.
>
> (Peillon, 1982, p.95)

As we will see in this chapter, the centrality of the family within Catholic corporatism had considerable implications for the position of Irish women.

Peter Williamson has argued that Catholic social teaching conceived of the social order 'in terms of a natural, and therefore immutable, hierarchy of status, with different privileges, rights and duties being granted to those of different status' (1989, p.23). This patrimonial hierarchical society offered the possibility of realizing social consensus in a manner that individualistic free market liberalism and totalitarian communism could not. In order to reproduce harmonious social relations, Catholic social teaching believed in the necessity of a corporatist approach to social and economic affairs. There should be institutional structures linking different interest and status groups together and these structures should have formal representation within the state. And, finally, this corporatist approach stressed that there should be a common set of moral values – provided by Catholicism – which would bond society together. Corporatism also dovetailed neatly with the principles of subsidiarity and family solidarity because 'the collective solidarity of a guild, fraternity or mutuality was clearly closer to the family unit, and hence more capable of serving its needs than was the more remote central state' (Esping-Andersen, 1990, p.61). Thus, Catholic social teaching argued for:

> ... a society in which socio-professional groups organize themselves into corporations and collaborate in decision making, and in which the independence of the family and voluntary organizations from the state is guaranteed. This Catholic corporatist organization ensures [in principle] that all voices are heard and that institutionalized dialogue is geared towards producing class harmony.
>
> (Peillon, 1982, p.96)

Although Catholic corporatism believes that, ideally, the state should have a minimal role to play in the provision and delivery of welfare, there is not the liberal or neo-liberal obsession with strictly adhering to free market principles. Subsidiarity allows the state to intervene if the family's capacity to care for its members is exhausted and/or when it is socially necessary. Furthermore, Catholic corporatism does not necessarily preclude state expenditure on welfare so long as subsidiary organizations retain responsibility for the actual delivery of services and it is geared towards the 'social good' and support of the family. Although there is no commitment to redistributive or egalitarian social policies or full employment, the state should not preside over extreme inequalities or manifest social injustice. Thus, Catholic corporatist welfare regimes can embody both liberal and social-democratic welfare principles. As a consequence, they can lay claim to offering a distinctive 'Third Way' in debates about social welfare.

1   CATHOLIC CORPORATIST SETTLEMENT, 1922–45

1.1   CHURCH AND STATE

The political order established in Ireland in the aftermath of the war of independence (1919–21), partition (1920) and civil war (1922–23) embodied both liberal democratic and authoritarian features (Prager, 1986; Garvin, 1996). The ideologies of Catholicism and nationalism fused to shape both the nature of the state and the relationship between the state and society. In no other European state, with the exception of Poland, was such a close relationship established between the Catholic Church and national identity and it played the pivotal role of bestowing legitimacy and authority on the new nation state (Schmitt, 1973). Organizationally, the Church provided the institutional links between the new political, economic and social élites and the masses. It was able to perform such a hegemonic role in the shaping of the new state because: first, the aspirations for Irish nationhood were inextricably linked to the Church; second, in the course of the nineteenth century it was allowed by the British colonial administration to broaden its influence throughout the social infrastructure; and, third, over 90 per cent of the country was Catholic. The Church was able, as both a 'state-in-waiting' and the moral guardian of constitutional nationalism, to ensure that 'post-colonial' Ireland made the transition to Catholic nationhood (see Whyte, 1980; Keogh, 1996; Inglis, 1998). As a consequence, 'the Catholic hierarchy assumed a major role in determining the social and moral climate within which the Free State was to be governed' (Cooney, 1986, p.42).

Nationalism played a double role in the shaping of post-colonial Irish society. First, the divisions created by the civil war shaped the core of Irish politics and society. The two main political parties that emerged – Fine Gael and Fianna Fail – represented the different sides in the civil war. The enduring legacy of the civil war, therefore, was the virtually unbridgeable gap between the victors who accepted the partition of the country (Fine Gael) and those who opposed it (Fianna Fail). The bitter debate about the 'unfinished' nationalist-republican project came to dominate all others and even today these two political parties do not divide on any recognizable right/left basis on political, economic and social issues. Both are essentially centre-right in the mould of European Christian Democratic parties. An electoral system based upon proportional representation has reinforced the need for both parties to project themselves as representing the national, as opposed to class, interests, and during the 1990s forced them into coalition with smaller political parties. Fianna Fail has been more successful in this respect, appealing to a coalition of the small farmers, significant sections of the working class and the lower middle class. Fine Gael, by contrast, has traditionally had difficulty in securing electoral support outside of the large farming class and professional middle classes. Thus partition, the resultant civil war and the electoral system adversely affected the significance of class politics and, as Whyte (1974) has argued, a 'politics without social bases' was created.

The labour movement failed to win a leading role in the shaping of the Irish state. Its political influence was directly affected by partition because the industrial heartland of the country was located within the six counties of Northern Ireland (O'Connor, 1992). In the late 1920s as little as 5 per cent of the population in southern Ireland was engaged in manufacturing. As a consequence, it was the economic interests of the conservative farm-owning class that initially took precedence within the new state. In addition, the idea was promulgated that, because British rule and the Protestant Establishment had been overthrown, Ireland was somehow a classless society. This linked into a wider social acceptance of a hierarchical society where deferential social relations were ordained by the Church as being natural.

The integrative ideologies of Catholicism and nationalism shaped the Irish state and the national identity into an exclusive, culturally homogeneous, conservative one. A concerted attempt was made to subordinate all socio-economic interests to the nationalist-populist project of constructing and consolidating a Catholic, Gaelic and pastoral 'imagined community'. Both ideologies stressed the importance of national consensus, and social movements which were deemed to threaten this project – particularly ones espousing secularist ideologies – were neutralized (Girvin, 1984; Lane, 1997). The state, for example, in the immediate years after independence dealt with its enemies – for instance, trade unions, the rural 'soviets' and farm labourers' organizations, the fascist 'Blueshirts' and the IRA – in a ruthless manner. Thus, the divisions caused by the civil war and partition left deep scars on the national psyche and deeply conservative political and social entities rapidly unfolded, both north and south of the border (see Munck, 1985).

So how did this ideological framework impact upon Irish social policy? After gaining independence, Ireland was faced with a series of possible pathways in relation to social welfare and social legislation. The new state was bequeathed a variety of British welfare policies and insti-tutional arrangements, ranging from the Poor Law to public health, housing and educational provision. Irish citizens had experience of state provision of old-age pensions and compulsory social insurance for manual workers and low-paid white-collar employees (Powell, 1992; Burke, 1999). In theory, therefore, the new state under the 1922 constitution could have committed itself to building a secular welfare infrastructure. However, there was also considerable opposition in the 'new' Ireland to the whole idea of state involvement in social policy. First, middle-class nationalists had consistently complained about excessive taxation under the British and argued that they could run a more efficient administration. Second, there was a shift supported by the Department of Finance towards laissez-faire economic policies and sound public finances with the result that severe restrictions were imposed on public expenditure and taxes were lowered. Third, there was the emergence of the powerful Catholic Social Movement in the 1920s and 1930s which argued that the state should limit itself to overseeing the activities of the various subsidiary welfare organizations. Hence, 'Catholic social philosophy, economic exigencies, and the nationalist tradition, all argued for a state whose role would be less substantial than in most European nations' (Lyons, 1979, p.476).

The Church took the lead role in the provision and management of the education and health services and in organizing public charity and assistance for the poor. As a consequence of the Catholicization, the social policy changes that did take place were haphazard and primarily administrative in nature (Fahey, 1998). Although some progress was made during the 1930s (for example, the 1933 Unemployment Assistance Act, the 1939 Public Assistance Act, and the public housing programme), the social services which existed at the end of the Second World War differed little in their essential residual characteristics from those of the early 1920s (Maguire, 1986; Burke, 1999).

1.2   THE IDEOLOGY OF 'MOTHER IRELAND'

The ideologies governing social policy determined that the family should take primary responsibility for welfare. In order to make sure that this happened, women were allocated a 'special' role by the Irish state and Catholic Church. The welfare of the family, Church and nation and the renewal of the post-colonial Irish 'race' were directly linked to the position of women in Irish society.

There were general improvements in the status of women in Irish society in the early twentieth century and the suffragette movement pressed nationalists and trade unionists on the question of women's rights in the new Ireland (see Cullen Owens, 1984). Women played a central role in the war of independence and the electorate enabled Constance Markiewicz, a leading Republican, to become the first woman ever elected to Westminster. However, as Kelly and Nic Giolla Choille have argued, 'independence for Ireland did not mean independence for women' (1990, p.11). In the 1930s the Fianna Fail government, under Eamon de Valera, and the Catholic Church decided to confront these 'unmanageable revolutionaries' and to clarify once and for all the role and rights of women in Irish society (see Ward, 1983).

In the 1930s the Land Commission, which was set up to implement the government's land redistribution policies, refused women the right to inherit land. In 1932 a marriage bar (similar to that which then operated in Britain) was instituted when the government banned the employment of married women as civil service employees. This policy of compulsory retirement upon marriage was subsequently adopted by many sectors of the Irish economy, particularly after the passing of the 1933 Conditions of Employment Act which allowed the government to prohibit female employment in any form of industrial work and to set quotas for particular sectors. Women's groups opposed this legislation arguing, unsuccessfully, that it contradicted the 1922 constitution which had given equal rights and opportunities to all citizens of the new republic (Owens, 1983).

Women's fears that the state and the Catholic Church were determined to push through enforced domestication were confirmed when de Valera unveiled the 1937 constitution. The new constitution created a theocratic state by legislating a set of principles which ensured that state policies remained within the parameters set by Catholic social teaching (Inglis, 1985). It gave formal recognition to the 'holy trinity' of the family, Church and nation and outlined a series of social policy principles which were intended to re-establish and reinforce traditional gender relations by removing women from the labour market and public life. Article 40 qualified the commitment to equality before the law by allowing the state to have 'due regard to difference of capacity, physical and moral and social function'. De Valera argued that:

> In regard to labour and in regard to work, our aim ought to be that the breadwinner, who is normally and naturally in these cases, when alive, the father of the family, should be able by his work to bring in enough to maintain the whole household and that women ought not to be forced by economic necessity to go out and either supplement his wages or become breadwinners themselves.

(quoted in Moynihan, 1980, p.324)

Women's groups fought against the retrogressive provisions of the new constitution. They demanded restoration of clauses of the old constitution which guaranteed the equality of all citizens of the republic. Although women won back the clause which guaranteed political participation 'without distinction of sex', they failed to reverse the economic and social policy clauses. The constitution made it clear that women's primary role in Irish society was looking after the welfare of the family (Daly, 1981). Thus, Article 41 on 'The Family' stated:

41.1.1   The State recognizes the Family as the natural, primary and fundamental unit group of Society, and as a moral institution possessing inalienable and imprescriptible rights antecedent and superior to all positive law.

2.   The State, therefore, guarantees to protect the Family in its constitution and authority, as the necessary basis of social order and as indispensable to the welfare of the Nation and the State.

41.2.1   In particular, the State recognizes that by her life within the family home, woman gives to the State a support without which the common good cannot be achieved.

2.   The State shall, therefore, endeavour to ensure that mothers shall not be obliged by economic necessity to engage in labour to the neglect of their duties in the home.

The constitution legally established that the family was the principal institution in Irish society and that women were mothers, carers and dependants whose lives lay in the home. As a result:

> For almost thirty years after the constitution was adopted, the position of women in Irish society hardly changed at all. The common law regulation of women to domesticity and powerlessness continued. Laws based on the premise that women's rights were inferior to those of men survived in, and indeed even appeared on, the statute books.

(Scannell, 1988, p.127)

The state and the Church were at one in ensuring that family law and reproductive rights legislation reinforced the position of women in the family. The constitution banned divorce, and the sale, advertising and importation of contraceptives were legally prohibited under the Censorship of Publications Act 1929 and Section 17 of the Criminal Law Amendment Act 1935. As Pyle has pointed out: 'Males were granted the right of sexual access to their wives, which, combined with the difficulty in obtaining contraceptives, reinforced female subordination in the household by precluding female control over reproduction and via the increased work load for women that the resultant higher fertility rates involved' (Pyle, 1990a, p.95).

Women were denied access to legal aid; no welfare was available as of right to unmarried mothers, deserted wives or prisoners' wives. A battered wife could not exclude her violent husband from the home. There was no divorce: if a wife left home, her husband had the right to claim damages from anyone who 'enticed' her away, or who harboured her or who committed adultery with her. And, until the 1965 Succession Act, her husband could legally disinherit her (see Scannell, 1988). Irish women were left with stark 'choices': either accept their allocated position in Irish society or emigrate. Many thousands chose to emigrate to work in low-paid sectors of the UK and US economies. In so doing they also played a crucial welfare role by sending money back to their relatives and establishing an informal infrastructure for assisting new migrants (O'Sullivan, 1995).

The constitutional settlement of the 1930s also had considerable implications for the 8 per cent of the population who were non-Catholics because, in addition to the above-mentioned restrictions, the constitution also forbade 'the publication or utterance of blasphemous, seditious or indecent material' and qualified freedom of speech and assembly if the authorities thought it would undermine public order and morality. Furthermore, the state's acceptance of the *Ne Temere* decree meant that children of mixed marriages were brought up as Catholics. As Joseph Lee has argued: 'It was difficult to avoid the impression that the state considered it a duty to impose specifically Catholic doctrine on all citizens, irrespective of their personal convictions' (1988, p.203).

2 TOWARDS A POST-WAR WELFARE STATE?

Ireland missed out on the first period of economic prosperity experienced by western societies in the 1950s and early 1960s. Such was the depth of the economic crisis that, between 1956 and 1961, 43,000 people emigrated every year forming a global diaspora not seen since the 1880s. Ireland was one of the few Western European countries to experience a dramatic population decline. In the period 1950–59 national income expanded at less than 1 per cent per annum. Net industrial output expanded by a meagre 1.3 per cent, whereas, for example, in Denmark it expanded by 3.5 per cent, in Spain by 8.5 per cent and in West Germany by 9.3 per cent. Industrial employment actually fell by 14 per cent in this period. These were startling statistics given that the international economy was expanding. In comparative terms, the wage levels of those who remained were low: in the late 1950s nearly six out of ten industrial workers earned less than £10 per week, while in Britain the equivalent figure was less than one in ten (Cassells, 1986, p.72).

2.1 THE CHANGING NATURE OF THE STATE'S ECONOMIC POLICIES

The depth of the economic crisis and the nature of the post-war international economic order resulted in a radical rethink of the Irish state's involvement in the economy. The state subsequently acquired considerable interests in the energy, steel, transport and communication sectors of the economy, as well as the ownership of banking and insurance companies. However, in order not to transgress the sacred principle of private property, state and semi-state ownership was achieved not through nationalization but by creating new 'partnership' enterprises (Chubb, 1982, pp.270–86).

Economic planning was adopted as part of a modernization strategy in 1958 and between 1959 and 1972 three programmes for economic expansion were implemented (Whittaker, 1986). Protectionism was abandoned and the principles of free trade and economic expansionism were embraced. The Anglo-Irish Free Trade Agreement was signed in 1965. This was followed by accession to the General Agreement on Tariffs and Trade (GATT) in 1967 and membership of the European Community (EC) was finally achieved in 1973. Entry into this competitive economic arena demanded the creation of an internal environment advantageous for industrial development. Since indigenous industry was not capable of generating the necessary employment or successfully competing in the export market, this meant enhancing Ireland's position as a base for foreign investment. The shift to an export-dominated strategy for growth was achieved by offering a generous package to persuade multi-national corporations (MNCs) to relocate in Ireland. The state, through the Irish Development Authority (IDA), announced to international capital that Ireland was the country 'where private enterprise is public policy' and administered the world's first free trade zone.

As Wickham (1980) has noted, because of the restructuring of international capitalism after the Second World War, Ireland quickly accessed the global economy. A major inflow of foreign investment occurred, especially in the latter half of the 1960s, and was maintained throughout the 1970s as a result of accession to the EC. With agricultural exports also benefiting from higher prices and unrestricted access to the European Community market, the annual growth of Irish exports was 8.2 per cent in the late 1960s and 8 per cent in the 1970s. It has been estimated that between 1960 and 1974 the change in government economic policy generated an additional 75,000 jobs. The major political parties committed themselves to producing full employment and, as a consequence, Ireland actually became a country of net in-migration in the 1970s.

Economic corporatist tendencies emerged in Ireland, as elsewhere in Western Europe, in the post-war period. Successive governments agreed that the future economic well-being (and indeed the economic survival) of the nation depended on partnership between private enterprise, the trade unions and the state. The 1946 Trade Union Act licensed unions for the purposes of collective bargaining. In the same year an Industrial Relations Act established an industrial tribunal, the Labour Court, on which employers and employees had equal representation. In the 1960s Fianna Fail governments attempted to incorporate the trade union movement into their economic strategy. A number of tripartite and bipartite consultative bodies were established to stabilize relations between the state, the unions and the employers. A National Pay Agreement was reached in 1964 and between 1972 and 1976 four bipartite wage agreements were reached. In the second half of the 1970s there was a shift to formal government involvement in tripartite discussions which culminated in the National Understandings for Economic and Social Development in 1979 and 1980. These represented the most serious attempt to develop a neo-corporatist relationship between the state and producer groups, involving very complex trade-offs between union commitments to pay restraint and state action on a wide range of economic and social issues (Roche, 1982; Hardiman, 1988). What is significant is that it turned out to be an approach that the Irish state would return to in the 1980s and 1990s.

It is in this context that the Irish state reoriented itself in relation to social welfare and social policy, and the exact reasons why are still debated by economists and political scientists. Coughlan has argued that:

> The Republic's welfare state could not be said to have been moulded by the pressures of a politically powerful social democratic movement, as in Britain, Scandinavia or West Germany ... Nor did the Republic, in contrast to Britain and several other countries, pass through a war time period when the requirements of a national war effort and the need to build social solidarity in face of a common enemy encouraged radically redistributive social policies.

(Coughlan, 1984, p.39)

From this perspective, the Irish state took the lead organizing role as part of its programme to promote and institutionalize economic development (Goldthorpe and Whelan, 1994).

2.2   SOCIAL CHANGES

It is also important to recognize, however, that the state's shift in attitude towards welfare was a response to wider social and cultural demands for change in Irish society. Politicians had always argued that increased social expenditure depended on a period of sustained economic growth. In the 1970s that growth was achieved and the rejuvenated labour movement was in a position to make renewed demands for improvements in social welfare. This demand for reform was also fuelled by comparison with developments in Britain and Northern Ireland (Bew *et al.*, 1989).

The health services were criticized because of their continuing association with the public welfare system. Housing statistics indicated that considerable overcrowding and substandard conditions still existed. There was also pressure for broadening the range of the social insurance system to cover more risks and to include sections of the population excluded from the existing system. In addition, the social strain resultant from a major change in demographic patterns forced the state to become involved. The censuses of 1971 and 1981 registered population increases of 5.5 and 14.4 per cent respectively and the 1981 census recorded a net in-migration of 100,000. By the beginning of the 1980s, the birth rate was 21 per 1,000 compared with the EC average of 12, and the rate of natural increases in the 1970s was six times that of the EC average. There was thus considerable political pressure for change and the main political parties began to view welfare expenditure as a form of 'largesse' with which to secure votes from an increasingly critical and demanding populace.

2.3   THE CHANGING POSITION OF THE CATHOLIC CHURCH

Of crucial importance was the shift in the attitude of the Catholic Church. In the immediate post-war period the Irish Church, more than anywhere else in Western Europe, retained its dominance at all levels of society and Catholic social teaching remained a powerful ideology: 'It was conditioning the language of public discourse, and concepts such as vocationalism, the principle of subsidiarity and the danger of excessive State control were current to an increasing degree' (Whyte, 1980, p.163).

In the 1940s and 1950s the Church remained wary of liberalism, individualism and state intervention and, for example, reacted unfavourably to calls for a comprehensive social insurance system, stressing that it would undermine the voluntary sector, result in higher taxation and violate Catholic social teaching because 'it aimed at doing away with poverty and consequently the opportunity of practising Christian charity' (Kaim-Caudle, 1967, p.43). Because of the opposition of the Church, the reforms that were introduced in the form of the 1952 Social Welfare Act were much more limited than originally proposed. However, in the course of the 1960s and 1970s, in the aftermath of Vatican II, the Church moved left of centre on issues of poverty and inequality. As a consequence, it was willing to sanction state expenditure on welfare on grounds of social justice. How far this constituted a departure from 'classic' Catholic corporatist principles we shall examine in the next section.

Thus, to summarize section 2, a social and political consensus emerged which pushed the Irish state towards a more expansive mixed economy of welfare provision. In the 1970s comprehensive social insurance schemes were introduced, including invalidity and retirement pensions. The philosophy underpinning income maintenance payments also changed. From the 1960s, the practice of pegging payments to subsistence levels was abandoned and more groups were deemed to be deserving of assistance. In 1977 a Supplementary Welfare Allowance scheme was introduced and the remaining traces of the Poor Law were removed from social welfare legislation. A standard basic minimum income, payable as of right, was provided in place of arbitrary and variable payments made under the 'Home Assistance' scheme. The state also committed itself to increased expenditure in housing provision, education and health services.

As a consequence of this modernization programme, by the 1980s the share of the national output designated to welfare in Ireland was comparable with the European norm, despite the fact that per capita gross domestic product (GDP) was well below the European average: in 1981 social expenditure was 23 per cent of GDP (11.7 per cent in 1960) compared with an OECD (Organization for Economic Cooperation and Development) average of 25.6 per cent (13.1 per cent in 1960). By this time Ireland ranked twentieth in the OECD in terms of per capita GDP, but eighth in terms of GDP share of social expenditure (Maguire, 1986, pp.286–7, 345).

3   THE IMPACT OF POST-WAR SHIFTS IN SOCIAL EXPENDITURE

There are three interrelated dimensions that need to be considered if we are to understand the outcomes of the Irish state's economic and social modernization strategy: first, whether the economic policies delivered full employment; second, the repercussions for the taxation system; and, finally, the impact of social welfare expenditure.

3.1   EMPLOYMENT

Ireland depended heavily on mostly American multi-national corporations which, as they became increasingly capital-intensive, could not deliver sufficient employment opportunities for the expanding labour force. Furthermore, as a result of changing global economic conditions and two global recessions, the state, through the Irish Development Agency, was forced to spend all its efforts recruiting new MNCs to keep pace with the relocation decisions of other MNCs. Hence, despite the considerable shifts in macroeconomic policy in the late 1970s and early 1980s, unemployment levels began to increase dramatically. By now, Ireland was registering the highest levels of unemployment in the EC. These levels would have been considerably higher still had not 240,000 people emigrated between 1980 and 1990. *The Economist* (1988) survey of Ireland documents how, even before the record increases in unemployment had been reached, Ireland's social security expenditure, as a proportion of GDP, had surpassed those of Japan and the USA. In the early 1990s state welfare payments were the only source of income for a significant percentage of the population.

3.2   TAXATION

The income distribution implications of the move to a welfare state depend on how the expansion is financed. In the 1970s and 1980s the structure of Irish taxation differed considerably from that in other Western European countries. Taxes on expenditure provided a significant share of total tax revenue and, in comparison with elsewhere in Western Europe, there was a marked decline in the revenue share from tax on property, inheritance tax and corporation income tax. Property tax declined through a series of electoral promises, most notably in 1978 when there was a removal of all taxes on domestic dwellings.

Until 1973 estate duties were the only form of capital taxation in Ireland and the government became increasingly concerned that these were being evaded. A series of reforms was attempted. Capital acquisition tax (1974) and a wealth tax (1975) were introduced to replace the old estate duties, and a capital gains tax (1975) focused on profits from speculative activities. The stated aim of these changes was to introduce a greater degree of fairness into the tax system. However, the considerable opposition to the proposal for a wealth tax meant that the reforms were rendered ineffectual and the wealth tax was finally abolished in 1978. Other forms of capital taxation were also nullified by generous exemptions, tapered relief and provisions for indexation with inflation. Such was their ineffectiveness that, in 1980, capital taxes represented 0.5 per cent of total taxation, a drop of 50 per cent on 1970.

Similarly with corporation income tax. In order to attract MNCs, export earnings were effectively protected from taxation after 1958. In 1978 this was replaced by a policy of a general tax on all profits from manufacturing at the low rate of 10 per cent. The Irish state's attitude to corporation and profit taxes meant that employers' contributions to

Pay Related Social Insurance (PRSI) was the only contribution made by many companies to the exchequer and this contribution was the second lowest in Europe (Breen *et al.*, 1990, p.82).

Whilst every effort was made to limit taxation on capital and corporate income, there were considerable rises in personal income tax revenue and social insurance contributions. In real terms, the yield from personal income tax grew more than fivefold between 1965 and 1980. This occurred because of a lack of a coherent policy in a period of ever-increasing inflation. Tax allowances and the starting-points of tax bands were not indexed to inflation. Consequently, the proportion of personal income being taxed increased, as did the proportion being taxed at the higher rather than the standard rate. Despite a protest by one million PAYE ('pay-as-you-earn') workers in 1979 against the glaring in-equalities of the punitive tax system, tax payments by the PAYE sector actually increased in the 1980s.

In the early 1980s Ireland's PAYE taxpayers were shouldering 87 per cent of the income tax burden. At 35 per cent, a single person started to pay tax at the developed world's highest starting-rate. Because of the steep progressiveness of the tax code, almost half of taxpayers were incurring higher rates of 58 per cent which took effect below the average male wage. No account was taken of the considerable difference in levels of income encompassed by the tax band. When 7.7 per cent for various social security deductions was added on, economists were agreed that Ireland had 'the industrial world's poorest super-taxpayers' (*The Economist*, 1988, p.13). The situation was compounded by the fact that, through preferential treatment and non-payment, the self-employed and farmers avoided this crippling tax system.

Thus, the evidence suggests that the burden of increased taxation underpinning the move to a welfare state was unevenly distributed among the various social classes, with the employee class in general bearing a relatively large share, while the tax burden on employers and proprietors remained relatively light.

3.3   WELFARE EXPENDITURE OUTCOMES

There was considerable investment in the fields of education, health and housing. However, this did not challenge Catholic corporatist principles because the state limited its role to the provision of resources. As a consequence, private and voluntary institutions, under the tutelage of the Catholic Church, retained the strategic role of delivering these social goods. And, as Breen *et al.* (1990) argue, this meant that the middle-class interests embedded in the existing infra-structure were not challenged by increased state expenditure.

Core sectors of education and health care remained under the control of the Catholic Church and were imbued with Catholic social principles, with the state's role limited to one of funding. Two-thirds of secondary schools were privately owned and managed, mostly by religious orders.

Such was the degree of autonomy enjoyed by these schools that the OECD argued that, by international standards, education in Ireland was 'privatized to an extraordinary degree' (OECD, 1991, p.36).

The state also became heavily involved in expenditure on health and by the early 1980s was spending a higher proportion of its gross national product (GNP) on health than were many richer OECD countries. However, provision of a free national health service was never an objective of state policy (Rafferty, 1985). Only medical card holders were entitled to free services which effectively meant that only social welfare recipients and their dependants could have access to comprehensive health care. The rest of the population was encouraged to take out health insurance under the state-regulated Voluntary Health Insurance Scheme (McDowell, 1990). The Church still played a considerable role in the provision of health care, approximately half of hospital beds in Ireland being provided by the non-state sector. In addition, Irish doctors jealously guarded the balance of private and public health care and the independence of the non-state sector.

A series of Housing Acts and budgets affirmed the government's belief in free market forces and owner-occupancy as the preferred form of tenancy. If we look at the consequences of the state's preferred housing policies, we find that inequities within the housing market widened. Rates on domestic dwellings were abolished, grants for first-time buyers were introduced and mortgage interest subsidies were subsequently added. In 1987 the government subsidy to owner-occupiers was £218 million, whereas the subsidy to local authority housing programmes was £194 million. It is not surprising, given the level of subsidies and the ideological orientation, that in the period between 1966 and 1987 the owner-occupier sector increased from 59.8 per cent to 78 per cent with 47 per cent of homes owned outright. Ireland was moving to having the highest percentage of owner-occupied housing in Western Europe (see McCashin and Morrisey, 1985; Daly, 1989).

Although there was a commitment to maintaining local authority housing to meet the needs of lower-income groups, it was not a government priority. Expenditure on social housing fell from 8.42 per cent to 5.8 per cent between 1971 and 1981, and between 1982 and 1987 capital expenditure on local authority housing was halved. Commentators identified a situation where a growing underclass was living outside the property-owning democracy on inferior social housing estates (NESC, 1986, p.112). Low-income, lone-parent families, for example, had particular problems because they were given low-priority status by local authorities. As a consequence, they had the choice of accepting accommodation on unwanted estates or competing in the minuscule private sector where rents are largely uncontrolled. The travelling people also found themselves adversely affected by the state's housing policies. Despite the fact that their numbers increased from 11,000 families in 1972 to 50,000 in 1992, their right to serviced sites was not being met and they were deemed not to be deserving of local authority housing.

Increased state intervention was justified on the grounds that economic development would result in a more equitable sharing of the substantially augmented national wealth. As indicated above, a massive increase did take place in the state's commitment to income maintenance programmes and to social services. However, the redistributive process operated unevenly from a social class perspective, treating the property-owning classes in a relatively favourable fashion (Maguire, 1986, p.320).

Breen *et al.* reached similar conclusions, claiming that: 'despite the enormously bloated role of the state as an economic intermediary, it has been monumentally unsuccessful either in ensuring sustained economic growth or in moderating inegalitarian tendencies in the class system' (1990, p.209). They argue that the main beneficiaries of economic modernization and the increases in state expenditure on welfare were those classes which paid the least in taxation. Thus, existing inequalities were compounded and new ones generated by Ireland's particular mix of welfare. The only option seemed to be to maintain disadvantaged sections of the community in their marginality.

4   SOCIAL PARTNERSHIP: THE BASIS FOR A NEW WELFARE SETTLEMENT

The tensions and contradictions generated by state policies resulted in economic and political crisis. Ireland was one of Europe's poorest societies, and bracketed with Greece and Portugal for European funding purposes. Governments were forced to expand public-sector employment as a compensatory measure and by the early 1980s this accounted for almost 30 per cent of the employment total (see Bew *et al.*, 1989, Ch. 3). This public employment programme worked with the increased social expenditure and spiralling unemployment to push public expenditure to record levels. Given that government expenditure was being financed by foreign borrowing and the crippling taxation system, political commentators began to notice the similarities between Ireland and so-called 'Third World' countries (Walsh, 1991). The strains and pressures caused by the manifest inequalities, the economic downturn and the public expenditure crisis were driving Ireland towards chronic political instability. Richard Kearney, in an overview of the state of the nation, concluded that:

> ... our present state of affairs is, by most accounts, bleak. One third of the population of the Republic live below the poverty line; fifty thousand young people emigrate each year; one quarter of a million are unemployed, with rates of up to 60 per cent in the new developments in Dublin; and inequality is growing rather than diminishing, with social welfare insufficient to meet the minimum

needs of a large proportion of the people. The continuing bloodshed of the North speaks for itself. These factors combine to produce a state of aimlessness.

(Kearney, 1988, p.7)

However, during the 1990s a dramatic turnaround in fortunes took place and the Irish economy ('the Celtic Tiger') was transformed into the OECD success story (Ó'Riain, 2000). The cumulative growth of almost 60 per cent in GNP since 1993 is without parallel in any OECD country and has very few historical precedents. Independent reports predict economic growth averaging 5 per cent between 2000 and 2005 (OECD, 1999). Between 1993 and 1999 the number of people in work grew by over 30 per cent, with employment opportunities in manufacturing, hi-tech industries, construction, financial services, tele-services and tourism. Unemployment fell from 15 per cent in 1993 to 6 per cent in 1999, with forecasts that full employment could be realized. Long-term unemployment and youth unemployment fell sharply, with significant rises in the number of female participants in the workforce, training schemes and further and higher education. As a consequence, it is argued that Ireland has finally unshackled itself from its colonial inferiority complex and become the epitome of a late modern, post-industrial, post-colonial European society.

Section 4.1 below assesses how Ireland's change in fortunes impacted upon social policy debates.

4.1 SOCIAL PARTNERSHIP

When Fianna Fail regained power in 1987 it announced that it was essential to reduce the national debt and that there would be public service redundancies, privatization, commercialization and public expenditure cutbacks. However, it was made clear that this retrenchment agenda would be carried out by agreement rather than by the neo-liberal tactics adopted by successive New Right governments in the UK during this period. Nor would there be a concerted effort to stigmatize those dependent on welfare provision.

In 1987 the Irish government negotiated a Programme for National Recovery with the 'social partners' of the state – that is, the trade unions, the employers and the farmers. The key to this complex agreement was a public-sector pay deal to secure minimal wage increases for three years. The government's strategy worked and borrowing was brought down to 3.3 per cent – the lowest rate for more than 20 years. In January 1991 the coalition government of Fianna Fail and the Progressive Democrats (a 'radical right' party formed in the mid 1980s) negotiated a new Programme for Economic and Social Progress with the 'social partners' and continued with its retrenchment, tax reform and privatization programmes (see Bew et al., 1989; Collins, 1992).

The government committed itself to mobilizing a 'triple consensus', consisting of: an agreement between employers and employees regarding pay and working conditions; agreement between the government and the 'social partners' over economic and social policies; and a national consensus to put the good of the country above sectional interests. The first problem to be confronted was that of spiralling unemployment rates. A series of government committees, with representation from all the 'social partners' and groups representing the interests of the unemployed, was set up to produce a co-ordinated approach to the problem. It was agreed that a fundamental shake-up of the economy and social welfare was necessary if unemployment was to be brought down to the European Community average and the gap in living standards closed (see Tansey, 1991).

The influential Culliton Report, which was published in January 1992, recommended a radical approach to the formulation and implementation of industrial policy. It argued for government policies to produce a competitive, flexible regional and local economy with a 'thriving enterprise culture' and 'spirit of self-reliance' in order to bring about convergence between Ireland and the rest of Europe and to break the dependence on MNCs. The key targets of reform were the taxation and welfare systems which, it was argued, had created work disincentives, a welfare dependency culture and an unacceptable state burden. Government attempts to reform the tax system began to take effect when the 1992 budget lowered the top income tax rate from 52 per cent to 48 per cent and the standard income tax rate from 29 per cent to 27 per cent. In May 1992 the Irish Minister for Social Welfare told the Fifth European Conference of Social Security Ministers that the present levels of unemployment benefits and eligibility could not be sustained and that Ireland would not have the resources to look after old people, sick people and others who may be deserving of support. He announced that proposals would be implemented to tighten eligibility criteria, to remove work disincentives and to integrate the tax and welfare systems.

As the rest of Europe withdrew from 'corporatist' approaches to economic and social issues – primarily as a consequence of the dominance of neo-liberal ideas – Ireland consolidated its social partnerships framework (O'Donnell and Thomas, 1998). The Programme for Competitiveness and Work succeeded the Programme for Economic and Social Progress and Partnership 2000 came into existence. The key objective was to construct a stable macroeconomic and fiscal framework capable of generating high and sustainable levels of economic growth and job creation. However, as a result of sustained campaigning, the 'social dialogue' was wider and deeper (Callan and Nolan, 1998). Policymakers began to take heed of mounting evidence that the economic boom was not benefiting all sections of Irish society. Most of the new investment and employment opportunities were occurring in the Dublin region. Rural and border areas were losing out and pockets of extreme deprivation were identified in the main cities. Partnership 2000 committed the state to formulating a co-ordinated approach to tackle inequality and social exclusion. Partnership 2000 was defined as a 'watershed' in the neo-corporatist approach because the interests of the socially disadvantaged and excluded were placed at the strategic centre of policy deliberation. Partnership 2000 even provided an expansive definition of social exclusion:

> ... cumulative marginalization: from production (unemployment), from consumption (income poverty), from social networks (community, family and neighbours), from decision-making and from an adequate quality of life. Social exclusion is one of the major challenges currently facing Irish society. To minimise or ignore this challenge would not only result in an increase in social polarisation, which is in itself unacceptable, but also an increase in all the attendant problems such as poor health, crime, drug-abuse and alienation, which impose huge social and economic costs on our society.

(Government of Ireland, 1996, para. 4.3)

In February 2000, in keeping with the conclusions of the National Economic and Social Council review (NESC, 1999), it was announced that agreement had been reached, between the Irish government and the social partners, on the terms of a new national programme. The Programme for Prosperity and Fairness is intended to deepen the partnership approach and produce the economic and social stability required to compete successfully in the globalized economy. Like its predecessor, the programme commits the government to implementing measures to address the needs of those on low incomes; the demand for social and affordable housing; support for childcare and family-friendly employment practices; and equality of opportunity. The programme also institutionalizes the government's anti-poverty strategy.

4.2 SOCIAL INCLUSION AND THE NATIONAL ANTI-POVERTY STRATEGY

At the United Nations World Summit for Social Development held in Copenhagen in March 1995, the Irish government committed itself to a Programme of Action to reduce global poverty and inequality. As a consequence, the government approved the development of a National Anti-Poverty Strategy (NAPS) which would set out the extent of poverty and social exclusion in Ireland as well as identifying policy solutions.

The strategy was developed within the framework of Partnership 2000, and, after consultation with the voluntary and community sectors of the social partnership, was launched in April 1997. The following principles underpinned NAPS:

- to ensure equal access and encourage participation for all;

- to guarantee the rights of minorities, especially through anti-discrimination measures;

- to reduce inequalities and, in particular, to address the gender dimensions of poverty;

- to develop a partnership approach, building on national and local partnership processes;

- to actively involve the community and voluntary sectors;

- to encourage self-reliance through respect for individual dignity and the promotion of empowerment;

- to engage in appropriate consultative processes, especially with users of services.

The overall intention is, over the period 1997–2007, to reduce the numbers of those who are consistently poor from 9–15 per cent of the population to less than 5–10 per cent. In addition to establishing an overall target, NAPS also identified five specific problems of social exclusion and set objectives, targets and time-frames for each of them:

1   Unemployment:

Paid employment should be available to all men and women currently in poverty and seeking employment. This should be capable of providing adequate income, either on its own or when combined with other forms of support, sufficient to lift people out of poverty, and should be available without barriers of discrimination.

2   Income adequacy:

Policies in relation to income support, whether these policies relate to employment, tax, social welfare, occupational pensions or otherwise, should aim to provide sufficient income for all those concerned to move out of poverty and to live in a manner compatible with human dignity.

3   Educational disadvantage:

To ensure that children, men and women living in poverty are able to gain access to, participate in and benefit from education of sufficient quality to allow them to move out of poverty, and to prevent others from becoming poor.

4   Urban disadvantage:

To bring about sustained social and economic development in disadvantaged areas in order to improve the lives of people living in such areas, by empowering them to become effective citizens, improving the quality of their lives, helping them acquire the skills and education necessary to gain employment and providing them with employment opportunities.

5 Rural poverty:

> Poverty and social exclusion in rural areas will be tackled by ensuring the provision of adequate income, through employment and/or income support, and access to adequate services and infrastructure, co-ordination of responses and empowerment of local people and communities.

It is difficult to reach a definitive conclusion on the likely impact of the National Anti-Poverty Strategy. It will require independent monitoring to establish whether NAPS achieves its objectives and carries out its functions as claimed. Questions have already been raised about the unambitious nature of the targets, given the favourable macroeconomic and political contexts; unresolved gender equality issues; foregrounding labour market participation as the key to social exclusion and disadvantage; and the lack of analysis of how wealth is being distributed as a consequence of the taxation system.

However, it is important also to think through the broader significance of the social partnerships and NAPS. The institutionalization and democratization of the partnership approach has the potential to produce a radical reconceptualization of the role, capacities, responsibilities and organization of the Irish state; and a considerably more inclusive and pluralistic notion of citizenship. In terms of the organization and delivery of social welfare, the outcome is equally potentially far-reaching. The Department of Social, Community and Family Affairs, whose remit was reviewed, has the role of providing citizens with the opportunities and incentives to participate fully in social and economic life.

The strategic nature of NAPS was reinforced during 1998 when the government introduced a 'poverty proofing' system whereby significant policy proposals would be assessed at formulation stage for their likely impact on groups in poverty or at risk of falling into poverty. Particular attention is to be paid to inequalities which may lead to poverty – that is, inequalities based on age, gender, disability, ethnicity and sexual orientation.

5   THE OTHER SIDE OF PARTNERSHIP: WOMEN, WELFARE AND CITIZENSHIP

It has not been easy to achieve any form of consensus over the relationship between Irish women, the Catholic Church and the state. It is this relationship, rather than any manifestations of social exclusions, that has periodically traumatized Irish society and threatened to destabilize the Irish state. While the Church has given its blessing to state efforts to resolve economic problems, it has been less prepared to condone any liberalization of state policies which it views as threatening family life (Hannigan, 1990). As a consequence, throughout the 1980s and 1990s conservative and liberal social forces, and increasingly Church and state, have clashed over the status of women. As we shall see in the following sections, women's groups have increasingly used EC institutions and legislation in their struggle to reform discriminatory state policies and practices.

5.1 DISCRIMINATION IN THE LABOUR MARKET

Jean Pyle (1990a) has documented how, in the post-war period, the state's economic policies were consciously geared towards the twin objectives of promoting economic development and the reproduction of traditional familial relations. Given that the state opted for export-led development, a strategy that usually involves increases in the use of female labour, it could be assumed that the participation of Irish women in the labour force would have increased in the post-war period. However, this did not happen. Initially, women did gain new employment opportunities, but the state responded by formulating a set of economic and social criteria for evaluating proposed industrial projects. Included in the criteria was an explicit statement regarding the preferred gender composition of the workforce. Irish Development Authority reports in the early 1970s stressed the need for proposals which would have a workforce composed of 75 per cent men.

There was a range of other practices and social policies which remained in force until the 1970s and which reinforced women's non-labour force status. The marriage bar, instituted in the 1930s, continued to operate. In addition, there were no legal provisions for ensuring that women had the right to adequate leave of absence for maternity and guaranteed right to reinstatement in their original employment. 'Protective' legislation, in the form of a ban on night work for women, was also implemented, restricting women's access to industrial work.

The income tax code discriminated against the participation of married women in waged work. According to various Finance Acts, the income of a married woman was considered for taxation purposes as the income of her husband, therefore added to his income and taxed according to the schedule for married couples, which moved them rapidly into higher bands. When combined with the lower rates of pay for women, the financial incentive to participate in the economy was offset by the crippling taxation rates. In addition, provision for childcare was lacking. In the early 1980s only 3 per cent of pre-school children of working parents were cared for in daycare centres or pre-schools; the rest were cared for by relatives and neighbours:

> The lack of provision by state personnel of this social service was as constraining on women's options as protective legislation or the marriage bar. The absence of child-care facilities co-ordinated well with the general tenor of state policy, which was still rooted in the belief that mothers belonged in the home and which reinforced traditional gender roles.

(Pyle, 1990b, p.97)

The state's attempted regulation of women extended into health matters. In 1947 and 1950 proposals were introduced to provide universal maternity and child health services free of charge, a compulsory school medical health inspection service and measures to combat infectious diseases. This scheme ran into outright opposition from the Irish Medical Association in conjunction with the Catholic Church on the grounds that it was bureaucratic, centralizing and infringed on the rights of the family. One of the most sensitive areas in the 'mother and child scheme' was the proposal to 'safeguard' the health of women in respect of motherhood. Such a proposal was completely unacceptable to Catholic social teaching and the proposals were not implemented (see Whyte, 1980).

5.2 REFORM, REACTION AND FURTHER REFORM

During the years from the 1970s through to the 1990s there were significant changes in the position of women in Irish society. In 1969 the National Commission on the Status of Women was set up and it condemned the extent of the discriminatory treatment of Irish women (see Brennan, 1979; Beale, 1986). In its deliberations it drew upon the views of the emergent women's movement. In addition, membership of the EC also required that Ireland conform with Community directives on equal pay and equal treatment with regard to access to employment (Laffan, 1991). As a consequence, a series of wide-ranging reforms was implemented in the 1970s and 1980s. The marriage bar was removed, employment equality legislation was passed and, in 1981, maternity allowance was finally introduced. In the late 1970s the policy of subsidizing male employment opportunities came under renewed pressure for change. Given the intense competition for multi-national relocation, it became evident that, in order to attract MNCs, countries would have to accede to the MNCs' demands to have freedom in hiring their workforces. As Pyle (1990a) shows, although the Irish government did persevere with attempts to 'fix' the composition of the workforce by offering higher incentives to those companies which would adjust their labour requirements, it did effectively have to abandon this policy. The significance of these shifts cannot be underestimated. The labour force participation of married women increased from 7.5 per cent in 1971 to 19.5 per cent in 1984 and the rates for young married women aged 25–34 increased from 8.8 per cent to 26.9 per cent in the same period (Fine-Davis, 1988). Ireland's economic transformation in the 1990s tilted state policy towards maximizing female participation in the labour market and this is forcing the government to address provision of adequate childcare and pre-school facilities and is putting pressure on firms to implement family-friendly work place policies and practices.

Welfare reforms were also implemented. The disqualification of women upon marriage from being entitled to short-term social welfare benefits was removed, as were the discriminatory tax laws. Social assistance for unmarried mothers, prisoners' wives and deserted wives, and a single woman's allowance (for elderly single women), were introduced. The

Family Home Protection Act of 1976 also established that the permission of both spouses is required before a family home can be sold.

In response to an EC directive (79/7/EC) on equal treatment of men and women in social policy, the state finally implemented further reforms in the mid 1980s. Under the terms of the directive, the Irish government had to implement changes in four areas affecting married women: reduced rates of benefit; duration of entitlement to unemployment benefit; admission of married women to the unemployment assistance scheme; and payments of increases in benefits to married women for adult and child dependants. Whyte (1992, p.134) argued that the change 'was one of the most controversial and far reaching reforms our welfare system had ever undertaken' because, prior to this directive, the core value underlying the social welfare code was that the husband was the breadwinner and, consequently, the person to whom increases of benefit for his dependent wife and children should be paid. Married women could only receive increases in benefits for husbands who were incapable of self-support as a result of mental or physical infirmity. Similarly, child dependant increases were not payable to a married woman except where the husband was an invalid or where she was living apart from and not supported by him. A married man, on the other hand, could receive increases for his wife and children regardless of her employment or financial status.

Murphy-Lawless and McCarthy (1999) argue that, for Irish women to 'achieve full personal agency in law', they needed to achieve access to contraception, information about abortion and legalization of divorce. And as will become clear in the next sections, in each area policy shifts unfolded in order to catch up with the choices many women were already making. As a consequence of the intense public debates generated, the state was forced to rethink the constitutional settlement on the rights of women in Irish society.

5.3   CONTRACEPTION

Women's groups realized that, until Irish women obtained full reproductive rights (that is, having information about, access to and control over technologies which regulate fertility) and the right to divorce, they would not be able to obtain further substantive social, political and economic rights. In addition to circumventing legal proscriptions, they looked to the courts in their campaigns to liberalize Ireland's prohibitive contraception, abortion and divorce laws. In 1979 the European Court of Human Rights ruled that the Irish government was in breach of two articles of the European Convention on Human Rights and Fundamental Freedoms – Article 6 which allows all citizens access to the courts, and Article 8 which protects family life. Mrs Josie Airey claimed that the Irish courts would not protect her from her violent estranged husband; they would only issue an injunction against him if a judicial separation was in force. The cost of procuring a judicial separation was beyond her means and she was not eligible for legal aid.

Her case, therefore, was that she was unable to obtain justice because the Irish High Court was only accessible to the wealthy. As a result of her successful appeal, the Irish government was forced to revise its rules on injunctions (Higgins, 1981, p.82).

Supreme Court interpretations of the constitution also seemed to be supporting this tentative liberalization process. In the early 1970s it declared that the right to marital privacy included the right to import contraceptives for personal use. This resulted in the 1979 Health (Family Planning) Act which decreed that contraceptives could be supplied on bona fide family planning purposes. This was described by Charles Haughey as 'an Irish solution to an Irish question'. In 1985 legislation was further amended to permit the sale of non-medical contraceptives without prescription for those aged 18 or over (Healey, 1988). In March 1991 a fresh row broke out concerning contraception. The government proposed to make contraceptives more widely available and to reduce the age at which one could buy them from eighteen to sixteen. The bishops attacked the proposals saying that it would lead to familial and social disaster by encouraging promiscuity and AIDS. The Fianna Fail government retreated by ruling out contraceptive dispensing machines and setting the age limit at seventeen. However, in 1997 the Department of Health published a five-year plan for women's health committing the state to developing equitable, accessible and comprehensive family planning services. Murphy-Lawless and McCarthy (1999) argue that this signalled the final move to women-centred (as opposed to state-centred) reproductive health care which recognized the need for dialogue and consultation.

5.4 ABORTION

There were also indications that increasing numbers of women were more prepared, after the enactment of the 1967 Abortion Act in the UK, to travel to Britain to terminate unwanted pregnancies. The official figure for 1977 was 2,183 and by the mid 1980s it had risen to almost 4,000 per annum. Pro-choice groups were also able to point to the wide-ranging implications of the 'British solution to an Irish problem':

> The presence of a total ban on abortion in the 26 counties of Ireland has led to a definite gap in the health services in other gynaecological and maternity areas. Family planning advice is not available to women in all maternity hospitals. Only one hospital in the country is equipped to respond to women victims of rape, and abortion referral is not offered. For fertile women there is no genetic counselling service. One of the consequences of this underdevelopment is greater difficulties for many women in dealing with miscarriage and spontaneous abortion.

(Jackson, 1986, p.159)

In 1980 the Women's Right to Choose Group was launched and it opened a pregnancy counselling service, offering information to pregnant women, including, if requested, information about abortion services in Britain.

Powerful conservative Catholic organizations complained vociferously about the 'radical' changes that were 'afflicting' Irish society, warning of the threat to the traditional Irish family and familial relations. As far as they were concerned, such changes had to be challenged and constitutional referendums on abortion in 1983 witnessed a reversal of this liberalization (Jackson, 1986; Mahon, 1987). Under the 1861 Offences Against the Persons Act abortion was (and is) illegal. But it was not explicitly prohibited in the constitution. Anti-abortionist groups expressed concern that a court decision, particularly a European Court decision, could legalize abortion even if the country was hostile to such legislation. In a bitter moral civil war the Catholic Church called for a 'yes' vote on the grounds that it would finally guarantee unborn human life the constitutional protection guaranteed to all citizens. In September 1983 the electorate voted for a constitutional amendment which stated that: 'the state acknowledges the right to life of the unborn and, with due regard to the equal right of the mother, guarantees in its laws to protect, and as far as practicable, by its laws, to defend and vindicate that right.' Galligan (1999, p.187) argues that the 1983 referendum 'altered the nature of women's citizenship during pregnancy from one of full individual citizenship to that of a shared citizenship with a being as yet unborn.'

In November 1991 the Irish government, in order to pacify the vociferous anti-abortion lobby, requested that a protocol be inserted into the Maastricht Treaty to provide that nothing in the Treaty should affect Ireland's constitutional ban on abortion. However, the whole issue was put back on the political agenda in February 1992 when an Irish High Court ruling prevented a 14-year-old rape victim from travelling to Britain for an abortion. The Attorney General attempted to use the 1983 amendment to prevent someone travelling to an EC country to avail themselves of a legal medical service. When the Supreme Court subsequently lifted the ban, the issue of abortion had once more displaced all others on the political agenda (Smyth, 1992; Porter, 1996; Smyth, 1996).

Two issues were raised. First, the court determined that abortion was constitutionally permissible if it was established that there was a real and substantial risk to the life of the mother. And in this case, given that the girl was suicidal, the court decided that this requirement had been met. The message was clear – abortion was legal in Ireland in certain limited circumstances. Second, it affirmed the right of EC citizens to travel and avail themselves of services, including medical ones. The anti-abortion groups were appalled by the reasoning that the Supreme Court used to overrule the Attorney General. Given that there was to be a referendum on the Maastricht Treaty and that it seemed as if EC law guaranteeing the right to travel could be used to overrule the

Irish constitution, the anti-abortion groups committed themselves to making abortion *the* issue in the referendum. Irish and European politicians realized that the furore over the case could lead to a rejection of the Treaty.

The Irish government successfully disentangled the ratification of Maastricht from the abortion issue by promising to hold a referendum on abortion after the Maastricht referendum. An all-party consensus was constructed around the economic and social need to vote 'yes' for Maastricht. It was made clear to voters that the nation's economic future was at stake in the referendum and a concerted effort was made to sideline the conservative Catholic pressure groups by defining them as a sectional interest. The government was helped by the fact that the Catholic Church supported Maastricht. The perennial concern with 'the national interest' was raised and the Church would have found it difficult to challenge the political party consensus that had been created. Allied to this was the fact that the major socio-economic classes, who had solidly supported the Church, desired a 'yes' vote. Furthermore, it became apparent in the course of this referendum that the Church had a wider political agenda. The Irish bishops conveyed their vision of a united Europe in which Ireland could 'give witness in the Councils of Europe to Christian values, which themselves help to form a society of justice and peace'. Hence, the Church agreed that the ratification of Maastricht should be separated from the constitutional debate on abortion.

The issue of women's reproductive rights did not disappear from the political agenda in the aftermath of the Maastricht referendum because of the government's commitment to hold a referendum on abortion in 1992. The Church made it clear that it would not countenance abortion in Ireland under any circumstances and the anti-abortion lobby received a considerable boost in their anti-liberal campaign when the Pope personally intervened to remind Irish Catholics that:

> ... the malaise of contemporary society revolves around family life and family values ... Where the family is weakened, society descends into confusion and conflict. Neither society nor the state can substitute for the family's educational and formative influence. To defend the family, that is, the institution based on human nature and the deepest needs of the human person ... and the bulwark of civilization, is an imperative task for society's political representatives.

(quoted in *The Irish Times*, 26 September 1992)

However, Patricia Redlich, commenting in a Dublin newspaper, pointed out the consequences for women if the anti-abortion lobby succeeded in their constitutional campaign to ban abortion in Ireland once and for all:

As always the poor, vulnerable and less informed will pay the heaviest price, this time to keep Ireland cosmetically clean. Families will cripple themselves to help a daughter in distress, young girls will walk the streets of London alone, and abortions will take place later rather than sooner. It's hard not to feel that a great hatred of women stalks the streets of Ireland today.

(*Sunday Independent*, 11 October 1992)

In November 1992 the Irish electorate voted to allow women the right to abortion information and the right to travel to clinics abroad. However, the proposal to legalize abortion where the life of the mother was at risk failed to win approval. Galligan (1999, p.186) notes how the referendum and subsequent legislation for the provision of information on abortion services 'did not address the central issue of its availability'. As a consequence, the government came under renewed pressure to legislate for the right to abortion. Amid the debate and prevarication, another case surfaced in November 1997 which highlighted Ireland's abortion law chaos. The High Court found that the termination of the pregnancy of a 13-year-old rape victim, authorized by a district court, was lawful under the constitution. Psychiatric evidence, that the real and substantial risk to the life of 'c' could only be avoided by the termination of her pregnancy, was accepted. In the traumatic aftermath of the case, opinion polls indicated that over 70 per cent of those questioned were prepared to accept that abortion should be introduced in Ireland to deal with particularly difficult cases. As a consequence, the government produced a Green Paper in September 1999 which would resolve Ireland's contradictory and socially discriminatory position on abortion.

5.5   DIVORCE

In 1986 the Fine Gael government attempted to amend the constitution to allow for divorce. Although opinion polls had demonstrated clear majorities in favour of removing the ban, the government was defeated in a referendum with a result which was almost an exact replica of the abortion vote. The Church was even more actively involved in this referendum than in the one held in 1983 on abortion and during the campaign the issue of the future of the Irish family was centre-stage. Anti-divorce groups such as 'Family Solidarity' used statistics about the poverty of families headed by lone parents in the USA as an example of what could befall Irish women if divorce was introduced. Nell McCafferty, sardonically, made the connection between women's legal and economic position and their attitude towards the divorce referendum:

What else could we do in a country where children are totally dependent on full-time mothering, and mother's function as unpaid dependent wives? It was open to Messrs Fitzgerald, Spring and Dukes [government ministers] ... when they proposed divorce, to offer a proper package that would have included an increase in children's allowance, vigorous enforcement of equal pay and enhanced job prospects for women. A nod in the direction of crèche facilities for civil servant females ... would have indicated an understanding of the difficulties that a divorced mother could face. It did not occur to them. They still have not understood that child care and money are an essential feature of a free woman's life.

(McCafferty, 1988, p.40)

In November 1995 voters decided by the narrowest of margins to support lifting the ban on divorce. And at the end of 1996 legislation permitting divorce was finally passed. By this time the rate of marital breakdown was over double what it had been in 1986.

As we have seen, through the constitutional referendums of the 1980s and the campaigns of the 1990s, conservative Catholic groups attempted to force state and society into defining Irish women, first and foremost, as mothers in order to bolster the stability of the conventional Catholic family. However, despite the set-backs in the referendums, women's groups have made significant advances in a relatively short period of time and they have been able to use EC directives, the national courts and the construction of a liberal-left consensus to challenge the constitutional 'settlement' on the position of women in Irish society:

> The women's movement in Ireland has matured and gained real political strength. The movement is now demanding, as never before, that a women centred analysis of policy decisions and women's input into social and health care policies become part of the institutional framework of government. Gender-proofing these institutional structures would help copper-fasten the state's over-due intentions to respect and secure women's reproductive freedom and physical well-being, as well as to actively support a diversity of forms of family life. These are moves which could fundamentally transform the meanings of motherhood in a country where woman as wife and mother, has so long been conflated.

(Murphy-Lawless and McCarthy, 1999, p.86)

5.6 THE FUTURE OF THE IRISH FAMILY

Following the example of several other European countries, Ireland established a Commission on the Family in October 1995 to examine the effects of government legislation on families and make recommendations which would strengthen the capacity of families to carry out their functions in a period of rapid social, cultural and economic change:

Like many other European countries, our families are coming under increasing economic and social pressure as we adjust to a more open and rapidly developing society. Over the past ten to twenty years, many of the social indicators in our society: the birth rate, the participation of women in paid employment, the marriage rate, have changed dramatically. People now have more choice about lifestyle, education and where to live. Economically we are better off too. However, unemployment and social deprivation persist with concentrations of it in certain areas. Families in these situations are particularly vulnerable to social and economic pressures.

(Proinsias De Rossa, Minister of Social Welfare, Press Release, May 1996)

The government was of the view that the establishment of a Commission on the Family signalled an important ideological shift in the relationship between the state and the family:

Not so long ago the family was regarded as a stateless space, an area where the State did not intervene. This no longer applies. The family cannot be immune from public policy decisions. The challenge we face is to provide the right kinds of support to families in all their diversities. The issue is not the abandonment of tradition but rather how we assist families to deal with changing social and economic realities.

(Press Release, 27 November 1996)

The first in-depth analysis of the state of the Irish family formulated six 'essential truths' which should underpin policies pertaining to families:

- Recognition that the family unit is a fundamental unit providing stability and well-being in our society.
- The unique and essential family function is that of caring and nurturing all its members.
- Continuity and stability are major requirements in family relationships.
- An equality of well-being is recognised between individual family members.
- Family membership confers rights, duties and responsibilities.
- A diversity of family forms and relationships should be recognized.

(Commission on the Family, 1998, pp.7–8)

Its recommendations were informed by the number of families bringing up children in difficult circumstances – for example: unemployment, low incomes, lone parenting, or living in socially and economically disadvantaged communities; glaring gaps in government policies; and a lack of co-ordinated approach of government departments.

In policy terms the Commission's report overlapped with NAPS because it concentrated on the needs of vulnerable families coping with considerable disadvantage. The Commission recommended a policy approach which concentrated on building strengths in vulnerable families through the introduction of a network of family and community services resource centres, and the development of customized local welfare services.

The state was informed that, if families were to carry out their functions and retain stability in changed social and economic circumstances, there would need to be:

- investment in the care of young children;

- provision to enable parental choice in the care and education of children;

- practical support and recognition for those undertaking primary caring responsibilities for children;

- support for families balancing work commitments and family life;

- support for unemployed families in getting access to the labour market.

Particular attention was also paid to the needs of lone-parent families in line with international research findings. Not surprisingly, the Commission favoured a US-style employment-led approach:

> Participation in employment presents the best prospects for improving income and hence the living standard of lone parents and their children. Lone parents are able to secure a higher income in countries where they are supported in finding employment ... Employment has further advantages in terms of offering choice and promoting self-esteem, less isolation and more active involvement in society, which is particularly important for young single mothers.
>
> (Commission on the Family, 1998, part 3, p.6)

The Commission concluded that the state should direct its efforts to ensuring that its welfare policies facilitate participation in the labour market, including access to childcare. In relation to teenage parenthood it opted for a mixed policy approach which would encourage deferment of parenthood and increased levels of support for teenage mothers in order to keep them in the education system.

The Commission supported retention of Article 41.3.1 of the constitution which commits the state to protecting the institution of marriage. However, ideologically, it committed itself to a concept of marriage as a partnership of equals and made it clear that families not based on marriage should not be disadvantaged by state policies.

6   CONCLUSION

Until the 1960s Catholic teaching largely determined the nature of Irish social policies, and strict adherence to the subsidiarity principle ensured that the austere state had a limited welfare role. It was left to the Church to provide a rudimentary mixed economy of social welfare. The idealized role allocated to the family in the delivery of the nation's welfare had considerable implications for Irish women. As mentioned in section 1.2 above, the constitution, in effect, gave women the choice of staying in Ireland to rear and look after families or emigrating to work in low-paid sectors of the UK and US economies.

From the 1960s onwards Ireland, as part of its modernization strategy and because of social and cultural change, invested heavily in welfare. Although adherence to Catholic corporatist principles meant that the role of the state in the delivery of social services was not as extensive as in other countries, the investment programme marked a dramatic change in attitude towards welfare issues. The state committed itself to providing increased welfare as a fundamental right of citizenship in modern Ireland. However, the core principles of Catholic corporatism determined the manner in which state welfare was delivered and this had a considerable impact on the outcome of this increased expenditure. During this period there were also shifts in the position of women in Irish society. Women's groups, with the help of EC directives, began successfully to challenge discriminatory state policies and practices.

In the 1980s both welfare and women suffered set-backs. Economic crisis, mass unemployment, record levels of emigration and spiralling public expenditure prompted a fundamental rethink of the state's social and economic policies. The Irish state, through a precarious balancing act with its 'social partners', was able to mobilize a national consensus in favour of modified neo-liberal solutions. It was able to do so on the grounds that Ireland needed to have a competitive economy, low levels of inflation and tight control of public expenditure in order to meet EC convergence criteria. This, it was argued, would guarantee further structural and regional funding which could be channelled into job creation projects. However, the same could not be said for the renewed debate over the rights of Irish women. The referendums and campaigns of conservative Catholic pressure groups in the 1980s and early 1990s split Irish society as they tried to block efforts to liberalize the divorce, contraception and abortion laws. This posed a fundamental problem for the Irish state as it has linked the future prosperity of the country with the European Union and it has been forced to reconsider its position on traditional family policies. As a consequence, there was an historic divorce between the state and the Catholic Church in the wider national interest. The controversy and campaigns surrounding women's role, rights and welfare finally forced a new pluralistic settlement upon which campaigners can build.

Having grappled with the institutional and cultural paralysis which resulted from decades of economic failure, policy-makers are now confronted by the complex of social problems generated by rapid economic transformation. In the past the overriding priority of economic policy had been job creation and even pursuing this goal had to take second place to ensuring that the state did not slide into financial insolvency. This set strict limits on the types of welfare provision that could be countenanced. However, the last years of the twentieth century and the onset of the twenty-first saw a dramatic turnaround in economic fortunes and the space was created in which to force a change in the institutional mind-set of policy-makers. For the first time since independence, Ireland found itself confirmed in membership of the club of rich western nations.

The state realizes that its ability to control the overall level of economic activity is limited, given the commitment to an open, flexible economy and the consequences of European monetary union. Its primary role is maximizing the overall efficiency and performance of the economy and to do so it has had to centre the notions of social partnership and social inclusion. This, in conjunction with a buoyant economic situation and a significant restructuring of the ideologies of welfare, has radically redefined the Catholic corporatist welfare regime as it had previously operated in Ireland.

There is one final point worth making before we leave this discussion of Ireland's welfare regime. In line with the rest of the European Union, during the late 1990s Ireland began to receive an unprecedented number of asylum seekers, primarily from eastern Europe and Africa. As a consequence, one of the most 'white' societies in Europe is now having to imagine what the shift to a multi-ethnic, multi-cultural future might mean in terms of notions of 'citizenship', 'national identity', 'belonging' and 'social inclusion'. The challenge will be to ensure that its reformed social welfare and social partnership arrangements reflect the new European Union-wide multi-cultural realities rather than producing new racialized forms of marginalization and social exclusion.

REFERENCES

Beale, J. (1986) *Women in Ireland*, London and Basingstoke, Macmillan.

Bew, P., Hazelkorn, E. and Patterson, H. (1989) *The Dynamics of Irish Politics*, London, Lawrence and Wishart.

Breen, R., Hannan, D.F., Rottman, D.B. and Whelan, C.T. (1990) *Understanding Contemporary Ireland*, Dublin, Gill and MacMillan.

Brennan, P. (1979) 'Women in revolt', *Magill*, vol.2, no.7, pp.34–6.

Burke, H. (1999) 'Foundation stones of Irish social policy, 1831–1951' in Kiely, G., O'Donnell, A., Kennedy, P. and Quinn, S. (eds) *Irish Social Policy in Context*, Dublin, University College Dublin Press.

Callan, T. and Nolan, B. (1998) 'Poverty and policy' in Healy and Reynolds (eds) (1998).

Cassells, P. (1986) 'Living standards' in Kennedy (ed.) (1986).

Chubb, B. (1982) *The Government and Politics of Ireland*, London, Longman.

Collins, S. (1992) *The Haughey File*, Dublin, The O'Brien Press.

Coman, P. (1977) *Catholics and the Welfare State*, London, Longman.

Commission on the Family (1998) *Final Report*, Dublin, Stationery Office.

Cooney, J. (1986) *The Crozier and the Dail*, Dublin, Mercier Press.

Coughlan, A. (1984) 'Ireland's welfare state in crisis', *Administration*, vol.32, no.1, pp.31–41.

Cullen Owens, R. (1984) *Smashing Times: A History of the Irish Women's Suffrage Movement*, Dublin, Attic Press.

Culliton Report (1992) *A Time for Change: Industrial Policy for the 1990s*, Dublin, Stationery Office.

Daly, M. (1989) *Women and Poverty*, Dublin, Attic Press.

Daly, M.E. (1981) 'Women in the Irish workforce from pre-industrial to modern times', *SAOTHAR*, no.9, pp.74–83.

Economist, The (1988) 'Poorest of the rich: an *Economist* survey of the Republic of Ireland', 16 January.

Esping-Andersen, G. (1990) *The Three Worlds of Welfare Capitalism*, Cambridge, Polity Press.

Fahey, T. (1998) 'The Catholic Church and social policy' in Healy and Reynolds (eds) (1998).

Fine-Davis, M. (1988) 'Changing attitudes to the role of women in Ireland' in *First Report of Second Joint Committee on Women's Rights*, Dublin, Government Stationery Office.

Galligan, Y. (1999) 'Women's issues in Irish politics' in Collins, N. (ed.) *Political Issues in Ireland Today*, Manchester, Manchester University Press.

Garvin, T. (1996) *1922: The Birth of Irish Democracy*, Dublin, Gill and MacMillan.

Girvin, B. (1984) 'Industrialization and the Irish working class since 1922', *SAOTHAR*, no.10.

Goldthorpe, J.H. and Whelan, C.T. (eds) (1994) *The Development of Industrial Society in Ireland*, Oxford, Oxford University Press.

Government of Ireland (1996) *Partnership 2000, for Inclusion, Employment and Competitiveness*, Dublin, Stationery Office.

Grogan, V. (1978) 'Towards the new constitution' in MacManus, F. (ed.) *The Years of the Great Test, 1926–39*, Dublin, Mercier Press.

Hannigan, J.A. (1990) 'Containing the Luciferine spark: the Catholic Church and recent movements for social change in the Republic of Ireland' in O'Toole (ed.) (1990).

Hardiman, N. (1988) *Pay, Politics and Economic Performance in Ireland, 1970–87*, Oxford, Clarendon Press.

Healey, G. (1988) 'Body politics', *Fortnight*, no.259, pp.14–15.

Healy, S. and Reynolds, B. (eds) (1998) *Social Policy in Ireland: Principles, Practice and Problems*, Dublin, Oak Tree Press.

Higgins, J. (1981) *States of Welfare*, Oxford, Blackwell.

Hynes, E. (1990) 'Nineteenth-century Irish Catholicism, farmers' ideology, and national religion: exploration in cultural explanation' in O'Toole (ed.) (1990).

Inglis, T. (1985) 'Sacred and secular in Catholic Ireland', *Studies: An Irish Quarterly Review*, vol.7, no.4.

Inglis, T. (1998) *Moral Monopoly: The Rise and Fall of the Catholic Church in Modern Ireland* (2nd edn), Dublin, University College Dublin Press.

Jackson, P. (1986) 'The women's movement and abortion: the criminalization of Irish women' in Dahlerup, D. (ed.) *The New Women's Movement: Feminism and Political Power in Europe and USA*, London, Sage.

Kaim-Caudle, P. (1967) *Social Policy in the Irish Republic*, New York, Humanities Press.

Kearney, R. (1988) 'Thinking otherwise' in Kearney, R. (ed.) *Across the Frontiers: Ireland in the 1990s*, Dublin, Wolfhound Press.

Kelly, K. and Nic Giolla Choille, T. (1990) *Emigration Matters For Women*, Dublin, Attic Press.

Kennedy, K.A. (ed.) (1986) *Ireland in Transition*, Dublin, Gill and MacMillan.

Keogh, D. (1996) 'The role of the Catholic Church in the Republic of Ireland' in *Building Trust in Ireland: Studies Commissioned by the Forum for Peace and Reconciliation*, Belfast, Blackstaff Press.

Laffan, B. (1991) 'Women' in Keatinge, P. (ed.) *Ireland and EC Membership Evaluated*, London, Pinter.

Lane, F. (1997) *The Origins of Modern Irish Socialism*, Cork, Cork University Press.

Lee, J.J. (1988) *Ireland 1912–1985*, Cambridge, Cambridge University Press.

Lyons, F.S.L. (1979) *Ireland Since the Famine*, London, Fontana.

Maguire, M. (1986) 'Ireland' in Flora, P. (ed.) *Growth to Limits: The West European States Since World War Two*, Berlin and New York, de Gruyter.

Mahon, E. (1987) 'Women's rights and Catholicism in Ireland', *New Left Review*, no.166, pp.53–79.

McCafferty, N. (1988) *Goodnight Sisters*, Dublin, Attic Press.

McCashin, A. and Morrisey, M. (1985) 'Housing policy: north and south', *Administration*, vol.33, no.3, pp.291–326.

McDowell, M. (1990) 'Competitive health insurance: the implications of removing the VHI monopoly', *Administration*, vol.38, no.2, pp.138–56.

Moynihan, M. (ed.) (1980) *Speeches and Statements by Eamon de Valera, 1917–73*, Dublin, Gill and MacMillan.

Munck, R. (1985) *Ireland: Nation, State and Class Struggle*, Boulder, CO, Westview Press.

Murphy-Lawless, J. and McCarthy, J. (1999) 'Social policy and fertility change in Ireland', *European Journal of Women's Studies*, vol.6, no.1, pp.69–96.

NESC (National Economic and Social Council) (1986) *A Strategy for Development*, Dublin, National Economic and Social Council.

NESC (National Economic and Social Council) (1999) *Opportunities, Challenges and Capacities for Choice*, NESC Report No. 4, Dublin, National Economic and Social Council.

O'Connor, E. (1992) *A Labour History of Ireland, 1824–1960*, Dublin, Gill and MacMillan.

O'Donnell, R. and Thomas, D. (1998) 'Partnership and policy-making' in Healy and Reynolds (eds) (1998).

Ó'Riain, S. (2000) 'The flexible developmental state: globalization, information technology and the "Celtic Tiger"', *Politics and Society*, vol.28, no.2, pp.157–94.

O'Sullivan, P. (ed.) (1995) *Irish Women and Irish Migration*, Leicester, Leicester University Press.

O'Toole, R. (ed.) (1990) *Sociological Studies in Roman Catholicism*, Leviston, NY, Edwin Meller Press.

OECD (Organisation for Economic Cooperation and Development) (1991) *Review of National Policies for Education: Ireland*, Paris, Organisation for Economic Cooperation and Development.

OECD (Organisation for Economic Cooperation and Development) (1999) *Ireland*, Paris, Organisation for Economic Cooperation and Development.

Owens, R. (1983) 'Votes for ladies, votes for women: organized labour and the suffragette movement, 1876–1922', *SAOTHAR*, no.9, pp.32–47.

Peillon, M. (1982) *Contemporary Irish Society*, Dublin, Gill and MacMillan.

Porter, E. (1996) 'Culture, community and responsibilities: abortion in Ireland', *Sociology*, vol.20, no.2, pp.279–98.

Powell, F.W. (1992) *The Politics of Irish Social Policy, 1600–1900*, Leviston, NY, Edwin Meller Press.

Prager, J. (1986) *Building Democracy in Ireland*, Cambridge, Cambridge University Press.

Pyle, J. (1990a) *The State and Women in the Economy*, New York, SUNY Press.

Pyle, J. (1990b) 'Export led development and the under employment of women: the impact of discriminatory development policy in the Republic of Ireland' in Ward, K. (ed.) *Women Workers and Global Restructuring*, Cornell University, Ithaca, NY, ILR Press.

Rafferty, J. (1985) 'Health services: north and south', *Administration*, vol.33, no.3, pp.274–91.

Roche, B. (1982) 'Social partnership and political controls: state strategy and industrial relations in Ireland' in Kelly, M., O'Dowd, L. and Wickham, J. (eds) *Power, Conflict and Inequality*, Dublin, Turoe.

Scannell, Y. (1988) 'The constitution and the role of women' in Farrell, B. (ed.) *De Valera's Constitution and Ours*, Dublin, Gill and MacMillan.

Schmitt, D.E. (1973) *The Irony of Irish Democracy*, Lexington, MA, Lexington Books.

Smyth, A. (ed.) (1992) *The Abortion Papers*, Dublin, Attic Press.

Smyth, L. (1996) 'Narratives of Irishness and the problem of abortion: the x case 1992', *Feminist Review*, no.60, pp.61–83.

Tansey, P. (1991) *Making the Irish Labour Market Work*, Dublin, Gill and MacMillan.

Walsh, B. (1991) 'Interpreting modern Ireland', *Studies: An Irish Quarterly Review*, vol.80, no.320, pp.400–11.

Ward, M. (1983) *Unmanageable Revolutionaries*, London, Pluto Press.

Whittaker, T.K. (1986) 'Economic Development, 1958–85' in Kennedy (ed.) (1986).

Whyte, G. (1992) 'Report of the review group on the treatment of households in the social welfare code: a legal perspective', *Administration*, vol.40, no.2, pp.134–50.

Whyte, J.H. (1974) 'Ireland: politics without social bases' in Rose, R. (ed.) *Electoral Behaviour: A Comparative Handbook*, New York, The Free Press.

Whyte, J.H. (1980) *Church and State in Modern Ireland, 1923–1979*, Dublin, Gill and MacMillan.

Wickham, J. (1980) 'The politics of dependent capitalism: international capitalism and nation state' in Morgan, A. and Purdie, B. (eds) *Ireland: Divided Nation, Divided Class*, London, Ink Links.

Williamson, P. (1989) *Corporatism in Perspective*, London, Sage.

CHAPTER 8:
LOOKING FOR A EUROPEAN
WELFARE STATE

ALLAN COCHRANE, JOHN CLARKE AND SHARON GEWIRTZ

CONTENTS

	INTRODUCTION	262
1	THE GLOBAL CONTEXT	265
2	EUROPEAN WELFARE STATES	268
3	A SUPRANATIONAL EUROPEAN WELFARE STATE?	271
4	A WIDER EUROPE	280
5	CONCLUSION	284
	REFERENCES	286

INTRODUCTION

The earlier chapters of this book have concentrated on the experiences of particular countries, with both shared and contrasting features being drawn out from the discussion of individual cases. In Chapter 1, we looked at Esping-Andersen's typology of welfare regimes (Esping-Andersen, 1990), which provided some justification for the choice of cases examined in the chapters that followed, beginning with the 'hybrid' British welfare regime (in Chapters 2–3). The United States (Chapter 4) was introduced as an example of the liberal market regime; Germany (Chapter 5) and Ireland (Chapter 7) were considered as rather different variants of the conservative regime; and Sweden (Chapter 6) was chosen as the prime example of Esping-Andersen's social-democratic regime.

Some of the general weaknesses of Esping-Andersen's typology were acknowledged in Chapter 1, particularly the difficulty it had in dealing with matters of gender and 'race'. All typologies tend to emphasize some features at the expense of others and, in this typology, vital aspects of welfare are marginalized. However, in broad terms, the differences between the types of welfare regimes identified by Esping-Andersen are significant, and the notion of welfare regimes is helpful in promoting comparative study because it opens up the possibility of identifying a range of different features and processes that come together to form particular national regimes.

The earlier chapters of this book have highlighted the extent of diversity between welfare states, even where they can loosely be placed within the same broad regime type. Esping-Andersen's typology provided a useful starting-point from which to explore the complexity of welfare state formation and development at the *national level*; the diversity of welfare regimes *between* individual countries, however, can only be understood by exploring the ways in which already existing national institutional, political and social arrangements respond to, and generate, pressures for welfare (see, for example, Flora, 1986a, pp.xvi–xvii). Although a generalizing typology may be helpful in drawing attention to both key differences between broad categories of welfare regime and overarching issues, it cannot explain the detailed processes of interaction that lead to the formation of particular welfare systems. Nevertheless, recognizing the idiosyncrasies of national welfare systems should not stop us from acknowledging the importance of wider changes that take place across national boundaries.

In this chapter we shall be asking, first, whether common trends are encouraging a process of convergence between European welfare states and, secondly, whether it is possible to identify moves that may be leading to a cross-national or supranational welfare state, based on the structures of the European Union (EU). Although it is tempting to see these two aspects of change as closely related, in principle policy convergence between different countries might be taking place without the development of any supranational institutional arrangements.

Alternatively, new institutional (welfare) arrangements might be developing at the European level even if convergence were not taking place between the different national welfare regimes.

The remainder of this chapter is divided into four main parts to take account of these analytical distinctions. Section 1 examines the global context for developments at European and national levels, identifying wider trends and pressures. Section 2 explores the extent to which there has been convergence between countries within Europe, particularly Western Europe, and explicitly refers back to the arguments of earlier chapters. It asks whether it is possible to identify a 'European model' of welfare and sets out to explore what the main features of such a model might be. Section 3 follows a rather different path and seeks to assess whether there have been moves towards an EU-based welfare state and, if so, how it relates to, and differs from, the welfare regime types discussed earlier. Finally, the chapter looks beyond the current boundaries of the EU to consider the implications of taking a wider view of Europe, examining the consequences both of the continuing enlargement of the EU and the uncertain outcomes of social, political and economic change in Central and Eastern Europe.

It is possible to point to three main tendencies in the new world of welfare that have been hinted at in previous chapters. First, and most importantly, welfare states are now more accurately understood as 'mixed economies' rather than welfare states in the traditional sense, which implied a unified bureaucratic system of state-based provision. In retrospect it may be appropriate to analyse all welfare states as mixed economies (since they have always relied heavily on informal care), but the nature of the 'mix' is changing to such an extent that it seems reasonable to suggest there has been a significant shift in emphasis. The issue of state funding of social welfare remains politically and analytically contentious. Despite the challenges to welfare states, public expenditure on welfare in European countries has remained high and has even increased (see Kuhnle and Alestalo, 2000, p.4 and Table 8.1 below). The role of the state seems to be moving towards forms of regulation and licensing as much as, if not more than, direct provision (Kuhnle and Alestalo, 2000).

Secondly, there has also been a move towards an interpretation of welfare policy as an important element in economic competition between countries. In its earliest form this found expression in the argument that particular national economies could not afford to sustain existing levels of welfare spending and remain competitive. More recently there has been explicit discussion both of the extent to which countries may compete for investment by presenting themselves as having low welfare costs for investors, and the extent to which particular forms of welfare expenditure may be more or less attractive in offering social infrastructure for investment and the encouragement of economic innovation (see, for example, Hay, 2001; Jessop, 2000).

Thirdly, welfare may no longer be solely the responsibility of national governments. This is a more speculative interpretation of changes at

TABLE 8.1 Current expenditure on social protection as percentage of Gross Domestic Product at current prices.

	1980	1981	1982	1983	1984	1985	1986	1987	1988	1989	1990	1991	1992	1993	1994	1995
EC12/EU15	–	–	–	–	–	–	25.8	25.7	25.3	–	25.4	26.5	27.8	28.9	28.6	28.4
Belgium	28.0	30.1	30.2	30.8	29.4	–	29.5	29.0	27.7	26.7	26.6	27.0	27.1	29.0	29.0	29.7
Denmark	28.7	30.1	30.5	30.2	28.7	27.5	26.7	27.5	29.3	29.6	30.3	31.6	32.1	33.5	35.1	34.3
Germany	28.6	29.4	29.4	29.1	28.7	–	28.0	28.3	28.3	27.3	25.4	27.0	28.4	29.1	28.9	29.4
Greece	–	–	–	–	–	–	15.5	16.0	16.5	–	22.6	21.0	20.3	20.8	20.8	20.7
Spain	–	–	17.0	–	–	–	17.5	17.2	17.2	17.3	19.9	21.0	22.1	23.5	22.4	21.9
France	25.5	27.0	28.0	28.5	–	–	28.5	28.2	28.1	27.8	27.7	28.4	29.3	31.0	30.5	30.6
Ireland	20.6	21.3	23.0	23.9	23.3	23.9	24.3	23.6	22.4	20.6	19.1	20.2	20.8	20.9	20.3	19.9
Italy	19.8	21.7	22.4	23.7	23.3	23.4	22.5	23.0	23.1	23.2	24.1	24.6	25.8	26.0	25.8	24.6
Luxembourg	26.4	28.2	27.0	26.5	–	–	24.8	26.1	26.2	25.6	23.5	24.6	24.4	25.2	24.7	25.3
Netherlands	30.4	31.4	33.2	33.7	–	–	30.9	31.4	30.9	30.2	32.5	32.6	33.2	33.7	32.7	31.6
Portugal	13.0	14.5	14.3	–	–	–	16.4	16.7	17.0	–	15.5	16.8	18.7	21.0	21.0	20.7
United Kingdom	21.6	23.7	23.9	24.1	24.1	–	24.4	23.6	22.1	–	23.1	25.2	27.3	28.4	28.0	27.7
Austria	–	–	–	–	–	–	–	–	–	–	26.7	27.0	27.7	28.9	29.7	29.7
Finland	–	–	–	–	–	–	25.5	26.0	24.8	–	25.5	30.4	34.4	35.5	34.7	32.8
Sweden	–	–	–	–	–	–	33.7	34.7	36.0	–	32.9	34.2	36.9	38.6	37.6	35.6

Source: Eurostat, 1988 and 1991, Table 3.31, p.135; Eurostat 1999, p.264

the global level, but if in the past welfare regimes were explicitly national, it may now be possible to find examples of transitional or supranational aspects of those regimes. Deacon argues, for example, that agencies such as the International Monetary Fund, the International Labour Organization and the European Community have had a significant impact on the reshaping of social policy in Central and Eastern Europe in the wake of the overthrow of the communist regimes at the start of the 1990s (Deacon, 1997). Since the world is increasingly dominated by the three major economic (and political) blocs of Europe, North America and East Asia, it might also be reasonable to expect that welfare systems are also being reorganized at that level.

The first two of these three tendencies suggest that any similar pressures may be absorbed differently in different countries, due to the ways in which they are reinterpreted through their existing welfare regimes. Alternatively, if those pressures are strong enough, they might lead to a process of convergence between those welfare regimes. The next section of this chapter considers these issues more carefully in the context of developments in Western Europe. The third possibility goes beyond individual welfare states to suggest ways in which they might be superseded by emerging supranational state forms. That issue is taken up again in section 3 of the chapter where attention is focused on the extent to which the European Union is developing any of the characteristics of a welfare state.

I   THE GLOBAL CONTEXT

Discussions of globalization and how the global context affects European welfare states became increasingly significant during the 1990s. In this section, we explore two different ways of thinking about the relationship between globalization and welfare states. The first treats globalization as a force that has undermined welfare states in the 'advanced capitalist nations'. The second places greater emphasis on the diversity of national and regional responses (in their political and institutional forms) to the pressures and demands of a new global economy.

The first view treats globalization as the single dominant economic, political and social process in the contemporary world. In this view, globalization has driven epochal changes in economic relations; it has undermined the capacity of nation-states to be self-contained and self-directing; it has promoted global social and cultural uniformity; and it has made the continuation of the system of European welfare states impossible. The enhanced mobility of capital, demands for tax reductions, the vulnerability of government policies to financial markets and related processes have, it is argued, led to a continuous downward pressure on public spending (and especially on public spending on welfare). For example, John Gray has claimed that:

Bond markets have knocked away the floor from under post-war full employment policies. No western government today has a credible successor to the policies which secured welfare societies in the Keynesian era ... Social market systems are being compelled progressively to dismantle themselves, so that they can compete on equal terms with economies in which environmental, social and labour costs are lowered.

(John Gray, 1998, p.92)

Here globalization is understood as an irresistible economic logic, forcing 'a race to the bottom' in which social costs have to be reduced because they impair national economic competitiveness in an increasingly competitive world. The flows of money, goods, information and even production systems have undermined the weight and significance of national boundaries, producing what Ohmae (1999) has called a 'borderless world'.

There are a number of reasons for viewing this conception of globalization sceptically. First, borders continue to exist and affect people in significant ways. In particular, the movement of people is controlled and constrained by the ways in which regional and national boundaries are asserted, defended and policed (Sassen, 1998). Secondly, this conception of globalization is a particular narrative: an over-deterministic account of changes in the world that positions nations, governments, organizations, citizens and the state-less as its powerless victims (Massey, 1999). This is a convenient story, both for those who want to make the world like this and for governments and organizations who can use the 'necessity' of globalization as a way of accounting for their actions and inactions (Hay, 1998). Thirdly, this view of the destructive elements of globalization in relation to welfare states does not quite match the evidence about the fortunes of developed welfare states. As we have seen in the earlier chapters of this book, only in the US have there been decisive moves to bring about 'an end to welfare', and even these have been more partial than the globalization thesis would suggest. Table 8.1 above suggests that welfare spending in Europe has remained at levels that this view of globalization suggests could not have been sustained. A growing number of studies have argued that this epochal view of globalization resulting in the dissolution of welfare states is too crude and one-dimensional (e.g. Esping-Andersen, 1996; Hirst and Thompson, 1999; Kuhnle, 2000; Rhodes, 1996; Sykes, Palier and Prior, 2001). For example, Esping-Andersen has argued that:

We should not exaggerate the degree to which global forces over-determine the fate of national welfare states. One of the most powerful conclusions in comparative research is that political and institutional mechanisms of interest representation and political-concessions building matter tremendously in terms of managing welfare, employment and growth objectives.

(Esping-Andersen, 1996, p.6)

This leads us to the second view of the relationship between globalization and welfare states. Here, new global forces and conditions are seen as forming a new context to which national welfare states have to adapt. However, the process of adaptation is one in which national political and institutional pressures play a significant part, sustaining a diversity of national welfare systems. Rather than the drive towards convergence in the first model, this second view stresses the relative autonomy of national processes in shaping responses to globalization (Kersbergen, 2000). It is clear that the national welfare states that are discussed earlier in this book are marked by different trajectories: while the USA might exemplify the neo-liberal retreat from welfare (in some respects), other states have sought to maintain welfare systems, or resist economic demands to curtail public spending. At the same time, other distinctive features or conditions of national social and political formations have played a distinctive part in shaping welfare systems, from the re-unification of Germany to the modernizing effects of Ireland's entry into the European Union. This view of common (global or international) pressures and national adaptations is the dominant view of recent comparative studies of 'welfare states in transition' (Esping-Andersen, 1996). Like the national case studies in this book, such work also suggests that the dominant trend has not been the dismantling of welfare states, but a period of politics dominated by 'retrenchment' or 'austerity' (Chamberlayne, 1992) followed by a revival of welfare spending. Welfare spending has been slowed, rather than dramatically reduced, across most of the European nations (see Table 8.1 above).

The resilience of welfare spending suggests that the rather apocalyptic view of globalization needs to be tempered by an understanding of the continued capacity of national political institutions and processes to shape welfare choices, and by a view of social welfare as performing valued social and political functions. Kersbergen's discussion of the 'resistance of welfare states' to pressures for change highlights the 'political' and 'institutional' forces promoting the maintenance of social welfare provision in Europe (Kersbergen, 2000). In different ways, welfare is something more than the 'unproductive expenditure' denounced by neo-liberals.

It may be important to take a more differentiated view of globalization, rather than treating it as a homogeneous, and homogenizing, process or set of forces. We have already seen that there is no simple homogenizing effect in relation to welfare systems. But it is also significant that the new pattern of global processes does not press on every nation state in the same way: their national economic and social systems means that they were placed differently in the previous international order. The UK's distinctive economic, social and political relationship to the post-war US hegemony have, for example, meant a different relationship to the processes of globalization in comparison to nations in western Europe such as France and Germany. At the same time, it is worth noting that the processes of globalization are potentially contradictory rather than one-directional (Clarke, 2000).

For example, in social terms globalization is seen to promote social/ cultural homogenization sometimes called 'Americanization' or 'McDonaldization' (see Held, 2000). However, it also celebrates and proliferates forms of cultural difference, both in creating 'local' markets and in selling the culture of one place/people to others as 'exotic' or 'novel' (Jameson and Miyoshi, 1998). In a different way, supra-national institutions and corporations have increasingly come to recognize questions of social order and quality of life as matters of concern (not least because they themselves need somewhere to live, see Sassen, 1998). A 'good business environment' may imply something more than low wages and low taxes. These aspects of globalization require an analysis that stresses differentiation, unevenness and contradictions rather than homogeneity and uni-directional development (Massey, 1999).

For the study of welfare states, such an approach means moving away from simplistic or reductionist political economy views towards more complex studies of the institutional and political conflicts over globalization and the 'adaptations' to it (Clarke, 2000). As a result, the core issues involved in studying welfare states have begun to move from 'typologies' to 'transitions'. The classification of types of regimes was developed in the period of relatively settled Keynesianism. That settled period provided the context in which different variants – what Ginsburg (1992) called 'structured diversity' – were developed and could be categorized by researchers. Since the 1980s, however, we have seen new dynamics of welfare states: processes of restructuring, realignment and reform. These reflect the destabilization of the global context and the unsettling of national social and political conditions that underpinned the Keynesian welfare states. Most welfare systems are now in search of new alignments, new settlements and new arrange-ments. As Jessop (2000) has argued, this is not the same as arguing that the nation state has been abolished, nor even fatally wounded. It points to a need to understand 'scalar changes': the emergent relation-ships between local-national-regional institutions and processes in the new global context. Here, Europe – in the form of the EU – is both a force of globalization, shaping the new world economy, and a bulwark against some aspects of globalization (the neo-liberal Americanizing tendency).

In sections 2 and 3 we look further at some of these European dimensions.

2 EUROPEAN WELFARE STATES

So far in this chapter we have tended to refer to welfare states in advanced capitalist countries, without worrying too much about whether they are European or not. So what about Europe? Perhaps the first point to make is that defining Europe is a problematic matter because the boundaries, content and relationships of Europe are in the process of being remade (Hudson and Williams, 1999; Jönsson, Tägil and Törnqvist, 2000). In this context, Europe can mean a range of different things for the study of social policy. It can refer to the historically dominant axis of Western and Northern European states that have provided the models of advanced welfare states. To an extent, this meaning overlaps with a second conception of Europe that equates it with the European Union, as Sykes has observed:

> Most studies of social policy in Europe focus either explicitly or implicitly on the member of states of the EU ... Yet we should not forget that while the EU's economic and political dominance of Europe progresses, other political economic and social systems continue to exist with social policy systems that may or may not be converging with the EU.
>
> (Sykes, 1998, p.15)

At the same time, of course, the EU has itself changed and enlarged as new member states join the Union, bringing with them their distinctive welfare systems. Sykes highlights the processes of deconstruction and reconstruction under way in the former Eastern bloc nations as a further central strand in the problems of defining Europe in social policy (Ferge, 2000; Poole, 2000). The conventional North/West axis in the study of European welfare states is increasingly confronted by the developments in both Central and Eastern Europe and in the South. What are sometimes called 'Mediterranean' welfare states (Greece, Italy, Portugal and Spain in particular) are posing new questions about welfare state development (see for example, Leibfried, 1993; Ferrara, 1996; Guillen and Alvarez, 2001).

Although these questions about Europe and welfare states go beyond the case studies that we have examined, they raise important issues about what it means to talk about European welfare states and European social policy. European welfare states tend to be discussed in terms of patterns of convergence and divergence among national welfare states in Europe (e.g. Sykes and Alcock, 1998). European social policy, however, tends to be discussed in terms of *supra*-national policy institutions, particularly those of the EU (e.g. Geyer, 2000). In the remainder of this section, we examine issues surrounding the European welfare states before moving on to look at the EU as a social policy institution. Finally, in section 4, we return to some of the issues raised by thinking about a 'wider Europe'.

When viewed from outside, the general assumption seems to be that the welfare states of Western Europe take similar forms. Flora argues that 'the modern welfare state is a European invention' (Flora, 1986a, p.xii), and in developing their analysis of the American welfare state, Weir *et al.* emphasize that it is 'not a Western European-style welfare state' (Weir *et al.*, 1988, p.9). In such broad terms, the claim seems to be little more than that the more prosperous Western European states have traditionally taken it for granted that in some sense they have a responsibility for the provision of welfare, and that they have spent broadly similar levels of their national income on social welfare – and rather more than countries such as the USA and Japan. An implicit contrast is drawn between the assumption, in most Western European countries, that the state plays an active part in shaping welfare and the opposite situation, which tends to dominate in the USA, in which there is what Stoesz and Midgley describe as a 'cultural antipathy to state welfarism' (Stoesz and Midgley, 1991, p.26). In the mid 1980s most of the EC member-states spent between 20 per cent and 30 per cent of their GDP on activities defined by the OECD as 'social expenditure'. In the 1980s only Greece, Portugal and Spain spent a lower proportion, with levels of between 15 and 20 per cent of GDP (closer to the levels of the US and Japan). During the 1990s, however, the southern states began to increase levels of welfare spending above 20 per cent of GDP (see Table 8.1 above; see also Kuhnle and Alestalo, 2000, p.4 and Table 8.2 below). Such trends are not just a straightforward process of 'convergence' – in either numerical terms or the forms of welfare organization. Nevertheless, they are an important reminder that the southern European states are also engaged in processes of transition (Kuhnle, 2000; Sykes, Palier and Prior, 2001).

Some shared features do run through the different chapters: all have recognizable welfare states and the continued role of the state in the provision, funding and regulation of welfare is not in question; all of them have clearly had to cope with the increased pressures of 'austerity'; all have gone through some process of retrenchment, although to varying extents. Other key features have also remained consistent over time, since each has remained committed to a mixed economy based on capitalism, and, despite some rhetorical flourishes, welfare has continued to be delivered on the basis of a set of patriarchal assumptions and a set of more or less clear assumptions about who is eligible for welfare citizenship. However, there is a real danger of failing to acknowledge the equally significant differences between European welfare states. The points of similarity listed above are still very broad principles, which do little more than provide parameters within which, as we have seen, a wide range of social policy practices may exist (see also Sykes, Palier and Prior, 2001). The experience of Western European countries since 1945 has been characterized by shared patterns of political change and policy development existing alongside what Kastandiek calls 'an equally striking persistence of national diversity' (Kastandiek, 1990, p. 69). But that diversity does not mean that individual welfare states can exist completely autonomously with little reference to global economic changes or political changes in other countries. Some responses to the wider context of global change are particularly apparent in the European context. Even the strongest bastions of social-democratic welfarism such as Sweden and Denmark have been forced belatedly to acknowledge the pressures of financial constraint, affecting their abilities to maintain high levels of state spending. Others, such as Britain, have more or less consciously presented themselves as offering low-cost welfare, with guarantees of minimum regulatory interference by the state. Austerity welfare certainly dominates throughout Europe, and within the EU this may be reinforced by the need to compete with the relatively cheap labour and low welfare costs of southern European member states. Leibfried (1992b, p.255) suggests that the model most likely to dominate in this process is the liberal (or 'Anglo-Saxon') one in which welfare tends to be residual and targeted, and not based on clear entitlements to benefit or commitments to the maintenance of full employment. Indeed, one central role of Britain within the EU has been as promoter of the liberal/Anglo-Saxon model of social welfare against other models (particularly the corporatist commitments of Germany and France). In this way, Britain has occupied a critical place as a hinge between the European Union and the US in the conflicts over 'models of welfare'.

Within comparative studies, arguments have continued about the degree of diversity or convergence between European welfare states. This is partly as a result of the different features that form the focus of studies. For example, Greve's emphasis on a growing convergence towards a 'safety net' welfare system (1996, p.364) reflects his primary attention to patterns and programmes of public spending on social protection within EU member states. These, he argues, show a narrowing of differences in levels of, and approaches to, spending on social protection. In contrast, Daly's (1997) analysis of 'cash benefit systems' in Western European welfare states argues for a renewed attention to the diversity of welfare state responses to new demographic, social and economic pressures. Her study of the 'institutional architecture' and patterns of social rights in benefits systems emphasizes both common trends (towards a 'meaner' and more 'conditional' focus of benefit) and a striking diversity of patterns (and timings) of change. She suggests that there is a need for studies that are attentive to the dynamics of welfare state development, rather than static classificatory systems.

The studies within this book tend to confirm Daly's view of the balance between convergence and diversity, with a stress on the continued differences of approach and adaptation among European welfare states. The chapters have also emphasized the importance of viewing welfare states as being 'in transition'. While it is possible to see characteristics and trends that differentiate European welfare states from other models of welfare (e.g. the US or the former Eastern bloc state systems), it still remains difficult to discern one 'European model' of welfare state while comparing different national welfare states. However, this is not the only level at which Europe and social policy can be explored.

3   A SUPRANATIONAL EUROPEAN WELFARE STATE?

If a distinctive European welfare system is unlikely to be created as the result of an incremental process of convergence between existing European welfare states, the rise of the European Union (EU) as a supranational political institution might encourage the parallel develop-ment of a supranational European welfare state, linking together member states in a single framework and possibly even providing its own forms of welfare throughout the Union. Such a welfare state is unlikely to look much like existing national welfare systems, both because it will be reluctant to undertake tasks already performed at national level and because the EU has few powers to operate indepen-dently of its member states. The politics of the EU combine intergovernmental bargaining and negotiation (through the Council of Ministers and the Parliament) with a degree of autonomy for the European Commission and the European Court of Justice. Although the EU's institutions and those who run them are 'European', they are also 'simultaneously linked to the national' through a complex web of appointments, meetings and other networks (Sbragia, 1992a, p.4). In this sense, referring to the EU as if it was a singular entity runs some risks, particularly that of understating the different interests, powers and trajectories of its constituent elements. A fuller analysis than we can undertake here would explore the different impacts of member states, different European bodies and their relations with social part-ners and non-governmental organizations in the shaping of European social policy (for example, Geyer, 2000).

Much of what is usually referred to as EU social policy bears little relationship to welfare as it is generally understood in the welfare systems of the Union member-states. This point is often missed in popular discussions of the EU, in part because frequent references to 'the social dimension' suggest the existence of a developed European social policy. The Protocol on Social Policy (frequently referred to as the Social Chapter) attached to the Treaty of European Union (Maastricht Treaty) is often assumed to promise a fully rounded welfare state, although its provisions concentrate on defining the rights of workers. Its objectives are general, focusing on the promotion of employment, the improvement of living and working conditions, and the provision of nationally defined adequate forms of social protection. The Protocol encourages dialogue between management and labour, with effective consultation of workforces, as well as improved health and safety at work, equal employment opportunities for men and women and equal pay for equal work.

Such an explicitly labour-market oriented package clearly takes a different starting-point in comparison to most welfare states, and its provisions fit uneasily with welfare regimes that are close to the liberal model. The UK government refused to sign this part of the Treaty when it was first agreed by the other eleven member states in 1991. However, the Labour government elected in 1997 signed the Protocol as a key element of its commitment to giving Britain an enlarged role in Europe. Leibfried (1992a, p.17) suggests that the earlier Social Charter (Fundamental Social Rights of Workers, again agreed by eleven of the states excluding the UK in 1989), on which the Social Protocol was based, reflected a 'negative' view of social policy, which stressed rights and above all the right to freedom of movement (labour mobility) for workers. Its main purpose was to remove obstacles to the operation of a single market within Europe rather than to provide a positive statement of social citizenship.

There are, however, ways in which it is possible to conceive of something that would look more like a European welfare state, for example we could look more carefully at forms of income transfer to particular groups. We could also adopt a rather different way of looking at welfare, concentrating on the regulation of social policy from above and the promotion of shared goals across the member-states. For example, the Commission's *Social Policy Agenda*, developed after the Lisbon European council meeting of 1999, addresses 'the modernization of the European Social Model'. It aims to develop an integrated European approach towards achieving the economic and social renewal identified at Lisbon, ensuring 'the positive and dynamic interaction of economic, employment and social policy' (Commission of the European Communities, 2000a, p.2).

If the definition is drawn broadly enough, some of the EU's existing expenditure could be defined as welfare spending. The main elements of EU spending are on the so-called structural funds, that is the European Social Fund, the European Regional Development Fund and the Common Agricultural Policy. Despite its title (which to a British audience might imply the payment of welfare benefits), the Social Fund has been oriented towards the retraining and relocation of the European unemployed. It has provided support for training in areas of high unemployment with an emphasis on removing rigidities in labour markets rather than providing welfare. It has been part of a package of policies intended to smooth the operations of the market or to enable 'adaptation to market-induced changes' as some industrial and employment sectors decline while others rise (Cutler *et al.*, 1989, p.148). Insofar as it is welfare, it is welfare oriented towards servicing the needs of innovation and market-led economic change and restructuring. Geyer argues that 'EC social policy was an essential element in the creation of the internal market ... promoting the free movement of workers and reforming the structural funds to make them more effective were obvious elements of the market-supporting strategy' (Geyer, 2000, p.46).

The European Regional Development Fund (ERDF) has been used to encourage infrastructural development in the poorest regions of the EU and those in industrial decline. The bulk of spending has gone to Ireland and the southern countries of the EU. As a result, its operation implies a redistribution of resources from the north to the south. It could, therefore, be seen as a form of welfare policy, but again if it is, then this implies a changed notion of welfare in which the generation of economic growth and restructuring to fit into a wider European market is itself defined as welfare. The ERDF does not intended to provide financial support to people living in the countries of the periphery, but to integrate those countries into a single market with the help of necessary infrastructural spending. Any increase in prosperity for local residents will be incidental to the process of economic integration. The governments of the EU's southern member states and Ireland have been resistant to suggestions that the Union's spending should be explicitly redefined as welfare spending (for example, as income support to people in poorer countries) because they want to encourage self-sustaining economic growth as a basis for prosperity that may ultimately result in improvements in nationally provided welfare. Because their main competitive edge within the EU lies in their low labour costs, the governments of these countries see social policies that might increase costs as threats to economic growth. As a result the governments of poorer countries have preferred programmes that transfer resources 'in a way that improves infrastructure and enhances productivity without dramatically affecting wages' (Leibfried and Pierson, 1992, p.346).

The Common Agricultural Policy (through the Common Agricultural Guidance and Guarantee Fund), involving some 60 per cent of EU spending in the 1990s, incorporated welfare principles rather more clearly. It is the most supranationally organized system within the EU and regulates some 90 per cent of agricultural production and almost all of the incomes of EU farmers. Unlike the other structural funds, the dominant driving force of agricultural policy *is* the maintenance of the incomes of one section of the population, rather than a process of economic restructuring, and unlike expenditure under the ERDF, most agricultural spending remains in the more prosperous northern European states, although some poorer countries do benefit from it. It is, however, not based on a set of agreed social or citizen rights for farmers, but on an economic rationale – a response to the economic restructuring of European agriculture. The income transfers are hidden behind guaranteed sales for some products, and payment for withdrawing land from the active production of others. Leibfried (1992a) argues that if income transfers were to be decoupled from levels of output, then the Union agricultural policy would more clearly be seen for what it is, namely a rather complicated social policy mechanism for providing a basic income to European farmers. If this interpretation were accepted, however, Leibfried goes on to argue, it would then be difficult to justify shutting out other claimants. It would be logically consistent to develop a more comprehensive system of benefits, related to the risks of falling income, following from European integration.

The EU's role in developing social policy takes on rather different forms, through the identification of key issues and programmes that have a high profile, even if they do not have large budgets. Geyer (2000) identifies a range of policy areas that have been developed beyond the core areas of labour policy and the structural and social funds. These include the development of gender equality policies as a 'mainstreamed' feature of the EU's social dimension. Gender policy has linked labour policy issues (for example, equal pay and workers' rights) to wider social policy matters (Pillinger, 2000). The EU has also engaged, though less substantially, with issues of poverty, social exclusion and policies directed at the elderly, young people and disabled people (Geyer, 2000). The EU has funded three anti-poverty pro-grammes between the mid 1970s and the 1990s. Although spending on programmes such as these is small by the standards of the welfare states that they are intended to influence, it represents significantly increased resources to individual projects and the partners involved in running them. It has also encouraged research into the incidence of poverty across Europe, which helps to raise the profile of the EU in social policy and also influences the policies of national governments. The programmes have also helped to sponsor and develop a range of non-governmental organizations (NGOs) that have become involved in both implementation and further policy development (Geyer, 2000).

The EU has also defined combating social exclusion as a major policy objective. The European Council identified three key elements of its 'social inclusion strategy': 'promoting a better understanding of social exclusion ... ; mainstreaming the promotion of inclusion in member states' employment, education and training, health and housing policies ... ; [and] developing actions addressed to specific target groups.' (Commission of the European Communities, 2000b, pp.2–3).

However, while it is possible to point to aspects of the EU's activities that are welfare-state-like, it is also important not to exaggerate their significance. Most of these activities are not perceived as having much to do with social policy or welfare, either by the EU itself or, possibly more importantly, by the governments of its member states. However optimistically one views the possibility of a supranational European welfare state, it would be unlikely to operate like the individual welfare states that constitute the EU. EU expenditure represents only 1.2 per cent of Union national income and less than 4 per cent of the central government spending of the EU member states. Since the structural funds account for around 80 per cent of EU expenditure, there is not much scope for developing a significant budget earmarked for welfare spending (Leibfried and Pierson, 1992, p.348). The difficulties of reaching agreement between the countries of the European Union at the start of the 1990s, even on the relatively modest political union proposed in the Maastricht treaty, suggest that any more far-reaching moves towards building a supranational welfare state are unlikely to be realized in the near future. At best it is possible to identify the seeds of welfarism in the operation of programmes with other ambitions, and in the form of rather minor welfare programmes. It does not seem likely that the EU will be able to transform itself into a fully fledged welfare state with trans-European income support programmes and funding, operated from Brussels or any other European centre. However, perhaps other aspects of the EU's operation, particularly those connec-ted with ways of regulating the operation of national systems within a single market, raise the possibility of alternative welfare developments.

It was argued by many of the supporters of the European Union in the early 1990s that, as the move towards a single European market took place, the importance of the 'social dimension' should be recognised.

This social dimension was to be 'directed towards protecting and improving the rights and quality of life of workers throughout the Union as the integration process moves ahead. Social policy also works to ensure the widespread availability of the skilled and flexible workforce seen to be necessary for European industry to maintain and improve its competitive position' (Lange, 1992, p.228). The key point about the social dimension, therefore, was that it was explicitly linked to the EU's strategy for economic integration. Majone points to the Commission's own ambitions 'to increase its influence' and the difficulties of doing so through its limited spending options, but also stresses the interest of multinational export-oriented companies in Europe-wide regulation as a means of 'avoiding inconsistent and progressively more stringent regulations in various EU and non-EU countries' (Majone, 1991, pp.96–7). One of the arguments for the social dimension, therefore, was the need to maintain consistency to make longer-term planning and investment easier for companies such as these.

Two opposing positions can be identified in debates about the forms of social policy regulation that should be developed through the EU (Lange, 1992, pp.230–1). The first (minimalist) approach expects no more than basic rules (minimum rights on health and safety at work, gender equality at work, the access of disabled people to employment, the transferability of social security rights for internal migrants) to be delivered on a decentralized basis at member-state level, leaving individual countries to determine rights and how to protect them. The second (social-protectionist) approach seeks to raise standards of provision where they are low, and to maintain them where high through a process of 'harmonization'. It argues for the EC to work against 'social dumping' or the reduction of provision to the lowest common denominator through competitive bidding between states over labour costs. Supporters of this approach argue that, 'by fostering a trained, protected and therefore flexible work force, while at the same time gradually raising labour costs for firms, EC-level social policy would provide both carrots and sticks for firms to upgrade their technology and to compete in markets in which European firms have the most favourable prospects in the coming decade' (Lange, 1992, p.231). While acknowledging the limited scope of European social policy, Cram argues that:

> The use of regulatory policy increasingly allows the European Commission to take on the role of 'calling the tune without paying the piper' in the field of social policy ... [B]y making use of regulatory policies in the area of social policy, rather than those involving direct Community expenditure, EC social policy, in a number of specific areas, increasingly sets the standards to be adhered to in the member states while incurring minimum Community costs.
>
> (Cram, 1993, p.136)

The advantage to the EU of such an approach is two-fold: first it avoids the necessity of having directly to confront powerful member states, and secondly, it ensures that the costs are borne by national taxes and individual employers rather than the EU itself. Policy-making through regulation and rule-making also tends to mask the extent of any potentially embarrassing redistribution between states and regions, instead of highlighting them as the structural funds do. Cram suggests that the creation of an effective and extensive regulatory framework for social policy is a gradual process characterized by 'the incremental development of marginal, relatively innocuous measures in order to establish precedent and competence' (Spicker, 1991, p.9, quoted in Cram, 1993). She emphasizes the importance of non-binding 'soft law' at the European level being created outside the high controversy surrounding the signing of major treaties, and points to the ways in which the declaration of political commitment to general goals (for example, on basic levels of income support or on employment rights) may help to encourage changes, as may EU-sponsored research, such as that organized around the poverty programmes discussed above.

Key aspects of a regulatory framework are already present in provisions within treaties, Community directives and regulations (as well as the Social Chapter) even if, as noted earlier, the emphasis of these documents is on the position of people at work or in the labour market, and on health and safety at work, equal treatment of men and women, protection and social security for EU migrant-workers. A relatively modest European welfare state, building on labour-market policies, is easier to envisage than more grandiose structures that use a vision of a United States of Europe as a starting-point. It may nevertheless have a significant impact on how the national welfare states operate. Here some rules, which were initially oriented towards labour markets, have already had clear social policy impacts, particularly in the field of equal opportunities for women. The European Court of Justice has ruled that individuals can bring cases under Article 119 of the Treaty of Rome, which relates to equal pay, and the EU has used sex discrimination as an issue on which to challenge member-states 'as an entering wedge for expanded activity' (Leibfried and Pierson, 1992, p.338). It is one of the few areas in which the EU has felt able to enforce social policy harmonization.

Regulation of the European labour market has also given the European Union and the European Court the responsibility of ensuring that internal (EU national) migrants do not lose out – that is: to ensure that there is no discrimination against citizens of other member-states on 'social security' issues; to determine which state would decide legally contested cases; to protect the accumulation and transfer of insurance entitlement arising from spells of employment in different countries; and to protect the right to take social entitlements to any member-state (Leibfried, 1992a, p.35). This responsibility is, however, of limited significance for two reasons. First, it affects only a very small number of EU citizens (and there is no similar arrangement for non-EU migrant-workers whose numbers are more than twice as great). Only some 1.4 per cent of EU employees fit into this category. Secondly, and more significantly, in this model 'national systems are "co-ordinated" rather than harmonized' (Leibfried and Pierson, 1992, p.338) in the sense that there is no attempt to bring the different systems to the same level, only to ensure that nationals of one EU state working in another EU state have access to the same entitlements as nationals of the state in which they are working. Again the entitlement to welfare comes from a stress on the free movement of labour, rather than a commitment to wider welfare ambitions. The European Court of Justice has ruled that what it defines as 'welfare rights' (that is, benefits that are not employment-related) may be limited to a country's nationals, even if in practice welfare is defined so narrowly by the Court that few benefits are actually excluded. The benefit systems remain national and the EU and the European Court only regulate access to them.

Despite the EU's limited scope for practical intervention, there are nevertheless some features of these responsibilities that may influence the shape of welfare at member-state and European level. The first is simply that EU requirements may encourage changes in national systems in unintended ways. Those requirements stress the portability of many benefits between countries because they are defined as employment-related (this extends to benefits such as child allowances). This may encourage national governments to move away from universal benefits towards contributory benefits (whether state-provided or, as is more likely, provided through insurance or employment, for example in the form of occupational pensions) or ones that can be more easily targeted and less easily transported (such as housing benefit) (Leibfried and Pierson, 1992). The second is a more important aspect of the emerging system that echoes some of the early experience of welfare state development at national level. A great deal of EU-wide policy is concerned with the defining of rights for citizens of EU member-states within a single market. It explicitly avoids providing similar rights for migrants who are not citizens of member-states. Their 'rights' are directly employment-related: while employed on limited-term contracts with appropriate entry certificates and visas, they may call on some nationally provided benefits, but as soon as those contracts come to an end, they have no EU-guaranteed welfare rights. Their position is governed by national laws that differ from member-state to member-state. Migrant women from outside the EU without work permits who have entered as dependants of their husbands are unable to register as unemployed, or to receive unemployment benefit or many other benefits (Prondzynski, 1989, p.351).

Mitchell and Russell have discussed the contradictory effects of steadily tightening policies of immigration control in the EU, and the continuing process of migration towards Europe. They suggest that it is evident that significant migration flows are continuing both into Europe and between the EU member states. Various 'half-open doors' and 'narrow passages' facilitate the continued migration of groups of people, many of which are destined to end up on the wrong side of the law, (Mitchell and Russell, 1998, p.82). Growing political demands to control, exclude or reverse the flow of migrants, and asylum-seekers in particular, have intensified border control processes and forms of internal policing within the EU. Nonetheless, Mitchell and Russell also point to the importance of 'migrants' not being a homogenous group:

> Different types of migrant enter different EU states on different terms. In part, this is because there is a range of types of migration in Europe from high-status professional and managerial elite workers who are in short supply, thorough to migrant contract workers, reunited family dependants, asylum seekers and illegal immigrants. It is also due to the fact that nation states retain the capacity to determine access to citizenship rights and that significant variations continue to exist across Europe in the criteria used to determine the civic status of migrants.

(Mitchell and Russell, 1998, p.83).

Citizenship thus becomes one of the central issues in the continuing realignment of nation-states, the EU and the wider Europe (see also Soysal, 1994 and White, 1999). Optimistic readings of these developments have suggested the possibility of a European 'right-based' model of social citizenship above the level of the nation state (see, for example, Leibfried and Pierson, 1992).

While it is possible to see how these initiatives could lead to a more developed form of welfare state – or what Leibfried possibly more accurately describes as a 'social' state to highlight the difference between the welfare regimes of the EU's member-states and what might grow out of the EU – moves in this direction are still relatively limited. They are either only apparent in cases that are strictly labour-market oriented (for example, equal pay cases, health and safety at work cases) or in the limited case of women's pension rights. The legalistic emphasis on entitlement only relates to those in the labour market, and substantial trans-European pressure would be required for its extension to other sections of the population (for example, in the form of a guaranteed basic income). The notion of entitlement itself fits more easily with the welfare systems of some countries (such as Germany) than with others (such as the UK and Ireland) where 'largesse' remains the main welfare principle.

Leibfried has argued that while there is little sign of a *European* welfare state being constructed, the development of the EU has created a 'multi-tiered' social policy system with important effects on both national and European levels. Although welfare states continue to 'display a national character', he argues that the process of European integration means that 'both the sovereignty (that is, legislative power excluding all other authorities), and the autonomy (that is, the *de facto* capacity for independent development of national space) of the member states have been and are being eroded' (Leibfried, 2000, p.45). Leibfried draws out three types of European level impact on social policy development in member states:

- *'Positive' integration,* or activist reform, develops from the centre of the EU outwards, through more traditional social policy initiatives by the European Commission and the Council of Ministers, as well as through the judgements of the European Court of Justice (ECJ), in which European Law is interpreted.

- *'Negative' integration,* or impediment-eliminating reform, aims to produce the conditions required for market compatibility; as when the ECJ makes the welfare payments of the member states 'portable' and thereby limits social policy ... and remoulds it.

- Finally, the process of European integration gives rise to a multiplicity of *indirect pressures* which, in this respect, do not, admittedly, bind the national welfare states by law, but clearly push them forwards altering their social policy in order to avoid possible negative impacts of economic integration.

(Leibfried, 2000, pp.47–8).

In these ways, Leibfried suggests, national welfare states have become injected into a multi-tier social policy system, such that national policy dilemmas and choices are formed and shaped by European-level pressures and policies. Whether these framing processes produce national-level convergence remains a contested issue. For example, Geyer has argued that the European level may even encourage national level social policy regimes to diversify (Geyer, 2000, p.212). What is clear though, is that it is increasingly inappropriate to treat national welfare systems as separate from their place within 'multi-tier' processes of governance (Marks, 1993; Scharpf, 1994; Geyer, 2000).

4   A WIDER EUROPE

Most of the discussion so far has concentrated rather narrowly on the experience of the European Union, the extent to which the welfare states of its members may be converging and the extent to which the EU itself may be transforming itself into a European welfare state. Although similarities and tendencies towards convergence were identified, we have stressed the importance of acknowledging continuing differences. And, again, although some signs of moves towards EU-wide structures were identified, it was stressed that the extent of such moves should not be exaggerated. They are possibilities rather than certainties, or even likelihoods. In any case, the EU itself is part of a 'wider Europe'. The changing patterns and relationships of this wider Europe, in particular in Central and Eastern Europe, suggest that it would be unwise to base any predictions on the experience of countries that were EU member states during the 1990s.

There are two main changes at European level that seem certain to influence substantially the future of welfare states. The first process is that of 'enlargement': the addition of new member states to the EU. As the union has been expanded beyond the original western nations, so has the diversity of national economic and welfare systems contained within the EU increased. While there are some general trends (around the level of social expenditure as a proportion of GDP, for example), the current membership of the Union reveals some patterned differences. Kuhnle and Alestalo (2000) have drawn out different patterns of welfare state dynamics around four clusters of member states (Continental Europe, Scandinavia, Southern Europe and the UK). While demonstrating a degree of convergence, both the starting points and trajectories are different, as Table 8.2 shows.

TABLE 8.2 Social expenditure as a percentage of gross domestic product in different types of European welfare states, 1980–95: unweighted averages [a]

	1980	1990	1995
Continental Europe	28.1	29.6	30.1
Scandinavia	25.6	28.1	32.1
Southern Europe	15.0	18.0	22.2
United Kingdom	21.5	24.3	27.7

Sources: Sosiaali-ja terveyministeriö (1998) *Sosiaaliturva Suomessa 1996* (p.32; figures based on Eurostat and Nordic Social Statistical Committee); Nordiska Statiska Sekretariatet (1984) *Social trygghet i de nordiska länderna 1981* (p.93); Nordic Social Statistical Committee (1998) *Social Protection in the Nordic Countries 1996* (p.144).

Notes

[a] Classification of countries:

Continental Europe: Austria, Belgium, France, Germany, The Netherlands;
Scandinavia: Denmark, Finland, Norway, Sweden;
Southern Europe: Greece, Italy, Portugal, Spain.

The processes of enlargement accomplished by 2000 (with 15 member states) are likely to be overshadowed by the issues of integrating Central and Eastern European nations into the EU over the next decade. As Hudson and Williams argue, the processes of economic transition, combining both integration and differentiation, are vitally significant to the remaking of Europe:

> The most far-reaching political–economic change within Europe has undoubtedly been the re-definition of the relation between East and West into one between Central and Eastern, and Western Europe. This transition to capitalism in Central and Eastern Europe was intended to help insert it into at least the margins of the wider global economy ... The process of reform and transition

is creating new inequalities in the East, and re-defining the map of uneven development within Europe.

(Hudson and Williams, 1999, p.8).

Significant political and economic unevenesses have resulted from the different places of nations (and new nations) within the former communist bloc, and the trajectories that they have subsequently constructed. For example, there are differences between the experiences of nations created from the break-up of the former Soviet Union (such as Estonia, Latvia and Lithuania) and some of the continuing nations of the bloc (such as the Czech Republic, Hungary and Poland). Hudson and Williams point to the ways in which these re-alignments to the East are taking place at the same time as (and overlapping geo-politically with) the processes of Mediterranean (Southern European) integration and the North-South fractures and conflicts across the former communist states such as Albania, Romania and especially Yugoslavia. Alongside the more visible issues of social, political and economic dislocation and reconstruction, questions of social policy and welfare systems have also been central to these transitions. The strongly centralized and statist welfare systems typical of the communist bloc have been challenged by the social costs of transition (especially in terms of massive unemployment), assaulted by 'neo-liberal' ideology and expertise, and dislocated by economic changes that undercut their fiscal basis.

In one case, that of the German Democratic Republic (GDR), the issue was resolved by absorption into a Western European welfare regime. Even in Germany the costs of integration have been high and a final balance sheet on their social policy impact is still to be drawn up. The old GDR disappeared and was absorbed into an existing system, imposing new strains on Social Assistance budgets originally only intended to deal with relatively brief breaks in employment or people excluded from the labour market for reasons of disability or childcare. But the difficulties faced by the other countries of Eastern and Central Europe have been still greater. Their welfare base has been substantially undermined as all of them have faced mass unemployment and collapsing state budgets (see, for example, Ferge, 1997; Williams and Balas, 1999; Poole, 2000). Many have also faced substantial conflict between ethnic groups, sometimes leading to the break-up of existing state boundaries. State welfare is distrusted and other forms of provision are rudimentary. Notions of basic incomes and income support are only just being constructed in the process of 'post-communist transition' (Lauristin, 2000). It is currently difficult to identify any dominant trends in the development of welfare in the countries of Central and Eastern Europe. Elements of liberal, market-based, residual welfare systems seem to be combining with conservative forms designed to protect powerful groups (such as some members of the former state bureaucracies and some sections of the working class). There are also signs of authoritarian, nationalist and racist political mobilizations that challenge EU conceptions of a socially inclusive and pluralist Europe (see, for example, Deacon, 1992, pp.178–83; Ferge,

1997 and White, 1999). However the changes are characterized, it is clear that state funding for social protection is not viewed as a high priority in any of these states, for whom economic development is paramount. The argument that welfare is dependent on economic success (or indeed survival) underlies social policy developments still more sharply in all these countries than in the rest of Europe. Integration into the EU 'economic space' is thus a critical political objective for many post-communist states.

There are proposals to expand the EU to include many of these countries, and these proposals are supported by the governments of the core European states. This programme of enlargement will have immense implications for the EU and its social policy. The EU has been basically what Leibfried calls a Western European 'closed shop' with a reasonably manageable periphery (Leibfried, 1992a, p.28). The implications of this are clear from some of the current debates about excluding non-EU nationals from its borders except on a clearly licensed basis. One social policy that has spread through the states of the EU like wildfire is that which restricts asylum to those with clear and narrowly restricted political grounds for claiming it. Since the fall of communism, few of those from Central Europe would be eligible, as they would be defined as 'economic' migrants.

If the EU is expanded to include these countries, it would almost certainly have to be on a different basis. The countries of Central and Eastern Europe could not begin to think of meeting the existing regulatory standards on employment or social protection (Sbragia, 1992a). One way of allowing expansion would be to move away from any pretensions to developing a social policy, so that an expanded EU would simply be a customs union (that is, a free trade area surrounded by a protective tariff wall designed to restrict lower-cost imports from elsewhere), and even then it is difficult to believe that some distinction might not have to be made between the different parts within an explicitly 'two track' Europe (Leibfried, 1992a, p. 28). Some EU members would only be members in a strictly limited sense, for example having access to markets on preferential terms, while others continued to seek closer integration (through social policy as well as economic policy and monetary union). In the 1990s the main emphasis of the EU's policies towards Eastern Europe was on assisting with the building of economic infrastructure capable of working in markets, but the scale of assistance was very small in comparison with the schemes already operating within the EU.

Hudson and Williams suggest that many of the tensions about conflicting social, political and economic objectives that have characterized debates over the future of Western European welfare states are implicated in the integration of the 'East' – but in a profoundly intensified way:

> Within Europe, the problems of socio-spatial inequality have become a focus of growing concern, not least as they are seen as one facet of the threat to cohesion posed by the continuing

deepening of the European Union and the creation of a homo-geneous economic space. Attaining an ambitious array of economic integration goals while maintaining a certain level of social cohesion clearly implies, *inter alia*, the need for strong redistributive, as well as facilitating and enabling, state policies. But the issue remains of the appropriate territorial level at which to formulate and implement policies to tackle social inequality and territorially uneven development.

(Hudson and Williams, 1999, p.11)

Once more, we are returned to the question of whether the European Union can provide the level, or the forum, through which what Leibfried (2000) calls the 'welfare state compact' can be revived, reconstructed and reasserted.

5   CONCLUSION

In the last decade of the twentieth century the differences between the welfare states of Western Europe remained as important as the similarities between them (Kersbergen, 2000). Despite the similar pressures they have faced since the late 1970s, they have tended to respond in ways that are based on past arrangements rather than choosing to make dramatic new departures based on templates drawn from any particular existing (or theoretical) system. Although the influence of market-based ideas was strong in the 1980s and 1990s, that did not mean that each country transformed its welfare state along neo-liberal lines. Even the changes that took place in the UK (whose politics are generally presented as the prime example of new right ideology in practice) cannot be understood simply in this way. There was a shift in the overall social policy agenda, but the way in which that changed agenda was interpreted varied significantly between different countries.

Europe has become a more important focus for social policy debate than ever before, both in the sense that lessons (and ideas) are increasingly drawn from the experience of other European countries and in the sense that Europe itself (through the EU) is understood to have a role in the development of social policy. Although we argue that the extent of this should not be exaggerated, it is nevertheless possible to identify ways in which the EU has begun to influence developments at member-state level and begun to set its own agenda for welfare. The most important aspects of this have been the increasingly explicit moves towards defining social policy in terms of the labour market and employment-based rights, and the extent to which legal forms of regulation and definitions of entitlement have become universally accepted aspects of social policy throughout the EU. The first of these fits in with and reinforces a more general shift towards an emphasis on the necessary relationships between economic and social policy. In this argument social policy is seen to have a key role in reshaping labour markets to fit with the needs of economic competitiveness, so that social policy becomes a form of infrastructure underpinning that competitiveness. The increased emphasis on regulation fits in with moves away from direct state welfare provision. This is likely to be of particular importance in the longer term for countries such as the UK in which notions of entitlement and legal rights have in the past played little part in the distribution of welfare.

Some aspects of change at the European level tend to be lost in the language of legal regulation. So, for example, the stress on employment-based rights helps to marginalize those who are not fully involved in paid employment, and leaves decisions on their benefit 'entitlements' to the member-states. In practice this continues to leave many women in a clear position of dependence on men within families or suffering the consequences of not being so dependent in lone-parent families. The dominant assumption remains that the norm around which social policy should be constructed is that of families centred around a single 'breadwinner', which in many, although not all, EU countries is assumed to be the man (Lewis, 2000). The emphasis of European regulation on internal EU migrant-workers also helps to marginalize and exclude those who are not EU citizens. It helps to create another (and much larger) category of migrant-workers whose position is precarious and much less protected, except by the uneven principles of national legislation.

We have seen that European welfare states have survived the pressures and challenges of the last two decades of the twentieth century, although their survival does not mean that they have emerged unscathed and unchanged (Kuhnle and Alestalo, 2000). Although national diversity continues to be a defining feature, national welfare states are placed within developing global and regional contexts that have profound implications for the future possibilities of welfare development. It is clear that welfare states can no longer be treated as hermetically sealed entities, capable of being studied separately from such contexts. The European Union has come to occupy a central place in these contextual conditions of national welfare systems. For member states, it mediates their relationship to the global political economy, being both the means of their insertion into that world and a regional bulwark against unchecked international competition.

This changing context has led to an interest in concepts of multi-tiered or multi-layered governance in relation to both Europe and welfare systems (e.g. Marks, 1993; Scharpf, 1995; Leibfried and Pierson, 1992; Leibfried 2000). Such concepts emphasize the interaction of different social (and territorial) levels in the making of social policy. Some studies have examined the rise, and rising influence, of institutions at the global level, such as the International Monetary Fund and World Trade Organization (Deacon, 1997; 2000). Others have concentrated on the growth of European level institutions, both the formal political and judicial European bodies and the increasing numbers of non-governmental organizations (NGOs) involved in social policy developments at the European level (Geyer, 2000). The interactions between these levels and the nation-state, as well as local level developments, form the focus of studies of multi-level governance. Such interactions, together with the changing political, economic and territorial contexts that make up Europe, are likely to play larger roles in shaping the future of European welfare systems.

REFERENCES

Chamberlayne, P. (1992) 'Income maintenance and institutional forms: a comparison of France, West Germany, Italy and Britain 1945–90', *Policy and Politics,* vol.20, no.4, pp.299–318.

Clarke, J. (2000) 'A World of Difference? Globalization and the Study of Social Policy', in Lewis, G., Gewirtz, S. and Clarke, J. (eds) (2000).

Commission of the European Communities (2000a) *Social Policy Agenda.* Communication from the Commission to the Council, the European Parliament, the Economic and Social Committee and the Committee of the Regions, com (2000) 379 final.

Commission of the European Communities (2000b) *Proposal for a Decision of the European Parliament and of the Council Establishing a Programme of Community Action to Encourage Cooperation between Member States to Combat Social Exclusion*, Brussels, com (2000) 368 final.

Cram, L. (1993) 'Calling the tune without paying the piper? Social policy regulation: the role of the Commission in European Community social policy', *Policy and Politics*, vol.21, no.2, pp.135–46.

Cutler, T., Haslam, C., Williams, J. and Williams, K. (1989) *1992 – The Struggle for Europe,* Oxford, Berg.

Daly, M. (1997) 'Welfare States under Pressure: Cash Benefits in European Welfare States over the Last Ten Years', *Journal of European Social Policy*, vol.7, no.2, pp.129–46.

Deacon, B. (1992) 'The future of social policy in Eastern Europe', in Deacon, B. *et al.*, *The New Eastern Europe: Social Policy Past, Present and Future*, London, Sage.

Deacon, B. (1997) *Global Social Policy: International Organizations and the Future of Welfare,* London, Sage.

Deacon, B. (2000) 'Globalization: a threat to equitable social provision?', in Dean, H., Sykes, R. and Woods, R. (eds) *Social Policy Review 12,* Newcastle, Social Policy Association.

Esping-Andersen, G. (1990) *The Three Worlds of Welfare Capitalism,* Cambridge, Polity Press.

Esping Andersen, G. (ed.) (1996) *Welfare States in Transition*, London, Sage/UNRISD.

Eurostat (1988 and 1991) *Basic Statistics of the Community*, Brussels, European Commission.

Ferge, Z. (1997) 'The changed welfare paradigm: the individualization of the social', *Social Policy and Administration*, vol.31, no.1, pp.20–44.

Ferge, Z. (2000) 'Welfare and "ill-fare" systems in Central – Eastern Europe', in Sykes R., Palier B. and Prior P. (eds) *Globalization and European Welfare States: Challenges and Change*, Basingstoke, Macmillan.

Ferrara, M. (1996) 'The "Southern Model" of Welfare in Social Europe', *Journal of European Social Policy*, vol.6, no.1, pp.17–37.

Flora, P. (ed.) (1986a) *Growth to Limits: Volume 1*, Berlin, de Gruyter.

Flora, P. (ed.) (1986b) *Growth to Limits: Volume 2*, Berlin, de Gruyter.

Flora, P. and Heidenheimer, A. (1981a) 'The historical core and changing boundaries of the welfare state', in Flora, P. and Heidenheimer, A. (1981b).

Flora, P. and Heidenheimer, A. (eds) (1981b) *The Development of Welfare States in Europe*, New Brunswick, Transaction Books.

Geyer, R. (2000) *Exploring European Social Policy*, Cambridge, Polity.

Ginsburg, N. (1992) *Divisions of Welfare*, London, Sage.

Glennerster, H. and Midgley, J. (eds) (1991) *The Radical Right and the Welfare State: An International Assessment*, Hemel Hempstead, Harvester Wheatsheaf.

Gray, J. (1998) *False Dawn: The Delusions of Global Capitalism*, London, Granta Books.

Guillén, A. and Alvarez, A. (2001) 'Globalization and the Southern Welfare States', in Sykes, R., Palier, B. and Prior, P. (eds) (2001).

Hay, C. (1998) 'Globalization, welfare retrenchment and the "logic of no alternative": why second-best won't do', *Journal of Social Policy*, vol.27, no.4, pp.525–32.

Hay, C. (2000) 'Globalization, economic change and the welfare state: the "vexatious" inquisition of taxation"?', in Sykes R., Palier B. and Prior P. (eds) *Globalization and European Welfare States: Challenges and Change*, Basingstoke, Palgrave.

Held, D. (2000) *A Globalizing World? Culture, Economics, Politics*, London, Routledge.

Hirst, P. and Thompson, G. (2nd edn) (1999) *Globalization in Question*, Cambridge, Polity Press.

Hudson, R. and Williams, A.M. (1999) 'Re-shaping Europe: the challenge of new divisions within a homogenized political – economic space', in Hudson, R. and Williams, A.M. (eds) *Divided Europe: Society and Territory*, London, Sage.

Jameson, F. and Miyoshi, M. (eds) (1998) *The Cultures of Globalization*, Durham, NC, Duke University Press.

Jessop, B. (2000) 'From KWNS to SWPR', in Lewis, G., Gewirtz, S. and Clarke, J. (eds) (2000).

Jönsson, C., Tägil, S. and Törnqvist, G. (2000) *Organizing European Space,* London, Sage.

Kastandiek, H. (1990) 'Convergence or a persistent diversity of national politics?', in Crouch, C. and Marquand, D. (eds) *The Politics of 1992: Beyond the Single European Market*, Oxford, Political Quarterly/Basil Blackwell.

Kersbergen, K. van (2000) 'The declining resistance of welfare states to change?', in Kunhle, S. (ed.) *Survival of the European Welfare State,* London, Routledge.

Kuhnle, S. and Alestalo, M. (2000) 'Introduction: growth, adjustments and survival of European welfare states', in Kuhnle, S. (ed.) *Survival of the European Welfare State,* London, Routledge.

Lange, S. (1992) 'The politics of the social dimension' in Sbragia, A. (ed.) (1992b).

Lauristin, M. (2000) 'Social reforms as part of post-communist transition', Paper presented to Social Policy Association Conference, Roehampton, July.

Leibfried, S. (1992a) 'Social Europe: welfare state trajectories of the European community', in Otto, H.-U. and Flösser, G. (eds) *How to Organize Prevention: Political, Organizational, and Professional Challenges to Social Services,* Berlin, de Gruyter.

Leibfried, S. (1992b) 'Towards a European welfare state? On integrating poverty regimes into the European Community', in Ferge, Z. and Kolberg, J. (eds) *Social Policy in a Changing Europe*, Frankfurt, Campus Verlag, and Boulder, CO, Westview Press.

Leibfried, S. (1993) 'Towards a European Welfare State?', in Jones, C. (ed.) *New Perspectives on the Welfare State in Europe*, London, Routledge.

Leibfried, S. (2000) 'National welfare states, European integration and globalization: A perspective for the next century', *Social Policy and Administration,* vol.34, no.1, pp. 44–63.

Leibfried, S. and Pierson, P. (1992) 'Prospects for social Europe', *Politics and Society,* vol.20, no.3, pp.333–66.

Lewis, G., Gewirtz, S. and Clarke, J. (eds) (2000) *Rethinking Social Policy,* London, Sage.

Lewis, J. (2000) 'Gender and welfare regimes', in Lewis, G., Gewirtz, S. and Clarke, J. (eds) (2000).

Majone, G. (1991) 'Cross-national sources of regulatory policymaking in Europe and the United States', *Journal of Public Policy*, vol.11, no.1, pp.79–106.

Marks, G. (1993) 'Structural policy and multi-level governance in the European community', in Caffany, A. and Rosenthal, G. (eds) *The State of the European Community*, New York, Lynne Rienner.

Massey, D. (1999) 'Imagining globalization: power-geometries of time-space', in Brah, A., Hickman, M., and Mac an Ghaill, M. (eds) *Global Futures: Migration, Environment and Globalization*, Basingstoke, MacMillan.

Mitchell, M. and Russell, D. (1998) 'Immigration, citizenship and social exclusion in the new Europe', in Sykes, R. and Alcock, P. (eds) *Developments in European Social Policy: Convergence and Diversity*, Bristol, The Policy Press.

Morokvasic, M. (1991) 'Fortress Europe and migrant women', *Feminist Review*, no.39, pp.69–84.

Ohmae, K. (1999) *A Borderless World: Power and Strategy in the Interlinked Economy*, HarperBusiness.

Pillinger, J. (2000) 'Redefining work and welfare in Europe: New perspectives on work, welfare and time', in Lewis, G., Gewirtz, S. and Clarke, J. (eds) (2000).

Poole, L. (2000) 'New approaches to competitive social policy: the changing face of control and Easter European Welfare', in Lewis, G., Gewirtz, S. and Clarke, J. (eds) (2000).

Prondzynski, I. (1989) 'The social situation and employment of migrant women in the European Community', *Policy and Politics*, vol.17, no.4, pp.347–54.

Rhodes, M. (1996) 'Globalization and West European Welfare states: A critical review of recent debates', *Journal of European Social Policy*, vol.6, no.4, pp.305–27.

Sassen, S. (1998) *Globalisation and its Discontents*, NY, The New Press.

Sbragia, A. (1992a) 'Introduction' in Sbragia, A. (ed.) (1992b).

Sbragia, A. (ed.) (1992b) *Euro-politics*, Washington, D.C., Brookings Institution.

Scharpft, F. (1994) 'Community and autonomy: multi-level policy making in the European union', *Journal of European Public Policy*, vol.1, no.2, pp.219–39.

Soysal, Y.N. (1994) *Limits of Citizenship: Migrants and Postnational Membership in Europe*, Chicago, Chicago University Press.

Spicker, P. (1991) 'The principle of subsidiarity and the social policy of the European Community', *Journal of European Social Policy*, vol.1, no.1, pp.3–14.

Stoesz, D. and Midgley, J. (1991) 'The radical right and the welfare state', in Glennerster, H. and Midgley, J. (eds) (1991).

Sykes, R. (1998) 'Studying European social policy – issues and perspectives', in Sykes, R. and Alcock, P. (eds) *Development in European Social Policy: Convergence and Diversity,* Bristol, The Policy Press.

Sykes, R., Palier, B., and Prior, P. (eds) (2001) *Globalization and European Welfare States,* Basingstoke, Palgrave.

Weir, M., Orloff, A.S. and Skocpol, T. (eds) (1988) *The Politics of Social Policy in the United States*, Princeton, NJ, Princeton University Press.

White, P. (1999) 'Ethnicity, racialization and citizenship as diverse elements in Europe', in Hudson, R. and Williams, A.M. (eds) (1999).

Williams, A. and Bolaz, V. (1999) 'Transformation and division in Central Europe.' in Hudson, R. and Williams, A. (eds) (1999).

ACKNOWLEDGEMENTS

Grateful acknowledgement is made to the following sources for permission to include material in the book:

TABLES

Table 2.1: Central Statistical Office (1982) National Statistics © Crown Copyright 2001. Reproduced with the permission of the Controller of Her Majesty's Stationery Office; *Tables 2.2 and 2.3:* Sleeman, J.F. (1979) *Resources for the Welfare State: An Economic Introduction*, Pearson Education Limited; *Tables 2.4 and 2.5:* Halsey, A.H. (ed.) (1988) *British Social Trends Since 1900: a Guide to the Changing Social Structure of Britain*, Macmillan Press Limited. Reproduced with the permission of Palgrave; *Table 3.1:* Glennerster, H. (1998) 'Welfare with a lid on', in Glennerster, H. et al. *The State of Welfare*, with the permission of Oxford University Press. *Table 4.1:* Organisation for Economic Co-operation and Development (OECD); *Table 4.3:* Katz, J. (1986) *In The Shadow of the Poorhouse: a Social History of Welfare in America*, Basic Books. *Tables 6.1 and 6.2:* Burniaux, J-M., Dang, T-T., Fore, D., Forster, M., Mira d'Ercole, M. and Oxley, H. (1998) *Income Distribution and Poverty in Selected OECD Countries: Economics Department Working Papers No. 189*, © OECD. *Table 8.1:* Eurostat: *Basic Statistics of the Community*, 1988, 1991 and 1999, Office for Official Publications of the European Communities, Luxembourg; *Table 8.2:* Kuhnle, S. and Alestalo, M. (2000) 'Introduction: Growth, Adjustments and Survival of European Welfare States', in *Survival of the European Welfare State*, Kuhnle, S. (ed.), Routledge.

FIGURES

Figure 2.4: Central Statistical Office (1982), National Statistics © Crown Copyright 2001. Reproduced with the permission of the Controller of Her Majesty's Stationery Office; *Figure 2.5:* Halsey, A.H. (ed.) (1988), *British Social Trends Since 1900: a Guide to the Changing Social Structure of Britain*, Macmillan Press Limited. Reproduced with the permission of Palgrave; *Figure 2.6:* Gough, I. (1979), *The Political Economy of the Welfare State*, Macmillan Press Limited. Reproduced with the permission of Palgrave; *Figure 3.1:* Glennerster, H. (1998) 'Welfare with a lid on', in Glennerster, H. et al. *The State of Welfare*, with the permission of Oxford University Press.

INDEX

Abel-Smith, Brian 52
abortion
   in Britain 65
   in East Germany 170, 171,
     177–8
   in Ireland 248–51
   in Sweden 214
ADC (Aid to Dependent Children)
   116–18, 142
AFDC (Aid to Families with
   Dependent Children) 122, 124,
   130, 131, 134, 136, 140, 144,
   145
ageing population 4
   in Britain 50–2
   in Germany 167
aggregate statistics 9–10, 14–16,
   18
agriculture, European Union
   Common Agricultural Policy
   273, 274
Airey, Mrs Josie 247–8
Amenta, E. 115, 119
American model of welfare *see*
   liberal welfare regimes
'Americanization', and
   globalization 268
Ashford, D. 7–8
asylum-seekers
   in Britain 82, 97, 99
   and the European Union
     183–4, 279
   in Germany 166, 169, 181–4,
     186
   in Ireland 256
   in Sweden 204, 211
Auletta, K. 133
Australia
   as a liberal welfare regime 11
   race regime in 17, 212
Austria
   as a conservative welfare
     regime 11
   race regime in 17, 212
   social expenditure as a
     percentage of GDP 264

Baldwin, P. 197
Bartlett, W. 87
Bauman, Z. 101
Belgium, social expenditure as a
   percentage of GDP 264
Berentsen, W.H. 173

Beveridge Report (1942) 2, 18, 35,
   64
   challenges to the social
     assumptions of the 66, 67
   and citizenship 42
   and full employment 39, 40, 67
   and means-tested benefits
     40–1
   and universalism 62, 99
black people
   in Britain 61, 62–4
   and the racialized division of
     labour 17
   in the United States
     and careers in the welfare
       services 129
     and the Civil Rights
       movement 121
     and the New Deal 118,
       119–20
   women
     and motherhood 63–4, 65
     and work 64, 142
   see also race
borderless world, globalization
   as a 266
Boris, E. 142
Borschorst, A. 218
Breen, R. 239
Britain 2–3, 18–19, 30–105
   challenges to the welfare state
     in 66, 72
   citizenship in 41–2, 53, 60, 62,
     102, 103, 104
   class in 19, 37
     and education 38, 63
     and infant mortality 65
     middle-class welfare services
       79
     and race 63
   continuity and change in the
     welfare state 100–5
   early years of welfare reform
     32–4
   economic recession in 66–7,
     72
   and the European Union (EU)
     98, 271
   expansion and modernization
     of the welfare state 44–61
   family, nation and work in 19,
     30–1, 35, 42–3, 53, 64–6,
     91–100
   family policies in 59–61

and New Labour 97, 98–9
and New Right ideology 89,
   91–2
gender in 19
   and the division of labour
     37–8, 61–2
   and full employment 40
   and inequality 94
and globalization 267
and imperialism 3, 32, 33–4,
   35
Job Seeker's Allowance 209
and the legacy of 1945 43–4
legislation
   Abortion Act (1967) 65
   Aliens Act (1905) 33
   Child Support Act (1991) 92
   Commonwealth Immigration
     Act (1962) 60, 62
   Crime and Disorder Act
     (1998) 92
   Criminal Justice Act (1991)
     91–2
   Education Act (1944) 38
   Education Act (1988) 93
   Immigration Act (1971) 60, 62
   Local Government Act (1988)
     92
   National Health Service Act
     (1946) 38
   National Health Service and
     Community Care Act (1989)
     87
   National Insurance Act
     (1911) 33
   Pensions Act (1908) 33
   Race Relations Act (1968) 62
   Social Security Act (1986) 82
local government 8
mixed economy of welfare in
   30, 37–8, 43, 44–5, 90–1,
   101–2
and Northern Ireland 30
periodization of social change
   in 31–2
post-war construction of the
   welfare state 31, 34–44
and the post-war political
   consensus 19, 36
poverty in
   and benefit reforms 84
   'familialization' and
     'feminization' of 83
   and New Labour welfare
     policies 84–5

and the 'new poor' 101
and pro-poor policies 78–9
'racialization' of 83
rediscovery of 52–3
private sector in 38, 45, 46
public expenditure and the
  welfare state in 47–50, 53–7,
  58, 59
quasi-markets in 88, 95, 101
race in 17, 19, 60, 62–4, 94, 97,
  104, 212
  and asylum-seekers 82, 97,
    99
  and migrant labour 61, 62–3
  and poverty 83
and Scotland 30
social expenditure as a
  percentage of GDP 125, 264
and social movements based
  on identity 94–5
and the state 30, 31, 32, 45, 59–
  60, 86, 103–4
and universal welfare benefits
  43, 62, 99–100, 104
unmarried mothers and the
  poor law in 210
voluntary sector in 32, 37, 45,
  52, 86, 88
and welfare pluralism 87–9,
  90–1, 101–2
welfare regime 11–12, 34–5,
  105, 270
welfare rights movement in
  52–3
see also Conservative New
  Right (Britain); New Labour
  welfare policies (Britain)
Bryan, Beverley 63–4
Buckley, M. 179
Bush, George 136
Bussiere, E. 142

Canada
  as a liberal welfare regime 11
  race regime in 17, 212
Castles, F. 9, 10, 17, 18
Castles, S. 212
Catholic Church
  and conservative welfare
    regimes 10
  and the German welfare state
    154, 155, 156–7, 158, 161
  in Ireland
    and abortion 249, 250
    and corporatism 22, 224–31,
      234–5, 255
    and divorce 251, 252

and education 237–8
  and women 244–5, 246
and the principle of subsidiary
  154, 156–7, 158, 161, 225,
  226
Child Benefit, and the British
  welfare state 53, 81
Child Poverty Action Group 52
childcare provision
  and international statistics 15
  in Ireland 245
  in Sweden 217
citizenship
  in Britain 41–2, 53, 60, 62,
    102, 103, 104
  and the European Union (EU)
    279
  in Germany 155, 158, 161,
    167, 185–6
  in Ireland 249
  in Sweden 211
Clarke, J. 60, 126–7
Clasen, J. 2
class
  in Britain 37
    and education 38, 63
    and infant mortality 65
    middle-class welfare services
      79
    and race 63
  and conservative welfare
    regimes 10
  in Ireland
    and politics 227–8
    and redistributive policies
      239
  and social democratic welfare
    regimes 11
  in Sweden 220
    and access to welfare benefits
      21
    inequalities 196
    and pensions 204
    and social policy 197, 198
  underclass 92, 131, 132–4, 136
  in the United States
    inequalities of 146, 147
    and New Right ideology 135–
      6
    and poverty 135
    underclass 131, 132–4, 136
  and welfare citizenship in
    Britain 19
  in West Germany, divisions
    and solidarity 159–60
Clinton, Bill 137, 139, 140
Clinton, Hilary Rodham 139

Cloward, R. 121
Coard, Bernard 63
Cochrane, A. 64, 83, 92
Cold War, end of the 5
collective bargaining, erosion of 4
community care policies, and
  New Right ideology in Britain
  89, 92
competitive tendering, and the
  British welfare state 86
Conservative New Right (Britain)
  73–93, 94–5, 96, 284
  and benefit targeting 78–9,
    80–1, 82, 84, 103
  and British/English culture
    92–3, 97
  deindustrialization,
    disincentives and
    demoralization 73–5
  family, nation and work in
    91–3, 94
  and primary care 89–90
  and privatization 85–91
  and public expenditure 74–5,
    76–9, 81
  and quasi-markets 87, 88
  and the 'three E's' 86–7
  and the voluntary sector 88
  and welfare pluralism 87–9
  welfare policies and
    expenditure 10–11
conservative welfare regimes
  10–11, 20, 24
  in Germany 11, 20, 21, 154–5,
    156–9, 201
  in Ireland 20, 22
consumerism, and the new
  welfare mix in Britain 88, 95,
  102
contraception
  and black and disabled women
    in Britain 65
  and women in Ireland 231,
    247–8
corporate management, and the
  British welfare state 59
corporatist welfare regimes
  Catholic corporatism in
    Ireland 22, 224–31, 255
  in Germany 154, 271
  in Ireland 22
Coughlan, A. 233
Cousins, C. 208
Cram, L. 276, 277
cultural essentialism, and New
  Right ideology in Britain 93

Dadzie, Stella 63–4
Dallos, R. 94, 96
Daly, M. 271
Davin, Anna 33
De Rossa, Proinsias 253
De Valera, Eamon 229, 230
Deacon, B. 265
deindustrialization, and New
  Right ideology in Britain 73–4,
  75
demographic changes
    and the British welfare state
      44, 50–2
    challenges to welfare states 4
demoralization, and New Right
  ideology in Britain 73, 75
Denmark, social expenditure in
  264, 270
Dennis, M. 171
dependency culture, and New
  Right ideology in Britain 92
disabled people 65, 134
discrimination
    and the European Union 277
    and guestsworkers in Germany
      165, 166
    in the labour market in
      Ireland 245, 246
    legislation against racial
      discrimination in Sweden
      212
disincentives, and New Right
  ideology in Britain 73, 74–5
diversity of welfare states
  22–3
division of labour
    gendered 4, 13, 15–16
      in Britain 37–8, 61–2
      in West Germany 161
    racialized 17
divorce
    in Britain 59
    in East Germany 177
    in Ireland 231, 251–2
Djilas, M. 128
Dominelli, L. 6, 16, 17

early retirement, and German
  women 175
earnings-related benefits
    in Britain 44, 47, 53, 57, 81
    old age pensions in Sweden
      (ATP) 202–3
East Germans (after unification)
    relations with West Germans
      186–7
    women 174–5, 176–9

East Germany
    and income inequalities after
      unification 176
    welfare system 170–2
    women in 170–1
Eastern European states 282–4
economic competition between
  countries, and welfare policy
  263
economic growth, effects on
  welfare states 4
education
    in Britain 38–9, 44, 45, 53
      and black children 63–4
      New Labour reforms 79
      and New Right ideology 93
      private education 38, 46
    and Catholic corporatism in
      Ireland 237–8
    Operation Headstart in the
      United States 123
EJC see European Court of
  Justice (EJC)
employment see labour market;
  unemployment
equality
    and citizenship in Britain 42
    and social democratic welfare
      regimes 11
Esping-Andersen, G. 10–11, 12,
  13, 14–15, 18, 19–20, 22, 24, 34,
  262
    and the British welfare state
      100, 105
    and the German welfare state
      154, 159, 168
    on globalization 266
    and Ireland 224
    and the Swedish welfare state
      196, 207
    and the US welfare system
      114, 147
EU see European Union (EU)
European Court of Justice (EJC)
  272, 277, 278, 280
European model of welfare 148,
  263, 268–71
European Social Policy 269
European Union (EU) 5, 269
    and the Agreement (1990) 184
    asylum policy 183–4, 279
    and austerity welfare 270–1
    and the British welfare state
      98, 105
    and citizenship 279
    Common Agricultural Policy
      273, 274

convergence 262, 263, 280, 281
    and the German welfare
      state 169
    and enlargement 281–4
    and 'Fortress Europe' 23, 183
    gender policy 274
    and globalization 268
    harmonization of welfare
      policies in 23–4, 98
    immigration policies 23, 278–9
    and Ireland 22, 232, 233, 239,
      246, 247, 249–50, 267, 274
    and the labour market 277–8,
      279, 284–5
    and negative integration 280
    and non-governmental
      organizations (NGOs) 285–6
    and positive integration 280
    Regional Development Fund
      (ERDF) 273–4
    and the single European
      market 275–6, 278
    Social Chapter 272–3, 277
    social exclusion policy 275
    and social expenditure 270,
      275, 281
    Social Fund 273
    and social policy regulation
      276–8
    and the supranational welfare
      state 262, 263, 265, 271–80
    and Sweden 199, 218, 219
    women and social policy 278,
      279, 285

Faist, T. 182
families
    and the British welfare state
      19, 59–61
      black families 63–4
    decline of the traditional
      family 4
    and the German welfare state
      and patriarchy 155, 158,
        162–3
      and the principle of
        subsidiary 154, 157, 160–1
    and mixed economies of
      welfare 14
family allowances, and the
  British welfare state 41, 53, 54,
  57
Family Credit, and the British
  welfare state 81
family policies 6, 7
    in Britain 97, 98–9
      and New Labour 97, 98–9, 100

and New Right ideology 89,
91–2
and Catholic corporatism
225–6, 230–1
and conservative welfare
regimes 10
in East Germany 170–2
and international statistics 15
in Ireland 230–1, 252–4
and social democratic welfare
regimes 11
in Sweden 213–18
lone-parent families 213,
215–16
parental leave and daycare
216–17
population policy 209–10,
213, 214
reform of 213–15
in the United States
ADC 116–18, 142
AFDC 122, 124, 130, 131,
134, 136, 140, 144, 145
feminism 13
and New Right ideology in
Britain 92
in Sweden 214
Finch, Janet 92
Finland, social expenditure as a
percentage of GDP 264
Flora, P. 269
Foreman, S. 94
'Fortress Europe' 23
France
as a conservative welfare
regime 11, 271
and the European model of
welfare 148
immigration control in 23
local government 8
race regime in 17, 212
social expenditure as a
percentage of GDP 264
full employment
in Britain 39–40, 43, 67, 79,
84
commitment to 5–6, 9
and social democratic welfare
regimes 11
in Sweden 196

Galbraith, J.K. 75
Galligan, Y. 251
GDP (gross domestic product)
in Ireland 235
and public expenditure in
Britain 77

and social expenditure 200,
235, 264, 270, 281
in Sweden 198–9, 200
gender
in Britain 19
and the division of labour
37–8, 61–2
and full employment 40
and inequality 94
and definitions of full
employment 5–6
and the division of labour 4,
13, 15–16
in Britain 37–8, 61–2
in West Germany 161
European Union (EU) policy
on 274
in Germany
post-unification 176–9
West Germany 160–3, 166
in Sweden 220
inequalities 196
and the labour market 207–8
and old age pensions 203–4
and unemployment 206
in the United States 117, 129,
136
and welfare policies 7
see also men; women
Germany 148, 154–88
citizenship in 155, 158, 161,
167, 185–6
as a conservative welfare
regime 11, 20, 21, 154–5,
156–9, 201
gender in
in the post-unification period
176–9, 187
West Germany 160–3
income inequality 175–6, 200,
201
local government 8
and the principle of
subsidiarity 21, 154, 156–7,
158, 160–1, 162
race in 17, 23, 212
and asylum-seekers 166, 169,
181–4, 186
and ethnic Germans 182,
183, 185–6, 212
and guest-workers 164–6,
167, 169, 180–1, 182, 186
in the post-unification period
179–86
West Germany 164–7, 169
and Social Assistance 156,
157, 158, 167, 168
for lone mothers 168–9, 174

for non-citizens 169
post-unification 175, 282
social expenditure as a
percentage of GDP 264
and social insurance 154, 156,
161, 188
Social State (Sozialstaat) 155,
157
Solidarity Pact (1992) 175–6
taxation in 159, 162, 176
and unemployment, in the
post-unification period
174–5, 183, 185
unification of 21, 22, 154, 158,
169, 172–3, 267, 282
and the future of the German
model 187–8
and relations between East
and West Germans 186–7
and welfare services 156–7
welfare spending as a
percentage of GNP 125
see also East Germany; West
Germany
Geyer, R. 273, 274, 280
Ginsburg, N. 18, 160
Glennerster, H. 78
globalization 3–4, 5, 265–8
and the Swedish welfare
system 218, 219
GNP (gross national product)
and public expenditure in
Britain 48–9, 58
social expenditure as a
percentage of 125
Gordon, L. 117, 120
Gough, I. 56
Gray, John 265–6
Greece, social expenditure as a
percentage of GDP 264, 270
gross domestic product see GDP
(gross domestic product)
gross national product see GNP
(gross national product)

Hammar, T. 210
Handler, J. 122, 133
Hansson, Per Albin 198
Haughey, Charles 248
Hauser, R. 175, 176
health insurance in Britain 33,
65, 82
private health insurance 45,
46, 86
health services
in Britain 38–9, 44, 45
and the ageing population 52

expenditure on 78
see also NHS (National Health Service)
in Ireland
expenditure on 238
maternity and child health services 246
in the United States
corporate healthcare provision 138–9
failure of reform 137–40
and the medical-industrial complex 138
Medicare and Medicaid programmes 123, 137–8
Heclo, H. 197
Hernes, H. 217–18
Hobson, B. 215
Horschelmann, K. 186
housing
in Britain 44, 79
housing tenure 46
and migrant workers 62, 63
'right to buy' local authority housing 86
in Ireland 234, 235, 238
Hudson, R. 281–2, 283–4
Hunter, Allen 128

immigration control
in Britain 33, 60, 61, 62, 64
in Europe 23
in the European Union 23, 278–9
in Sweden 210–11
imperialism, and the British welfare state 3, 32, 33–4, 35
income inequality
in Germany 175–6, 200, 201
in Sweden 200–1, 203
in the United States 200, 201
Income Support, and the British welfare state 80, 82
individual countries, detailed studies of 8–9, 18
infant mortality in Britain 65
informal carers, role in welfare states 23
informal/household sector, and mixed economies of welfare 14, 91
insurance *see* health insurance; social insurance
International Labour Organization 265
International Monetary Fund 265, 285

Ireland 224–56
asylum-seekers in 256
Catholic Church in
and abortion 249, 250
and corporatism 22, 224–31, 234–5, 255
and divorce 251, 252
and education 237–8
and women 244–5, 246
and the 'Celtic Tiger' economy 22, 224, 240
citizenship in 249
civil war in 227
class in
and politics 227–8
and redistributive policies 239
Commission on the Family 253–4
as a conservative welfare regime 20, 22
constitution (1937) 230–1
economic crisis in 232
economic policies in 232–4, 256
emigration from 231, 232
and the European Union (EU) 22, 232, 233, 239, 246, 247, 249–50, 267, 274
and globalization 224
income maintenance payments in 235
nationalism in 227, 228
poverty in 235, 239
and the Anti-Poverty strategy (NAPS) 242–4, 254
public-sector employment in 239
social assistance in 246–7
social change in 234
social democratic policies in 22
social expenditure as a percentage of GDP 264
and social partnership 240–2
taxation in 236–7, 239, 241, 245
travelling people in 238
unemployment in 236, 239, 240, 241, 243
welfare expenditure in 235, 236, 237–9
women in 22, 244–54, 255
and abortion 248–51
and contraception 247–8
and divorce 231, 251–2
and the family 230–1, 252–4

and the ideology of 'Mother Ireland' 229–31
in the labour market 229–30, 245–6
and welfare reforms 246–7
Italy
as a conservative welfare regime 11
social expenditure as a percentage of GDP 264
Japan, and Western European welfare states 270
Jenkin, Patrick 90
Jessop, B. 268
Joppke, C. 164, 167, 182

Kastandiek, H. 270
Katz, J. 118, 120–1, 124, 130, 133, 134
Kearney, Richard 239–40
Kersbergen, K.V. 4–5, 267
Keynes, John Maynard 2, 35, 36
Kohl, Helmut 167, 168, 172, 182, 188
Kolinsky, E. 174, 177
Korpi, W. 196, 197
Krieger, J. 129

labour, decommodification of 13, 15
labour market
in Britain
deregulation 79–80
employment in public sector services 57
inequalities 47, 95–6
and migrant labour 61, 62–3
and New Labour 80, 84, 90, 96, 99
rising labour costs 56–7
changes
effects on welfare states 4
and the European Social Fund 273
and the European Union 277–8, 279, 284–5
in Germany
after unification 174–5, 178
and the East German welfare system 170
and guest-workers 164–6, 167, 169, 180–1, 182, 186
international statistics on labour market policies 15
in Ireland 232, 236
and discrimination 245, 246
in Sweden 210–11

and migrant workers 210–11
programmes 205, 206–7
and women 207–8, 210, 211,
  214–16
in the United States, and the
  New Deal 117, 119
and women 6, 15–16
  black women 64, 142
  in Britain 33, 40, 61–2, 64,
    90, 96
  in Germany 168–9, 170–1,
    174–5, 177, 178
  in Ireland 229–30, 245–6
  and social democratic welfare
    regimes 11
  in Sweden 207–8, 210, 211,
    214–16
  in the United States 141–2
see also full employment;
  unemployment
Langan, M. 15, 160
language differences 8
Lawrence, Stephen 97
Le Grand, J. 87
Lee, Joseph 231
legal rights, and citizenship 42
Leibfried, S. 271, 274, 279–80,
  283, 284
Lewis, J. 13, 15, 161, 163
liberal welfare regimes 11, 12,
  23–4
  and Britain 105, 271
  and Catholic corporatism 206
  as the dominant model 22
  in the United States 11, 20–1,
    22, 147–8, 201
liberalism, New Liberalism and
  citizenship 42
local government
  in Britain 45, 58, 60
  comparing different countries
    7–8
lone-parent families
  in Britain 41, 53, 59, 60, 83,
    90, 92, 215
  in Germany
    after unification 174, 177,
      179
    East Germany 172
  in Ireland 238
  and New Right ideology 92,
    131, 136
  in Sweden 213, 215–16
  in the United States 131, 136,
    141–3
  in West Germany 162–3, 167,
    168–9

Luxembourg, social expenditure
  as a percentage of GDP 264
McCafferty, Nell 251–2
Madsen, H. 197
Majone, G. 276
Major, John 73
managerial efficiency, and
  British welfare reforms 59
market economies
  and mixed economies of
    welfare 14
  and the post-war British
    welfare state 34, 36
Markiewicz, Constance 229
Marshall, T.H. 42
maternity benefits, and the
  British welfare state 54
'McDonaldization', and
  globalization 268
means-tested benefits
  and the British welfare state
    40–1, 42, 53, 57–8, 67
  and New Right ideology in
    Britain 78–9, 80–2, 84
  in the United States 116–18
'Mediterranean' welfare states
  269, 282
Meidner, Rudolf 219
men, and parental leave in
  Sweden 216–17
Miller, M. 17, 212
Mink, G. 143
Mishra, M. 76
Mishra, R. 5, 7
Mitchell, M. 278–9
mixed economies of welfare 7,
  13–14, 16, 263
  in Britain 30, 37–8, 43, 44–5,
    90–1, 101–2
  in Germany 21
  in the United States 20–1
Morris, L. 104
mortgage tax relief in Britain
  45–7
motherhood
  and the British welfare state
    33, 61
    and black women 63–4, 65
    and Conservative ideology 90
    and disabled women 65
  and the German welfare state
    158
    and childcare 178–9
    and East German women
      170–1, 178–9, 186–7
  in Ireland, and divorce 251–2
  in Sweden 215–16

in the United States, and
  welfare mothers 117, 136,
  142–3
see also lone-parent families
Murray, Charles 92
  Losing Ground 131–2
Myrdal, Gunnar 209
National Assistance, and the
  British welfare state 40–1, 57,
  64
national governments
  and the European Union 285
  responsibility for welfare
    263–4
  and welfare systems 267
National Health Service see NHS
  (National Health Service)
National Insurance, and the
  British welfare state 40, 41–2,
  43, 49, 57
Naylor, Fred 93
Netherlands
  race regime in 17, 212
  social expenditure as a
    percentage of GDP 264
New Labour welfare policies
  (Britain) 73, 79, 80, 95, 105
  and the European Social
    Protocol 272
  on the family 96–7, 98–9, 100
  on nation 99, 100
  and the new welfare mix 89
  on the NHS 87
  on pensions 83–4
  on poverty 84–5
  and privatization 86
  and the 'Third Way' 98
  on work 99, 100
    and welfare 80, 84, 96
    and women 90
New Liberalism and citizenship
  42
New Right ideology in the United
  States 20, 125–34, 143–4, 147
  and class politics 135–6
  and the problem of
    dependency 130–2
  and the state 127–30
  and the underclass 131, 132–4,
    136
  and women 129, 136
  see also Conservative New
    Right (Britain)
NHS (National Health Service)
  65
  and abortion 65
  and family care 89

and migrant labour 63
and New Labour reforms 79
quasi-markets in the 87
reorganization 57, 58
and the social services 60
Nixon, Richard M. 124
non-governmental organizations
(NGOs), at European level
285–6
Northern Ireland 30, 234
OECD (Organization for
Economic Cooperation and
Development) 9
Ohmae, K. 266
old age pensions see pensions
Organization for Economic
Cooperation and Development
(OECD) 9
Ostner, I. 15, 160, 163

parental leave, in Sweden 216–17
parental responsibility, and New
Right ideology in Britain 91–2
patriarchal welfare regime in
Germany 155, 158, 161–2, 163
Peillon, M. 225, 226
pensions
in Britain 54
and the ageing population 52
earnings-related (SERPS) 57,
81, 82
occupational pension
schemes 45, 46, 83
private pensions 82
'stakeholder' pensions 82–3
in Ireland 228
in Sweden 202–4
in the United States 145, 146
in West Germany, and gender
162
periodization, and the British
welfare state 31–2
personal social services, and the
British welfare state 45, 58, 60–1
Piachaud, D. 85
Piven, Frances Fox 121, 141–2,
144
political rights, and citizenship
42
population see ageing population;
demographic changes
Portugal, social expenditure as a
percentage of GDP 264, 270
post-fordist welfare systems 4
poverty
in Britain
and benefit reforms 84

'familialization' and
'feminization' of 83
and New Labour welfare
policies 84–5
and the 'new poor' 101
and pro-poor policies 78–9
'racialization' of 83
rediscovery of 52–3
European Union (EU) policy
on 274
feminization of 83, 135, 162
in Germany 202
post-unification 178, 202
West Germany 160, 162–3,
168
in Ireland 235, 239
and the Anti-Poverty
strategy (NAPS) 242–4, 254
reduction of, and full
employment 5
in Sweden 201–2, 204, 214,
215
in the United States 202
and the Civil Rights
movement 121
and class 135
and dependency 131–2
and gender 135
and the New Deal 115
and New Right restructuring
of welfare 129–30
numbers of families below
the poverty line 130
as a political issue 52
poor men and imprisonment
147–8
and the underclass 133
war on 122–3
prisons, poor men and
imprisonment in the United
States 147–8
private sector
and the British welfare state
38, 45, 46
and mixed economies of
welfare 14
privatization 7
in Britain 85–91
of pensions in the United
States 145, 146
public expenditure
in Britain 47–50, 53–7, 58, 59
and the Conservative New
Right 74–5, 76–9, 81
and globalization 265–6, 267
on welfare in European
countries 263, 264
and Western European

welfare states 270
see also social expenditure
public sector, and mixed
economies of welfare 14, 91
public service employees, in the
United States 128–9
public/private spheres, in the
provision of welfare 6, 14, 16
Pyle, J. 231, 245, 246

Quadagno, J. 119–20, 129, 146
quasi-markets, and British
welfare state 88, 95, 101

race
assimilationist multicultural
model of 17, 212
in Britain 17, 19, 60, 62–4, 94,
97, 104, 212
and asylum-seekers 97, 99
and migrant labour 61, 62–3
and poverty 83
and the division of labour 17
exclusionary regimes of 17
in Germany 17, 212
and asylum-seekers 166, 169,
181–4, 186
and ethnic Germans 182,
183, 185–6, 212
and guest-workers 164–6,
167, 169, 180–1, 182, 186
in the post-unification period
179–86
West Germany 164–7, 169
quasi-assimilationist post-
colonial model of 17
racialized minority
populations in Europe 24
in Sweden 17, 209–12, 220
and asylum-seekers 204, 211
ethnic minorities 203, 204,
205–6, 209, 211, 212
and immigration control
210–11
legislation against racial
discrimination 212
social eugenic policy 209–10
in the United States 17, 146–7
and the New Deal 117, 118,
119–20
and New Right ideology 131,
132, 136
and poverty 135
and the underclass 133
and welfare citizenship 16–17
in Britain 19, 60, 62
see also black people;
immigration control

Rao, N. 13
Reagan, Ronald 72, 74, 126,
128–9, 134, 139–40
Redlich, Patricia 250–1
refugees
in Britain 97, 99
in Europe 23
rights, and citizenship 42
Roosevelt, Franklin D. 115, 116,
120
Russell, D. 278–9

Sapsford, R. 96
Scafe, Suzanne 63–4
Scandinavian countries
and social democratic welfare
regimes 11
see also Sweden
Scannell, Y. 231
Scotland 30
Second World War, and the
British welfare state 3, 19, 34,
35, 38–9
sickness benefits in Britain 40, 44
Siim, B. 218
Simon, W.E. 128
Skocpol, T. 139–40, 145
social changes, challenges to
welfare states 4–5
social citizenship, and the British
welfare state 53
social democratic welfare regimes
11, 24
and Catholic corporatism 226
in Sweden 20, 21, 196–200
social exclusion, European Union
(EU) policy on 274
social expenditure
and the European Union (EU)
270, 275, 281
as a percentage of GDP 200,
235, 264, 270, 281
as a percentage of GNP 125
in Sweden 199–200, 270
Social Fund, and the British
welfare state 82
social insurance
and the British welfare state
37, 39–42, 42, 43
and full employment 5, 39–40
and the German welfare state
154, 156, 161, 188
in Ireland 228, 234–5
in the United States, and the
New Deal 115–16, 119
social rights, and citizenship 42

social security
in Britain 78, 79, 80
and New Right ideology
79–85
in the United States 124
social services, expenditure on in
Britain 78
Soviet Union
breakup of former 97, 282
and the British welfare state
3, 34, 35
and the European welfare
states 19
Spain, social expenditure as a
percentage of GDP 264, 270
Starr, P. 123
state provision of welfare 6–7, 14
in Britain 30, 31, 32, 45,
59–60, 86, 103–4
statistical analysis 9
Strachey, John 34
stratification, and welfare
regimes 13
structured diversity 18
Supplementary Benefit, and the
British welfare state 41, 60, 80,
81, 82
supranational European welfare
state 262, 263, 265, 271–80
Sweden 196–220
citizenship in 211
class in 220
and access to welfare benefits
21
inequalities 196
and pensions 204
and social policy 197, 198
development of the modern
welfare state in 197–9
economic crisis and recovery
(1990s) 198–9, 219
equality movement in 198, 201
and the European Union (EU)
199, 218, 219
family policies in 213–18
lone-parent families 213,
215–16
parental leave and daycare
216–17
population policy 209–10,
213, 214
reform of 213–15
full employment in 196
gender in 220
inequalities 196
and the labour market 207–8
and old age pensions 203–4

and unemployment 206
and globalization 218, 219
income inequality in 200–1,
203
labour market 205, 219
and migrant workers 210–11
programmes 205, 206–7
and women 207–8
multi-cultural awareness in 21
old age pensions in 202–4
poverty in 201–2, 204, 214,
215
race in 17, 209–12, 220
and asylum-seekers 204, 211
ethnic minorities 203, 204,
205–6, 209, 211, 212
and immigration control
210–11
legislation against racial
discrimination 212
social eugenic policy 209–10
and social assistance 204–5
Social Democratic Party (SAP)
196–7, 198–9, 203
as a social democratic welfare
regime 20, 21, 196–200
social expenditure in 199–200,
270
as a percentage of GDP 125,
264
taxation in 200, 214
trade unions in 196, 197, 198,
203, 208
unemployment benefits in
208–9
unemployment in 196, 198,
204, 205–6, 211
and labour market
programmes 207
and lone mothers 216
univeralism in 198
Switzerland, race regime in 17,
212
Sykes, R. 269

Takahashi, M. 215
taxation
in Britain 41–2, 49–50, 74–5
mortgage tax relief 45–7
in Germany 159, 162, 176
in Ireland 236–7, 239, 241,
245
and New Right ideology 74–5,
127–8, 130
in Sweden 200, 214
in the United States 127–8,
130

Taylor-Gooby, P. 15
Thatcher, Margaret 2, 72, 73, 75
Tillet, Ben 33
Titmuss, Richard 35
Townsend, Peter 52
trade unions
    in Britain
        and immigration control 33
        and public-sector workers 64
        and rising labour costs 57
        and the 'winter of discontent'
            67
    in Germany 161, 174, 185
    in Ireland 233
    in Sweden 196, 197, 198, 203,
        208
transitional nature of welfare
    states 12
Trilateral Commission, *The
    Crisis of Democracy* 127
underclass 92, 131, 132–4, 136
unemployment
    in Britain
        changing definitions of 9
        and the long-term
            unemployed 53
        mass unemployment and
            welfare spending 72, 78
    in Eastern European states
        282
    and the EU Social Fund 273
    in Germany 168, 174–5, 178,
        179
    in Ireland 236, 239, 240, 241,
        243
    in Sweden 196, 198, 204,
        205–6, 211
        and labour market
            programmes 207
        and lone mothers 216
    in the United States
        and imprisonment 147–8
        and the New Deal 115
unemployment benefits
    in Britain 41, 54
        and black workers 62
        earnings-related 44
        and New Right ideology 80
    in Sweden 208–9
United Kingdom (UK) *see* Britain
United Nations 9
United States 114–48, 267
    and benefits to disabled people
        134
    and the British welfare state
        3, 34–5, 35–6, 37
    and the 'business agenda' 74

Civil Rights movement 121
class in
    inequalities of 146, 147
    and New Right ideology
        155–6
    and poverty 135
    underclass 131, 132–4, 136
'deviant' view of the 114
and the European welfare
    states 19, 114
and the Great Society 120–5,
    131
and healthcare
    corporate healthcare
        provision 138–9
    failure of reform 137–40
    Medicare and Medicaid
        programmes 123
income inequality in 200,
    201
'laggard' view of the 114
as a liberal welfare regime 11,
    20–1, 22, 147–8
and the New Deal 114–20,
    139, 146
and New Right ideology 20,
    125–34, 143–4, 147
    and class politics 135–6
    and the problem of
        dependency 130–2
    and the state 127–30
    and the underclass 131,
        132–4, 136
    and women 129, 136
and the Office of Economic
    Opportunity (OEU) 121–2,
    123
and the Personal
    Responsibility Act (1996)
    141–4
and the post-war
    reconstruction of Europe 35
and poverty
    and the Civil Rights
        movement 121
    and class 135
    and dependency 131–2
    and gender 135
    and the New Deal 115
    and New Right restructuring
        of welfare 129–30
    numbers of families below
        the poverty line 130
    as a political issue 52
    poor men and imprisonment
        147–8
    and the underclass 133
    war on 122–3

and public assistance 130–1,
    133, 134
    ADC 116–18, 142
    AFDC 122, 124, 130, 131,
        134, 136, 140, 144, 145
    TANF 140–1
race in 17, 121, 129, 146, 212
    and the New Deal 117, 118,
        119–20
    and New Right ideology 131,
        132, 136
    and poverty 135
    and the underclass 133
    and welfare 132
and social security 124, 130,
    133–4
    future of 144–6
and social welfare expenditure
    125, 134, 144
and taxation 127–8, 130
and unmarried mothers 210
and welfare policies
    and class 117
    and gender 117, 129
    and race 117, 118, 122, 129,
        130
and Western European
    welfare states 270
and workfare 114
universal welfare benefits
    in Britain 43, 62, 99–100, 104
    and the European Union (EU)
        278

voluntary sector
    in Britain 32, 37, 45, 52, 86, 88
    and mixed economies of
        welfare 14

wages
    concept of the family wage
        in Britain 37–8, 40, 42, 43, 67
        in Germany 158, 161
        in Ireland 232, 233
        and women in the United
            States 142
Wedderburn, Dorothy 52
welfare capitalism (regimes)
    10–13, 14, 19–22, 23–4, 262
    in Britain 10–11, 34–5, 105
    and globalization 268
welfare citizenship, and race
    16–17
welfare pluralism 13
welfare rights movement in
    Britain 52–3
welfare states, defining 5–7

welfare workers, motives of 6
West Germans (after unification),
  relations with East Germans
  186–7
West Germany
  benefit levels 159
  Christian Democratic Union
    (CDU) 155, 182
  class divisions and solidarity
    159–60
  constitution (Basic Law) 154,
    155, 161, 164, 172, 181
  feminist and Marxist
    criticisms of welfare policies
    155
  labour migrants in 158
  male unemployment in 168
  poverty in 160, 162–3, 168
  rights-based system in 155
  Social Democratic Party of
    Germany (SPD) 155, 182
Western European welfare states
  269–71
White, P. 17
Whyte, J.H. 228, 247
Wickham, J. 233
Williams, A.M. 281–2, 283–4
Williams, F. 16, 17, 19, 31
Williamson, Peter 226
Wilson, Harold 44
Wistow, G. 14

women
  and the British welfare state
    and abortion 65
    black women 63–4
    and citizenship 42
    as a contradictory
      relationship 64
    in the early years 33
    and the family 38, 59, 61, 89
    and healthcare services 65
    and 'primary carers' 89–90
  and European Union social
    policy 278, 279, 285
  and the 'feminization' of
    poverty 83, 135
  in Germany 158, 160–3, 166,
    167
    East Germans 170–1, 174–5,
      176–9
    post-unification 175, 177–9,
      188
  in Ireland 22, 244–54, 255
    and abortion 248–51
    and contraception 247–8
    and divorce 231, 251–2
    and the family 230–1,
      252–4
    and the ideology of 'Mother
      Ireland' 229–31
    in the labour market 229–30,
      245–6
    and welfare reforms 246–7

  role in welfare states 23, 24
  in Sweden 21
    and family policies 213–18
    and the labour market
      207–8, 210, 211, 214–16
    and old age pensions 203–4
    and social eugenic policy
      209–10
    and unemployment 206
  in the United States
    and careers in the welfare
      services 129
    and the New Deal 117–18,
      119
    and New Right restructuring
      of welfare 129, 136
    and poverty 135
    and welfare reforms 141–3
  and work 6, 15–16
    black women 64, 142
    in Britain 33, 40, 61–2, 64,
      90, 96
    in Germany 167, 168, 168–9,
      170–1, 174–5, 177, 178
    and social democratic welfare
      regimes 11
    in Sweden 210, 211, 214–16
    in the United States 141–2
  see also feminism; gender;
    motherhood
work see labour market
World Trade Organization 285